"This Is America?"

"This Is America?"

The Sixties in Lawrence, Kansas

Rusty L. Monhollon

palgrave

First published 2002 by PALGRAVE ™
First published by PALGRAVE MACMILLAN™ 2004
175 Fifth Avenue, New York, N.Y. 10010 and
Houndmills, Basingstoke, Hampshire, England RG21 6XS.
Companies and representatives throughout the world.

PALGRAVE MACMILLAN is the global academic imprint of the Palgrave
Macmillan division of St. Martin's Press, LLC and of Palgrave Macmillan
Ltd. Macmillan® is a registered trademark in the United States, United
Kingdom and other countries. Palgrave is a registered trademark in the Eu-
ropean Union and other countries.

ISBN 1–4039–6574–9 paperback

The Library of Congress has cataloged the hardcover edition as follows:
Monhollon, Rusty L.
This is America? : the sixties in Lawrence, Kansas / by Rusty L. Monhollon.
     p.   cm.
   Includes bibliographical references and index
   ISBN 0–312–29329–1
   1. Lawrence (Kan.)—Politics and government—20th century.
2. Lawrence (Kan.)—Race relations.   3. Lawrence (Kan.)—Social
conditions—20th century.   4. Nineteen sixties.   I. Title.

F689.L4 M66   2002
978.I'65—dc21   2001058018

A catalogue record for this book is available from the British Library.

Design by Letra Libre, Inc.

First edition: March 2004
10 9 8 7 6 5 4 3 2 1

Printed in the United States of America.

for Sonja

CONTENTS

LIST OF ILLUSTRATIONS

LIST OF ABBREVIATIONS

ASC	All Student Council
BSU	Black Student Union
CCBC	Coordinating Committee of the Black Community
CORE	Congress of Racial Equality
CRC	Civil Rights Council
DAC	Daughters of the American Colonists
DAR	Daughters of the American Revolution
DCCIA	Douglas County Community Improvement Association
DLAL	Dorsey-Liberty American Legion Post #14, Lawrence, Kansas
DPS	Department of Public Safety, Lawrence, Kansas
JBS	John Birch Society
KFU	Kansas Free University
KU	University of Kansas
KU-New Mobe	University of Kansas New Mobilization against the War in Vietnam
KU-Y	University of Kansas Young Men's Christian Association and Young Women's Christian Association
LBPWC	Lawrence Business Professional Women's Club
LCPI	Lawrence Committee for Peace in Indochina
LCPJ	Lawrence Coalition for Peace and Justice
LCPV	Lawrence Committee for Peace in Vietnam
LDC-NAACP	Lawrence-Douglas County National Association for the Advancement of Colored People
LDJW	*Lawrence Daily Journal-World*

LFHCC   Lawrence Fair Housing Coordinating Committee.
LHRC   Lawrence Human Relations Commission
LLF   Lawrence Liberation Front
LLPD   Lawrence League for the Practice of Democracy
LO   *Lawrence Outlook*
LPAC   Lawrence Peace Action Committee
LPC   Lawrence Peace Center
LSYLPC   Lawrence Support Your Local Police Committee
LWV   League of Women Voters, Lawrence, Kansas
OD   *Oread Daily*
PCCU   President's Commission on Campus Unrest
SDNE   The Sons and Daughters of New England
SDS   Students for a Democratic Society
UCM   University Christian Movement
UDK   *University Daily Kansan*
WILPF   Women's International League for Peace and Freedom
YAF   Young Americans for Freedom
YMCA   Young Men's Christian Association
YWCA   Young Women's Christian Association

ACKNOWLEDGEMENTS

Few periods in American history are as misunderstood as the sixties. Part of the reason for this is that the era was a critical period in American history, a moment when significant change took place in American society. Not surprisingly, many issues of the 1960s—racial and gender equality, for example—are still unresolved and provoke heated debate. So many Americans, whether they were on the barricades or not, lived through the decade, and thus the era is of intense personal significance to them, as it is in my own case. Claims of knowing the "truth" about the decade often are made because one "was there" during the sixties.

Although I never participated in a civil rights demonstration or an anti-Vietnam protest, never dropped acid, and did not grow my hair long until 1976, I, too, lived through the sixties, and am a product of those years. I was born in Topeka, Kansas, on the cusp of the baby boom in 1959, and raised in a working-class neighborhood with a large Mexican and German-Catholic population. Although I was too young to remember John Kennedy's death (my parents have told me where I was and what I was doing when the news was broadcast), I idolized the late president and his family, particularly his brother Bobby. I made campaign posters for RFK as part of a third-grade class project during the 1968 primaries. (The class, as I remember, was divided in its support for Kennedy, Richard Nixon, and Eugene McCarthy; several students supported George Wallace.) A large poster of RFK decorated my room, and I was devastated when I woke one morning to learn he had been shot. I struggled to understand why my aunt and mom were so worried when my cousin headed off to Vietnam, a place I had never heard of before. My bellbottoms went well with my extra-wide leather watchband. My hair was neatly trimmed above my ears, at my dad's insistence.

More significant than fashion concerns was my confusion over the racial slurs directed at my black and Mexican friends in our school and neighborhood. I understood less the racial violence that erupted at Highland Park High School in 1970, which my younger sister and I would have attended, had we stayed in Topeka. Instead, my parents, as did thousands of other white Americans in other communities, moved us from the urban turmoil of Topeka to the bucolic peace of Rossville, a racially and ethnically homogeneous town of some 1,000 people twenty miles west of Topeka, where I graduated from high school and later joined my father in his welding shop. I never stopped thinking about those years in Topeka. When I entered Washburn University in 1987, and later graduate school at the University of Kansas, I began to think seriously about them, American race relations, and the legacy of the 1960s.

This book is my effort to make sense of the sixties. It culminates a long journey, as much personal as it was scholarly. Along the way, I have incurred many debts from friends and family, which I would like to acknowledge here.

The history department and the Humanities and Western Civilization Program at the University of Kansas provided various kinds of financial support, for which I am very grateful. The George L. Anderson Dissertation Award provided support while I revised the manuscript; I thank the Anderson family for the endowment. My mentors at KU created a stimulating and supportive intellectual environment. I extend my gratitude in particular to Ted Wilson, Ray Hiner, the late John Clark, Ann Schofield, Carl Strikwerda, Joane Nagel, and David Smith, who read all or part of the manuscript and gave advice and support. The Dissertation Writers' Group at KU was a comfortable place to commiserate and bounce around new ideas; thanks to everyone in the group for your support. Scholars outside of the KU community offered criticism at various stages of the project. I sincerely thank Beth Bailey, Dominic Capeci, Mark Carroll, Timothy Chin, Ralph Crowder, Lawrence Christiansen, Bob Collins, David Farber, Mary Neth, Barry Riccio, Bill Wagnon, and the late Bill Cecil-Fronsman for their comments and suggestions. I am especially indebted to Linda Reed and Richard Blackett of the University of Houston Department of History and African-American Study Program for inviting me to participate in the Black History Workshop. I also thank all of the workshop participants for their comments and constructive criticism.

Part of chapter three appeared as "Taking the Plunge: Race, Rights, and the Politics of Desegregation, Lawrence, Kansas, 1960," *Kansas History* 20:3 (autumn 1997): 138–159. I thank Virgil Dean and three anonymous reviewers for their suggestions; thanks, too, to Virgil for allowing it to appear in this book. Parts of chapters three, five, seven, and eight appeared as "Black Power, White Fear: The 'Negro Problem' in Lawrence, Kansas, 1960–1970," in *Race Consciousness: African American Studies for the New Century,* ed. Judith Jackson Fossett and Jeffrey Tucker (New York: New York University Press, 1997), 247–262. I thank Judith and Jeffrey for including it in the collection and for their comments, and NYU Press for permission to include it here.

Through its Faculty Research Funds, Hood College provided important financial support at a crucial juncture in revising the manuscript. I am grateful to the Faculty Development Committee for granting the award, and to my new colleagues at Hood for welcoming me so warmly. A special note of thanks goes to Colette Cooney, Tiffany Taylor, and Mary Beth Molin for their help in preparing the manuscript. An Alfred M. Landon Research Grant, administered by the Kansas State Historical Society, supported part of the research for this project, which I gratefully acknowledge. Additionally, the staff at the KSHS was extremely helpful while I did my work there. I thank the good people at the Kansas Collection at the University of Kansas who patiently filled my seemingly endless requests for materials and took a sincere interest in my work. Ned Kehde and Barry Bunch at the University of Kansas Archives made digging through boxes of papers a little more enjoyable. I offer special thanks to Barry and Deborah Dandridge for finding and obtaining photographs to include here. Steve Jansen and his staff at the Douglas County Historical Society were similarly helpful and supportive. I also thank the staffs at the National Archives and Records Administration in College Park, and the Archives of Appalachia at East Tennessee State University for their assistance.

The people of Lawrence were exceedingly gracious in sharing their memories of a troubling time in their community's past. Max Rife gave me access to his personal papers, as did Alan Fisher, for which I am very grateful. Mr. Fisher also granted me access to the Dorsey-Liberty American Legion Post's files, which were very helpful. John Spearman, Jr., Jesse Milan, Harry Shafer, Vince Brown, Charles Oldfather, Stephanie Coleman, E. Laurence Chalmers, Dick Raney, and Ocoee Miller provided their recollections of the sixties in Lawrence. Al Sellen, the historian of the Plymouth Congregational Church, allowed me to read his work on Plymouth and its involvement in the civil rights movement in Lawrence. Ellen Garber provided Lawrence High School yearbooks and helped locate many people for interviews.

Several people deserve special mention. Chris O'Brien lived with this project for several years, read numerous drafts, raised important questions, and sometimes sprung for beer. He's a good critic, but a better friend. It was largely at the insistence of Professor J. C. D. Clark that this manuscript made its way to Palgrave. I am genuinely flattered by his interest in the project and eternally grateful for his efforts to see it published. Deborah Gershenowitz has been all a historian could want in an editor, and more. I could not have finished this book without her excellent advice, trenchant editing, and consistent encouragement. Many thanks go to production editor Donna Cherry, copy editor Jennifer Simington, and production assistant Erin Chan for their hard work and great advice. Phyllis Erickson read the manuscript and tactfully offered suggestions as only an English teacher and mother-in-law could. She and Don Erickson kept us well fed and gave me a place to work on trips to Manhattan. I am very thankful to them on all accounts.

I am fortunate that this book bears the imprint of both Bill Tuttle and David Katzman. Bill suggested that this study was worth doing and shaped it from start to finish, while David gave unselfishly of his time and expertise. They provided sharp criticism and valuable suggestions, for which I thank them. Moreover, Bill and David epitomize the highest standards of our profession and the purest values of a humanist. For this, and making me feel part of an academic community, I am most grateful. I owe David an additional note of thanks for the use of his personal papers and files.

Ron and Anne Monhollon have been a constant source of love and support, and this book is a testament to the values of hard work, persistence, and honesty they instilled in me. They also offered me the Rossville Machine and Weld, Inc., "Weld-Your-Way-Through-Graduate-School" fellowship, which gave me the financial means to support my family while pursuing my academic goals. I can never fully repay them, but I hope this book is at least a down payment.

Daniel and Richard Monhollon have exhibited patience and understanding beyond their years, especially when I missed a ball game or two to write or do research. They have never wavered in their support, have shared in my academic pursuits, have grown up with me, and have become fine young men, despite (or in spite of) their father. Richard also provided much-needed research assistance. Like their older brothers, Davis and Rachael Monhollon Erickson amaze me every day, and their insatiable curiosity and quest for knowledge has reinvigorated my own. My children, each in their own way, help me keep the past in perspective.

Above all, I want to thank my dearest friend, Sonja Erickson. An outstanding historian in her own right, she patiently read each word of this manuscript too many times, offered honest criticism, and gave nothing but abiding support. This is as much her book as it is mine (although I take all responsibility for errors or omissions). Thank you, Sonja, for sharing this with me, and for everything else. Although it is a small gesture compared to all that you've given me, I humbly, and lovingly, dedicate this book to you.

INTRODUCTION

Officer William Garrett of the Lawrence, Kansas, police department watched closely as Rick "Tiger" Dowdell, a nineteen-year-old African American and lifelong resident of Lawrence, got into a friend's red Volkswagen late on the night of July 16, 1970. Reports of gunfire had brought Garrett and other LPD officers to the area, and they believed Afro-House, a black cultural center, might have been the source of the shooting. As the car headed toward the campus of the University of Kansas, Garrett, joined by Officer Kennard Avey, followed. They turned on their sirens and flashing lights after a short distance, but the driver of the Volkswagen led them on a chase through the streets of Lawrence. The car struck a curb and stopped, and Dowdell jumped out and ran down an alley, followed by Garrett. The chase ended when Garrett shot Dowdell to death.

Four days later, while attempting to disperse a crowd gathered to protest Dowdell's death, Lawrence police officers in riot gear shot and killed Harry Nicholas Rice, a white, nineteen-year-old student at the University of Kansas. These two deaths precipitated a period of social and cultural upheaval not seen in Lawrence since the Civil War. For nearly two weeks, Lawrence, a mid-sized university town in northeast Kansas, teetered on the brink of civil insurrection.

These murders were not the first episodes of violence in Lawrence that year. In April and May the town had had a preview of the summer's fury. Bombings and arson, which had been common occurrences for more than a year, increased dramatically in April. Yippie Abbie Hoffman spoke on campus the first week of April, boring most KU students but angering Lawrencians with his cry for a revolution against "Amerika." A week later at Lawrence High School, after a walkout by black students to protest racial discrimination and the lack of an Afro-centric curriculum, fights between blacks and whites nearly exploded into a riot. During the racial tension at the high school, a late-night arson at the Memorial Union on the KU campus caused more than $1 million in damage, was never solved, and compelled local officials to ask the governor for an emergency proclamation; a dusk-to-dawn curfew lasted for three days. The president of the Black Student Union at KU encouraged blacks to arm themselves, while many whites stockpiled weapons, anticipating a guerilla war with blacks. In late April and early May, anti-Vietnam War demonstrations spilled off the campus and into Lawrence's streets. After the Kent State University and Jackson State University shootings, radicalized students and faculty campaigned to shut down the university, a move sternly opposed by the governor, the Board of Regents, and the Legislature. The semester ended with the university open (although the last week of classes was suspended) and the chancellor under fire but with no further violence. An uneasy calm gripped the city; it was easily shattered less than two months later.

Lawrence in late July resembled a combat zone. Between Dowdell's death on the sixteenth and the end of the month, firebombs, arson, and vandalism rocked the community nightly. Snipers blasted out streetlights and shot at police officers, firefighters, and ordinary citizens, including the local newspaper editor and radio station owner. The governor proclaimed a state of emergency, sent the Kansas Highway Patrol to relieve the beleaguered Lawrence Police Department, and mobilized the Kansas National Guard to protect property and keep the peace. These efforts were not enough for some residents. White vigilantes threatened to restore order by killing "nigger and hippie militants." Business owners guarded their property with shotguns and rifles; several exchanged gunfire with unidentified persons. Right- and left-wing radicals resented what each considered an invasion of their space, and both vowed an armed defense of that turf.

Rick Dowdell had been active in the Black Power movement in Lawrence, and his comrades vowed they would "avenge" his death "by any means necessary." They threatened to kill "any other muthafucka that gets in the way of the total liberation of our people."[1] The street people ("hippies" to local residents) and some KU students, who claimed to experience the same alienation and harassment from police as blacks, were similarly outraged at the shootings. One of the street people who lived in the Oread neighborhood where Rice had died promised that if the police "come in here again . . . there ain't gonna be any dead on our side." The underground newspaper *Vortex* published Garrett's photograph with the caption, "Wanted for Murder," which incensed the officer's supporters and advocates of law and order in Lawrence.[2]

For black and white radicals, Lawrence's (and America's) problems were rooted in oppressive racism, an unjust economic system, and American imperialism at home and abroad. Some Lawrencians, however, rejected this appraisal and saw the town's predicament as a matter of law and order, respect for property, and the decline in moral authority and standards, all of which had resulted from New Deal liberalism, misguided Supreme Court rulings, and social permissiveness. The local American Legion post passed a resolution supporting law enforcement's "conduct and handling of the conditions in Lawrence," which included the shooting of both Dowdell and Rice. A business owner circulated a petition expressing "gratitude and sympathy" to police wounded by sniper fire and praising the "courageous action of the police officer who fired the shot that killed Dowdell." A downtown merchant claimed he did "not like killing[, b]ut if it's going to take some killing to get the job done" and return Lawrence to normal, "then I say let's get on with it."[3]

Between April and July the small town of Lawrence seemed to experience the full brunt of what is commonly called the sixties: racial conflict, youth radicalism, division over the Vietnam War, cultural ferment and conflict, strained police-community relations, and a spiral of violence. The era is usually understood as one of great turmoil, characterized by massive social movements (led principally by women, blacks, and young people as part of the New Left or the Movement); a backlash from the "Silent Majority"; political assassinations, riots, and other violence; and a flowering of oppositional cultures. Today, depending on one's political perspective, the sixties was either an epic age when millions of Americans struggled valiantly for social justice and equality, or a dark age when the nation lost its moral compass amid cultural degeneration and youthful hedonism.

Much of what gave the era its distinctiveness was the vision of civil rights activists, peace workers, students, and other activists; they thought that all Americans should have full and complete access to the privileges and benefits of citizenship. Meaningful participation in society would empower citizens, they held, and politics could thus be transformed to reflect the dignity and worth of each individual.[4] Faith in the promise of America, however, was not the sole province of the New Left. Conservatives, right-wing radicals, and political moderates offered alternate narratives, their version of the nation's "freedom struggle" that encouraged supporters to resist the challenge of liberalism and the New Left. To be sure, these narratives typically were not democratic—certainly not in the sense that the New Left meant—and they sought to preserve rather than change the status quo. They did not, however, simply "react" to the New Left but instead offered their own vision of what constituted a just and democratic America.

After World War II, the strain of urbanization, shifting demographics, the nationalization of culture, and the expansion of the welfare state, as well as conflict over civil rights, Vietnam, feminism, the Cold War, oppositional cultures, and other issues, transformed the United States, forcing its citizens to reconsider the meaning and values of the American experience. Some Americans questioned the capitalist system, American imperialism abroad, and the "establishment" while others questioned New Deal and Great Society liberalism, the encroachment of the activist welfare state into social issues (especially civil rights), and the depth of the American commitment to combat communism at home and overseas. Activists and nonactivists from the Left and the Right drew from a well of similar experiences, discourses, symbols, and rhetoric to construct oppositional realities, all of which fit within the main of American political thought and culture.[5] This struggle to define the meaning of the American experience reshaped society and politics in the United States after 1945. The sixties was an important moment in American history because the issues and turmoil of the era politicized and socialized most Americans, regardless of political outlook. To understand the sixties more fully, we must examine how *all* Americans, not just the young or those on the Left, were politicized during those turbulent years.

This is, of course, a difficult task, unless we find a narrower frame of reference, a single community where we can measure and assess the full impact of the decade's political and social dislocations, and explore how individual Americans experienced and responded to those changes. Lawrence, Kansas, is just such a place. What happened in Lawrence in the 1960s is a compelling story, full of drama, humor, and intrigue, characterized by acts of human courage, folly, and tragedy. As a case study, *"This is America?"* explores how the residents of Lawrence responded to and tried to resolve political and social conflict over important issues, some of which do not typically define the sixties: the spread of the welfare state; economic growth; urban development; the Vietnam War; the civil rights, student, and feminist movements; communism and anticommunism; and oppositional culture, among others. The traditional images and characters of the sixties are included here—civil rights protestors, New Leftists, hippies, feminists, antiwar protestors—but they appear alongside nontraditional sixties' characters: conservatives, vigilantes, the "establishment," and anticommunists, to name a few. They, too, were significant historical actors who shaped the contours of the decade, and their voices need to be heard if we are to understand the era more completely.

In the following pages I examine how the residents of Lawrence, Kansas, contributed to and experienced the sixties. I try to strip away, as much as possible, the decade's myths to reconstruct the contested political and social terrain and examine the various ways that Americans constructed alternate visions of the good life in the United States. The driving force of the narrative is a community in turmoil, experiencing rapid transformation during a time of great social and political upheaval. Lawrence's conservative political order's attempt to hold on to power and defend its hegemonic ideology from the assaults led by blacks, women, youth, pacifists, and others on the margins of American society is at the heart of this story. This study helps us to understand why conservatism was such a potent force during the decade, despite a moderately successful leftist revolt. Most significantly, *"This is Amer-*

ica?" underscores the centrality of race and racial identity in understanding the political and cultural unrest of the sixties.

I chart this transformation by examining how the people of Lawrence constructed alternate worldviews that shaped their personal and group identities, redrew social boundaries, and competed for and redistributed political power in the community. The key to understanding why the era was so contentious is in understanding the ways in which Americans of all political perspectives personalized the issues debated in the public arena. Grounded in the notion of "personalism"—the political implications of the everyday choices individuals make about their lives, communities, and sense of self—this volume traces the ways in which Americans during the 1960s increasingly personalized their political responses to pressing issues. Some Americans personalized politics through their participation in grassroots, rights-based, or protest movements, such as the civil rights, feminist, or antiwar struggles. Others, however, did so through their resistance to these movements and their goals, or by appealing to a narrow definition of national citizenship expressed through the Cold War and anticommunism. Thus, the personalization of politics helped to create, or in some cases, recreate, new group and individual identities of some Americans, based on perceived racial or ethnic similarities and differences, a common past, shared cultural and political values, and economic status while challenging those of others. The personalization of politics gave new expression and meaning to the political process and the ways in which Americans participated in that process. It also helps to explain why the era was so divisive and often violent.

I make no claim here that Lawrence's experience in the 1960s was typical or representative of other American communities, although, at least on the surface, it shares many similarities. Regardless, Lawrence is an excellent place in which to examine the sixties more closely. Like other communities across the United States, the small town was transformed after World War II, yet its sixties experience was deeply ingrained in local conditions and circumstances, unique to itself. With 45,000 residents in 1970, the largest city in Douglas County was hardly a sprawling urban area with significant minority populations, like Los Angeles, Chicago, or New York. While it may have been the most atypical of Kansas towns—thanks largely to the liberalizing influence of the University of Kansas—Lawrence on the whole was politically conservative. The university and a modest industrial base provided a solid economic base that remained sound throughout the 1960s. Lawrence did not endure the economic dislocations of deindustrialization, the loss of jobs, or the flight to the suburbs as did other American communities after World War II. Average income increased during the decade for all groups, including the 5 percent of the population who were black. Race relations in Lawrence did not compare to either the Jim Crow South or the northern urban ghettos, although housing for African Americans was clustered and educational and employment opportunities were limited. In addition, blacks in Lawrence typically endured social ostracism and blatant racism.

Situated between the Kansas City metropolitan area and the state capital in Topeka, Lawrence in the 1960s was very much a small town, sharing attributes of both rural and urban America. Lawrence grew steadily after 1945, in both its population and boundaries. It was not cosmopolitan, although KU attracted individuals from across the nation and around the world with different backgrounds, experiences, and worldviews, which made Lawrence more diverse than most Kansas towns. The baby boom had great significance for the university, and by extension, Lawrence, as increasing numbers of students began attending the university after 1960, and the youthful population and their professors became frequent targets of conservative fears. Significantly, Lawrence's free-state heritage, born of the violence of "Bleeding Kansas" during the sectional crisis of the 1850s, resonated still, especially among those residents who denied the community had racial problems. On a different level, there was what some call the John Brown legacy in Lawrence, which attracted many people, especially the young, to Lawrence to join the struggle for freedom and equality.

Politics and daily life in Lawrence, especially in the 1960s, revolved around issues of legitimacy and authority with which the rest of the country was struggling: the growth and impact of the welfare state, the nature of American political and economic institutions, the integration of all citizens into public life, and the conduct of the Cold War, among others. Moreover, in trying to resolve these issues, social activism had transformed both the content and the context of the public culture in Lawrence, just as it had the rest of the United States.[6] In their homes and churches, in the media and in the streets, the people of Lawrence debated the meanings of freedom, equality, and justice and struggled to define the state and its role in society and what it meant to be an American. Civil rights activism in Lawrence since World War II had evolved from occasional direct action to integrate places of public accommodation and to obtain equal housing, educational, and job opportunities for blacks into an Afro-centric cultural and political movement called Black Power, which empowered many blacks, alienated most whites, and redrew the community's racial boundaries. Students at the University of Kansas, who had protested on campus against dorm closing hours, in loco parentis, and racial exclusion in university housing earlier in the decade were by 1970 defiantly taking to the streets of Lawrence to oppose the Vietnam War, American militarism, and what they saw as the impersonalization and dehumanization of American society. Women in Lawrence had always been active in both the civil rights and antiwar movements, and by the end of the decade they struggled for gender equality in the workplace and greater access to health care, child care, and reproductive rights. By 1969 Lawrence also had been transformed by an alternate culture of self-styled street people, hippies, freaks, dropouts, and others seeking to escape from middle America.

At the same time, however, politically moderate and conservative Lawrencians both protested and supported the war, attacked and defended segregation, and offered their own sense of the just society. Some even contributed to this discourse by becoming socially and politically active, banding together in a grassroots anticommunist movement or using existing civic organizations to protest the growth of the federal government, the extension of the welfare state, and the growing power of minority groups. The culture wars of the 1960s, therefore, had multiple narratives, multiple sources of power, and multiple languages and were expressed by Americans from a vast range of political orientations.

To understand how the people of Lawrence experienced the 1960s, I have mined manuscript collections, letters to the editors of local papers, interview transcripts and oral histories, constituent correspondence, newspaper accounts, and government documents. I have unearthed a rich vein of material, hundreds of letters and telegrams that Lawrencians sent to local newspaper editors, elected officials, and university administrators. These firsthand accounts provide a contemporary window into the writers' worldviews, their political ideologies, their sense of personal and group identity, and their views of what constituted the good life in the United States. Perhaps most significantly, these perspectives offer a sense of immediacy that other sources, such as oral histories, do not provide. Written by concerned and engaged Americans at the time the events and issues were being discussed, these sources form the actual substance of that political discourse, conveying the emotion of the participants and the urgency of their perceptions. Throughout the study, I have tried whenever possible to let the people of Lawrence explain in their own words how they interpreted events and ideas, to allow them to "reclaim their voices" amid the turbulence of the era. I also have made use of oral histories here—both those I have conducted and those done by other scholars—to add texture and detail to the narrative.[7]

As I hope will be apparent, I believe history is made by local actors responding to local conditions. The history of the sixties was a series of local histories, not confined solely to large urban areas or elite universities. The sixties was made in the homes, the streets, and the minds of citizens in places like Lawrence, as they and other Americans gave meaning to the rhetoric and symbolism that came from their experiences.

As Lawrence grew from a small, sleepy college town after World War II, it experienced acute growing pains. Nationally, television was almost singularly responsible for creating a national public culture that tugged at the authority and control of traditional centers of power, especially local elites and institutions. Similarly, federal legislation and Supreme Court decisions, most evident perhaps in the Civil Rights Acts and *Brown v. Board,* created national standards of conduct and behavior. Locally, economic development and population growth pushed at the traditional boundaries of authority and power in the small town. Not everyone in Lawrence welcomed these challenges or the changes that they would bring.

The *Lawrence Daily Journal-World* proclaimed on New Years Day, 1960, that Lawrence faced a "bright future." "The 1950s have been tremendous years here," the paper declared. "The1960s promise to be even better." Ten years later, most Lawrencians would have laughed at the *Journal-World's* optimism. Even as it foresaw a bright future, the issues that would dominate the sixties were evident elsewhere in the paper: the space race, nuclear proliferation and disarmament, confrontations with the Soviet Union, the rise of the Third World and decolonization, the black freedom struggle, oppositional culture, and women's issues, to name a few. These issues transformed Lawrence, creating a community unfamiliar to many residents. By 1970, Lawrencians from all walks of life looked hard at their town and asked, "This is America?"[8]

CHAPTER 1

"THE HOMESTEAD OF THE FREE"

Bert Carlyle disliked the leftward course of American politics in the 1960s. As publisher and editor of the *Lawrence Outlook,* in his editorials and weekly columns Carlyle frequently railed against liberalism, communism, and all the other "isms" in which he believed "Left-wing" college professors were indoctrinating students at the University of Kansas. "What the gifted intellectuals fail to explain to the wide eyed, fuzzy-faced students," he wrote after a 1965 student-led civil rights demonstration on campus, "is how their country and Kansas got where it is today; populated by the 'prairie protestants' who believe in corny ideals such as God, free enterprise and hard work." Carlyle believed intellectuals had rejected the values of God, country, and capitalism, which to him were the cornerstones of Americanism. Moreover, America's future rested in what Carlyle identified as the "real Americans," the simple folk like the "prairie protestants" who had pushed across the frontier and settled Kansas a hundred years earlier. To make sense of the present and find solutions for the future, Bert Carlyle, like others in Lawrence, looked to the past, to the nation's, and Kansas's, myths and legends.[1]

This view of Kansas was not unique to Carlyle. The progressive historian Carl L. Becker, who taught for fourteen years at the University of Kansas, wrote in 1910 that "Kansas was a state of mind," a sense of place that defied precise definition. Becker and other writers believed that Kansans were a peculiar mixture of New England Puritanism and moral idealism, tinctured with faith in individualism, liberty, equality, and materialism. These generalizations, however, belie the influence of southerners and other migrants in shaping Kansas's past. More significantly, faith in liberty and equality are contested values, with different meanings for different groups of people. Kansas has always been a place of contested meanings. During the national debate over the 1854 Kansas-Nebraska Act and the westward extension of slavery, Kansas took center stage in a national morality play. For the New England abolitionists who got credit for settling the state, Kansas represented the divine righteousness of their crusade to end slavery in the United States. To southerners from Missouri and the upper South, Kansas stood for the affirmation of states' and individual rights. For blacks leaving the South after the Civil War, Kansas was Canaan, the place of their deliverance where the promise of equality would be fulfilled. For others from the upper Midwest and Europe, Kansas was a place of opportunity, a chance for mobility and economic success.

Kansas is literally at the nation's crossroads. As the geographical center of the continental United States, its political culture reflects the diversity of ideas that flowed into the state with it early migrants. Kansas is as much North (Kansans fought on the side of the Union during the Civil War) as it is South (it had more migrants from Missouri and the southern states than any other state or region). At the same time, Kansas evokes the nation's frontier past, with visions of rugged pioneers crossing the prairies. The legends of cowboys and cowtowns like Dodge City (made famous by the *Gunsmoke* television series of the 1950s and 1960s) place Kansas solidly in Western mythology.

Strictly speaking, most geographers classify Kansas as part of the Great Plains, but that best describes the western two-thirds of the state. As one moves eastward from the Rocky Mountains, the vast plains in western Kansas give way to gently rolling hills and creek and river valleys. In the middle third of the state are the Flint Hills, a natural grassland covered with bluestem grasses and wildflowers, including the ubiquitous sunflower. The same glacier that created the Great Plains also left rich, dark soils in the eastern third of the state, where the Kansas River, or Kaw (as it is known), links together most of the major towns. From Salina it winds to Abilene (Dwight Eisenhower's hometown), Junction City, Manhattan, and then on to Topeka, Lawrence, and Kansas City, where it merges into the Missouri River. With an average annual rainfall of forty inches, the river bottom has some of the most productive farmland in the region. Although not heavily forested, the valleys are thick with cottonwood, hickory, walnut, elm, willow, and oak trees.

Nestled in the fertile Kansas and Wakarusa River valleys in northeast Kansas is Lawrence. Like the state in which it resides, from its beginnings Lawrence was a contested site. Before the Kansas Territory was organized in 1854, hundreds of migrants on the Oregon Trail passed through the area, and fur traders worked the Kaw on keel boats. When Congress passed the Kansas-Nebraska Act organizing the territory, fewer than 1,500 white persons were in Kansas, and nearly 700 of these were soldiers. At the time, the Kansa Indians (from whom the state takes its name) populated the area around present-day Lawrence, but they ceded most of the land to the government (except 200-acre tracts for each tribe member). White settlers prized the areas along the river not only for their agricultural value but for their commercial and transportation potential, and soon took control of the area.[2]

The Massachusetts (later the New England) Emigrant Aid Society, an antislavery organization, sent its first party of settlers to Kansas in 1854. They located west of Kansas City, on a site to the south of the Kaw, near a graceful hill (later the site of the University of Kansas) that provided a panoramic and strategic view of both the Kansas and Wakarusa river valleys. Although the fledgling settlement's official name became Lawrence (after Amos Lawrence, the principal benefactor of the Emigrant Aid Society) the community became known colloquially as Yankee Town.[3] Finding squatters, mostly Missourians, already at the townsite, the abolitionists evicted the southerners east to the lower ground along the river. The New Englanders settled west of Massachusetts Street, across a ravine in what later became known as west Lawrence, because it was on the higher ground, had a better view of the area, and had a good water supply. The Yankees deemed the river bottom east of Massachusetts (what became east Lawrence) "undesirable" because it was prone to flooding, had a poor water supply, and bred disease, but mostly because southerners lived there.

Some scholars claim that the Civil War began in Lawrence. In 1856, proslavery forces sacked Lawrence, burning the fledgling town nearly to the ground, in what abolitionists called the "crime against Kansas." The violence between proslavery and abolitionist factions continued, and the imagery of "bleeding Kansas" thrust the state into the national consciousness and embedded the town firmly in the nation's mythology. Just south of Lawrence, in 1856, the zealot abolitionist John Brown and his followers ruthlessly murdered five unprotected men and young boys who allegedly were linked to proslavery groups. In 1863, William Quantrill's band of Confederates burned the town down, the single bloodiest act of civilian terrorism of the Civil War.[4] Lawrence's early history is inextricably tied up with the cause of abolishing slavery and the rhetoric of freedom and equality. Like Brown, Lawrence became a martyr to the cause of freedom and equality, the essence of the town's official history. The "free-state" narrative is an identity that the town always has embraced. The narrative exerted a powerful influence on the town that to its nineteenth- and twentieth-century residents exemplified the triumph of good over evil, freedom over slavery, justice over inequity, and virtue over materialism.

The Sons and Daughters of New England, established in 1896 to celebrate the spirit of the pilgrim ancestors and founders of Lawrence, is an example of the enduring quality of and the cultural power attached to the free-state narrative. Many of Lawrence's leading citizens—newspaper publishers, judges and politicians, university administrators, business owners—were members. Well into the 1970s the organization held annual reunions at the Eldridge Hotel, once the Free State Hotel that Quantrill's men had destroyed. At each reunion, the Sons and Daughters of New England sang what they called the "Emigrants' Hymn," (actually, *The Kansas Emigrant*, written by the Quaker abolitionist and New Englander John Greenleaf Whittier) which combined religious and constitutional faith with a sense of place:

> Uprearing like the ark of old / The Bible is our van
> We go to test the truth of God / Against the fraud of man. . . .
> We'll tread the prairies as of old / Our fathers sailed the sea,
> And make the West as they the East, / The homestead of the
> free.[5]

These latter-day pilgrims allied their providential mission with the Republican Party, to saving the Union, and to freeing the black slaves in the South. They believed their crusade would make Lawrence a model of virtue that would triumph over base southern materialism. Lawrence would be, the abolitionists believed, nineteenth-century America's city on the hill. To most Lawrencians, the meaning of the free-state narrative meant that the town had paid its dues to the cause of justice and equality. To many Lawrencians in the 1960s, that idea operated as if true, even as racial strife, cultural change, demographic shifts, and political conflict challenged that narrative in their small community. The Yankee-influenced free-state narrative was solidly entrenched in local mythology, expressed through travel and visitor's guides, and embodied in community and civic organizations.[6]

Although only a small portion of Lawrence's population came from New England, these emigrants and their descendants formed much of the town's elite. They owned many businesses (especially newspapers), had access to capital, and had connections to local, territorial, and state government. Yankee newspapers appealed principally to New England sensibilities and largely ignored the town's cultural and ethnic diversity. By the end of the century New Englanders had published the town's "official" history.[7]

Yankee culture also came to dominate the town's official history through religion and education. New Englanders, more so than the Missourians and other southerners, were committed to the construction of churches, schools, and colleges in Lawrence. As early as January 1855, grammar school classes were held on the top floor of the Emigrant Aid Building. When the city's charter was amended in 1860, it established a school board; local government had assumed responsibility for public education and over the next decade built several elementary schools. The most important educational institution in Lawrence, however, was the University of Kansas (KU). One goal in the charter of the Emigrant Aid Society was to provide its settlers with the "advantages of education," so a "Harvard on the Kaw," as the New Englanders hoped, appeared inevitable. Thanks to some astute political maneuvering and the largesse of several New England benefactors, Lawrence in 1866 won a fierce competition among other Kansas towns to be the home of the state university. The university was located on a 974-foot promontory south of the town site, first called Hogback Ridge but later renamed Mount Oread, after the Oread Seminary in Massachusetts.[8]

The university has had a significant economic and cultural impact upon the community from its founding. The dominance of the Yankee culture was further enhanced in the late nineteenth century when the university became the town's economic center after the railroads failed. By the 1910s Lawrence was clearly a "college town." Many of the university's administrators and faculty were transplanted New Englanders, further embedding the narrative in the town's collective memory. The university was the town's largest employer, and with the influx of new students and governmental spending on higher education and research after World War II, the importance of the university to Lawrence's economy increased. Throughout the twentieth century KU was a magnet for alternate cultural, ideological, and social thought and activism, frequently to the disquiet of the townspeople, who often lamented "those people on the Hill." The contentious relationship between "the town and the gown," between a generally conservative (sometimes reactionary) and sedentary townspeople and a generally liberal (sometimes radical) and transitory university community helps to define Lawrence's character. It was also a major source of conflict during the 1960s. The anti-intellectualism of many townsfolk, who saw the university community as "eastern snobs," was counterposed by an antiprovincialism from many in the university community.

Another important educational institution in Lawrence was Haskell Institute (later Haskell Indian Junior College and now Haskell Indian Nations University). In 1884, the federal government established the United States Indian Industrial Training School in Lawrence, later renamed for Dudley C. Haskell, a Kansas Congressman and former chair of the House committee on Indian affairs. Haskell Institute emerged from the nineteenth-century westward migration of Euro-Americans, the confiscation of Indian lands, and the bitter and bloody Indian wars. The training school's purpose was ambiguous. As part of treaty obligations, it provided educational opportunities to Native Americans in exchange for their lands, but it did so by trying to separate young Indians completely from their native culture, language, and religion. The effort to "civilize" Native Americans included forcing them to wear uniforms and cut their long hair, and imposing harsh discipline. Living conditions were deplorable, and many students died from illness brought on by the cold winter. The curriculum focused trades and crafts, such as blacksmithing and harness-making for boys, and cooking and sewing for girls. By 1900, Haskell had become a normal school, and in 1927 the state of Kansas accredited its high school classes.[9]

Although there were about 2,000 Indians in Lawrence in the early 1970s (they were nearly as numerous as blacks), Native Americans did not shape the public discourse as significantly as did African Americans. Business owners, especially tavern owners, simply declined to serve Indians. On one occasion, a Lawrence restaurant owner declined to serve a group of Haskell students, declaring the 1964 Civil Rights Act decreed that she only had "to serve niggers."[10] During the 1960s, Haskell's mission, and paternalistic methods, had not changed much from the late nineteenth century. According to its superintendent, Haskell tried to meet the "special needs" of young Native Americans who "have not had ample educational experiences and have suffered from geographical and social isolation." Native Americans faced the same discrimination as blacks, as well as verbal abuse from local residents, including KU students. Haskell was more "structured" than KU, which led many student activists at KU to complain about its "quasi-military mentality" and the lack of liberation and voice for Indian students in campus affairs. There was little exchange of any kind between KU and Haskell, and many Haskell students felt "threatened by the Hill" and were "suspicious of overtures by whites who might be friendly." As one KU political group noted, Haskell was "an antiquated frontier institution which segregates the Indian and makes him a target of curiosity and scorn."[11] According to one poll, Haskell students, by a four-to-one margin, opposed the efforts of the American Indian Movement. Although there were some stirrings of unrest among some Haskell students, most were not participants in the turmoil in Lawrence in the sixties.[12]

In addition to importing education to Lawrence, Lawrence's settlers also brought their religion with them. In 1854, New England settlers founded Plymouth Congregational Church. The following year, recent migrants to Lawrence established Unitarian, Baptist, and Methodist Episcopal churches. A Presbyterian church was established in 1856, and Trinity Episcopal and St. John's Catholic in 1857. The Society of Friends began meeting in 1865, and two Lutheran churches were started in 1867 and 1868. As one settler remarked in 1868, in the early days "the town's social life fell oftenest in the groupings of church membership."[13]

Spirituality was an important element of daily life in Lawrence and helped to create identities for its residents. In both the nineteenth and twentieth centuries, the nation's churches were places where Americans disputed and debated, but did not always resolve, the meaning of freedom and equality. Religion and churches could be powerful forces for social change, or they could be irresistible defenders of traditional social boundaries.[14] In Lawrence and elsewhere, for example, black churches were key organizational and cultural resources for mobilizing support for the civil rights movement.[15] The student and antiwar movements also had religious roots. Conversely, segregationists and opponents of the civil rights movement used similar appeals to Christianity and the Bible.[16] The Cold War to many Americans was a religious war against godless communism, and the 1962 Supreme Court decision on school prayer was a rallying point for a resurgent Christian right. Religion was a crucial component of identity in Lawrence, regardless of what position its citizens occupied on the political spectrum. Throughout the decade, liberal theology and social activism confronted conservative orthodoxy.

Despite the power of the Yankee narrative, Lawrence was not a homogenous community. From its beginnings, Lawrence was an ethnically mixed community. Other regional culture groups migrated into Kansas territory, often in numbers greater than those of the Yankees. Farmers from the upper Midwest—Ohio, Indiana, and Illinois—black exodusters from the South, and foreign-born migrants, especially Germans and Scandinavians, were nearly as plentiful in Lawrence as the New Englanders. Unlike the Yankees, Lawrence's early immigrant settlers were more interested in the economic opportunity that Kansas offered than the morality and politics of slavery.[17] Missourians were the largest single contingent of migrants to Kansas. Indeed, southerners were important settlers in Lawrence and early occupation of land allowed them to gain an economic foothold and to create a government sympathetic to their proslavery interests.[18]

Although abolitionists intended to fill Lawrence with men who abhorred slavery, it did not mean that they welcomed African Americans. In its early days, there were no blacks in Lawrence, and even as it became known as a free-state stronghold, few African Americans lived there. Neither slave owners and their slaves, nor, ironically, free blacks, were welcome. African Americans, however, did begin settling in Lawrence just before the Civil War started. As a station on the underground railroad, and because of its free-state rhetoric, Lawrence seemed a logical place for black migrants to settle. During the war, runaway slaves, especially those from Missouri, made Lawrence their destination. Pastor Richard Cordley of Plymouth Congregational Church wrote in the late nineteenth century that the "colored people of Missouri" saw Lawrence as a "city of refuge." Cordley noted that "the slaves on the border took advantage of it to make sure of their freedom. They came by scores and hundreds, and for a time it seemed as if they would overwhelm us."[19]

That trend continued after the Civil War, when Exodusters (black migrants seeking land and opportunities outside the South) caught "Kansas fever."[20] For many former slaves, Kansas was the promised land. After the Civil War, African Americans began carving out a sense of place for themselves in Lawrence, building four churches, and black-owned businesses flourished in the late nineteenth century and into the twentieth until World War II. In the nineteenth century, many blacks from Kentucky settled in North Lawrence, across the river from Lawrence. Working class and semi-rural, North Lawrence was a separate political entity until 1870, when it was annexed into Lawrence. Together, Lawrence and North Lawrence in 1865 had 1,464 blacks. Physically separated from Lawrence by the Kansas River, blacks in North Lawrence achieved some measure of economic independence on the small plots of land they could purchase, till, and improve.[21]

While the percentage of blacks in Lawrence's total population has steadily declined since the nineteenth century, in the twentieth century the actual numbers of the black population have remained remarkably stable, growing by only 87 persons (to 1,849) between 1910 and 1915, and decreasing to only 1,658 by 1960. The stability of the black community is noteworthy, but the lack of growth suggests the powerful impact of white racism and limited housing, educational, and employment opportunities on the black community. According to a 1963 survey of blacks in Lawrence conducted by the Lawrence-Douglas County chapter of the National Association for the Advancement of Colored People (LDC-NAACP), 41 percent of Lawrence's blacks were born in the city, and 54 percent had parents who were born there. Moreover, 54 percent had lived in Lawrence more than twenty years, while only 31 percent had lived there less than ten years.[22]

Despite this stability, African Americans grappled daily with discrimination and exclusion in Lawrence. John Spearman, Sr., a longtime resident of east Lawrence, remembered growing up that "blacks were pretty invisible people." Born in Lawrence to social activists, Spearman recalled that the entire town "was segregated except the schools. Housing was segregated, the drugstores were segregated, the restaurants were segregated, jobs were segregated." Despite persistent discrimination, Jim Crow laws did not confine blacks to one specific area of the town. The 1917 *Lawrence Social Survey* remarked that there was no distinct "colored district" (by which the *Survey* meant "negroes, Mexican, and Indians") in Lawrence, nor had there ever been. But most black families everywhere in the city were clustered into substandard housing.[23]

In addition to Yankees, white southerners, and African Americans, Germans, Scandinavians, and Irish were among the early settlers in Lawrence. Germans were the largest foreign-born group in Lawrence, greatly affected the town's development, and sustained a distinct German ethnic identity into the twentieth century. The Germans began arriving in small numbers before the Civil War and tended to congregate on the first several streets east of Massachusetts Street. By the end of the century, a strong and lively German culture was evident in German churches, a German language newspaper, German-owned businesses (including several taverns and breweries), and a *Turnverien* (an athletic and social club). Through successful business and civic activities Germans assimilated easily into Lawrence's mainstream and were socially mobile, yet nativism and prejudice permeated the town. During World War I, anti-German sentiment eroded the outward signs of German culture in Lawrence, and by the Great Depression, it had all but disappeared.[24] Although in 1960 many Lawrencians were of German ancestry, they did not publicly celebrate their ethnicity, which had been subsumed into an American identity. Because of their light skin color, foreign-born Germans could easily transform themselves into white Americans.

As it had been throughout the twentieth century, in 1960 Lawrence was mostly a white community. Ninety-one percent of Lawrence's population, according to the 1960 census, identified itself as white. African Americans in Lawrence numbered 1,657, about 5 percent of the total population, slightly higher than the state average of 4.6 percent. Twelve hundred Native Americans comprised 3.7 percent of the population. The remaining 138 residents (less than 1 percent of the total population) were scattered among 29 Japanese, 42 Chinese, 6 Filipinos, and 61 "other races." Presumably, most of the Asian population was KU faculty or students.[25]

Like the rest of the United States, Douglas County, of which Lawrence is the county seat, had become increasingly urban, growing by 20 percent between 1940 and 1950. The rural population—and especially the number of family farms—decreased significantly. Reflecting another national demographic trend, the town was getting younger, too, as the baby boom hit Lawrence. Lawrence built a new high school in 1953, and enrollment pinches were felt at the elementary and junior high schools. Children fifteen years and younger comprised more than 25 percent of the total population in 1960, a 97 percent increase from 1950. More significantly, children under ten made up than 18 percent of the total population; the figure had been 13.4 percent in 1950. The median age dropped from 25 in 1950 to 23.8 in 1960, and residents under eighteen increased from 20.5 percent of the total population to 28.4 percent. Added to this were student registrations at KU. In 1951 6,000 students registered at KU. By 1960, the figured had swelled to 9,325 and ballooned to 17,947 in 1970.[26]

In the 1950s and 1960s, spurred on by urban renewal projects and federal funding, housing and commercial construction crossed Iowa Street (U.S. Highway 59), which had long been the town's western edge. New houses, shopping centers, and several motels and restaurants fueled the area's growth. Additionally, the city of Lawrence annexed new areas into its boundaries, which brought forth a series of angry letters to newspaper editors and heated city council and county commission meetings about the growth and power of local government. Annexation and economic growth also elicited complaints and misgivings from several residents about increased traffic, the lack of planning, commercial encroachment of residential areas, and other growing pains. Urban renewal, meanwhile, fed fears of an omnipresent and overbearing federal government and that the "few" (minorities in east and north Lawrence) would benefit at the expense of the "many."[27]

Like the rest of the United States, Lawrence also shared in the post–World War II economic boom, of which housing was an important element. Housing in Lawrence in the early fifties was scarce, and remained so until the National Defense Production Administration named Lawrence a "critical defense area." After that, new housing developments—occupied exclusively by whites—sprang up to house a growing residential and student population. In 1950, seventy-seven new houses were built in Lawrence. That number increased almost every year during the fifties, peaking in 1958 when 384 new homes were constructed. New housing tapered off after that, dropping to 108 in 1963. African Americans did not benefit equally, if at all, in Lawrence's housing boom. As late as 1964, the LDC-NAACP reported that of the 211 black family dwellings in Lawrence, 4 percent had no indoor water and 8 percent had no indoor toilet. Since 1950, there had been at least a dozen new housing developments in Lawrence; by 1964, none had been "populated with a single Negro family."[28]

A growing population and more college students created greater demands for jobs in Lawrence, but the black community did not share equitably in this growth either. In 1963–64, the LDC-NAACP surveyed 790 black Lawrence residents (80 percent of the black population) and reached some disturbing conclusions. It reported that the typical black person in Lawrence did not "need to worry about being able to register and vote [73 percent of Lawrence's eligible black voters were registered] nor avail himself of the protection of the law. However, he does face rather formidable obstacles in obtaining his share of the economic rewards and satisfactions which all Americans have a right to expect." The report noted further that "economically, then, the Negro in Lawrence is hardly better off than his counterpart in the Deep South or in the large urban slums." African Americans' "opportunities for employment [were] severely limited," their "expectations of earning anything but a subsistence wage" were "ill-founded," and the "possibility of obtaining decent housing" was "very much non-existent." Even those African Americans financially able to afford newer or better housing were prevented from doing so by racist realtors and landlords, who colluded to keep blacks confined to certain parts of the town, particularly east and north Lawrence. Jesse Milan, the first black teacher in the post-*Brown* integrated Lawrence schools, struggled for years to rent or purchase suitable housing for his family. Routinely, when he would arrive to inspect a house, the white landlord told Milan that it had "already been rented." Once, when shown a house with a dirt floor and no indoor toilet, Milan angrily told the realtor to call when he found a house in which the realtor would let his wife live.[29]

Low income and narrow educational and employment opportunities also contributed to the poor housing situation for Lawrence's African American population. The median income in 1960 for nonwhite families in Lawrence was $3,832, over a third less than the median income of $5,708 for all families in Lawrence. Further, the unemployment rate among people of color was significantly higher. The unemployment rate for white men and women in Lawrence was 3.4 percent and 3.5 percent, respectively; the rate for non-white men was 6.9 percent. Interestingly, the rate for black women was 2.9 percent, perhaps reflecting the fact that, as the NAACP reported in 1964, 57 percent "of all adult employed Negroes in Lawrence fall into the category of *domestic* employees (janitors, maids, busboys, cooks, and cook's helpers, etc.)" Magnifying blacks' economic condition was the problem of underemployment: seasonal and reduced hourly work, which further limited annual income.[30]

Mere statistics, however, do not describe the full extent of the social conditions African Americans confronted in Lawrence. Because the black population in Lawrence was small, the town's junior and senior high schools were not segregated. The Lincoln school in north Lawrence was a black-only elementary school until 1954, but it was integrated after the *Brown* decision; it later became a recreation center. Although the quality of education in Lawrence schools was generally good, the racist attitudes of some white teachers and students, and black students' ostracism and physical and cultural isolation, made young African Americans' educational experience less than ideal. Frequently there was only one black student in a class, and there were no black principals, counselors, or administrators in the Lawrence school system. Black history, literature, or culture, and African history were not part of the curriculum.[31]

Additionally, limited post-secondary educational opportunities (the median years of education was eleven for nonwhites in Lawrence, 12.5 for the entire population) further contributed to blacks' low economic status.[32] But even African Americans with high school diplomas were prevented from using the education they had received and were pigeonholed into low-paying, unskilled occupations. In 1963 the Lawrence Human Relations Commission (LHRC), an interracial body formed by the city council in 1961 to improve race relations in the city, observed that several black graduates of Lawrence High School did not use their high school training but worked in low-paying, menial jobs with "inferior status." Opportunities for African Americans in the professions were almost nonexistent. In 1960 there were few black teachers and no black physicians or lawyers in Lawrence (although there had been earlier in the century, when black-owned businesses thrived). Additionally, only 4.5 percent of employed blacks were in retail sales; of these, only a few "were in direct customer contact." The LHRC found that only two of 614 (.003 percent) full-time sales clerks in Lawrence were black; of 166 supermarket employees, only two (.012 percent) were black. The LHRC reported that business owners were "reluctan[t] to 'risk' having a member of a minority" in contact with the public, because they were concerned about the "reaction of other employees, and the image of the business." This attitude reinforced racial stereotypes and boundaries. Several businesses blatantly claimed that blacks were "'unqualified' and that these people must 'help themselves first,'" or that blacks would not "work regardless of opportunity."[33]

While educational opportunity had a clear racial dimension, it also was a dividing line throughout the town's population. More than 23 percent of Lawrence's residents had four or more years of college; presumably most these were university faculty and administrators. The median years of school completed for all persons over 25 was 12.5. In all, over 60 percent of persons in Lawrence 25 and over had at least a high school education. Nearly 40 percent, however, had less than a high school education, including nearly a quarter (23.6 percent) with an eighth grade education or less. These two extremes provide a partial explanation for a thread of anti-intellectualism and general disdain for the university that ran through the community.[34]

Regardless of education level, jobs open to whites in Lawrence abounded after 1945. Much of the community's economic growth in the twentieth century could be attributed first to World War II and later to the Cold War. During World War II, the federal government built a large gunpowder manufacturing plant, Sunflower Ordnance Works, in eastern Douglas County, about twenty miles east of Lawrence. The *Journal-World* reported that construction on the plant had turned Lawrence into a "boom town almost overnight," as the plant hired "three thousand new workers . . . most of whom were housed in Lawrence." The plant pumped much-needed capital into Lawrence's economy, moribund since the Great Depression. The plant shut down production after the war, severely crippling the local economy. It remained stagnant until the military reactivated Sunflower during the Korean War. A seventeen million-dollar expansion in 1952 stimulated an economic recovery throughout the fifties, even after production was cut back after the war.[35]

The key to Lawrence's economic fortunes after World War II was the University of Kansas. Although its free-state legacy provides Lawrence with a unique history in Kansas and the United States, it was the University of Kansas, especially during the twentieth century, that most significantly gave the town its identity, shaped its economy, and affected social relationships. KU athletic teams, like the 1952 NCAA national basketball champions or the 1956–58 teams that featured Wilt Chamberlain, gave national recognition to both the campus and the city and provided an entertainment outlet for local residents. During the twentieth century, national politicians, artists, writers, and other noted figures—including William Jennings Bryan, Billy Sunday, William Howard Taft, Allen Ginsberg, Robert F. Kennedy, and Dr. Benjamin Spock—spoke on campus. The city's cultural scene was enhanced by the university's ability to attract famous artists, musicians, and singers, and its museums, libraries, and theaters provided additional cultural outlets for Lawrencians. Faculty and students from across the country and around the world gave Lawrence a cosmopolitan feel unlike any other Kansas community.

The university was easily the largest employer in town, with over 2,000 staff and faculty in 1963 (more than the city's next eight largest employers combined) and an operating budget of $25,000,000. Annual growth in student enrollment at the KU never was below 4.4 percent during the sixties and averaged 6.8 percent.[36] These student consumers purchased clothing, housing, food, entertainment, and services, while simultaneously adding to the city's coffers through sales taxes. Restaurants, cafes, taverns, clubs, bowling alleys, and skating rinks, to name a few establishments, all relied on the financial support of KU students, which made those establishments available to the greater community, too. KU students provided service-oriented businesses with a large, low-wage employment pool.

Lawrence is often called the most politically liberal community in the state, a perception largely shaped by the university and its students and faculty. While the notion has a grain of truth, on the whole Lawrence is politically conservative. Because of the politics of slavery, Kansas and Lawrence were bulwarks of the Republican Party. New Englanders often claimed their moral superiority over southern materialism but vigorously promoted economic growth and development. Lawrence's Republicans were fiscally conservative, although many were socially moderate, and free market values guided their political outlook. The party of Lincoln had dominated both Kansas's and Lawrence's politics since 1861 and was never more in control than in the 1960s.

Richard Nixon overwhelmingly (two to one) carried Douglas County in the 1960 presidential race. While Lyndon Johnson carried the county in 1964, Barry Goldwater garnered 45 percent of the vote (he received 38.2 percent nationally). In 1968, Nixon garnered almost 49 percent of the Douglas County vote, Hubert Humphrey got 32 percent, and George Wallace took about 10 percent. Local and state races give a better indication of the Republican dominance of local politics. In United States Senate races between 1960 and 1968, the Republican candidate consistently received well over 50 percent of the vote, and often more than 60 percent. The vote for

Republican congressional candidates was even greater.[37] Republicans usually won the lesser state, county, and local political offices, too. The Republican dominance of local politics contributed to the perpetuation of the
town's official narrative. It is not surprising that the prevailing cultural values of the early New England settlers—free enterprise, thrift, promotion of
business, education, and organized religion—are also core values of traditional Republicanism.

Religion, ancestry, ethnicity, class, and a sense of place all were key elements in the construction of a dominant narrative in Lawrence that prescribed social boundaries and created social identities for its residents.
Lawrence was contested space since Kansas's organization as a territory and
remained so in the twentieth century. Its identity and history, encoded in
the rhetoric of freedom and liberty and centered around the free-state/slave-
state turmoil of the 1850s, was given new meaning in the 1960s. Lawrence's
experiences in the 1960s illustrated the continued struggle in the United
States to define and give meaning to freedom, liberty, and equality. The
town remained placid as long as these traditional boundaries went unchal-
lenged. When this happened in the early 1960s, however, conflict was sure
to result.

CHAPTER 2

"KANSAS MUST DECLARE WAR"

During a July 1960 protest to integrate a swimming pool in Lawrence, Ed Abels, the publisher of the weekly newspaper *Lawrence Outlook*, claimed that the picket followed the "pattern of those" protests "staged by the Communists in other parts of the world. The same phrases are used by the picketers, the same tactics are followed," all of which, he argued, were "entirely contrary to the teaching of Christianity." Nine years later, in the aftermath of a student protest against the Reserve Officers Training Corps (ROTC), Lawrence's state senator Reynolds Shultz asserted there was "some connection" between the ROTC disruption and "an international communist conspiracy." Shultz, an ex-marine, professed that he "would rather fight communism in Vietnam than in the wheat fields of Kansas." Later that year, KU chancellor E. Laurence Chalmers refused a demand by the KU Black Student Union (BSU) to crown a black homecoming queen during halftime of the Kansas-Iowa State football game. For even considering the request, K. S. (Boots) Adams, Chair Emeritus of Phillips Petroleum, assailed Chalmers for allowing the "colored minority communistic group" to dictate university policy.[1]

These comments reveal deep-seated antagonism toward social activism and 1960s protest movements. What is more revealing, however, is that each man linked social activism with a communist conspiracy. Organized communists and communism were, at best, tangentially related, through the rhetoric some activists used, to the civil rights, student, and antiwar movements. Abels's and Adams's conviction that the black freedom struggle was communist-inspired perhaps obscures their racist beliefs but reaffirms their own racial (white) identity. Fueling Shultz's political conservatism was the view that student activism, opposition to the Vietnam War, and political liberalism were part of a larger communist plan to overrun the United States. Additionally, by comparing his religious values with atheistic communism,

Abels constructed a Christian, and national, identity out of his anticommunism. Fighting domestic subversion during the Cold War was a dominant force in creating symbolic boundaries and in shaping the perceptions of a significant portion of the American public throughout the decade. Anticommunism activism, by creating and defending specific social boundaries and identities, and by limiting the parameters of the national discourse on the nature and meaning of American society, was an important source of many Lawrencians' experience in the sixties.

A 1960 editorial cartoon in the *Lawrence Daily Journal-World* showed a nervous and quite disturbed John Q. Public, who exclaimed, "I'm Gettin' Sick an' Tired of This Darned Ol' Cold War." In the background, a grinning Nikita Khrushchev clasped his hands in joy. One message was clear: American weariness or apathy in fighting the Cold War was exactly what the communists wanted, and each such expression was tantamount to a victory for Khrushchev or Mao.[2]

Ten years later, Louraine Mulally, a homemaker and a Quaker, succinctly expressed the concerns of many residents of Lawrence: "I [wish] there was something we could do to stop communism."[3] The willingness to confront or contain communism always was a significant aspect of life in Lawrence during the 1960s, and into the 1970s, and was perhaps at times a majority opinion. Mulally's simple plaint suggests the uncertainty and powerlessness felt by many Americans during the era. The Cold War, however, manifested more than fear and trepidation. For Lawrencians it was a prism through which they refracted the world and a cultural source on which they drew to create an American identity and define the "American way of life." Conversely, it also provided a way for them to identify and explain what was not American.

Domestically, the Cold War with the Soviet Union created seemingly irrational fears of internal communist subversion. An anticommunist crusade, fed by the McCarthy witch hunts of the early 1950s, impelled American involvement in the Korean War and escalated a nuclear, missile, and space race with the Soviets. The federal government poured money into defense contractors to fund these projects, resulting in a great economic boom and an affluence never before known. Missile silos, military hardware, and bases were obvious products of Cold War spending, but so too was an interstate highway system (part of the 1956 National Defense Highway Act) and increased funding for education (part of the 1958 National Defense Education Act). A nuclear culture entered the American vernacular and remade daily life. Government agencies, national magazines, and local newspapers gave citizens instructions and plans on how to build fallout shelters. The Cold War also provided a context in which millions of Americans defined, negotiated, and attempted to resolve issues like civil rights, campus unrest, urban crime, school prayer, and the national debt, among others. The Cold War gave form and expression to many social and political issues, acting as a brake that limited social reform during the era.[4]

The Cold War was daily news, and the local media, particularly the *Journal-World*, an afternoon daily that reached perhaps 90 percent of the town's households, kept Lawrencians informed of its progress.[5] Dolph Simons, Sr., the son of the *Journal-World*'s founder and the paper's publisher and editor, and Dolph, Jr., the associate editor, were both ardent cold warriors and staunch defenders of free enterprise and economic growth. They were cautious, even wary, of social change, however, because it threatened the town's tranquil image and thus its ability to attract new industry and investment. The Simons's political and economic views were particularly evident in the weekly "Saturday Column," which three generations of Simons had penned. The column was a frequent forum for assailing communism and America's apparent "softness" toward the Soviets. On one occasion, Dolph Simons, Jr., condemned Americans as ill-prepared to face the challenges of fighting communism, which, to him, was symptomatic of a nation-wide malaise. "It is too bad but it seems there is nothing that can change this attitude—short of an attack on America." In another column, Simons observed "America is the target of all communists, whether it is Khrushchev, Mao, Castro, or some small-time Red agitator. The odds are big enough as it is—let's don't make it worse by being soft, apologetic and unwilling to stand up for our government."[6]

Although the Simons were moderate Republicans, they used the patriotic rhetoric of Americanism to take a hard line on communism, a view that also shaped their take on social issues. Additionally, they defined their Americaness in large measure by how they opposed, and thought others should oppose, communism. This was evident in 1960, when the *Journal-World* endorsed Arizona Senator Barry Goldwater's "back to basics" program to fight communism. Goldwater urged the United States to formulate "sharp, positive aggressive maneuvering," develop an "offensive" strategy, "achieve military superiority," "[k]eep America economically strong," act like a "great power," and "[a]dopt a discriminating foreign policy." Goldwater contended, and the *Journal-World* concurred, that "[c]ommunism is not superior to freedom," and that the "American Revolution meant progress for the world. The Communist revolution means retrogression."[7]

In addition to keeping the community informed about the Cold War and urging greater vigilance in the anticommunist struggle, the *Journal-World* also helped Lawrencians prepare for a nuclear attack. In 1960, for example, the paper featured a sketch of a concrete block fallout shelter that could be built in a basement and would "provide protection from radiation and storms," the latter a persistent concern in the unpredictable Kansas weather. The state's director of civil defense commented that "requests . . . have nearly doubled recently as a result of more tornado activity and alarm over world events," a reference to fears of radioactive fallout from the Soviet Union's atmospheric nuclear testing in 1960. In October 1961, one Lawrence lumberyard reported that during the previous month it had sold material for twelve shelters. The Lawrence Jaycees even built a model fallout shelter in the basement of the community building as "a civic project."[8]

The fear of nuclear war was greatest before and during the 1962 Cuban missile crisis, but it remained a concern throughout the decade and into the 1970s. In 1971, for example, the *Journal-World* published a pullout section on civil defense that included a family emergency plan, a checklist of necessary supplies, and a list of approved fallout shelters in Lawrence. There also were instructions for converting a storm cellar and a basement corner into a fallout shelter. If no other shelter was available, readers were advised to "dig a hole about 2 feet wide by 8 feet long and 4 or 5 feet deep," place two doors over the top, cover with the doors with dirt, and place a blanket or tarp over the entrance to the hole. This promised to "provide excellent protection."[9] Although some Lawrencians did build bomb or fallout shelters during the 1960s, there is no way of determining how many were constructed; it would appear that the number was low. Civil defense planning, however, and especially the designation of public buildings as fallout shelters, continued well into the 1970s.

Cold War culture in Lawrence entailed more than merely reading about civil defense or how to survive a nuclear attack: Citizens became social activists and organized to fight communism at home. Through an intricate web of fraternal and civic organizations, church and work associations, and personal relationships, a grassroots anticommunist movement flourished in Lawrence throughout the 1960s and 1970s.[10] The Lawrence Committee for a Free America was an example. It ran frequent advertisements in the *Outlook,* and invited other "concerned" Lawrencians to learn more about the "Communist menace" and "conspiracy which threatens our very survival as a free nation" and to join its crusade.[11]

Some heeded the call. Merle L. Jackson, an office worker at Norris Brothers Plumbing, asked Congressman Robert F. Ellsworth, a Republican from Lawrence, "for a list of the more than 200 organizations that the Communists use for a front so" he could "help publicize the fact" in Lawrence. Jackson felt he was not alone in fighting domestic communism, as there was "a great many of us wanting some decisive action taken on these things." Perhaps one of those people was Richardson T. Conner, a facilities operations worker at the university. Conner and several friends had been meeting weekly to contemplate the "menace of communism." They listened to recordings from "experts" and perused literature from the House Un-American Activities Committee (HUAC), which had given them a "glum picture on this subject." He asked Ellsworth what Congress was doing "about this menace, and what we as citizens of this great country can do to help eliminate the dangers involved." Connor probably belonged to the Save America from Communism Council, where members studied such topics as "You can Trust a Communist to be a Communist," "The Naked Communists," and Congressional reports on communism, and listened to FBI-approved tapes. Mr. and Mrs. O. H. Garber—he was a plasterer at KU—were members of the study group. They declared that they led "a Christian life and do not want to see our country taken over by the Communists. We ask that you use your good judgement in your part of the law making. We are opposed to Medicare, to [sic] much foreign aid, to all the Subsidys [sic] that are handed out to farmers and many other present day problems which lean toward socialism and eventually to Communism." Ellsworth received "a lot" of correspondence from Lawrence about anticommunist study groups and commended their efforts. "It is absolutely vital that a free people be intelligently informed," he wrote, "and I can think of no better way to do this than to read and discuss."[12]

Grassroots anticommunism in Lawrence also was evident through social, fraternal, and veterans' organizations, like the American Legion and the Veterans of Foreign Wars (VFW). The VFW, for example, sponsored the showing of *Operation Abolition,* the staunchly anticommunist and grossly misleading film produced by HUAC, in the spring of 1961.[13] The American Legion was a steadfast proponent of Americanism and fighting communism. In its early years, especially during the first Red scare after World War I, legion vigilantism was used against communists and other radicals. Concerned with its image, the legion later discouraged such methods and used its institutional resources, political clout, and patriotic rhetoric to organize local and national efforts against subversion. The organization was largely responsible for keeping the issue of domestic subversion before the American public, ultimately leading to the creation of HUAC in the 1930s. Additionally, each local post had a standing "Americanism" committee that promoted American ideals through programs, speeches, loyalty oaths, patriotic observances, and other events.[14]

In Lawrence, the Dorsey-Liberty American Legion Post #14, consisting primarily of veterans of World War I and World War II, sponsored grassroots programs to fight communism. In November 1963, it held an "Americanism Program" at the Lawrence community building, attended by over 200 Legionnaires and guests. The featured speaker was W. Cleon Skousen, the author of *The Naked Communist* and a former FBI agent and chief of police in Salt Lake City. Skousen's appearance was headline news in the *Outlook,* which described him as a "man on a mission" seeking "grass-roots support for a firmer policy toward Communist nations," and he found an eager audience in Lawrence.[15] In February 1964, the legion held an initiation meeting followed by a speech by Clarence Oakes, the director of the Institute for American Strategy, and over 200 people attended. Oakes, a KU graduate and former member of Post #14, outlined communist propaganda techniques and how best to fight them.[16]

Veterans were not the only cold warriors in Lawrence. Other organizations, perhaps not as obvious as the legion and VFW, also devoted time and resources to fighting communism. The Lawrence Kiwanis Club, a civic and service organization comprised mostly of businessmen and white-collar professionals, participated in the public discourse about communism by supporting the "Freedom Academy Bill." The bill would have created "a Freedom Commission and a Freedom Academy to train government personnel, private citizens and foreign students in the non-military science of the global struggle between freedom and communism."[17] The club also hosted speakers who discussed Cold War themes. In May 1961, Colonel Beverly Finkle, an Army instructor at Fort Leavenworth, warned the club that "ignorance, indolence, lethargy and lack of understanding . . . [could] sound the death knell of the freedoms we cherish." Alan Stewart, who worked for the Centron Corporation, a local company that made films, said the talk "impressed" the club "with the urgency of combating communism at home."[18]

Like the Kiwanis Club, the Lawrence Knife and Fork Club, a social organization, frequently hosted "experts" on communism. In March 1960, the club brought to Lawrence the noted anticommunist Herbert A. Philbrick, the author of the best-seller *I Led Three Lives: Citizen, Communist, Counterspy*. Philbrick had infiltrated the Communist Party USA for the FBI in the late 1940s and early 1950s and later recollected his experience in *I Led Three Lives,* which also became a popular television show in the 1950s. He warned the Knife and Fork members about the National Council of Churches and its National Program of Education and Action for Peace to Promote World Order Study Conference, which, he noted, some Lawrence churches were using. Radio station KLWN taped and aired his speech twice "because of popular demand," the cost of which was paid by Knife and Fork member Warren Zimmerman, a fervent cold warrior who personally bore the financial cost of spreading anticommunist literature.[19]

KLWN also brought the anticommunist crusade into the homes of Lawrencians by broadcasting "Life Line" every morning at 6:30.[20] Financed by the eccentric Texas billionaire H. L. Hunt, "Life Line" was a syndicated program produced by the Washington, D.C.-based, nonprofit Life Line Foundation (which included John Wayne on its advisory board). "Life Line" sprinkled religious commentary with political messages, presenting what Hunt called the "constructive" side of an issue; those on the other side of an issue, especially communists, were called the "Mistaken." Although it had a distinct rightist political bent, "Life Line" eschewed the demagoguery and redbaiting of other anticommunists like Joseph McCarthy, Billy James Hargis, or Robert Welch. Hunt directed "Life Line" commentators to moderate opinions on African Americans, Jews, and other minorities, and even encouraged commentators to "praise a well-known Jew so that 'LIFE LINE' would be given the credit of extolling and memorializing a Jew." Although the program was myopically patriotic, it used communism as a springboard to attack "liberal" Supreme Court decisions, the "tyranny" of the federal government, and the expansion of the welfare state.[21]

Lawrencians were receptive to "Life Line" and even welcomed several of the show's hosts. The first "Life Line" shows in the 1950s were hosted by the Reverend Wayne Poucher, a minister in the Church of Christ and the campaign manager of Strom Thurmond's successful write-in senatorial campaign. Poucher preached at the Lawrence Central Church of Christ in 1961 about the threat to religion from communism. Another "Life Line" commentator, Melvin Munn, came to Lawrence in 1965 to discuss the evils of communism; he "was well received" by an enthusiastic audience.[22]

Grassroots anticommunism in Lawrence remained strong throughout the 1960s. By 1970, at the height of Lawrence's violence and turmoil, it was fueled by concerns over the war, urban crime, race riots, campus unrest, and a deteriorating respect for authority, especially for police officers and police departments. President Richard Nixon's Commission on Campus Unrest (PCCU) in August 1970 sent a team to investigate the sources of violence and unrest in Lawrence. A significant potion of the respondents to a questionnaire circulated by the commission believed that communists or "outside agitators" were responsible for the town's troubles. A thirty-six-year resident of Lawrence claimed the town had never "had any serious trouble" until "Communists" and other "outsiders" infiltrated the community. Katherine Tarr, a twenty-seven-year-old housewife believed Lawrence suffered from the "same tension that is causing *world wide* tension and unrest—communist conspirators and agitators trying to create . . . fear from 'below.'" Her husband Kenneth was "fed up with people . . . who pooh-pooh the idea that Communists (and other outsiders) are central to our problems." L. V. Feuerborn, a KU student, believed the problem was "[a]bout 1% a racial problem and 99% caused by communist agitators aided by the news media." Postal Clerk Floyd L. Shields knew, "as does everyone, the root of the trouble is caused, instigated and kept going by the communistic element that has so thoroughly infiltrated . . . all branches of our government with the express and only purpose being to destroy our freedom, our way of life and even our very lives and existence."[23]

Kenneth and Katherine Tarr were members of the Lawrence Support Your Local Police Committee (LSYLPC), which most likely was affiliated with the John Birch Society (JBS). The LSYLPC gave unbridled support to Lawrence's police, and believed that a communist conspiracy was the primary source of the community's problems. In 1971, it sponsored a speech by FBI counterspy Gerald W. Kirk, an African American who had been a student at the University of Chicago. He reported on "revolutionary activities" among Communist Party "fronts" in the area by infiltrating peace group and student organizations like SDS, working for Stokely Carmichael and Dr. Benjamin Spock, and obtaining grants from the government to help the Black Panthers buy weapons. "The Communists, Black militants, and revolutionaries will never succeed in overthrowing the government," Kirk asserted, "[b]ut unless they are stopped, they will scare the American people into accepting socialism from Washington. This is what it is really all about.[24]

The grassroots effort to fight communism in Lawrence was part of a larger, national movement. It is likely that many of Lawrence's cold warriors probably were members of JBS, an organization committed to combating communism and that was strong in Kansas, particularly in Wichita. The majority of Lawrencians, however, probably shared Senator James B. Pearson's view of the Birchers. Although Pearson did not back away from fighting communism, he distanced himself from extreme right-wing groups like JBS. "If their goal is to fight socialism and Communism in this country—well and good," Pearson said about the Birchers. "[B]ut when the leadership of this society brands some of our great public servants such as President Eisenhower as a 'fellow traveler' then this represents a lack of responsibility."[25]

It is not clear if there was an official JBS chapter in Lawrence, but many Lawrencians shared the society's goals and general worldviews, even if they were not members. Lawrencians used the same language, allusions, and rhetoric in their attacks on the federal bureaucracy, social programs, and Supreme Court decisions as did the JBS. The people in the grassroots anticommunism movement in Lawrence did not consider themselves to be extremists or even out of the mainstream of American politics. Their anticommunism was informed by what they understood as threats to their own identity, their religious values, and to the cultural values they associated with the American economic and political system.

If there was an official Birch cell in Lawrence, it might have been led by Edwin (Ed) A. Abels, the founder, publisher, and editor of the weekly *Outlook* and a tenacious anticommunist and notorious red-baiter. Abels established the *Outlook* in 1926, and for the next forty-three years his paper, not unlike the larger *Journal-World,* was a forum against Franklin Roosevelt, New Deal liberalism, the growth of the welfare state, and most frequently, communism. Abels and his wife Marie often sang the praises of the Birchers and invited readers to come by the *Outlook* office to purchase the most recent Birch Society Blue Book.[26] While the *Journal-World* participated in the anticommunist effort by providing information and preaching Americanism, the *Outlook* was the unofficial organ of—and an active participant in— a grassroots anticommunist movement in the community until the paper folded in 1970.[27]

A native of Douglas County, Abels earned an A. B. degree at the University of Kansas in 1914, where he also served on the staff of the *University Daily Kansan.* He later worked for the *Parsons [Kansas] Sun* and did a stint as teacher and superintendent in a small Kansas school district before launching his own his publishing career in 1922 in Humansville, Missouri. He sold that paper after four years and used the proceeds to start the *Douglas County Republican,* which he later renamed the *Lawrence Outlook.* Additionally, Abels served two terms as a state legislator from Douglas County, was president of the National Editorial Association, and was a member of numerous civic and fraternal organizations, including the Masons (in both Lawrence and Kansas City), the Lawrence Kiwanis, the Lawrence Co-op Club (now Sertoma Club), and was director of the Kansas Chamber of Commerce. He often was linked with the Ku Klux Klan.[28] Abels wrote two weekly columns, "Ed Abels' Column" and "Comments on Local Affairs" (which was broadcast on KLWN radio each Sunday). Abels's wife Marie worked beside him at the *Outlook* until her death in 1961. She also wrote a weekly column, "Information to Encourage Loyalty for Citizenship," which was full of commentary and advice on combating communism. They both admonished each Lawrencian to "help win the cold war by being an informed citizen."[29]

Ed and Marie Abels both believed communists were responsible for creating labor strife and undermining authority through the student and civil rights movements, which threatened the nation's security and values and had resulted in a national malaise and cultural decline. Taking their lead from the Birch society, the Abels believed the United Nations, the New Deal, the Marshall Plan, Americans for Democratic Action, most of the students at the University of Kansas, and the majority of Lawrence's churches were communist dupes, a view that was widely shared throughout the community.

Marie Abels, like many women in the United States, was a cold warrior in her own right. Once a Sunday school teacher at First United Methodist Church, Marie Abels withdrew from the church after becoming convinced that church leaders "were compromising with evil rather than taking a firm stand against it," a likely reference to the National Council of Churches' ecumenical movement and the call for a détente with the Soviets in the 1950s. Like her husband, Marie was active in Kansas Republican politics and was a member of the Daughters of the American Revolution (DAR) locally and nationally. Proud of her Virginia ancestors, who owned the estate next to

George Washington's, she traced her heritage prior to the signing of the Magna Carta. Her activity in the DAR was more than an ancestral hobby, her husband recalled, it "gave her an opportunity to teach patriotism and the necessity for checking the communist movement."[30]

The liberal welfare state, as it emerged in the twentieth century, was a site of cultural debate among Americans as they struggled to understand its meaning and its power. When this conflict melded with the Cold War, it resulted in an augmented "illiberal patriotism" and a veneration of national might.[31] Cold War culture was highly masculinized, pervading all areas of American society, including the family and gender roles. Within this culture, a true patriot—male or female—need not risk his or her life through military service, but must exhibit his or her love of country through the conduct of their everyday life. Social conventions and cultural ideals promoted a particular way of life and brand of patriotism by linking hegemonic social expectations with political goals. As well, the values of capitalism, pitted against the communist menace, were embedded in domesticity. Thus, the Cold War reinforced traditional gender roles, notions of domesticity, and the centrality of the nuclear family as a refuge against the threat of nuclear attack and communist subversion. Women were to be the custodians of this struggle. Although during the 1950s, and certainly by the 1960s, many Americans (especially women) came to challenge these notions, women still remained important sources of gendered and national identity, markers of social boundaries, and obstacles to meaningful social change.[32]

Women played important roles creating and sustaining the culture of anticommunism and created specific social boundaries around that culture. Many women in Lawrence felt a particular threat from communism, not only to their identity as women but also to their identity as Americans. It was evident in the frequent letters about the perils of communism that women in Lawrence wrote to their elected leaders and local newspapers and in the activities of several women's clubs. The John Pound chapter of the Daughters of the American Colonists (DAC), for example, frequently held talks on patriotism and fighting communism. The Betty Washington chapter of the Daughters of the American Revolution in Lawrence invited anticommunists to speak on topics such as the United Nation's efforts to abolish the Constitution, communist "double-speak," and New Deal threats to private property, youth, local autonomy, and the control of agriculture. They believed that a bigger federal government, the progressive income tax, and the centralization of credit and money were evidence of the American drift toward socialism and communism.[33]

It is significant that these women professed a particular social identity (white, Anglo-Saxon, Protestant, old-stock immigrants) and a particular Americaness through their participation in the DAC and the DAR, an identity that they believed communism threatened. They used the DAC and the DAR and their resources and rhetoric to defend that identity and maintain the boundaries it prescribed. Moreover, the DAR's glorification of the nation, the military, traditional gender roles, a philosophy of service and sacrifice, and subordination of personal attainment to duty and the greater good effectively created a civil religion with the family and ancestry at its core. The DAR and the DAC used the culture of anticommunism to reaffirm their own Americaness and woman's traditional place in sustaining that collective identity.[34]

The culture of anticommunism was evident in Lawrence in other forms, particularly as it promoted the values of American capitalism. Local businesses, for example, used anticommunism not only to display their patriotism but also to attract customers. The Standard Life Association, whose home office was in Lawrence, frequently ran half- or full-page advertisements that promoted Americaness. In June 1961, its ad claimed "Liberty Needs Your Protection" and encouraged citizens to "Do More Than Defend—Fight For Freedom! Be an informed, active citizen." The First National Bank of Lawrence believed "we must fight to keep our freedom and rights alive in a world threatened by Communist control. We need the faith our forefathers showed when they stood up and fought for their right to freedom." Another advertisement played on an important American value, property ownership, by claiming "RUSSIANS don't have private property to insure but Americans do and that's what keeps the George Hayes Insurance Agency in business."[35] Defending capitalism through consumption, therefore, was an act of patriotism. Buying a house and insuring it made as strong a statement against communism as did rooting out atomic spies.

Indeed, defending the capitalist system and property rights was an important element of the anticommunist crusade. Many Lawrencians in the early 1960s believed that the greatest threat to American freedom and values came not from the Soviet Union's nuclear arsenal but from the United States government. Since the 1930s, the New Deal had increased the size of the liberal, interventionist welfare state, with a corresponding increase in its power and involvement in the lives of American citizens. The *Journal-World's* attacks on communism belied a subtle assault on big government, liberalism, obstacles to economic growth, and New Deal-type legislation. For example, an August 1960 editorial entitled "Maddening, Isn't It?" bemoaned the revelation that it "costs roughly $33 billion" to pay eight million government workers." On another occasion, Dolph Simons, Jr., wrote that "[e]veryone likes to get something for free," but noted that the "freeloader bandwagon cannot be expected to roll on forever without disastrous consequences somewhere along the road." He suggested that Douglas County, which saw its welfare expenditures rise from 1950 to 1960, require "local welfare chiselers" to work for their support.[36]

The *Journal-World* merely expressed concerns shared by many Lawrencians. The rise of the welfare state, in lockstep with the Cold War struggle, suggested to many Americans a trend in the United States toward socialism, which they believed was only a step away from communism. James R. Thomen, an assistant manager at the DuPont chemical plant near Lawrence, encouraged Congress to "guide this nation away from . . . expecting the government to solve the problems of life." In another letter, Thomen proclaimed, "Free enterprise is dead! . . . choked at the hands of TOO MUCH GOVERNMENT." A. B. Weaver, who owned Weaver's Department Store on Massachusetts Street, believed a minimum wage law was "a threat to the general welfare" and "an issue that strikes at the most important principle—States Rights—Main Streets."[37]

As these letters suggest, after World War II the debate over the proper role of the federal government and its relationship to the states and the people intensified. The discussion was complicated by fears of communism. After World War II, America's cold warriors had formulated a stinging critique of American society and the liberal state. Theirs was not a radical assessment, for it never questioned the foundations of the American socioeconomic system and sought a return to "traditional" values. But it did question the authority and legitimacy of the federal government and the relationship between it, on the one hand, and the states and the people, on the other.

According to several Lawrencians, New Deal, New Frontier, and Great Society legislation and programs played right into the hands of the communists, threatening capitalism and free enterprise by undermining individualism and promoting socialism. Elmer Pond, a barber, opposed Medicare, government "interference with our free enterprise system [and] farm subsidies." These were all part of the same "trend toward socialism" that he felt "should be reversed." Similarly, Doris Zeller, a research associate at KU, believed Medicare was an example of "the insidious socialization taking place in our country which is stifling individual incentive." Weldon H. Sickles, the owner of the Pancake Man restaurant, opposed the repeal of section 14(b) of the 1947 Taft-Hartley Act (which permitted states to pass and enforce right to work laws), which, he claimed, would force him to raise prices, lay off some employees, and throw them "onto government relief rolls." The move to repeal 14(b) indicated to Sickles that the nation needed "[l]ess federal control." Such control was "leading us toward socialism and undermining individual initiative which made this country great."[38]

Likewise, L. W. and W. H. Blevins, the owners of Blevins' Bike Shop, were "deeply concerned with the socialistic trend of our country." Their fear of socialism, however, seemed to be driven less by any ideological concerns and more by what they perceived as a loss of their own identities as Americans. The Blevins worried that the United States was "rapidly becoming a nation of subsidies and pressure groups" rather than a unified nation of "Americans," a not-too-oblique reference to the civil rights movement.[39] This point is crucial. The Blevins and their neighbors—who were all white—felt threatened by the expansion of the federal government and the increase in social welfare programs. Consequently, these citizens linked their marginalization to a communist plot or a socialist government. In their minds, such programs were usurping power from hard-working people and were helping "undeserving " minorities.[40] Moreover, the welfare state, by re-distributing power and resources, threatened these people's sense of them-selves and their place in the community.

Similarly, communism was quite personal for Douglas County State Bank president Chester G. Jones because it attacked the values and symbols around which he constructed his own identity as an American. What Jones felt was at stake was "the American way of life," an ambiguous notion that he defined only as the opposite of communism and that subsumed any racial, ethnic, or gendered identity he might have professed. Like the Blevins brothers, Jones decried the idea of "hyphenated Americans." He was Amer-ican, there were only "Americans," and he claimed this identity because his values and personal identity stood in stark opposition to the values of com-munism. To Lawrencians like Chester Jones communism meant slavery, col-lectivism, and the destruction of free enterprise. The American way of life stood for timeless and absolute truths: liberty, freedom, and individualism. Fighting communism was a matter of life and death, and nothing could be worse than living under communist rule. "Of course, no one wants war," Jones reminded Senator Pearson, "but there are infinitely more terrible ex-periences than war and possible death."[41] The Blevins, Jones, and their fel-low Lawrencians, confronted with increased governmental regulation and taxes as well as an economy and society in transition, looked to the past to sustain a sense of who they were, an identity that was largely constructed by their vision of who is and is not an American. The culture of anticommu-nism gave them a means to do this.

The rhetoric of the Cold War reduced the world to simple terms: one was either a communist (a red), sympathetic to communism (pinks, pinkos, fel-low travelers), or an "American" who opposed communism and believed in the "American way of life." Moreover, Cold War rhetoric obscured other possible social identities, severely constrained social space, and left little room for the dominant boundaries to be challenged. In this view, how could one be an American if one charged that America was racist, sexist, or impe-rialistic? There was little, if any, public space for blacks, students, women, and others who questioned the narrative. The naive assumption that those who challenged America's social inequities were tacitly un-American masked the complexity of the Cold War, of course, but it provided a convenient way for "true Americans" to identify who was and was not an American. To what extent one contained, fought, or stood up to communism became, for millions of Americans, the principal criterion that measured one's Americaness and set the boundaries prescribed by that identity.

Letters from Lawrence residents to local newspapers depicted communists as duplicitous and conniving people who never could be trusted, all qualities that, to cold warriors, made communism antithetical to American values. Mrs. H. M. Brownlee, who lived in rural Douglas County, claimed "to the Communists the word 'peace' means the time they have conquered the world." Brownlee demanded a potent, large American nuclear deterrent, because the Soviets would not "hesitate to attack a nation without defense." The Cold War was not unlike World Wars I or II to Brownlee, and she asked why "some people regard[ed] the cold war as sort of a football game when in reality it is worse than a shooting war because of the Commie double-talk? It poisons the mind."[42]

To many Lawrencians, communism was not only a threat to their freedom and a challenge to how they defined the "American way of life" but also an attack on religion and Christian values. Anticommunists assumed the United States was a Christian nation, and "atheistic" or "Godless" communism, in the eyes of cold warriors, was immoral and incompatible with Americanism and Christianity. The Christian religion became yet another indicator of who was and was not an American. Hattie McClain, the widow of a clerk for the Standard Life Association, believed a proposed "atheist colony" in western Kansas was "an insult to all red-blooded American citizens." McClain proclaimed that Americans needed "to prove to the atheists and the communists that we are going to keep America the Land of the Free and the Home of the Brave."[43] Mrs. Lee Morgan was suspicious of the ecumenical National Council of Churches (NCC) since news accounts had linked it to the Communist Party and it had opposed a Constitutional amendment protecting prayer in schools. Many on the right feared that the NCC's ecumenicalism—participation in a world-wide Christian church—was leading the United States down the path to one worldism, and thus to the loss of a distinctive American identity. "[I]f if the accusations are correct," she warned, "the very basis of our American belief is on the threshold of destruction." Morgan was not alone in Lawrence in asserting that the United States and "its laws and standards" were built "on faith in God and in the church of our choice."[44] Citing J. Edgar Hoover as an authority, Morgan concluded that "[b]ecause they despise the church, the Communists continually attempt to infiltrate unsuspecting religious organizations.'" Morgan believed that communism was "a terrible way of life, and not one of us who love God and our country want to live under Communist controlled government or churches."[45]

The battle for the religious values of the United States was waged on many fronts. None, however, was more disconcerting to Lawrencians than the 1963 Supreme Court decision prohibiting mandatory prayer and Bible reading in public schools. The decision "shocked" Daisy Reynolds, a member of both the John Pound chapter of the DAC and the Betty Washington Chapter of the DAR. "What under the Sun" she asked, was "the Supreme Court thinking of to permit the Atheists to take over the running of the country." It was "time for AMERICA TO WAKE UP," Reynolds said, and it was up to elected officials to "stamp out this Atheist plan, as YOU KNOW its the fore runner to commonism [sic]." The DAC supported legislation that would keep Bible reading and references to God in the Pledge of Allegiance and on coins.[46] The court's decision so upset Elmer Pond, a barber at Jayhawk's Barber Shop, that he believed Congress should investigate Earl Warren "and maybe the entire supreme court." Pond did not think Warren was "an idiot, so he must be a communist." The Birch Society had initiated an "Impeach Earl Warren" campaign in the early 1960s, but Pond made it clear that he was "not a Bircher," although he thought they were right about Warren. Moreover, Pond thought it was "unfair to let a very small minority deny the majority their privalige [sic] that our constitution guarantees."[47]

In the eyes of Lawrencians and other Americans, communism threatened not only American religious beliefs and institutions but also the nation's educational system. Cold warriors in Lawrence saw the University of Kansas as a "hotbed of Communism and socialism," a source of domestic unrest and moral decay, and a challenge to traditional authority. In 1970 many Lawrencians resolutely believed that all of the town's problems could be traced to a communist conspiracy. A typical response came from Robert Ammel, a thirty-eight-year-old painter, who professed "[t]here are communist type people in the university here and elsewhere." Katherine Tarr stated that "the 'insiders' behind the campus and other disorders are communists," while a sixty-five-year-old life-long resident believed the town's travails were the fault of KU faculty and "other pinks and reds."[48] Yet KU and other universities employed a large number of politically conservative faculty (particularly in the hard sciences, business, law, and architecture) as well as a great many liberal anticommunists.[49] Raymond G. O'Connor, a history professor at KU, warned that Americans must "defeat the communist threat" and "do whatever is necessary to preserve our beliefs, our fundamental values and our way of life." O'Connor claimed, with a hint of nostalgia, that this would require the same level of commitment and sacrifice the United States had exhibited during World War II to defeat "a system dedicated to our extinction."[50] Throughout the 1960s, the nation's universities were as much a place of conservatism as they were of liberal or radical reform. Although the university was often seen as a bastion of liberalism, it only reflected the society of which it was a part, and KU faculty reflected the range of political perspectives. University of Kansas geographer Walter Kollmorgen, for example, was a liberal on many social issues but also an ardent anticommunist virulently opposed to bigger government and social welfare programs.

Kollmorgen's colleague Fred C. Bates, an associate professor of mechanics and aerospace engineering at the University of Kansas, expressed his views on America's struggle against communism in a January 1963 article in the *Journal-World*. The "pressures of the cold war," he argued, had dangerously enlarged the powers of the executive branch, increased the size of the "welfare state" at the expense of individualism, and pushed the nation down the road to socialism. The United States had to win the Cold War, he asserted, because communism threatened to enslave America. "[S]elfish objectives" and "factionalism" (another reference to the civil rights movement) undermined social order. The country was "drifting" from the "democratic, capitalistic ideology" on which the nation was founded. So "Kansas must declare war," Bates concluded, and "must contribute far beyond its relative status among the States" to winning the Cold War.[51]

Bates was pessimistic but saw a solution. By applying faith in democratic capitalism, by practicing "individualism," by assuming leadership in the "psychological warfare" of the Cold War, and by increasing its production of "deterrent weapon systems," Kansas could help the United States not only to win the Cold War but also to create economic development. "Kansas companies, organized and led by Kansans, financed . . . by Kansas wealth, and producing things that have stemmed from ideas by Kansans developed by Kansans" would show democratic capitalism in action and provide an economic windfall to the state.[52]

Bates missed the paradox of his analysis: He wanted to trim the government yet expand the national security apparatus; he supported liberal economic policies for business but wanted to avoid the "factionalism" of liberal social legislation; he ultimately wanted collective action to fight collectivism. Democratic capitalism and liberal economic growth, spurred on by greater defense spending and a return to the "traditional" values of "rugged individualism," would be an economic boon for Kansans, resolve pressing social issues like inequality and poverty, eliminate bloated government bureaucracy, and win the Cold War to boot.[53]

Fred Bates was no demagogue, no McCarthyite in academic robes hunting for communists lurking in each corner. But he was a cold warrior, not unlike Ed Abels, Warren Zimmerman, or any number of other Lawrencians. Like Abels, Dolph Simons, Jr., the banker Chester Jones, and others, Bates believed in the unlimited benefits of capitalism and free enterprise. Although he might typically be branded as a "liberal" because he was in academia, Bates was as socially conservative as Abels or Zimmerman. The free exchange of ideas was perhaps a guiding principle of the academy, but like other Lawrencians, Bates decried the dissent and "factionalism" that threatened the fabric of an ordered society. Bates used a sense of place as a shield against communist intrusion, but beneath his adulation of Kansans, his disdain for communism, and his critique of the Cold War, Bates articulated a distinct political perspective that combined elements of traditional American conservatism (individualism, smaller government, moral order) with economic liberalism (democratic or unfettered capitalism), which ultimately would make the United States triumphant over communism.

Bates pointedly decried the "factionalism" created by the civil rights movement that he, and others, feared was threatening the nation's strength. The link between Cold War Americanism and race became clearer as the decade progressed and was painfully obvious at the height of Lawrence's unrest in 1970. There was no ignoring the racial overtones of Rick Dowdell's death, although many Lawrencians saw it as a matter of law and order rather than race. A substantial portion of the community believed that racial problems in the United States, and especially in Lawrence, were communist inspired. Margaret Lockard, who identified herself as a member of the white race, gave a typical response: "We have many fine negro families in Lawrence who are honored and respected. Unfortunately, they are being linked to all the outrages perpetrated by various subversive groups. They too are frightened and need to be protected and in some way separated from the agitators." Lewis O. Sale, a U.S. letter carrier and longtime resident of Lawrence, believed that the town's racial unrest was merely "a front used [to] muster other subjects into this Unit. All of the town Rascals (colored) are anxious to join in the plundering." Katherine Tarr, a twenty-seven year old housewife and officer in the LSYLPC, believed that "Black radicals" were mere "'dupes' to help promote socialism in America." An auto repair shop and car wash owner concluded that the unrest was caused by "Communist[s] . . . agitating the black people and passing out narcotics to them," while a postal clerk thought "trained outside revolutionarys [sic] with a few local recruits in Lawrence" were "trying to drive a wedge between the races."[54]

What this suggests is that throughout the 1960s and well into the 1970s there existed a strong, highly masculinized and racialized anticommunist ideology in the United States that was a significant factor in mobilizing political opposition and placing very real limits on liberal reform efforts. Additionally, anticommunism was a crucial factor in creating what scholars have called the "conservative backlash" or the "rise of the new right."[55] Anticommunist activism has received little attention as a social force in shaping the 1960s. The anticommunist crusade, to be sure, was undemocratic, racist, regressive, and repressive. But for millions of Americans, it refracted the world, and thus was a powerful social force in shaping the content and the context of a public discourse to define America and Americaness. Anti-communism was not monolithic—there were radical, moderate, and even liberal anticommunists—but the culture of the Cold War was all around and many Lawrencians drew heavily on that culture to construct their world. It provided them a means (although certainly not the only one) of interpreting what they considered the failings of American society, in particular the New Deal and the liberal welfare state. It also allowed them to interpret and understand, in their own way, the civil rights and student movements, the Vietnam War, feminism, and traditional gender roles, among other issues, and colored their responses to the changes wrought by these movements. It was perhaps reactionary and undemocratic but it should not be underestimated as a social force, a form of social activism, and a brake on social reform.

At the heart of the Cold War (and especially the anticommunist crusade) was a debate to define the state and its role in allocating privilege and benefits to citizens. Because dissenters were seen as "un-American," American Cold War culture, with the defeat of communism at its core, severely constricted the choices of identities available to Americans and drew tight the acceptable boundaries of American society. Although there were significant challenges to this culture and cracks began to form in the Cold War consensus during the 1960s, anticommunism remained strong throughout the era. With the boundaries drawn so narrowly, identities too became constrained; one was either an American and believed in the American way of life, or one was a communist, or a communist sympathizer or dupe. Fighting communism was one way to create an identity for oneself, set the boundaries prescribed by that identity, and proscribe the identity and boundaries of the "other." As such, it contributed to the transformation of American political culture.

In Lawrence, Kansas, the Cold War culture was dominant. Whether conscious of it or not, the residents of the community negotiated the meaning(s) of freedom, citizenship, patriotism, and an American identity, configured their social, political, and economic life within the context of this culture, and created and recreated social boundaries and identities. This struggle between good and evil became the metaphor through which many Lawrencians interpreted and explained both domestic and international affairs.

Understanding how the Cold War shaped these boundaries is crucial for understanding the responses to the racial, ethnic, and gender mobilization that often defines the 1960s. It also is vital for understanding the conservative political resurgence and the decline of liberalism in the 1960s. In decisive ways, those responses shaped the mobilization of identity during the decade. Anticommunism claimed to be neither racially specific (although most of its proponents used it to affirm their whiteness) nor ethnically specific (although its zealots, as far as I can tell, were old-stock immigrants) nor gender specific (although the rhetoric was clearly masculinized). Moreover, the claim to an "authentic" American identity also included the right to claim who was "un-American."

The Cold War created a dominant culture in the United States that deflated the world into a simple dichotomy: The "good" values of American democratic capitalism were pitted against the malevolence of international communism. In language not unlike that used by civil rights activists, anticommunist activists constructed their own "freedom struggle." The culture of the Cold War contained several elements, but central to it was a bipolar narrative of struggle: between capitalism and communism, between democracy and totalitarianism, between individualism and collectivism, and, most importantly, between freedom and slavery.

At the very core of American Cold War culture was opposition to communism: combating, containing, or destroying it, although there was never any unanimity on how this should or could be accomplished. Tactics, strategies, and action ran the gamut from the liberal promotion of economic growth to the reactionary creation of a police state. Always, however, the goal was to confront communism, because millions of Americans perceived it as the antithesis to fundamental American values. Communism and American capitalism could not coexist; they were mutually incompatible. Capitalism was democratic, based on individual freedom; communism was authoritarian and denied freedom to the individual. Capitalism encouraged individualism, private ownership of property, and hard work; communism encouraged collectivism, state ownership, and indolence. Capitalism acknowledged a creator and encouraged spiritual values; communism was atheistic. Americans were free; Communists were slaves. As we will see in the next chapter, any challenge to this model, especially racialized challenges, were vigorously resisted.

CHAPTER 3

"THE RIGHT TO THESE THINGS"

In March 1965, Justin D. Hill, the president of the Lawrence Paper Company in Lawrence, Kansas, wrote to University of Kansas chancellor W. Clarke Wescoe about a recent civil rights demonstration on campus. He commended Wescoe for having the protestors arrested, calling it a "stand for law and order and the protection of the rights of others." His comments on the substance of the protest, however, were more revealing. Hill, who lived in Lawrence's racially exclusive West Hills area, was astounded that African Americans in Lawrence, and across the nation, were "demanding housing in suburbs developed by whites, jobs in companies developed by whites, the right to eat in restaurants and go to stores owned and developed by whites." Declaring that "white people must earn the right to these things, it is not given to them," Hill concluded that the "coloreds should earn the right to these things," too.[1]

Hill, a grandson of one of the town's most successful entrepreneurs, president of the largest locally-owned business, a member of the chamber of commerce, and an elder in the Plymouth Congregational Church, here offered a vision of a society at odds with the dream of Dr. Martin Luther King, Jr., and civil rights activists in Lawrence. While Hill did not refer to the dominant white superiority/black inferiority model that typified the American South, he nonetheless seems to justify racial segregation. Hill identified himself as white, in opposition to "the coloreds" who were "demanding" the "right" to eat, shop, or live wherever they chose. In language not unlike the Supreme Court used in its 1896 landmark decision *Plessy v. Ferguson,* Hill implied that the property interests of individual white Americans, as homeowners or as businesspeople, superseded the rights of blacks, as a group, to equal opportunity and protection under the law. Ironically, Hill made this proclamation based on a group identity, as a "white person" and for other "white people." Hill did not close the door to racial equality someday, but made clear it would be opened wide only when blacks "proved" themselves worthy; moreover, "white Americans" like himself should control the process of opening the doors.

For thousands of Lawrencians like Justin Hill, group identity and social boundaries were based on skin color, and they used arguments for property rights to defend those boundaries. This particular protest, and the movement more generally, provided Hill with an opportunity to affirm his whiteness and reject the collective goals of the black freedom struggle. Moreover, clearly Hill felt that his own identity as a "white" person, and the privilege and power that accompanied it, was being challenged by civil rights activists.

Perhaps the most enduring legacy of the freedom struggle, especially that part of the struggle since 1945 that is commonly called the civil rights movement, is that it politicized and socialized—to one degree or another—nearly all Americans, whether they were active participants or not. Their resistance to the goals of the civil rights movement was a source on which many Americans drew to construct or reconstruct their own identity and to set racial boundaries within their communities. In his opposition to civil rights activism, Justin Hill revealed a great deal about the civil rights movement in the United States and the limits of liberal reform. Moreover, views such as Hill's reveal how basic values like freedom, equality, and citizenship in the United States were contested in the 1960s, which gave the era much of its character.

Significantly, racial identity, both "blackness" and "whiteness," was crucial in how these values were defined and acted upon. On the one hand, most Lawrencians who identified themselves as white had full access to the community's political economy as consumers of goods and labor and were citizens by virtue of their skin color, no matter their socioeconomic standing. Whites in Lawrence did not need to demand the "right" to eat or shop or live wherever they wanted; they already had "earned" that privilege, as part of the psychological wage of whiteness.[2] On the other hand, African Americans in Lawrence did not have full access to Lawrence's political economy, as either consumers or workers. Moreover not all public spaces, especially the city's housing market, were open to them, thus they could not enjoy the full benefits of citizenship. Their struggle for full citizenship and the resistance to that struggle by many white Lawrencians was an essential factor in shaping Lawrence's sixties experience.

Of all the towns in Kansas, Lawrence might have seemed the least likely to experience racial problems. Because of its free state status, and the influence of abolitionists in settling the town, Lawrence had been a symbol of the African American struggle for freedom and equality since before the Civil War. In practice, however, most white Lawrencians never did welcome blacks, despite the fact that by 1890 almost 2,000 African Americans, about one-fourth of the population, called it home. To be sure, Lawrence never resembled the Jim Crow South, but racial exclusion and clustered housing characterized the town and the University of Kansas in the nineteenth century and well into the twentieth century. Blacks had voted freely in Lawrence since the end of the Civil War, but most could buy or rent only substandard housing in clustered neighborhoods scattered around the town. As workers they typically earned a third less than whites, suffered higher rates of unemployment and underemployment than whites, and confronted limited educational and employment opportunities. As well, they were socially excluded and frequently endured the indignities of racial slurs and ostracism. Like other African Americans outside of the South, those in Lawrence had some of the trappings of equality but were not afforded the opportunity and respect that accompany first-class citizenship. The persistence of these conditions compelled hundreds of black and white Lawrencians to continue the struggle for racial justice, and by the end of World War II grassroots activism had begun to challenge the dominant racial structures and hierarchies in the community.

At the vanguard of civil rights activism between 1945 and 1960 was the Lawrence League for the Practice of Democracy (LLPD), an interracial organization dedicated to social justice and racial equality through nonviolent, liberal reforms. The LLPD's members, many of whom were employed by the university, pledged to "foster and encourage" racial harmony and cooperation through the practice of grassroots democracy. Members swore not to abide racial or religious intolerance or to perpetuate racial or religious stereotypes. The close connection between the LLPD and the university community, however, was often a source of contention for those in Lawrence opposed to the organization's efforts. Some conservative residents of Lawrence frequently sneered at LLPD members as "outsiders" who had no real commitment to the community and sought only to stir up trouble. The LLPD's most active members were KU faculty, their spouses, and students, most of whom were born outside of Kansas. They, too, lived in Lawrence, however, and felt justified in fighting racial injustice in the place they called home.[3]

Racial exclusion and discrimination were not confined to the town proper. While blacks had been "welcomed" at KU since the university's founding, once they arrived in Lawrence they were shunned, both on campus and in the greater community, a trend that continued well into the twentieth century.[4] Jesse Milan, who first enrolled at KU in 1946 and received a B. S. in 1953 and an M. S. in education in 1954, recalled enduring this inferior social status. Blacks then could not participate in intercollegiate athletics (this was true until the early 1950s), were segregated at the cafeteria in the union, were not allowed to take part in activities like the orchestra or the glee club, and were not invited to join white fraternities or sororities. There were no African Americans on the university faculty, Milan recalled; janitors or other menial jobs were the only positions held by blacks at KU. Milan claimed that while he was grudgingly accepted by fellow students and instructors in the classroom (although he believed his grades were lowered because of his teachers' prejudice), he was never invited to participate in social activities.[5]

Between 1943 and 1960, the LLPD, Lawrence's chapter of the National Association for the Advancement of Colored People (NAACP) and the university-based Congress of Racial Equality (CORE) had made important progress in eliminating racial exclusion in Lawrence and at the university. While backed by the moral authority and activities of local churches, the effort was aided by the institutional power of KU chancellor Franklin D. Murphy and the presence of KU basketball star Wilt Chamberlain. Murphy, who served as chancellor of the university from 1951 to 1960, epitomized the liberalism that characterized early civil rights activism. He used the chancellor's office as a lever for social change by threatening to show first-run movies and open barbershops and cafes on campus that would compete with Lawrence's segregated businesses, which convinced many business people to open their doors to blacks. Chamberlain played an important role in breaking down racial barriers, but business owners typically welcomed the seven-foot-tall All-American and selectively excluded other African Americans. The progress that Murphy and Chamberlain helped attain proved illusory. After Murphy left Lawrence to become the chancellor at the University of California, Los Angeles, and Chamberlain departed for professional basketball, white Lawrence business owners and city officials often ignored antidiscrimination laws, excluding African Americans at their own discretion.[6]

The struggle continued without Murphy and Chamberlain. Since an abortive "sit-down" in a local cafe in 1947, civil rights activists had shied away from direct action, opting instead to use legal or other economic means to end racial exclusion in the community.[7] That changed in July 1960 when, inspired by the southern sit-in movement, about thirty civil rights activists picketed the Jayhawk Plunge, a privately owned swim club that let whites, but not blacks, swim as "guests" of members.[8] Inexplicably, the pool for years had evaded, through deceit or a lack of enforcement, a city ordinance requiring the licensing of swimming pools. White children could swim safely at the Plunge by paying the twenty-five-cent admission fee, while black children could only peer in through a chain-link fence surrounding the pool.[9]

In March 1960, civil rights organizations began applying pressure on Bertha Nottberg, the owner of the Plunge, to integrate the pool. Harry Shaffer, a refugee from Nazi persecution in Austria and an economics professor who had just assumed the presidency of the LLPD from Jesse Milan, announced that the group would use legal, nonviolent methods to accomplish that goal, including mass-meetings, boycotts, and direct action. As president of the recently reconstituted Lawrence-Douglas County NAACP (LDC-NAACP), Jesse Milan joined the battle, despite some friction between him and Shaffer over tactics and strategy. The LDC-NAACP preferred to seek a court injunction to prevent anyone from swimming at the pool.[10]

Supporters of the segregation policy decried the involvement of "outsiders" from KU and the encroachment on the property rights of the pool's owner.[11] Lawrence homemaker Norma McCanles, for example, wondered why "all of a sudden, the pool has to be considered to belong in the inalienable rights category. What about the rights of business owners? Have they lost their right to run their business as they see fit[?]" McCanles was not alone in her views. Charles C. Spencer declared "an individual still has the inalienable right to pick or select his own friends and associates."[12] Rather than integrate, Nottberg closed the pool, then leased it to two investors a week later, who promised to operate it as private club. The LLPD could do little but promise to monitor the club's guest policy.[13]

Ed Abels wrote in the *Outlook* that Lawrence had "advanced far since the days when Negroes were hanged from the Kansas river bridge."[14] Confronted with attitudes such as this, it is not surprising that the picket failed to integrate the pool and only compelled a private club to operate as such. The picket upstaged the NAACP's injunction strategy, sowed the seeds of dissension among civil rights activists in the community, and polarized public opinion. Just as significantly, the resistance to the picket testified to the potent forces impeding racial equality in Lawrence and the limits of liberalism in challenging those forces. Unadulterated racism was one such force, but many Lawrencians, like Americans throughout the land, defended segregation through their opposition to the activist, liberal state and a steadfast belief in the rights of private property. Rather than arguing against integration around the nexus of white supremacy/black inferiority, these individuals—consciously or not—effectively resisted integration by painting themselves as defending freedom, individualism, and private property against the encroachment of the liberal state and special interests. The result was a defense of segregation with a "moral" voice, a more rational defense than one based on racial hierarchies. By defining freedom as the right to own and dispose of property without interference from the state, white Lawrencians, in effect, challenged liberalism and the activist state by defending white-only public spaces and by reaffirming existing racial boundaries.[15]

The Plunge protest failed to desegregate the pool but laid the groundwork for a decade of social activism for full access to public accommodations, open housing, and equal employment and educational opportunities. The struggle to integrate private clubs like the Plunge illustrates the contested definitions that Americans gave to ideas such as freedom and equality. To segregationists the Plunge signified the right of free association and the right of business owners to use their property how they saw fit. Civil rights activists argued that publicly licensed, segregated pools implicated local governments for tacitly accepting, if not outright promoting, racial exclusion.

Perhaps most significantly, the demonstration raised an awareness of racial exclusion in the community, which most white Lawrencians claimed had not existed previously. In response, the Lawrence City Commission created the Lawrence Human Relations Commission (LHRC) in May 1961. The *Journal-World* acknowledged that Lawrence had a human relations problem but questioned whether it was "serious enough for local government participation." Dr. Ted Kennedy, a city commissioner and LLPD member, argued that the LHRC would be the "first time the city in its official capacity has shown an interest in the Civil Rights problem." Like many white residents of Lawrence, Kennedy believed the existence of a racial problem was ambiguous. One "could get an argument on this" from some parts of the community, he declared, 'but "I think the action at the pool this summer . . . [has] pointed out that the students feel there is a problem." Commissioner Phillip Godwin asserted that the LHRC could "solve discrimination problems without creating tension," as he claimed the LLPD and the Civil Rights Council, a KU student organization, were doing. "They are making a lot of noise," he said, but church organizations were "doing more to solve the problem." Ed Abels of the *Outlook* spoke for many Lawrencians concerned about the involvement of "outsiders" sent to Lawrence as part of a "highly organized and carefully directed scheme to stir up trouble in the university and our community" and "to stir up bitterness and hatred." Abels believed that race relations were improving and would continue to do so as long as blacks were "ready and prepared" when opportunities came along. Quoting a "long time resident" in the wake of the Plunge picket, Abels claimed Lawrence never had "a race problem . . . until it was stirred up by the University people."[16]

Black Lawrencians knew there was a problem in Lawrence, the extent of which was made more evident as the civil rights movement gained strength and began to focus its energies on fair housing and employment. Following the 1963 March on Washington and the highly publicized atrocities committed by segregationists against blacks and freedom workers in the South, President John F. Kennedy sent legislation to Congress that would eliminate racial exclusion and discrimination in federal employment, contracts, and housing, and that was passed as the Civil Rights Act of 1964. A year later, President Lyndon B. Johnson proposed legislation that eventually became the Voting Rights Act of 1965.[17] While many Lawrencians believed that the legislation was a positive and much-needed step, others felt that this swing in public opinion was shortsighted and ill advised. They argued that Congress was passing legislation too quickly and without sufficient debate, that such laws were unconstitutional or already provided for in the Fourteenth and Fifteenth Amendments, and that the federal bureaucracy created by new legislation would usurp individual freedoms.

Opposition to civil rights legislation was an important factor in a revival of political conservatism and the transformation of the nation's political culture. Scholars often point to Barry Goldwater's unsuccessful 1964 presidential campaign as the key moment of this resurgence, but the grassroots core of the movement had always been active in places like Lawrence, where people criticized the New Deal and liberalism and sought an issue or issues that might galvanize a rebirth.[18] Civil rights legislation and activism, among other issues, provided such an opportunity. As civil rights activists challenged Lawrence's racial boundaries, defenders of those boundaries mobilized to maintain the status quo.

The intimate connections between civil rights legislation and conservative politics became clear as the struggle progressed. "I certainly am not pleased with your liberal votes," retiree Anne Gill scolded Senator Pearson, "So I shall appreciate your voting against the Civil Rights Bill." Regarding "the negro question in the South," H. A. Puckett, a laborer, asserted that blacks "should be given some consideration but not overdone." M. S. Winter, the owner of Ship Winter Chevrolet, put it succinctly by urging Senator Frank Carlson to "oppose" civil rights legislation and "to preserve the individual freedoms which are the foundation of this republic." Civil rights legislation, Winter believed, not only threatened the individual but the security and well-being of the nation as well. Additionally, he declared that he was "*still high for Goldwater,*" which suggests that he believed only a conservative resurgence could roll back this tide of governmental intrusion and usurpation of power. Warren Zimmerman, a vice president at Kansas Key Press and an ardent cold warrior, supported the "Goldwater idea" on civil rights. The proposed civil rights bill would "wreck . . . private enterprise," he declared. A year later Zimmerman was still concerned about the "infernal civil rights bill," which he believed "ultimately" would lead to "government control of everything."[19]

To be fair, many Americans, including Goldwater, opposed civil rights legislation out of sincere conservative beliefs and convictions, such as statist or constitutional concerns. Goldwater opposed civil rights legislation because he believed moral issues could not be resolved through new laws. These principles, however, clearly became racialized and perverted by segregationists, who in their desire to maintain racial separation found the Arizona senator a vessel for their own convictions. Similarly, numerous

Lawrencians appropriated the rhetoric of traditional conservatism to maintain the existing racial boundaries in their community.[20]

The fear of federal mandates legislating racial equality or "forcing" whites to "accept" blacks as equals was heard frequently in Lawrence. "You can't legislate equality; you have to deserve it," wrote E. W. King, of rural Douglas County, citing an article in *New Age* magazine (the organ of the Masons, Southern Jurisdiction), and "[y]ou can't demand success; you have to earn it."[21] In this view, the goal of civil rights legislation, racial equality, was something that had to be earned by blacks and given by whites. In some distorted way this perhaps reflected traditional conservative fears of big government and the loss of local control. But it also was a construction of American society that fed into a white identity by claiming that whites already had earned, and therefore deserved, every opportunity and success. The dichotomy was clear and racially based: Whites deserved full participation as American citizens, blacks did not; whites should decide when blacks deserve that equality.

Like E. W. King, others feared the effects of federally mandated racial equality if Congress passed a civil rights bill. Even a proponent of civil rights legislation, like Lawrence resident and Second District United States Representative Robert F. Ellsworth, was ambivalent in his support. In justifying his sponsorship of the 1963 Civil Rights Bill, Ellsworth declared that he was "committed" to strong civil rights legislation "because it is right." "I am going to fight for this legislation all the way," he wrote in his weekly *Journal-World* column. During the floor debate on the bill the following year, however, Ellsworth proclaimed that "CIVIL RIGHTS DON'T COME FROM CIVIL WRONGS," aping the rhetoric of southern states' rights and far-Right organizations. Without naming specific protests or individuals, he also chastised the "[e]xtreme and irresponsible demonstrations led by some of the so-called Civil Rights leaders." These protests, Ellsworth claimed, did "more to harm the cause of true equality of opportunity in America than the discredited misrepresentation of the very worst racist." Moreover, Ellsworth declared, "the American people have never appreciated having ideas or principles shoved down their throats" a position that others in Lawrence seconded.[22]

Perhaps Ellsworth was just following the lead of his constituents. During the floor debate on the Civil Rights Bill, noteworthy for an eighty-two-day southern filibuster, Lawrencians weighed in on the proposed law. Fred Bremer, an insurance agent, wanted more "amendments" to the bill "to protect the rights of both white and black from the absolute dictatorship of the bureaucrats." Bremer claimed that "[v]ery few reasonable people are against giving the colored people equal rights," but that moving too fast would create a situation worse than Prohibition. Although he claimed to support racial equality, Bremer also claimed it was not yet the right time to give it to African Americans. Similarly, Harry Westergren, a plumbing and electrical contractor, felt that other proposals should be "considered so that the majority [would] . . . have a say" and "not just the commies and the coloreds." Likewise, Otto Lohrenz, an assistant instructor of history at KU, professed concern in "protecting the rights of minorities," but was "more concerned about the rights of majorities."[23]

Like anticommunists in Lawrence, opponents of civil rights legislation also feared the further growth of the federal government, which they associated with a loss of individual liberty and freedom. As the Plunge protest had made clear, Lawrencians also feared that civil rights legislation would violate the rights associated with private property. Mrs. Richard B. Stevens, whose husband was an attorney, urged Senator James B. Pearson to support a civil rights bill that would "protect any person's right to associate privately for lawful purposes." Eugene L. Hardtarfer, a sales associate at Ship Winter Chevrolet, did not feel that anyone "should be required to rent or sell his home or real estate to someone not of his own race." He declared that fair housing could only be achieved "through gradual and willing cooperation rather than shoving it down the throats of property owners." Basil Parris, a supervisor at Hallmark Cards, agreed, claiming that the 1966 fair housing bill was "taking all rights away from a man to own his own property!" Parris also believed that the Constitution declared that the "rights of one man stops [sic] when it infringes on another mans [sic] rights. I think it is time we started practicing what our forefathers fought and died for." Victor Melton, the manager of the Douglas County Humane Society, was "up to here in so-called Civil Rights bills," which he believed were "destroying our freedoms." Melton and others felt that home owners, landlords, and business people had a "right" to sell, rent, or do business with whomever they wanted, simply because their rights as property owners were superior to the rights of blacks to equal opportunity and equal treatment before the law. Melton avowed, "the spirit of heroes is bred into Americans and someday in concert with an awakened leadership they will throw off the yoke of Racial Equalitarianism, and take action to ensure [sic] that a bankrupt philosophy of appeasement and defeat shall not endanger them again."[24]

Additionally, invoking the rights of property owners often included an "economic" argument against integration that was appealing to many Lawrencians. A Lawrence apartment building owner defended his refusal to rent to black students in 1965 by asking the leaders of CORE and the NAACP if they "were prepared to reimburse him for the loss of income" that would result from the "exodus of white students" unwilling to live near blacks. His refusal to rent to blacks was justified, he argued, because the individual property owner should not have to bear the costs of integration.

Even a junior high student believed that privately owned businesses "should not have to serve everyone—only who [the owners] want to serve."[25]

Although this prevailing attitude tacitly acknowledged the lower socioeconomic status of blacks, it held the black community responsible for creating and maintaining that condition. "Progress depends on the individual and his qualifications," Ed Abels wrote in 1960. There was "no law, prejudice or anything else preventing a Negro" from practicing law or medicine in Lawrence. One only need "make the necessary sacrifice to earn a degree. He cannot qualify in a picket line."[26] The underlying assumption to this reasoning, which had broad support in Lawrence, was that blacks had the same educational, occupational, and social opportunities as whites, which clearly was not true. If African Americans did not take advantage of these chances, the argument went, it was not the fault of whites. Moreover, even as Abels and others of a like mind tried to distance themselves from race, they constructed social identities based on race and drew clear social boundaries between whites and blacks. This ideology put sole responsibility on African Americans to "prove" themselves worthy of American citizenship but left it wholly in the hands of white Americans to decide when blacks had reached that point.

Many Lawrencians opposed civil rights legislation because they feared race mixing. A Lawrence physician, W. R. Palmer, claimed his "father and father in law [sic] had risked their lives that the negro be free," but he did "not want any unnecessary mixing." While conceding that blacks should be entitled "to certain accomodations [sic] when their own people don't take advantage," he also asserted that "too much intermingling in our schools will result in intermarriage which would be as unpopular as the mixing of canaries and black birds. They are very happily separate in their own homes."[27] This was likely not a minority opinion. An unofficial poll conducted by a KU political behavior class in 1964 suggested that "most Lawrencians" believed racial discrimination to be "morally wrong," yet they were opposed to their children having a black roommate. While a majority supported a city ordinance prohibiting racial exclusion in athletic clubs or veterans' organizations, they did not believe it should apply to private organizations such as country clubs, churches, fraternities, sororities, or women's organizations.[28]

A thread that ties segregation to Cold War concerns was the fear of outsiders, and, in particular, communists. Specifically, many Americans, north and south, contended that integration was a "communist-backed conspiracy." Although this concern ostensibly was about national security, it effectively impeded the move to racial equality and obscured the larger issues sustaining racial separation. Moreover, this worldview reinforced racial identities around the rhetoric of freedom and slavery and, as such, was of great symbolic importance.

This was apparent in Lawrence, once the heart of free-state abolitionism. A Lawrence woman claimed that civil rights legislation had "gotten way out of hand" and feared that "white people will have to sell their property to Negro's [sic] or [be] forced to run their businesses according to Federal Law—What is that??? Communism?" What angered her the most, however, was that civil rights activism was "forcing" her to associate with blacks. "We are not forced to associate with undesirable whites," she noted, "but Negro's [sic]—thats [sic] different." African Americans, she declared, were "basically lazy, easy going, highly emotional, mentally [and] . . . physically—and morally corrupt. There are few exceptions." Although she conceded that blacks "can have equal rights, we are for that," she first expected them to "prove they are worthy." It is "not the American way to do things forcefully." Finally, she linked racial unrest with a communist plot and called Martin Luther King, Jr., a "tool of Communism." If blacks "are unhappy here let them try Russia or help build up Africa." She closed by pleading for a return to "States Rights."[29]

This woman was a blatant racist wanting to maintain segregation and white supremacy. Segregationists believed that they were decent, honest, hardworking, God-fearing people, concerned with family, community, and the future of America. Integration threatened all of their ideals, as well as their personal identity and sense of self. As the White Citizens' Councils proclaimed, the separation of blacks and whites was "the essence of all things good—the freedom to choose one's associates, Americanism, state sovereignty, and the survival of the white race." The alternative, they believed, was "'darkness, regimentation, totalitarianism, communism, and destruction." Lawrencians hid their desire for a segregated society in a language that emphasized traditional American conservatism, using it to defend the dominant social boundaries in the community. This rhetoric, when tinted with the town's free-state mythology, was a powerful impediment to meaningful social change in Lawrence. Clearly, two conflicting ideals were at the heart of early 1960s civil rights activism: the rights of property owners to use their property however they choose, on the one hand, and, on the other, the legal right of all Americans to equal opportunity.[30]

Although resistance was strong in Lawrence, there also was significant, if not majority, support for civil rights legislation. Building on the momentum provided by the passage of the 1964 Civil Rights Act, local civil rights activists turned their attention to equal employment opportunities and fair housing. In 1963, the LLPD, the LDC-NAACP, and other groups and individuals worked to open up for blacks such traditionally "white" jobs as store clerks, checkers, and salespersons in the downtown stores. Their efforts were not immediately successful. In the spring of 1963, some forty African Americans reportedly had been turned down for sales and clerk jobs in downtown shops. Dolph Simons, Jr., the editor of the *Journal-World,* asserted that more could be accomplished in race relations by "reasoning and common sense" than by "forc[ing] an issue down the throats of any people." Simons scoffed at the existence of discriminatory hiring practices in Lawrence. In addition to the forty African Americans denied employment, he asked, had forty whites similarly been turned down? Simons suggested that blacks had not been hired because of their skin color but because they were not qualified.[31]

Like many economically liberal but socially conservative people, Simons believed race was a relative matter.[32] Race relations in Lawrence clearly were better than those in the deep South. Unlike blacks in the South, daily existence for African Americans in Lawrence was not a matter of life and death, at least not in 1963. Civil rights activists' charges of discrimination and exclusion perplexed Simons, who was oblivious to the seriousness of the claims. He asserted that discrimination in Lawrence was not a matter of race but of character and economic standing, claiming, for example, that realtors did not show all homes for sale to blacks, but neither did they do so for white clients. Although the lack of an integrated municipal pool was one problem, Simons admitted that he and other "long-time residents" were unaware of any "major, possibly explosive, racial problems in Lawrence compared to other cities." When the LHRC was created in 1961, however, "racial problems involving housing . . . lack of employment opportunities, and discrimination in some beer halls" suddenly appeared. Fearing "factionalism" and the disruption of business growth he believed crucial to the town's prosperity, Simons wondered why his fellow Lawrencians took the "negative" and not the "positive viewpoint."[33] What Simons meant by "positive" was not altogether clear, but it clearly did not include protesting, picketing, or making demands.

There were, in fact, several examples of black citizens and civil rights activists expressing a "positive viewpoint" in Lawrence. In May 1963, the city's predominantly black churches—St. Luke African Methodist Episcopal, the First Regular Missionary Baptist, St. James African Methodist Episcopal, the Ninth Street Baptist Church, and the Second Christian Church—joined forces to show sympathy with the Southern Christian Leadership Conference's campaign to integrate Birmingham, Alabama and gain passage of a national civil rights bill. Beyond financial contributions to the campaign, the churches held a peaceful march down Massachusetts Street, displaying their moral support for the southern movement.[34] In July 1963, the LDC-NAACP conducted "without incident" a racially mixed "Freedom March" down Massachusetts Street. Escorted by local police, close to 300 hundred people marched from St. Luke to the Douglas County Courthouse, including NAACP leaders from Kansas City and Topeka. Carrying signs reading,

"I want to swim in Lawrence," "Wanted: A Desegregated Heart," and "We Want to Work Where We Shop," the march was intended to publicize the problems confronting blacks in Lawrence rather than to directly challenge the system. Its leaders encouraged local banks and newspapers to become equal opportunity employers and strive for the full social and economic integration of blacks in Lawrence. The *Journal-World* ran a front-page photograph of the marchers; ironically, above the heads of black marchers, who had been denied decent housing and employment by Lawrence realtors, bankers, and merchants, was a business sign reading: "LOANS for better living." The marchers were not asking for a change in the system but only access to that system, principally as consumers and workers.[35]

The *Journal-World* praised the marchers, who were "serious" but "well-mannered," whose "desires for greater economic advancement" and for "better housing" were "entirely reasonable." "Lasting good can come to all residents of this community through the manner in which" the "protest was staged and received," an editorial read, and "other communities could benefit by following the reasonable and dignified pattern established by our Negro leaders." The *Outlook* offered a different view on civil rights marches, although it was responding more to racial tensions in the South than to local conditions. Ed Abels claimed that racial tension in the United States is "exactly what the enemies of the nation want." The "situation grows worse day by day" and will "continue to do so," Abels predicted, "as long as the principal appeal of those responsible for the situation continues to be the emotion of the Negroes as they are induced to form mobs in which there is singing, praying, cheering and resistance to law and order."[36]

Despite resistance, civil rights activists and organizations continued to struggle to obtain equal access to public accommodations for African Americans and to improve their educational, employment, and housing opportunities in Lawrence. The efforts of activists focused on two objectives: the construction of a municipal swimming pool open to all residents and open housing legislation. Throughout the 1960s, the LDC-NAACP, along with local churches, the LLPD, the League of Women Voters (LWV), ad hoc groups, and concerned citizens, lobbied for a fair housing ordinance and for a bond issue to build a public swimming pool, both of which came to fruition in 1967.

The task confronting other civil rights activists was daunting. Unlike whites, African Americans in Lawrence did not have the option to live in any house in the community they could afford to purchase. Landlords refused to rent to blacks, while real estate agents refused to show them houses for sale in particular neighborhoods. In 1964, the LDC-NAACP reported that there were many black consumers who could afford "low or medium priced housing," and that Lawrence's African-American community "would be a sound investment for home ownership."[37]

In addition, African Americans in Lawrence encountered an entire set of white attitudes about race, held not only by hard-core racists but also by alleged "moderates" sympathetic to the rhetoric of freedom and equality. These attitudes were perhaps best illustrated in a 1964 *Journal-World* editorial, which recounted the story of one family's search for housing in Lawrence. They were "good substantial people. . . . clean and decent, a credit to the community." Forced to sell their home because of a city building project, the family could not find a new home, even after several months of going to realtors, several of whom were long-time acquaintances of the family. The family was, of course, "a Negro family," one that had "done nearly everything that could be expected to bring respect and dignity to the race and yet" could not purchase a "satisfactory" house in Lawrence. As a result, the family built a new home in Kansas City.[38]

Clearly, the *Journal-World* noted, this was a mark against the goodwill of the community. While it chided local realtors for not having "'the guts' to do what was right and proper, for fear of being classified as agents who were trying to break the 'color line'," it added that "[n]ormally, the problem is not so clear-cut because the economic position of most Negroes is such that area-housing problems do not develop." The paper also minimized the fact that white realtors had taken down "For Sale" signs when the family expressed interest. The *Journal-World* was willing to allow black citizens to live wherever they wanted only when they had "proven" themselves worthy of living next to whites, as this family had by being "clean and decent," and "bringing respect and dignity to the race." Acknowledging that being white was akin to owning property, the *Journal-World* suggested that if blacks conducted themselves properly, then they "could expect to enjoy the economic privileges of the white man."[39] It refused to label as "bigots" those whites who would not sell to blacks because it was a "fact" that sales to blacks lowered property values. Race relations drove market values. The "great majority of potential purchasers prefer an all-white neighborhood. There is no hatred in the hearts of most such people," the editorial rationalized, it was simply "an economic situation which cannot be disregarded."[40] While the *Journal-World* deplored the problems confronting this particular family, it still defended the existing racial boundaries in the community.

The resistance to equal housing did not deter local activists, who began a publicity campaign against racial exclusion in housing in Lawrence. The LLPD and the CORE urged the passage of fair housing legislation by encouraging realtors to rent and sell to blacks, publishing a list of several local realtors opposed to fair housing legislation, and voicing their disapproval of housing discrimination based on race to real estate agencies.[41]

Church-based groups were also at the center of this struggle. Many activists were inspired by their religious beliefs to work for social change, and their faith was integral to their own identity.[42] African American preachers had long been prominent leaders in the local movement. Rosa Sims and her husband, the Reverend W. S. Sims of the Ninth Street Baptist Church, originally had organized the Lawrence NAACP in December 1942. When the organization was reconstituted in 1960, Ninth Street served as the meeting place for the LDC-NAACP, and several of its members were officers of the organization. The Reverend Richard Dulin, pastor of the Second Christian Church, was the head of the Lawrence Fair Housing Coordinating Committee (LFHCC). Several predominantly white churches were inspired by the Christian ethos to join in the struggle for racial equality, including Plymouth Congregational, the town's largest church; the First Christian Church; and the Oread Meeting of the Society of Friends.

Through its Social Action Committee, for example, Plymouth Congregational encouraged local realtors to attend an upcoming civil rights conference in Lawrence because fair housing was "a major item on the agenda." The Social Action Committee gathered information for church members and compiled its own report on housing in Lawrence in 1964. In September 1964, 845 Lawrence residents signed a "Statement on Equal Opportunity Housing," which the Committee on Christian Social Relations of the United Church Women of Lawrence (UCW) had distributed. The UCW, an interracial and mostly middle-class group, had been disseminating information on integrated housing since at least the beginning of 1964. Signers of the statement pledged not to discriminate in the buying, selling, or renting of housing and "agreed to accept as a neighbor any lawabiding, responsible person, regardless of race or creed." The UCW also pointed out that property values did not decrease when blacks moved into a neighborhood, as the *Journal-World* had claimed. The UCW asserted that while most Lawrencians did not object to having an African American for a neighbor, they were reluctant to sell their home to a black buyer "for fear of displeasing their present neighbors." This, the UCW argued, was the biggest obstacle to integrated housing in Lawrence.[43]

Activists tried to topple that barrier through promoting education and building personal relationships, which they believed, in the long run, would be a more effective remedy than legislation. In May 1966, the Interfaith Committee, an arm of the United Church Women, sponsored interracial home visits to "improv[e] . . . interracial understanding in Lawrence." A host selected a suitable date, and then a member of the Interfaith Committee escorted guests to the home for an "evening of conversation in an interfaith and interracial group."[44]

In addition to the churches, the university faculty gave generally solid support to the goal of fair housing. Physics professor Richard Sapp and his wife Phyllis wanted Senator Pearson to support a fair housing provision in the 1966 Civil Rights Bill. "[S]uch a law is needed," they claimed, "in order to redress an unjust imbalance in rights of buyers and sellers of housing, and to provide further encouragement for minority group citizens who are advancing in the other areas of employment and education." Other KU faculty wrote letters to the *Journal-World*, pointing out the inconsistency of whites, but not blacks, having the right to choose their own neighbors. One pointed out that the ancestors of Lawrence's black population had come to the community at about the same time as the New Englanders who settled in west Lawrence. "One look at Lawrence today," she wrote, "with its pretty new housing developments all lily-white, and one might wonder just who really did win that Free State-Slave [S]tate controversy after all. For what purpose did the Lawrence settlers come two thousand miles and [a] world away?"[45]

Support for fair housing grew as the decade progressed, and coordinating the campaign for fair housing was the ad hoc LFHCC, created in January 1965. Instituted as a clearinghouse for civil rights activity, the LFHCC included representatives from the LLPD, the LHRC, the NAACP, CORE, the UCW, the Council of Churches, and the Lawrence League of Women Voters, among others. Other groups helped, too, including the KU-YMCA and YWCA and the Lawrence chapter of the Women's International League for Peace and Freedom.

Sensing a change in attitude among the state's lawmakers, brought on by the national civil rights struggle, in 1965 the LFHCC lobbied Lawrence's state representatives to propose a state fair housing law. Its strategy was to publicize and inform people about the problem, encourage well-known African Americans, such as athletes, to talk to legislators, and use advocates from the business and legal community to point out the economic disadvantages of racial exclusion. During the 1965 Kansas legislative session, a bill was introduced in the Kansas Senate to broaden the Public Accommodations Law by forbidding racial or religious discrimination in housing sales or rental. The bill failed to pass, and Kansas did not have a fair housing law until the late 1960s. The LFHCC also lobbied for a real estate licensing law, which would require realtors to show houses to blacks if the seller requested, which the LFHCC believed would render moot the real estate industry's argument that many whites did not want to sell their homes to blacks.[46]

Indeed, the real estate business in Lawrence was perhaps the biggest defender of the racial status quo. For many reasons, most notably a fear of losing sales, few realtors shared the commitment to fair housing of the LFHCC or the UCW. Local realtor Geneva Simmons, for example, called the proposed creation of the Department of Housing and Urban Development "down right frightening." It was "[n]ot just a drift but a huge stride toward centralized federal control." In April 1965, the Lawrence Real Estate Board (LREB) placed a full-page advertisement in the *Journal-World* opposing the proposed federal Fair Housing Bill, charging that it would "eliminate the basic right of any citizen to control his own property." The ad employed language eerily similar to the rhetoric of the Coordinating Committee for Fundamental American Freedoms (an ad hoc group headed by former American Bar Association president John Satterfield that fought against the 1964 Civil Rights Act), states' rights groups, White Citizens' Councils, and the John Birch Society, as well as respected conservative politicians. The LREB charged "discrimination and inequality in housing provide an ideal vehicle to advance [the] . . . cause" of the "Marxist-Socialistic doctrine" of "curbing the property-owning class." Arguing that proponents of the bill were misguided and inexperienced in buying and selling property, the LREB declared that its members worked for the "desires of the Owner" and were "limited to the buyer's or renter's willingness to agree" to the seller's terms. Open negotiation between a willing buyer and a willing seller was the "ONLY basis" for real estate transactions. The LREB asserted the bill would "force" a property owner to sell or rent "against his will and judgement." Arguing that racial exclusion in housing was caused more by "social and economic reasons, rather than by racism and bigotry," the LREB suggested that many property owners were "willing to sell or rent without restrictions," and that "more would be willing in the future if they are not intimidated or forced to defend their rights against proposed housing laws and ordinances designed to remove the freedom of choice and contract."[47]

Despite this opposition, the efforts of the LFHCC and its allies paid off in 1967, when the Lawrence City Commission passed a fair housing ordinance. One justification for the ordinance, in addition to it being a long-time goal of the LHRC, was Lawrence's sense of place and identity. "Lawrence is a center of culture, whose democratic principles are being constantly observed by foreign students and foreign visitors," read the preamble to the ordinance. The law declared that racial discrimination was "against public policy"; made violations punishable by a $100 fine, up to thirty days in jail, or both; and gave enforcement power to the city.[48]

At the same time, however, the city faced a critical housing shortage, which only exacerbated the problems of African Americans. Even with the passage of the fair housing ordinance, little change could be noted. For example, *Disorientation,* the newsletter of the radical New University Conference, claimed in 1970 there had only been "token" integration of any of the city's new housing developments and "no discernable change" was evident in the town's housing patterns. As well, local real estate agents, except one, still inhibited integration. That single exception was Glenn Kappelman, who claimed that many realtors discriminated against "anyone who might be a little 'foreign.'" Evoking the spirit of John Brown and Bleeding Kansas, Kappelman lamented that "too many people" ignore racial exclusion. "Kansas history is based on freedom, tolerance, the Christian way and fair play; we must not lose this foundation," he pleaded.[49]

By tapping into Kansas's free-state past and the ethos of Christianity, Kappelman wielded powerful rhetorical imagery in the fight to establish equal housing and open new public spaces to African Americans. At the same time, many white Lawrencians offered significant resistance both to liberalism and the civil rights movement. Some opponents of integration in Lawrence were simply racists, wishing to preserve the racial status quo. Between the white/black hierarchy of unreconstructed racists and freedom workers' dream of a color-free society, however, were many Lawrencians who claimed to support the principle of equal opportunity but who placed the rights of association and private property above racial equality and the civil rights of African Americans. By not framing their opposition around the nexus of white superiority/black inferiority, and by grounding their rhetoric in appeals to the Constitution and mainstream American conservatism, these Lawrencians wielded a powerful means of resisting racial integration and maintaining existing boundaries.

As Lawrence's example suggests, the struggle for racial equality was not solely a southern phenomenon. Although there were regional differences in conditions, tactics, and strategies, the movement itself transcended regional boundaries. Between 1960 and 1967 in Lawrence the civil rights struggle facilitated a public discourse on the meaning of freedom and equality, the role of the state in allocating privilege and power to citizens, and the definition of a citizen, a discourse that altered the community's social boundaries. For some Lawrencians, freedom and equality meant the elimination of distinctions based on race, equal access to the community's political economy for all citizens, and an activist state to ensure and protect these most basic of rights. For others, however, freedom and equality meant the right to own property and to do with it whatever one chose, the right to choose one's associates, and a nonactivist state whose primary function was to protect property and property rights. Either way, for many Lawrencians the politics of the discourse had become quite personal and intense.

Civil rights activism empowered both blacks and whites. Drawing on Lawrence's free-state heritage, America's promise of equality, and shared cultural and religious values, the movement allowed people to put their beliefs in freedom and democracy, or their moral and religious convictions, into action. It allowed some activists to use personalist values to redefine citizenship, especially African Americans, who now were closer to redeeming their full rights as American citizens. The results of this struggle, however, were ambiguous. Although civil rights activists could point to successes such as the Lawrence Fair Housing Ordinance, in reality such changes made little immediate impact in the lives of African Americans in the city. Employment and educational opportunities did not increase, and not many blacks had the financial means to purchase homes in Lawrence's new housing developments. Few African Americans saw their power within the community's political economy change.

At the same time, this process led Lawrencians to defend the town's traditional racial boundaries and recreate dominant social identities. White Lawrencians resisted civil rights protests, open housing ordinances, civil rights legislation, and other liberal measures, which they saw as encroachments into their territory and the usurpation of their power. Civil rights legislation strengthened their belief that the liberal welfare state was too large and out of control, gave special treatment to minorities, and marginalized and dispossessed white folk. In Lawrence in 1967, this notion did not reflect reality, but the perception was a powerful force shaping the sixties experience in Lawrence.

CHAPTER 4

"THE PROPER SENSE OF VALUES"

In January 1967, *Time* named the twenty-five-and-under generation as its man of the year. "Never have the young been so assertive or so articulate, so well educated or so worldly," the magazine wrote. "Predictably, they are a highly independent breed, and—to adult eyes—their independence has made them highly unpredictable. This is not just a new generation, but a new kind of generation."[1] *Time* noted that the sixties' youth were well educated (40 percent were in college), raised in material comfort, impatient with the slowness of social change, and characterized by a sense of immediacy.

Youth activism since 1960, in a variety of forms, had much to do with that generation's selection as man of the year. Between 1960 and 1970, perhaps the greatest challenge to Lawrence's traditions came from students at the University of Kansas and young people generally. Young Lawrencians were both leaders and foot soldiers in the black freedom struggle, effectively challenging and reconfiguring the community's traditional racial boundaries. Many also confronted racism and racial exclusion on campus, as well as what they believed was their own oppression as students through outdated rules and regulations governing their personal lives. In redefining their role in the impersonal, corporate multiversity, young men and women sought to remake and reform American society. Student activism and changing perceptions of youth in the United States created new identities of young people, both as students and citizens, that defined politics more personally and helped to transform the whole community.

The challenge offered by student and youth activism did not go unnoticed or uncontested in the community. Because youth activists offered a fundamental challenge to the traditional racial, gender, class, and cultural boundaries of the nation, and thus challenged the identities of millions of Americans, a struggle resulted within the country, and within Lawrence, to define the nation's values and standards and to act upon those definitions to decide who was, and who was not, an American.[2] The nation's universities were important places for social change in the 1960s, where the values of American society were debated and new options were offered. The effects of this discourse, however, extended far beyond academia's ivied walls.[3]

W. Clarke Wescoe, in his installation address as chancellor of the University of Kansas in 1960, remarked that "a new era" had arrived for the university, one that would provide "stimulating challenges." Enrollments at KU had increased steadily since 1951, and the 1960 class of 2,376 first-year students was 25 percent larger than that of the previous year. Equally significant was the increased number of women attending college. During World War II, women had made up more than half of all students, but by 1950, men, many former soldiers and sailors on the GI Bill, accounted for nearly three-fourths of the enrollment. In 1960, men still comprised two-thirds of the total, but the number of female students began to increase at a greater rate than those for men. The number of women students rose 13.4 percent between 1959 and 1960, and 14.5 percent between 1960 and 1961; the same figures for men were 4.3 and 4.7 percent, respectively. It also was apparent in the male-to-female student ratio, which was 2.79 to 1 in 1950, 2.3 to 1 in 1960, and fell to 1.49 to 1 by 1970.[4] The growing number of students entered a campus culture that was generally racist, sexist, and conservative, reflecting the culture at large. In the late fifties and early sixties most KU students were more intent on making grades and seeking the credential for a job and status in corporate, Middle-Class America than in learning.[5] Those perceptions, however, cloud the impact that this generation would have on American society.

Youth-led civil rights activism by young Lawrencians had an immediate impact on the community. In Lawrence and elsewhere, the black freedom struggle was the catalyst for a great social awakening and mobilization of people, especially the nation's youth, in other areas of public life after 1945. As freedom workers struggled for fair housing in the city, KU students turned their attention to the same issues on campus and created their own organizations to end racial exclusion. Their efforts, bolstered by both their religious beliefs and faith-based institutions, provided a space and a language for challenging exclusion in the academy, and the experience allowed student activists to consider their own marginalization as consumers of education.

Students at the University of Kansas found compelling reasons to speak out in the early 1960s. Although KU had enrolled black students from its inception, and despite Chancellor Franklin Murphy's liberal activism in the 1950s, racism and racial exclusion existed on campus well into the 1960s. The *University Daily Kansan* still accepted racially discriminatory advertising in 1965. The university registrar used information forms that racially identified ("coded") students and paired black students with whites as roommates only with the consent of the white student, while the School of Education only sent African American students to school districts that would accept blacks as teachers. Additionally, several fraternities and sororities had racially exclusionary clauses in their national charters.[6]

The growing awareness of discrimination and exclusion in Lawrence and at KU was evident in the number of student organizations that addressed these issues. The search for fulfillment in their personal lives on campus led many young people to seek fulfillment in the larger world, and some activists used very traditional means in their quest. The University Christian Movement (UCM) was a campus-based religious organization that tackled problems of racism, war, and the spiritual emptiness of the modern world. Established in September 1966, the UCM was an ecumenical coalition of several KU religious organizations, including the Young Men's Christian Association (YMCA), the Young Women's Christian Association (YWCA), and the United Campus Christian Fellowship. The UCM staff included civil rights, peace, and antiwar activists.[7]

The KU-UCM was not formally affiliated with the national movement of the same name, which also was founded in 1966, although they did share common goals.[8] The KU-UCM sought to recreate a community of faith and justice in the greater Lawrence community by transforming social relationships through education, activism, and the teachings of Christianity. The UCM defined itself as an ecumenical movement in which all of the KU campus ministers joined together in "an expression of the 'community' we are and share!" It confronted racism on the campus by offering a course on white racism in the fall of 1968 and one on institutional racism in the spring of 1968. Two hundred eighty-seven people enrolled in the first course, which featured lectures by four KU professors and four weeks of discussion groups led by nineteen faculty members. Students who participated in the first course helped to plan the second, in which 230 people enrolled. About 450 people attended a Sunday lecture series and one hundred fifty local church people were involved in the course.[9]

The UCM also sponsored the "Eros Urban Plunge," a program which allowed its "participants to comprehend the repression, oppression, and suppression inherent in white, middle-class society . . . which prevent[s] lives of openness and freedom, which keeps us isolated from the injustices which are taking place. The entire syndrome must be the focus of the revolution as organized and theorized within the white community." Additionally, in November 1968 the UCM participated as part of the "peace contingent" during a Veteran's Day Parade, which brought a "mixed reaction" from the rest of the community.[10]

Two other campus religious organizations that took an activist approach were the YMCA, which began at KU in 1883, and the YWCA, which was founded two years later. In the late 1950s, the YMCA and the YWCA created the KU-Y to coordinate their activities. The KU-Y applied the teachings of Christianity as a means to enrich the lives of university students and the entire campus, beliefs that led the group into the struggle for racial equality. Both the YMCA and the YWCA welcomed students regardless of religion and race, a departure from the racially exclusive policies of most campus organizations, particularly fraternities and sororities. From the 1940s until the late 1950s, the YMCA owned and ran Henley House, a cooperative for KU women students that was among the first integrated student housing in Lawrence.[11] Although seldom involved in direct action, from their inception the YMCA and YWCA provided forums for discussion of pressing social issues, a tradition that continued throughout the 1960s. The issue of civil rights was important to the KU-Y, and the organization became an important voice for racial equality in Lawrence.[12]

Religion, in particular Christianity, played a significant role in the youth activism of the 1960s. The impersonal, alienating mass society of Cold War America led many young Americans to Christianity as a means to find fulfillment and contentment. It also provided them with a language (the teachings of Christianity) and a space (churches and ministries) from which they could try to resolve problems such as racial inequality, poverty, sexism, and, later in the decade, war. Of these issues, however, the most significant was the civil rights movement. The student Christian movement of the post–World War II era, a legacy of the early twentieth-century social gospel movement, provided black and white youths with the opportunity to interact.[13]

The confluence of religion and church in the civil rights struggle was as clear within Lawrence as it was on campus. In 1960, the KU-Y increased its membership to 310, a gain of 20 percent over the previous year. That year it gave its "full support" to the lunch counter sit-ins in the South and declared that segregation was "still a problem" in Lawrence and at KU. It proclaimed in 1962 a "sense of fellowship" with the University of Mississippi's YMCA, as the southern group struggled to integrate Ole Miss. The Y's 1961–1962 program included weekly meetings, speakers, and films on race relations.[14]

The KU-Y, however, soon discovered it would take more than writing letters and passing resolutions to overcome campus apathy over civil rights. In the fall of 1960, it created the Civil Rights Council (CRC) as one of its standing committees, largely in response to the sit-in movement sweeping the South and spreading to northern campuses. Although it had its greatest impact in challenging Jim Crowism in the deep South, the sit-in movement had great significance throughout the country, including Lawrence.

As the civil rights arm of the KU-Y, the CRC focused its efforts on education and the investigation of racial exclusion on campus and in the community. Like the Y, the CRC's membership was racially mixed, although most members were white.[15] Several also belonged to the Lawrence League for the Practice of Democracy and had picketed the Jayhawk Plunge in 1960. One black member of the CRC was Marion Barry, a KU chemistry student (who later would become the mayor of Washington, D.C.) and the first chair of the Student Nonviolent Coordinating Committee. Although the CRC mainly focused on investigating racial discrimination, on election day in November 1960, two interracial groups of CRC members marched peacefully from Allen Field House to various polling places around the city, urging the city to take "meaningful civil rights action." The "March for Freedom," however, garnered only an occasional curious onlooker, a few honking horns, and several "wary glances." The *Kansan* reported only that one white man remarked, "[a]in't that a white girl walking between them two colored guys?"[16]

The CRC investigated barbershops, taverns, and other businesses that refused to serve blacks. In the spring of 1961, Barry, who left KU at the end of the semester, and the CRC threatened direct action against any business that excluded African Americans. The CRC never officially followed through on these threats (although individual members did), but it did begin investigating another issue that would be significant later in the decade: racial exclusion in campus fraternities and sororities.[17]

The CRC was part of a radical social and political movement called the New Left, which drew its first breath from the experience of the civil rights struggle. The New Left was strongest on college campuses, as young people were its primary constituency. If there was a guiding philosophy to the New Left, it was probably best expressed through the "Port Huron Statement," the manifesto of the best-known New Left organization, Students for a Democratic Society. In general, the New Left rejected consensus politics and mass society, was wary of liberals and conservatives, and wanted to restore the dignity of the individual and remake American society through the radical, community-based notion of "participatory democracy."[18]

To that end, several KU students and faculty established a chapter of the Congress of Racial Equality (CORE) in August 1964. A vibrant organization after World War II, the original Lawrence CORE chapter had disbanded a few years later, after an unsuccessful attempt to integrate a local cafe. Most members of the new CORE chapter were white and determined "to change the [racial] situation in Lawrence." CORE's early efforts, however, mirrored action previously taken by other civil rights organizations: protesting at private swimming clubs, investigating housing discrimination and noncompliance by taverns and barber shops with the Kansas public accommodations law, and lobbying for civil rights legislation.[19]

Like other New Leftists, many CORE members also belonged to KU's chapter of SDS. Don Olson, a former SDSer at San Diego State who had transferred to KU; Laird Wilcox, an SDS member-at-large and the publisher of the *Kansas Free Press* (a local alternative newspaper); and several CRC members formed the KU chapter in the spring of 1965, three years after the national organization was founded. By May the chapter had some thirty-five members, including eight faculty. Initially, KU-SDS sponsored speeches (the peace activist Norman Thomas was its first speaker), participated in campus teach-ins on the Vietnam War, and encouraged a dialogue on civil rights, the war, and university reform. There was some discussion of SDS and CORE joining forces during the summer of 1965 for a community organization project in north Lawrence, probably inspired by SDS's Economic and Research Action Projects (ERAP). That plan fell through, apparently because many CORE members "went south" to join in the black freedom struggle.[20]

Like other SDS chapters, the records of the KU affiliate are sparse. It is likely that SDS attracted only a handful of students, perhaps never more than fifty. The KU chapter, however, illustrates how the lines between the civil rights, student, and antiwar movements became blurred.[21] At its first meeting in the fall of 1965, for example, KU-SDS announced it would not focus solely on Vietnam but would target other issues as well, specifically capital punishment and in loco parentis. The fledgling group did not plan any demonstrations or pickets, but wanted to open "channels of communication" to educate students, faculty, and others in the community about these issues. If this failed, however, SDS vowed to "use whatever is necessary to be effective." It was most interested in university reform, particularly the trend toward the corporate university, racism on campus, and what it saw as the elitism of the Greek housing system.[22]

Largely autonomous, the KU-SDS chapter, like other local chapters, did not always agree with the national organization. While the latter used marches and pickets, especially as Vietnam became the dominant issue of the day, the former preferred to use education and public awareness, such as teach-ins. KU-SDS felt its position in "conservative Kansas" did not allow it "especially profound opportunities to challenge basic power structure and social attitudes." It preferred to "emphasize [the] education part of [the] SDS constitution." To underscore the point, a 1965 *Kansan* editorial applauded KU-SDS for using "valid" teach-ins on the Vietnam War rather than "meaningless demonstrations" as the national organization had done.[23]

Student organizations such as SDS offered a critique of American society that met real resistance from those who did not share the group's views. For many Lawrencians, including some KU students, leftist youth activism was simply a communist-inspired plot. *Lawrence Outlook* publisher Bert Carlyle claimed that KU-SDS was "one of the most active communist cells in the

U.S." and implored Governor William Avery and Chancellor Wescoe to "stop this movement [SDS] before it snowballs." Carlyle accused SDS of threatening the "American way of life" and the country's future. "What harm can the Kansas University SDS organization do," he asked rhetorically, "besides attempt to convert our sons and daughters to the communist and socialist causes?" Carlyle predicted "somebody is going to have to take responsibility for allowing it [SDS] to remain as a 'recognized campus organization.'"[24]

Despite such opposition, leftist student activists, including SDS, the CRC, and the All Student Council (ASC), did take action on at least one campus issue: the racially exclusionary policies of campus fraternities and sororities. The national charters of many fraternity and sorority houses specifically forbade local chapters from pledging racial or religious minorities and forced local houses to pledge only individuals acceptable to every member of the fraternity nationwide. During the 1950s, under pressure from civil rights activists, several fraternities and sororities had removed these discriminatory clauses from their charters, but this often only moved racial exclusion "underground."[25] At the University of Kansas, several fraternities, most notably Sigma Nu, still had the offending clauses well into the 1960s, and alumni, benefactors, and national officers continued to pressure local houses not to accept minorities. While SDS, the ASC, the CRC, and other civil rights activists found this practice undemocratic and racist, the fraternities, sororities, and their supporters asserted they had the right to associate with whomever they wished, echoing a refrain commonly heard throughout the community in defending racist practices.

The lines of the debate were sharply drawn. No one, not even the fraternities or sororities, denied that Greek-letter houses discriminated. The fraternities and sororities argued that they excluded on character, income, and status, not race or religion. Individual members, however, could blackball any perspective member, making it nearly impossible for a minority member to pledge. Although there had been all-black fraternities and sororities at KU for some time, their charters did not exclude any prospective member on account of race.[26] Moreover, for civil rights advocates dedicated to an integrated society, separate, white-only institutions that used race as a criterion for membership were unacceptable.

With the arrival of SDS on campus in 1965, however, the issue of exclusion by fraternities and sororities was transformed into a referendum on the existence of the entire Greek system. Both SDS and the CRC believed the system was a microcosm of the elitism and class divisions in American society and the mere existence of fraternities and sororities was anachronistic and undemocratic. The Greek system conflicted with SDS's vision, shared by the CRC and other activists, of what America should be: a participatory democracy, with all people enjoying complete political rights and representation.

Fighting the Greek system, though, would not be easy, in part because university officials denied that racial exclusion in fraternity and sorority housing existed. Wescoe claimed in March 1961 that the university was integrated and that racial segregation was confined to the city. The CRC disputed the claim and was vindicated when it revealed that the national constitution of Sigma Nu prohibited any local house from pledging blacks. This disclosure contradicted Wescoe's claim, but the administration rather disingenuously maintained that fraternities and sororities were not directly under university control, and thus it could not compel integration as it could in other campus organizations. Fraternities and sororities were privately owned and operated but dependent on the university's support and recognition. Wescoe recognized that Greek houses were outside of the university but also an integral part of it. Moreover, Wescoe was a fraternity man, and according to longtime KU administrator Francis Heller, the "fraternity had in fact opened important doors" for Wescoe, further complicating his decisions.[27] More significantly, the issue illustrated a conflict of worldviews and values. The fraternities' defenders saw exclusiveness, homogeneous communities, and discriminatory practices as positive and beneficial, while their critics viewed them as undemocratic and harmful.

Civil rights activists began their assault on Greek housing in earnest in 1964. Since 1961, the CRC had tried to negotiate with local fraternity and sorority houses to remove the exclusionary clauses but had not taken direct action to challenge their discriminatory membership practices because it considered segregation in Lawrence businesses a more pressing issue. In the fall of 1964 the ASC passed a resolution setting a deadline of one year for university-recognized organizations to remove all "discriminatory clauses" from their constitutions, or suffer the loss of university recognition. Meanwhile, KU-SDS member Laird Wilcox claimed that his lawyers, working with the NAACP, were preparing a court case against the university. Wilcox believed that the university had violated the Civil Rights Act of 1964 by accepting federal funds while condoning discriminatory policies and practices (the fraternities' and sororities' exclusionary clauses). SDS's strategy was to force the university to withdraw recognition of Greek houses, which would force such groups off campus and cause them ultimately to wither away. It is unclear if SDS implemented this legal side of the strategy, but, by early 1965, it and the CRC were pressuring the university to repeal its recognition of all fraternities and sororities with exclusionary clauses. By linking civil rights and class with the discriminatory practices of Greek houses, SDS and the CRC brought into focus the external forces and structures that propped up and perpetuated racism in the United States, in particular class distinctions and white privilege. Together they led an assault on the university's

Greek housing system, an effort that in many respects illustrates the complex nature of the struggle for social change during the sixties.[28]

That complexity was evident within the Greek system itself. Fraternity and sorority members who did not agree with the exclusion clauses faced great pressure to maintain the status quo. Anonymous affidavits given by sorority and fraternity members in 1965 confirmed the charges the CRC had leveled against the houses. Some members suggested that their houses were genuinely interested in admitting qualified minorities and were disappointed that "alumnae pressure" constrained their "right of individual choice of association." The sorority Chi Omega, for example, denied membership to a Jewish student from St. Louis after a Kansas City alumna objected that "they [Jews] would take over the house." National offices claimed that local chapters had the right of free association but had to select only those members who were "considered personally acceptable as a [member] . . . by any chapter or any member anywhere." In effect, this meant that a chapter in New York or Mississippi could veto membership for a chapter in Kansas.[29]

The CRC and SDS stepped up the campaign, with the CRC taking the lead. It had threatened to demonstrate during the 1964 homecoming activities but called off the protest when the administration agreed to cooperate in ending discrimination. On March 2, 1965, the Sigma Nu fraternity, the prime target of civil rights activists, received permission from its national office, after having been turned down several times, to waive the exclusionary clause in its charter. This news, however, did not hearten activists, who still saw plenty of racial issues on campus to address.[30]

On the evening of March 7, 1965, at a meeting at Alpha Phi Alpha, a black fraternity, the CRC's two white leaders resigned and were replaced by three black students. Immediately, the new leadership made plans to sit-in at Chancellor Wescoe's office the following morning, marking a dramatic shift in the CRC's tactics. The change in leadership was crucial. One student recalled that at the CRC meeting "it had been made clear to the [white] officers that it would be better for the leadership to be Negro." Jim Masters, a white graduate student and a member of both the CRC and SDS, claimed that Wescoe had been putting the CRC off for two years and "finally, the Negro students themselves got aroused after a hot session" and "the leadership was turned over to them." Several white CRC members told black members to "be a little less emotional . . . about the matter." It is not clear exactly what "the matter" was, but there were several possibilities. Perhaps blacks saw the news of the Sigma Nu waiver as just another tactic to sidestep the issue of racism and exclusion. The most likely explanation was that black CRC members were angry after watching (as did the rest of the nation) television coverage of police viciously beating civil rights marchers in Selma, Alabama, earlier in the day. The brutal assault of the marchers became known as "Bloody Sunday."[31]

The next day, 150 students, most of whom were black and members of the CRC, sat down in the Strong Hall office of Chancellor Clarke Wescoe to protest racial exclusion at the university. Specifically, they wanted racially exclusionary clauses removed from the charters of university-approved organizations, especially fraternities and sororities. They also demanded that the *University Daily Kansan* refuse discriminatory advertising, insisted that the university housing office stop listing segregated rentals for off-campus housing, and that the School of Education not send student teachers to segregated schools. Additionally, they asked that the ASC pass, and Wescoe sign, pending resolutions that would accomplish their goals in one bold stroke. To insure compliance, they encouraged the creation of a faculty, student, and administrative board to hear grievances concerning discrimination and exclusion. One account suggested that the events in Selma, coupled with what the students perceived as Wescoe's years of stonewalling on civil rights, played a significant role in the demonstration. The protestors were "determined to get arrested and re-arrested and rot in Strong Hall if necessary to get action." Wescoe politely listened to the students, but he was "apparently shook up" by the students' actions. He warned them if they remained in his office when the building closed they would be arrested. At 5:00 P.M., with more than one hundred students still quietly occupying his office, Wescoe ordered the Douglas County sheriff to arrest the students for trespassing, although he also offered to post bail, guaranteeing the bond with his personal check. His gesture was unnecessary, as two local ministers and Jesse Milan, a Lawrence school teacher and civil rights activist, signed the $25 bonds for all the protestors, secured by property put up by several blacks in Lawrence. The protestors were released later that night. Wescoe also suspended the students, notifying their parents by telegram.[32]

Although unconcerned with the possible legal ramifications, one of the protestors, Norma Norman, knew that this was a turning point in her life. She was concerned about several things: her parents' reaction, the involvement of the police, and the potential for violence. She was both nervous and uncertain about her actions, yet never considered backing away. Paradoxically, she found strength in being part of the group and but also felt "peer pressure" to participate in the demonstration. After their release from jail, many protestors gathered at a local church, with family, friends, and supporters, where they sang "We Shall Overcome" and discussed what to do next. Norman described the meeting as "a psychological release" from the exhilarating but tense protest.[33]

Under white leadership, the CRC had targeted the racially exclusive clauses of Greek houses; under black leadership the goal had broadened to include other issues of discrimination and exclusion. As one CRC leader noted, "frats aren't the issue, discrimination is." The following day protests continued as other students sympathetic to the cause joined the original group. They picketed in front of Strong Hall, held silent vigils, and marched to the chancellor's campus residence, a move that "alarmed" Wescoe. Late in the afternoon of March 9, Wescoe signed the ASC civil rights bill. The protests ended soon thereafter when the chancellor and the CRC promised to cooperate in ending racial exclusion at the university; Wescoe also dropped the protestors' suspensions. Within weeks, almost all of the demonstrators' goals had been met. An ASC resolution, signed by Wescoe, created a University Human Relations Council (UHRC). Wescoe also prohibited racially discriminatory advertising in campus publications, banned rental listings that excluded blacks, and directed the School of Education to sever all connections with school districts that would not accept black student teachers or hire black full-time teachers. That fall, the Kansas Board of Regents required that all student organizations, including Greek houses, sign an affidavit stating that they did not discriminate because of race, creed, or religious belief. With a rush of student government resolutions, administrative orders, and a stroke of Wescoe's pen, racial exclusion had been banned from the campus of the University of Kansas.[34]

The 1965 demonstration was perhaps the most successful civil rights protest ever in Lawrence. Why it succeeded is not entirely clear. In part, the timing was right, and the administration was simply catching up with the tide of civil rights reform sweeping the nation. The assumption of leadership by black students gave the protest greater urgency and legitimacy, and the events in Selma no doubt played a role, if only symbolically. As well, the students' demands challenged vestiges of racial exclusion that could easily be removed and did not cost the university much financially or administratively. Whatever the reason, the protest broke down the remaining legal and institutional boundaries to racial equality at the university, which had been under assault for more than two decades; it also polarized public opinion on the issue of racial equality. Significantly, the issues were very personal to the student protestors, affecting how they thought of themselves. Thus, the effort created new social and political identities for its participants, and spaces and forms in which they could speak and act, paving the way for the next generation of African American activists in Lawrence. Inspired by the national civil rights movement but responding to local conditions, the sit-in was an "emotional rite of passage" for the demonstrators, almost a spiritual experience that created a "sense of urgency" within them to remain involved in civil rights activity and working for racial justice.[35]

The reactions to the protest also suggest the extent to which Lawrence and Kansas were becoming divided over race. KU alumni, faculty and students, and ministers, local businesspeople, doctors, lawyers, and several national Greek organizations overwhelmingly approved of Wescoe's handling of the sit-in, which they believed was fair and open-minded. The Kansas Board of Regents gave its "full support" to the chancellor. While lauding Wescoe, most Kansans disapproved of the students' "confrontational tactics," which they feared would lead to violence. Predictably, Bert Carlyle wrote in the *Outlook* that the sit-in was initially "stirred up" and "staged" by "the Communist front organization, the American Civil Liberties Union, and outside agitators belonging to other organizations." The *Journal-World*, too, was pessimistic about the future, declaring that "traditionally" KU had always welcomed "ambitious Negro youths" from Missouri, Arkansas, and Oklahoma. Ironically, according to the *Journal-World*, "outsiders," students who were "accepting the assistance of Kansas taxpayers," were leading the protests. Similarly, Ed Abels wrote in the *Outlook* that it was "terrible for the Kansas taxpayers . . . to provide college facilities for these grotesque characters from all parts of the world . . . encouraged to come here by cheap out of state fees." It is unlikely, however, that Kansas students would have participated in the protest had they not shared, with their out-of-state schoolmates, moral outrage over racial exclusion. The contention that the protest was not indigenous underestimated the role of Kansans in the protest. Of the 110 arrested, 13 gave Lawrence addresses, 50 more were from Kansas, and another 17 were from states bordering Kansas. The remaining activists came from across the United States and overseas.[36]

Additionally, national youth activism shaded perceptions of the KU protest. Several people unfavorably compared the KU protest to the Free Speech Movement at Berkeley. Marcia Fleagle, a 1942 KU graduate from Wichita, urged that Wescoe "take a lesson from the Berkeley disaster" and discipline students more frequently and harshly. Similarly, another alumnus, Mrs. Robert D. Love, also of Wichita, believed Wescoe had mishandled the sit-in, as officials had done in Berkeley. "Co-existence with the devil breeds destruction finally!" she exclaimed, threatening to withhold financial contributions to the university, a warning issued by others as well.[37]

Many students shared this opposition to the protest. KU editorialist Linda Ellis argued that the protestors were wrong because they were "step[ping] on the rights of others to give minorities rights," although she never explained who the "others" were or what rights minorities were to be "given." KU student Roger Meyers agreed with her "sound reasoning," asserting that the protestors lacked "common sense" and were only looking for publicity. Gary Noland, another KU editorial writer, claimed that the CRC's demand to prohibit discriminatory advertising in the *Kansan* was a violation of free speech. With strained logic he reasoned that a "majority of students [were] not discriminated against," thus other students were "denied the opportunity to read where they may seek accommodations. This amounts to an infringement upon the rights of the majority by a minority."[38]

In the fall of 1965, after the sweeping changes brought on by the demonstrations, the CRC conducted anonymous interviews with members of over twenty fraternities about their reaction to the sit-in and the university's response. One fraternity member claimed that the university "can't legislate attitudes" and that the Board of Regents' requirement that campus groups sign nondiscriminatory affidavits was "idealistic and unrealistic." Another member thought his house was "open-minded" but that "forced integration" would create "social problems in [the] House." Still others felt that race was a southern, not a Kansas, problem. "Perhaps [forced integration is] justified in South, but here it was more of an antagonism than anything," stated one opinion. Others agreed, adding that the "feeling is generally that Negroes should sit back [and] . . . wait" for conditions to improve. Still others believed that the CRC was too radical and did not "have good campus standing" because too many of its members were identified with KU-SDS. Another person said that the CRC and its members were "spooky people."[39]

The consequences of the demonstration, like most civil rights victories, were mixed and point to the difficulty in achieving racial integration in private housing. The protestors had achieved their goal of forcing the university to work toward ending segregation on campus. By the fall of 1965, no part of the university was officially segregated, and a new structure was in place to hear grievances and give redress to victims of racial discrimination and exclusion. The protest did not, however, alter racist attitudes on campus; if anything, it intensified opposition to racial inclusion. Most fraternity members did not change their positions about integration after the Strong Hall demonstration, and discriminatory practices continued at KU's fraternities and sororities. The first African American did not pledge a previously all-white KU fraternity until 1969.[40] As happened after the protest at the Jayhawk Plunge, the limits of liberal reform again were exposed.

The Strong Hall sit-in left many Lawrencians fearing future demonstrations. In August, the *Outlook* claimed that demonstrations would begin on campus in October and that the March sit-in was but a "test demonstration" and "a warning for Lawrence." Protests at KU were part of a nationwide conspiracy, and, according to Ed Abels, the dismissal of charges against the protestors made "Lawrence an ideal spot for a big one this year." He further claimed that there were "many experienced rioters within an hour's drive of Lawrence who will be only too happy to take part if it is decided to smash store windows or harass the police."[41]

Abels's prediction soon came true. Demonstrations did take place in October, directed not at racial exclusion but at increased U.S. involvement in the Vietnam War. Several hundred KU students and faculty participated in a national protest against the war. The shift in focus to the war among white student activists and white liberals coincided with the fragmentation of civil rights activity on campus and the emergence of Black Power and black nationalism. Over the next several years, the war became the dominant issue on the nation's campuses, and many activists formerly involved in the civil rights movement turned their energies to protesting the war. Although they did not abandon their commitment to social justice and racial equality, they saw the war as a more pressing issue; indeed, they saw war and racial inequality as products of the same unjust system. American imperialism abroad, they believed, was symptomatic of American racism and neglect of issues at home. Moreover, the costs of the war, in lives and money, gave them an opportunity to address issues of poverty, low-paying jobs, and inadequate housing for the nation's poor, many of whom were racial minorities. Although racial politics most significantly transformed Lawrence during the 1960s, the conflicts surrounding America's involvement in the Vietnam War were nearly as important.

The first organized, public opposition to the Vietnam War in Lawrence came from the KU chapter of the Student Peace Union (SPU). Quaker students active in the civil rights and nuclear disarmament movements and with ties to pacifist organizations like the Fellowship of Reconciliation and CORE founded SPU at the University of Chicago in 1959. By 1960, SPU's membership had swelled to 5,000, with over 10,000 subscribers to its newsletter. The thrust of the SPU's activism was directed at nuclear disarmament and a test ban treaty, but it opposed militarism of any kind, which led its members to protest the Vietnam conflict. The KU chapter was organized in 1963, and, although the national organization folded in 1964, students at the University of Kansas apparently continued to use that name later in the decade.[42]

In 1963, however, most KU students were ambivalent about the war, and many supported the United States' effort as part of the larger Cold War struggle. The SPU, however, offered a sustained critique of the war.[43] Its first target was the Reserve Officers Training Corps (ROTC), which it saw as a glaring on-campus symbol of American militarism. In October 1963 and May 1964, the SPU picketed without incident ROTC reviews, which it called a "public demonstration of the military machine on campus." After that, protests at ROTC reviews became something of an annual event on campus. Although the SPU was committed to peaceful protest and nonviolent direct action, not all antiwar protestors shared this commitment. A few days after the May demonstration, an unknown person or persons set an ROTC jeep on fire.[44] It was not clear whether the incident was a statement against the military or a case of vandalism. Although no one was injured, it served as a portent of a changing mood in Lawrence, and especially on campus, about the war.

Public demonstrations and pronouncements against the war became more frequent in 1965, although they remained, as they did across the nation, small. In addition to picket lines and vigils, the SPU distributed leaflets, held meetings, and tried to educate the community about the war. In February 1965, the SPU led an antiwar demonstration on campus, which was marked by a counterdemonstration, symbolic of how Vietnam was polarizing the community. As the SPU peacefully marched, twenty or so supporters of the war "sang the Marine's Hymn" and carried signs that said "Beatniks Go Home." The prowar group followed the SPU as it marched from Lawrence's city hall to the post office, but no violence resulted. The following month, the SPU challenged any group in Lawrence to a public debate on the war. KU students created several new organizations opposed to the war, including a Stop the War in Vietnam committee.[45]

By 1965, the war had become central to daily discourse and the life of both the community and the campus. University of Kansas faculty increasingly opposed the war, and not only the younger, radical, or liberal members. Donald R. McCoy, a professor of history and a Republican, encouraged Pearson to consider Senator Wayne Morse's proposal of a negotiated settlement. McCoy declared that the United States should "extricate itself from a situation that is disturbing us so much emotionally that it threatens not only the unity but the sanity of the nation." In May, fourteen KU students, including several members of the SPU and SDS, signed a letter to Pearson strongly urging "action . . . to stop this inhuman, mistaken war, before it is escalated to the destruction of mankind." The University of Chicago political scientist and critic of American foreign policy Hans Morgenthau spoke at KU in March about U.S. policy. In July, on behalf of SDS's forty members, president John Garlinghouse demanded that the United States halt its bombing of North Vietnam.[46]

When the fall semester began, antiwar activity picked up, and the intersection of the antiwar movement and the student movement made them nearly indistinguishable. The SPU, SDS, Student Union Activities (SUA), and the KU-Y organized a campus teach-in on the war. A steering committee of students and faculty in September created the KU Committee to End the War in Vietnam (KUCEWV), fashioned after the national group of the same name. KUCEWV promised to use teach-ins, invite speakers, and confront Congress to raise public awareness of the war. "As a university is supposed to be a center for exchange of ideas," the new group declared, "it is the responsibility of students to inform themselves about a situation [to which] they might have to give their life."[47]

The SPU again picketed the Lawrence draft board in October 1965, as part of the nationwide teach-ins and an International Day of Protest organized by the National Coordinating Committee to End the War in Vietnam.

George Kimball, then a twenty-one-year-old KU student and SDS member and later a prominent member of Lawrence's counterculture, and another student were arrested by Lawrence police for carrying a sign that read "Fuck the Draft," but neither were part of the SPU demonstration. During the picket, an "active member of a veterans organization" punched an SPU protestor with his fist. The veteran was not charged, according to the *Outlook,* because the "bearded and sandaled youth who was struck apparently doesn't want to fight for his country or self." Although the *Outlook* preferred to stereotype protestors, the picture that accompanied the article showed Tom Kellogg, the SPU president from Wichita, and other picketers, all of whom were clean shaven with short hair, wearing coats, ties, and oxford shirts.[48]

Attitudes and action toward the war remained mixed. The SPU in November 1965 sponsored a blood drive "for victims of LBJ's war" and held a discussion panel urging the U.S. government to "bring the boys home." As American involvement in the war increased and the number of Americans in Vietnam grew, young men who faced the prospect of conscription grew more interested. The administration professed that student unrest was of benefit to the university because it offered new ideas about social problems, but Dean George Waggoner declared the "primary concern of the university is ideas, not action." The *Kansan* opined in November that the United States could not withdraw its troops from Vietnam now, for that would mean certain defeat and a communist takeover.[49]

If the volume of letters that Senator James Pearson and Representative Robert Ellsworth received is an accurate barometer, it appeared that by 1965 more Lawrencians opposed the war than supported it, although there was still significant support. Moreover, many who opposed the war urged a reconsideration of current policy or a negotiated settlement rather than an immediate and unilateral pullout of troops and support. In addition, it is clear from these letters that the crux of antiwar sentiment in Lawrence was centered in Mount Oread and the university community. Students, faculty, and staff generally opposed the war on moral or humanitarian grounds. Lawrencians not affiliated with the university also opposed the war, but their opposition typically centered on economic issues or concerns over American prestige.

At mid-decade the war was supported by many college students such as Jay Weiss, who planned to send a "letter of support and appreciation" to General William Westmoreland, the U.S. military commander in Vietnam. "There is such a small percentage of demonstrators who are against U.S. action compared to the number of students who are in favor," Weiss asserted, "that we would like for our side, which I feel is the definite majority, to be heard." The letter, addressed to the "fighting men in South Viet Nam," read that the undersigned students "heartily disagree with recent demonstrations by misguided minorities claimed [*sic*] to represent the majority view of

Kansas University students and faculty." The *Outlook* applauded the effort, as did the *Kansan.* Similarly, in October 1965, the College Young Republicans (CYR), the College Young Democrats (CYD), and the Young Americans for Freedom sponsored a letter writing effort at KU to support the U.S. position in Vietnam and boost morale. In November 1966, three KU undergraduates from Corbin Hall gathered "bits of Christmas"—a Christmas candle, pine cones, and candy canes, all wrapped in the November 16 *University Daily Kansan*—to send to United States airmen in Vietnam. Similarly, in 1967, Vicki Henry, a student at KU and president of the Junior Auxiliary of the American Legion in Lawrence, along with other KU students initiated a letter-writing and Christmas gift campaign for American troops in Vietnam, a tradition which continued for several years. They placed deposit boxes in downtown stores and at the high school. The Dorsey-Liberty American Legion post sent a form letter to American troops explaining Henry's efforts. "Vicki, we think," the letter read, "is more typical of the kind of young people we have here than most of those we hear about in the news media."[50]

By the end of the decade antiwar protests—and the responses they elicited—had become confrontational. Antiwar demonstrations, including the SPU's protests, were directed at symbols of American militarism. In Lawrence, these included the ROTC, the draft board, the National Guard armory, and the Sunflower Munitions Plant about ten miles east of Lawrence.

ROTC bore the brunt of antiwar protests, especially after 1965. By 1969, physical attacks against ROTC were commonplace. The military science building at KU suffered $500 in damage from a firebomb in February 1969. In April, student protestors waved toy guns in the faces of ROTC cadets during an awards review in front of Allen Fieldhouse. Then, on May 9, around 200 students disrupted the annual chancellor's review of ROTC in Memorial Stadium, dancing around the football field, shouting antiwar slogans, and taunting the cadets. Fearing violence, Chancellor W. Clarke Wescoe abruptly canceled the event. Wescoe blamed KU's chapter of Students for a Democratic Society, whom he criticized as "dedicated anarchists," for the protest. Although SDS had distributed handbills encouraging people to demonstrate at the review, not all of the demonstrators were SDS members.[51]

Prior to the review, Wescoe had agreed to turn control of the university over to the adjutant general of the Kansas National Guard should the protest become violent. Before the review began, two battalions of Kansas National Guardsmen were brought to the area. One was positioned on U.S. Highway 40 (Sixth Street), a major east-west artery through Lawrence, and the other on U.S. Highway 59 (Iowa Street), a major north-south trafficway. Wescoe later remarked that if the review not been called off, "Kent State would have happened here, and *we* would be the university that would be blackened." It is not clear from his comments if Wescoe understood that the violence he so feared might have resulted had he allowed the National Guard onto campus, which he was prepared to do. Perhaps he believed that calling off the review would keep the guardsmen off campus and allow him to remain in control of the university. Regardless, Wescoe was clearly perplexed by student activism. He told student supporters after the demonstration that "there was little left for the administration to do in regard to student unrest" and that because of the democratization of university governance, students were deeply responsible for maintaining peace on campus. Wescoe resigned as chancellor shortly after the incident.[52]

The controversy over the demonstration persisted into the fall. Conservative politicians demanded that the university harshly discipline the protestors and release their names, which the university resisted.[53] The May protest marked a turning point in the antiwar movement in Lawrence. Alongside the peaceful protests led by pacifists and religious groups came confrontational, street theater demonstrations led by students and radicals. It also hardened the resistance from the political far Right.

E. Laurence Chalmers, a liberal opposed to the war in Vietnam, succeeded Wescoe. While Chalmers came to a campus—and community—rife with social tensions, he also inherited a new university governance system with increased student participation. The democratization of university governance signaled to Chalmers a means for channeling the energy of student dissent into positive directions. Chalmers maintained, however, that the greatest threat to academic freedom came from campus radicals. In his installation address, he stated that the "intolerance of disruptive members of the academic community may be as threatening to academic freedom as the intolerance of those in the larger community who would use their influence to suppress the free expression of thoughts, beliefs, and opinions. . . . *We have the right and indeed the obligation to defend our institution against both of these destructive forces.*"[54] Although he sympathized with the ideals and aims of student, and particularly antiwar, activism, Chalmers assured alumni, parents, legislators, and Lawrencians that he would be firm if demonstrations became confrontational and threatened the university. Chalmers's failure to make good on his promise, at least to the satisfaction of alumni and local residents, had a negative impact on his tenure at KU.

In September 1969, Chalmers spoke to the River Club, the most exclusive Kansas City businessman's club. There Chalmers avowed that "the war in Vietnam is perceived by our students as politically unjustifiable and morally indefensible, and I agree with them on both accounts." Although Chalmers's candid antiwar stance garnered the support of many students and faculty, he underestimated the political fallout of his position among conservative Kansans, alumni, politicians, and the Board of Regents, and he struggled to maintain their support.[55]

Youth activism helped to transform the University of Kansas and Lawrence. Young people were active makers of the decade's history. From both liberal and conservative perspectives, young Lawrencians offered a critique of American society and did what they could to change its failings, which often conflicted with the desires of their parents. Indeed, youth activism, the democratization of campus governance, and greater student control over matters of personal behavior increased the gap between parents and alumni on the one hand, and students, faculty, and the administration on the other. Students, often to the chagrin of their parents, wanted a greater say in the direction of their lives and took their cues from the New Left and national events like the Free Speech Movement at Berkeley and the founding of Students for a Democratic Society. This provided a critique of society that resounded in the minds of many KU students, even those who did not become part of the New Left or who, indeed, rejected the radicalism of the New Left. Parents, doubting the maturity and wisdom of student activists, responded with a critique that implored the university to continue its traditional parental role. Moreover, students disagreed over issues like Vietnam and civil rights.

Not all youth activism was inspired by the New Left. Many students offered a critique of America not from the Left but from the Right and formed a grassroots campus core of young conservatives. Although New Right activism typically was out of the public eye, youth conservatism provided a counterpoise to New Left activism, especially as civil rights and the Vietnam War became referenda on American values and the meaning of citizenship.

Youth activism forced mainstream society from its apathy as the challenges from students and other young people grew stronger. Many Lawrencians were simply bewildered by youth activism and looked to the past to make sense of it. One Lawrencian sent Clarke Wescoe an article by Kansas City journalist Tom Leathers that expressed his own skeptical views on the value of student activism. Leathers, writing in *The Squire* in April 1966, noted that "when we were in school we didn't sign protest petitions, we didn't pass resolutions demanding this or that. . . . We went to the college of our choice, and if we didn't like it, we could just change *schools*—not try and change the *university*. We respected the rights of the administration to set the policy." Like many other Americans, Leathers believed that learning the proper respect for tradition and authority was "just as important to a college boy's growth as what he might have learned from an experiment in freedom."[56]

Others in Lawrence shared Leathers's view, and many looked warily at the challenge that America's youth posed to accepted boundaries, traditional authority, and their sense of themselves. Youth activism—in civil rights, women's liberation, and cultural dissent, among other issues—challenged the ideals and values on which many Lawrencians had constructed their own identities. Content amid the material comfort of postwar America, some Lawrencians took the young people's critique of American society as a criticism of them, their values, and their way of life, a plebiscite on the nation's identity and its future.

"It starts with our youngsters," the *Lawrence Daily Journal-World* editorialized in 1960. "If this trend of moral decay is to be reversed," the paper predicted, "then the children are going to have to grow up in the close association with parents and teachers and acquaintances who have the proper sense of values."[57] The *Journal-World* had a clear sense of what values were proper; the values of the sixties' youth generation were not as clear. Some activists used their religion to reform American society and create a "beloved community," some joined with the New Left to recreate American society based on "participatory democracy," while others joined to remake American society on free market principles and "true conservative" values. Some sought their niche in corporate America while others rejected the system; some dropped out of the system altogether and still others wanted to destroy it. Youth activism, in a variety of forms, wanted to transform the community, but not all young people in Lawrence agreed on how to do that.

Compounding the complexity of youth activism, especially after 1965, was the Vietnam War. As the United States became more entangled, the prospect of military service made the war increasingly tangible for millions of male college students. Moreover, Vietnam became symptomatic of what the New Left and other student, civil rights, and antiwar activists saw as the larger problems in American society: racism, imperialism, arrogance, and a capitalist economic system. Vietnam created problems for conservatives who, as supporters of the war, found themselves increasingly marginalized as the war lost its popular support. As a result, both a critique of American society and a social movement to reform that society emerged after 1965, offering a challenge to the existing power structures in the United States and traditional social boundaries and identities.

CHAPTER 5

"Our Way of Life"

Pharmacist Dick Raney wore many hats in Lawrence, a town he had called home since he left Osborne, Kansas, in 1945 to enroll at the University of Kansas. The owner of several drugstores in Lawrence, in the early 1960s Raney and his father built the Hillcrest shopping center on the western edge of town, a venture that foreshadowed the town's growth in that direction. A moderate Republican, Raney was elected to the city commission, was mayor for four years, and served on the board of directors of Headquarters (a drug counseling center), the Ballard Center (a black-oriented community center in north Lawrence), and other community organizations. The coffee shop in his south Massachusetts Street pharmacy was like an informal town meeting, where people of different backgrounds and perspectives met to discuss politics, problems confronting the city, or the latest scientific discoveries. As a pharmacist, Raney had a broad range of customers, but he knew little about them and their problems, especially his black customers. Raney recalled that he had been aware of some protests over racial exclusion in Lawrence, but he and other whites who frequented the coffee shop believed "those were isolated events." He noted that he and other Lawrencians "were not well enough acquainted with the black perspective" in the early 1960s to fully comprehend matters of race. In time, however, as a civic leader Raney was forced to examine racial issues in his community.[1]

Dick Raney recalled the night in April 1968 when he learned that Martin Luther King, Jr., had been murdered. "By coincidence, I was meeting with some black activists," he remembered. "God, I will never forget how they looked, how they reacted when the news came. . . . I knew then that blacks have to threaten our way of life; if they're going to get back what the past took away, they've got to look us right in the eye and say 'Screw you.' I came away from there a different man—not more liberal, not more patronizing. If anything, I took my heart off my sleeve. I knew the black man was going to make it without me. I knew things were about to start changing in Lawrence."[2]

A great transformation occurred in Lawrence after 1967, one that Raney, but few other white residents, recognized or understood. Raney knew that for real change to occur, racial boundaries in Lawrence, and especially his "way of life," had to be challenged and reconfigured.

The civil rights movement culminated with the passage of the Civil Rights Act of 1964 and the Voting Rights Act of 1965. Even with these impressive victories, the promise of racial equality had not been redeemed. Jim Crow blatantly lingered in the South, and in the North, blacks struggled for better educational and employment opportunities, with moderate but painstakingly slow progress. Although the movement had raised expectations, many African Americans discovered that legislation did not eliminate poverty, job ceilings, police harassment and brutality, or the barbs of racial exclusion and discrimination. Liberals believed that progress in race relations was being made; to many African Americans, especially young blacks, progress was an illusion.

By mid-decade, when black frustrations over continued racial inequality became clear, several northern and western urban areas exploded in racial violence. From the Watts riot of 1965 through the upheavals in Newark, New Jersey, Detroit, Michigan, and twenty-three other American cities in 1967, race riots seemed to characterize the mid-1960s. The National Advisory Commission on Civil Disorders (the Kerner Commission), in studying the causes of violence in America, concluded that the underlying cause of riots was white racism. "What white America had never fully understood—but what the Negro can never forget—is that white society is deeply implicated in the ghetto," the commission declared in 1968. "White institutions created it, white institutions maintain it, and white society condones it."[3] The commission also asserted that police brutality and a double standard of justice for racial minorities contributed to the violence.

Although white racism and racist institutions were important contributing factors to the violence, the unfulfilled expectations and unredeemed promise of racial equality were equally important. With the failure of liberalism to correct racial injustice, African Americans increasingly took to correcting the problem themselves. Frustration and anger led to racial violence, whether it was in Watts, Newark, Detroit, or Lawrence, Kansas. While there was no section of Lawrence that could be called a ghetto, the same forces that existed in Newark and Detroit were at work in the small Kansas university town. Given these conditions of life in America, it is little wonder that many African Americans rejected the liberal/integrationist approach to racial equality and adopted other means: self-help, black nationalism, and cultural nationalism, among others. Part of what Dick Raney saw emerging in his town was a powerful political and cultural movement called Black Power, a force that redefined race relations in Lawrence and radically challenged and redrew Lawrence's social boundaries.

In 1966, the Student Non-Violent Coordinating Committee's (SNCC) chair Stokely Carmichael's cry for "Black Power" quickly became an exhilarating alternative to traditional civil rights goals and action.[4] A year later, Carmichael's book *Black Power* (co-authored with Charles Hamilton) defined the inchoate idea "as a call for black people to unite, recognize their heritage, . . . build a sense of community, . . . define their own goals, [and] to lead their own organizations."[5] Black Power did not cause the riots that racked the nation between 1964 and 1968, but through the "Black Power" slogan Carmichael and SNCC constructed "a political vocabulary" that allowed many African Americans, especially young, urban blacks, to articulate their anger.[6]

As a movement, Black Power was not confined only to the nation's large urban areas. Many African Americans in Lawrence, lured by the emphasis on cultural and racial self-identification, and armed with a rhetoric that allowed them to release their own anger, quickly embraced the movement and redirected the course of race relations in their community. Black Power empowered African Americans psychologically, culturally, and politically. It provided them with a language to create new spaces in the community in which they could act. Moreover, it changed the terms of the community's discourse on race, terms now set by both blacks and whites. The Black Power movement challenged not only Lawrence's dominant free-state narrative and the racial status quo but also the identities that most whites in the town had created for themselves. Fearful and distrusting of a movement that they were unable or unwilling to understand whites in Lawrence hardened their defense of the town's traditional racial boundaries and their own sense of who they were. This racial dynamic transformed the community.

This process was evident in the long struggle to build a municipal swimming pool open to all Lawrencians. In November 1967, Lawrence voters narrowly approved issuing bonds to build a municipal swimming pool. A critical factor in the election was the anger and frustration of African Americans, especially young African Americans, and the response to them by the all-white city commission, white civic and business leaders, and other white residents. In demanding immediate resolution to a twenty-year issue, black youths displayed the first stirrings of the Black Power movement in the community and set the tone for future race relations in the town. Lawrence narrowly escaped a full-blown race riot in the summer of 1967, but the threat seemed very real, at least to many white residents. This perception is a key to understanding the shifting racial boundaries in Lawrence.

Lawrence voters in 1961 and 1963 (as they had in 1956) turned down a bond proposal to build a municipal pool. Opposition to the pool bond issue centered on resistance to higher taxes and the proposed pool's location. Additionally, there was little incentive for white voters to approve a municipal pool, since at least four private swim clubs were already providing facilities at which their children could swim. New apartment complexes on the south end of town (several of which excluded blacks from renting) had swimming pools, too, and nearby Baldwin City, Eudora, Oskaloosa, and Tonganoxie all had pools in their small towns, accessible to whites willing to make the drive.[7]

Undeterred, the NAACP, the Lawrence League of Women Voters (LWV), the Lawrence Human Relations Commission (LHRC), and other civil rights and civic organizations campaigned for a municipal pool with petition drives and information campaigns and kept the issue alive. The lack of a public pool was a civic embarrassment, as Lawrence was one of only three first-class cities in Kansas not to have a municipal pool. The pool bond election in 1963 was closer than previous votes (3,817 no to 3,155 yes), and over 75 percent of the registered voters had cast a ballot. "[S]ome say the racial issue is still hot," the *Journal-World* reported, but the paper preferred to believed the bond issue failed because people did not want to pay higher taxes.[8]

In 1966, the Lawrence City Commission established the Citizens Advisory Group (CAG) to plan for capital improvement projects needed to keep up with the town's growth. The CAG recommended the city issue bonds for a new airport west of town, new fire stations, and other city building projects, including a municipal swimming pool. Before putting the pool bond question on the ballot, in June 1967, the city applied to the state's Park Resources Authority for a $203,800 grant to build a pool. The authority denied the request when a Midwest Research Institute study concluded there was no need for additional swimming facilities in Douglas County, citing the private swim clubs in Lawrence and the municipal pools in nearby towns. The study did not, however, address the exclusion of African Americans from these pools. Although denied the grant, the city commission accepted the CAG recommendation to put before the voters in November a bond proposal for constructing a municipal pool.[9]

The denial of the grant added to the growing frustration among some of Lawrence's young African Americans. This generation of African Americans, who came of age after the 1954 *Brown v. Board of Education* decision, grew up expecting the promise of racial equality to be fulfilled. They found their lives in Lawrence, however, at odds with the town's free-state narrative. They endured racial slurs and wary glances from their white peers and found that not all of the city's public spaces were open to them. They confronted racist teachers and administrators, had few black role models in the schools, and learned little about African culture and history in the classroom. They were excluded from most recreation and employment and viewed with suspicion by police. In early August 1967, frustrated by the lack of local progress in the nation's century-old promise of equality and enraged over the lack of summer recreational and employment opportunities, the apathetic attitude of Lawrence's city officials and other whites in rectifying the situation, and police harassment, a large group of angry young blacks gathered on Massachusetts Street and, according to local educator Jesse Milan, threatened to burn the town.

What really happened is difficult to discern, as detailed accounts of the incident are scarce. The *Journal-World* reported only that the town had experienced "several nights of minor incidents involving mostly Negro teenagers." Another account asserts, without any documentation, that "armed black male youths were threatening violence in the downtown area; some were on the roofs," and that the crisis ended when "influential blacks convinced them to attend a special meeting of the Human Relations Commission." The minutes of that meeting, held on August 8, 1967, which might help to clarify the incident, unfortunately are missing from the LHRC records and presumed lost or stolen. Some sources suggest the incident was overblown. Lawrence Chief of Police Bill Troelstrup scoffed at suggestions that the city had been on the threshold of a race riot, claiming that his department did not "act on rumors." While Troelstrup's comment diminishes Milan's claim that a riot was imminent, it reinforces the notion that rumors convinced many people in Lawrence that such an event could happen.[10]

Jesse Milan, however, distinctly recalled the incident. Absorbed in working on his master's degree at Emporia State University that summer, Milan was out of town and not as active in the community as he had been in other summers. When, on August 4, young blacks assembled downtown, however, it alarmed enough Lawrence citizens that Mayzelma Wallace, the chair of the LHRC, turned to Milan to diffuse the situation. Whether or not the threat of a riot was as serious as Milan remembered, the LHRC took it seriously, as did many other whites. Milan told Wallace that city officials had been saying the "same damn things" for years, and, in the eyes of these young African Americans, no real progress had been made in race relations in Lawrence. Milan, who had taught the youths since they had started school, agreed to talk to them and to seek a solution.[11]

Reasoning with the embittered teens, Milan told them that violence was only a temporary solution. Afterward, the town would have to be rebuilt, which would push the concerns of African Americans to the background. Offering the students his assistance, Milan promised them that if they did get not any results, "then the town is yours." The young men and women wanted Wallace to chair a public meeting with the LHRC and the city commission. Milan told the LHRC that the black youths had "dialed the phone" and that the city had "to pick it up and listen." The LHRC agreed, and the meeting was set for August 8.[12]

The swimming pool was symptomatic of the young blacks' grievances. For years, they had relied without success on the good faith of civil rights activists—black and white—and liberal politicians to make good on promises of equality and social justice. In their minds, little had changed and the prospects for change did not look good. John Spearman, Jr., a senior at Lawrence High School and one of the teenagers who spoke at the special meeting of the LHRC, was not present among the throng of black students gathered on Massachusetts Street. Nearly thirty years later, he vaguely recalled the incident, but he did not remember it as a near riot. Spearman, Jr., was angry, however, about the lack of progress in race relations in Lawrence. Moreover, he was at that time willing to express that anger, which he did at the LHRC meeting. He had reached a point in his life where he was weighing alternatives to the mainstream civil rights movement, which he believed "had failed to get it done."[13]

Milan and Spearman, Jr., both remembered that the special LHRC meeting was well attended by African Americans. The *Journal-World* reported that "more than 100 persons, most of them Negroes and mostly youngsters," were there. Milan encouraged the kids to talk for themselves, and many did. The *Journal-World* identified ten "spokesmen" for the black youths, all students at Lawrence High School, several of whom, including John Spearman, Jr., later became Black Power activists. The students voiced three, by then common, complaints: the lack of swimming facilities, of recreational facilities, and of job opportunities. Another student, sixteen-year-old Rick Dowdell, complained of harassment by Lawrence police officers.[14]

The meeting, however, focused on the swimming pool issue. Earlier in the day the LHRC and the city commission met at the Eldridge Hotel to find a way to provide a public swimming pool. According to the *Journal-World,* "several avenues [were] being explored." But the all-white city commission, led by Mayor Dick Raney, told the black youths that the city had neither the money nor facilities to provide swimming opportunities for them. Milan chimed in that there was a small pool at the Four Seasons Motel, near the southwest edge of town, that was sitting idle. Milan suggested that the city lease the pool temporarily and allow all of Lawrence's children to escape the summer heat. The *Journal-World* never explained why the pool, for which the city had approved a building permit, was not being used. It is also unclear whether this was one of the options discussed by the LHRC and city commissioners at the Eldridge Hotel meeting. According to Milan, city officials initially balked, but he pressed the issue. Again, city officials explained that they could not "make that kind of commitment." Milan allegedly retorted, "You don't have a choice. It's either [this] or burn the town."[15]

Nothing was done that evening, but the *Journal-World* reported the next day that approval of the temporary pool "appeared likely." On August 9, the city commission voted unanimously to lease the Four Seasons pool until Labor Day, at a cost of $10.00 per day. The city also agreed to clean up the vacant pool, including the filtering system and changing areas, and provide bus service to the pool several times a day. The total cost of about $850 would be paid out of a city contingency fund set aside for emergencies and offset by a twenty-five-cent admission. City officials, who had "worked all day" in search of a solution to the impasse, emphasized that the lease was "only temporary" and stressed that bonds for a permanent pool would again be on the ballot in the November election. The cleanup began on August 9 with several young African American volunteers helping city workers. They cut grass and chopped weeds, painted the changing areas, and removed a few catfish from the pool. Officials estimated that the Four Seasons pool would be ready by Friday, August 11.[16]

City manager Ray Wells put the city's efforts in a positive context, emphasizing that the city's summer recreation program, which had ended a week earlier, provided all youngsters—black and white—opportunities during the summer to swim in local private swim clubs. Wells played down the influence that the rage of young African Americans had had on the city's decision, remarking only that "recent incidents led us to investigate leasing a small pool." Ray Riley, an assistant city manager, insisted that the temporary solution was "not designed for one specific group and there was never an intention for it to be otherwise."[17]

After years of struggle, African Americans could, for the first time, swim in a publicly supported pool in Lawrence. The first weekend the pool was open, it received "steady use," although a *Journal-World* photo showed more white children swimming than black children. Black children, many of whom lived far away from the pool, continued to escape the summer heat in other ways: swimming in the Kansas River or other streams and ponds, playing with water hoses and sprinklers, and using a three-and-one-half feet deep corrugated steel pool lined with plastic at the Ballard Center in north Lawrence, the gift of an anonymous donor.[18] While the temporary lease was a step forward, the difficulty in making the long trip to the Four Seasons pool, even with bus service, prevented quite a few people, especially those from north Lawrence, from swimming there.

Not everyone in Lawrence thought the lease option was a good idea. Mrs. V. R. Rody, whose husband was a foreman at Morton Building Materials (owned by city commissioner Clark Morton), was angry that Raney "took it upon himself to rent at a great deal of expense for so short a time a pool for the 'city' of Lawrence." Rody, who lived in east Lawrence, claimed that the people had spoken when they voted down previous bond issues and the commission was ignoring the will of most "adult, tax-paying voters." Moreover, Rody was angry that "a few [black] teenage kids have dictated the terms and had them accepted." Similarly, general contractor Glen Roberts asked the commissioners to "accept the vote of the people," a reference to the history of unsuccessful bond elections.[19] Clearly, neither Rody nor Roberts wanted to pay for a public pool, and their response to the commission's action suggests a mistrust of government, and a thinly-veiled racism.

Nonetheless, angry black teenagers had transformed the public discourse and public space in Lawrence. By gathering en masse on Massachusetts Street and claiming the street as their own, they got the attention of white residents in the community. When given a public forum to express their desires, the youths had articulated their anger in a way that changed the tenor of the city's discourse on race. Through their expression of anger, they moved the city commission to act.

Perhaps the most ominous issue discussed at these meetings was the one Rick Dowdell raised: police violence toward and harassment of African Americans. Lawrence police chief Bill Troelstrup attended one of the special LHRC meetings and said that blacks' claims of racial discrimination and harassment by Lawrence police officers were "very hard to buy." Troelstrup admitted that the LPD had not hired an African American since he became chief in July 1964, but added that "Negroes [were] given an equal employment opportunity with the department." Verner Newman, one of three African Americans on the force, disputed the claim, noting that the department had passed him over for promotion many times, despite his superior qualifications over white officers. While Newman was promoted to lieutenant, he later was passed over for promotion to captain and chief.[20]

Police supervisor Charles Greer, who was white, believed that the police department was simply misunderstood. While he did not deny that isolated episodes of police brutality and harassment did occur, Greer thought such behavior had mistakenly come to dominate the image of local police. For example, he claimed that standard operating procedure was for more than one officer, often three, to arrest and handcuff a suspect, to prevent anyone from getting hurt. To onlookers, however, it gave the appearance of police "whipping" or "beating" an arrestee.[21]

Other Lawrencians, however, thought the police department needed revamping. Dick Raney remembered that too often Lawrence police officers used the "fat end of [their] . . . billy club" to resolve problems. Bill Simons, the director of the Ballard Center, recalled inviting about fifty kids, most of whom were black, to his house to listen to records and have some apple cider. "Well, you can imagine in an all-white neighborhood in the late '60s, when, all of sudden, carload after carload of blacks start pulling up and filing into this house," he recalled. Within minutes, three police cars pulled up to investigate. To Simons, the episode illustrated all too well the white community's paranoia and the fear that most black teenagers in Lawrence had about the police.[22] It is not surprising that the 1965 Watts riot (and other race riots throughout the twentieth century) had been precipitated by an incident between the police and black citizens. Increasingly, black radicals came to see police departments as "occupying forces" in black "colonial" enclaves. As Black Power grew in strength across the country, confrontation between police and militant blacks seemed inevitable. Most blacks in Lawrence, especially black youth, distrusted the police, who held values similar to the dominant white community they served.

The pressing issue in Lawrence, however, remained the swimming pool, in essence a racial issue. Civil rights activists had been working all summer to get a swimming pool built in Lawrence. Knowing in August that the Four Seasons pool was not a permanent solution, they stepped up the campaign to pass the pool bond issue. The LDC-NAACP and the Lawrence LWV led the attempt but also had the support of the *Journal-World,* the Lawrence Council of Churches, the Park and Recreation Advisory Board, and the chamber of commerce. Jesse Milan met with black teenagers in the South Park Recreation Center every Sunday in the summer and fall and organized them to canvass the town for the bond issue. The LWV also circulated petitions for a referendum vote. The LWV addressed questions that had plagued earlier elections: What would be the cost of the pool? How much would the bonds raise taxes? Where would it be located?[23]

On November 28, 1967, Lawrence voters, by a margin of only 544 votes (4,615 "yes" to 4,071 "no"), agreed to issue bonds for a municipal swimming pool. Over 70 percent of the city's eligible voters had cast their ballots. The residents of east and north Lawrence, areas which had the largest African American population in town, again voted "no" on the pool, suggesting that race perhaps was less of a factor than it was perceived to be and that economic concerns were greater than suggested. Lawrence had its pool, which opened, amid continued racial tension, on June 3, 1969.[24]

The approval of the bond issue culminated a struggle that dated back to at least 1946. The victory, however, raised the question: Why was the pool campaign successful in 1967? The efforts of the LWV, the NAACP, and other organizations and activists were crucial, as was the support of the city commission. These groups circulated reliable information that surely convinced some to vote for the pool. While these factors should not be discounted, the crucial variable for the "yes" vote was the changing the public discourse on race relations in Lawrence, of which the threat—or at least, the perceived threat—of violence against whites and the community by African Americans was an important element.

The sequence of events is clear. A large group of young blacks gathered on Massachusetts Street, and this prompted the LHRC to meet with young African Americans. Before the meeting the Lawrence city commission provided temporary swimming facilities and soon afterward leased a temporary pool open to all residents of the city. In November Lawrencians voted to construct a municipal pool open to all residents, after voting "no" on three previous occasions. Some white residents probably voted "no" because they did not want their children to swim with black children, and the threat of violence only reinforced their cultural stereotypes, while others voted for the measure out of a sincere belief that an integrated pool was a step toward racial equality and justice. It is likely that still other white voters said "yes" because they feared a "no" vote would result in racial violence; their votes were an effort to appease blacks in Lawrence.

While Lawrence escaped racial violence in the summer of 1967, the threat had been genuine. Jesse Milan, a committed follower of nonviolence, believed that this moment was "the first time black youths had really spoken out in this town about not being able to be a part of this town." Milan insisted that the teenagers were prepared to riot. Moreover, many whites in Lawrence shared Milan's concerns, their fears intensified by urban rioting in Newark, Detroit, and, nearer to home, in Wichita. The *Journal-World* ran disturbing headlines in the summer of 1967, which was an important factor in white's reactions to the teens: "Negro Outburst Follows Order Setting Curfew," "Wichita Feels More Violence During Curfew," and "Gangs of Negroes Shake U.S. Capital." Although the *Journal-World* characterized the menacing actions of black teenagers in early August as "minor incidents," the effects of such dramatic headlines were profound.[25]

Most of the community, and especially whites, perceived the potential for violence as real. It was these perceptions, and not the event itself, that were most significant. Jesse Milan may have overstated his role as mediator in the situation, but the LHRC did approach him to diffuse what it perceived to be a volatile situation; the LHRC's willingness to hold a special meeting to hear the black youths' grievances attests to this. Moreover, there is little reason to doubt Milan's testimony—even if it is self-congratulatory—because it follows the contours of the incident as reported in local papers and oral accounts. Even if all that happened was that a group of young African Americans congregated in the downtown area, the chain of events stands as powerful testimony to the depth of white fears, generated not only by local events but also by the growing unrest and militancy among urban African Americans across the country.

The growing militancy of blacks concerned many Lawrencians, black as well as white. Lawrence retiree Roy Hicks sent to Senator James B. Pearson a clipping that recounted a comment made by Stokely Carmichael. In response to Carmichael's words, Hicks asked, "[A]ren't Negroes supposed to obey the laws the you folks enact there in Washington? How far does a citizen have to go to commit treason? Must we have Benedict Arnolds preaching and teaching all over the country such doctrine as this?" Pearson also expressed "shock and dismay," and was "hopeful that responsible leaders of minorities can be encouraged so that the positive aspects of *our* efforts to help them will not be lost."[26] Pearson's comments, despite his good intentions, smacked of paternalism and held white ("our") efforts as the standards by which others should be judged. Pearson's opinion reflected those of many of his constituents. Whites who thought that race relations were improving were confounded by the anger of young radicals, as well as by the more "radical" pronouncements about poverty and against the war made by Martin Luther King.

Several currents in Lawrence coalesced in August 1967, mirroring national trends: rising anger among young blacks, new perceptions of racial identity and consciousness, and heightened militancy among young African Americans. Like their peers across the nation, young blacks in Lawrence were dissatisfied with the failure of the civil rights movement to attain its promise of racial equality. Black Power emerged as an alternative to traditional civil rights efforts, and many young blacks adopted confrontational tactics to achieve their goals. African Americans in Lawrence had tapped into a dynamic force that was reshaping the black freedom struggle.

Black Power stressed the need of blacks for self-determination and control over their lives and communities. It rejected integration and coalitions with whites without black control. In *Black Power,* Stokely Carmichael and Charles V. Hamilton used the language of third world nationalism to depict black communities as "colonies" of white society. To liberate these colonies, they focused on "militant racial consciousness," which enticed African Americans to create new racial identities that celebrated their African cultural heritage and distinction from white society. Racial consciousness, Carmichael and Hamilton claimed, would provide the means for radical social change, something that the civil rights movement had not been able to do. They accused the civil rights movement and Martin Luther King, Jr., of speaking in a tone acceptable to white liberals, which assured white liberal acceptance of King's nonviolent, integrationist tactics and hence forced blacks to resist from a state of weakness. Carmichael and Hamilton rejected black assimilation into middle-class America because it was "anti-humanist" and "perpetuate[d] racism." The failure of the civil rights movement, they asserted, rested with an oppressive capitalist system, institutional racism, and power relationships that excluded blacks; racial consciousness would provide the means for blacks to gain control of their lives and radically change American society. They also called for blacks to defend themselves. "There can be no social order without social justice," they wrote, and "if a nation fails to protect its citizens, then it cannot blame the citizens for protecting themselves."[27]

For whites, however, Black Power conjured up frightening images, especially the thought of armed black men. Black community control, pride, and self-esteem scared white Americans who believed that blacks wanted to dominate American society. Just as frequently, whites equated Black Power with a communist-inspired conspiracy to depose the American government. Blacks' militant and inflammatory rhetoric did nothing to assuage white fears, although clearly that was never the militants' intent.[28]

In addition to promoting black racial consciousness and black culture, a principle of Black Power was black control of black institutions. In Lawrence, this was apparent in a power struggle between Black Power advocates and white liberals, both of whom were fighting for control of the Ballard Center in north Lawrence and over public education in Lawrence. These battles illustrated the powerful and compelling qualities of Black Power and how it changed the course of race relations in Lawrence.

The Ballard Center was once the blacks-only Lincoln School, but by the mid-1960s was principally a recreation center for black youths and a center for the black community. Besides providing recreational and cultural activities, the center, under Bill Simons's direction, started an employment program for minorities, which addressed one of the issues young African Americans had raised before the LHRC. Simons recalled that race relations in Lawrence in 1967, when he was hired as the center's first full-time director, were characterized by a lack of communication between blacks and whites, which was evident in employment opportunities. For example, Simons claimed that blacks did not apply for jobs because they believed they would not be hired, while Dick Raney declared he would have hired blacks at his pharmacy but none applied. Several employers, including Raney Drugs and the Centron Corporation, committed to hire blacks as part of the Ballard Center's job program, and some jobs opened to young African Americans. However, according to Simons, the program was not completely successful because one or two workers "got into fights" and some white employers judged all blacks through these experiences and the distorted retelling of these stories.[29] Despite the best efforts by liberals like Simons, racial stereotypes and boundaries were resilient in Lawrence.

Simons felt awkward running a center that served blacks but that had none on staff. This changed when he hired Leonard Harrison as assistant director at the Ballard Center. Harrison, an African American, had moved to Lawrence from Wichita in 1967 so that his wife could finish a graduate degree in history at the University of Kansas. Harrison immediately put his mark on racial politics in Lawrence. Harrison, who had been an antipoverty worker in Wichita, argued that since the Ballard Center served the needs of the black community, it should be run by African Americans. During a 1968 speech at KU he proclaimed that "if you're black and don't believe in Black Power, you're either insane or a damn fool."[30]

Not surprisingly, a power struggle for control of the center ensued. Much to Simons's chagrin, Harrison, or "Shooby Do," as he was known, immediately took the view that "Blacks should do their own thing, whites should do their own thing," which was an affront to Simons's liberal and integrationist views on race (his wife was black). Harrison held meetings in his house for blacks only and put "tremendous pressure" on young African Americans not to socialize with whites. Violence became a frequent way to settle disputes, and not just black on white or white on black violence; much of it was black on black. "[L]ifelong friends were getting beat up by friends," Simons recounted.[31]

In 1968, Simons fired Harrison for meeting in "secret" with young blacks and encouraging them to use the center as a political forum. "[W]hen I fired him, shit hit the fan!" Simons recalled. "[M]y life was threatened, the center was fire bombed, [and] I had to send my children out of town." Police kept a close watch on Simons's house, and his father-in-law brought a shotgun for him keep in the house, where his family slept on the floor in the family room, for fear of an attack directed at their bedrooms. Some African Americans were angry when Harrison was fired and demanded a meeting with Simons. After a heated exchange among Simons, the center's board of directors, and an angry black audience (many of whom, according to Simons, were from Wichita) in the steaming basement of the Ballard Center, Simons and the white members of the board resigned. Immediately, Simons claimed, several blacks in the crowd "named themselves to the board" and hired Harrison as director at a greater salary than Simons had been earning.[32] Harrison remained the center's director until 1970.

Harrison shaped the town's racial discourse in his own terms and pointed it in the direction that many blacks were taking at the time. He helped found and became president of the Coordinating Committee of the Black Community (CCBC), a group that also included Jesse Milan and Vernell Sturns, the city's director of human resources and community social development. What makes Harrison such a pivotal figure in Lawrence's sixties experience is his complexity. Others described Harrison much as Simons had: dynamic, charismatic, articulate, proud, defiant, confrontational, and, at times, inflammatory. Frequently dressing in a dashiki, wearing his hair in dreadlocks, and refusing to defer to white society, Harrison was a nightmare to whites in Lawrence. His militant rhetoric and defiant swagger did little to assuage those fears. Harrison had been convicted of burglary in Oklahoma in 1961, for which he had served a jail sentence, and, like other black militants in the 1960s, his outspokenness and previous record made him a target of police surveillance. On October 29, 1968, Harrison, who then was Ballard Center director, and eight other men headed to the Wichita Holiday Inn to collect money they were owed by three men who worked for the Wichita Model

Cities program. A heated discussion ensued, and Harrison and his comrades allegedly badly beat two of the Model Cities men and dangled the third over the balcony, threatening to drop him if they were not paid. The police arrested the nine men and they were charged with kidnapping, extortion, and assault. Harrison contended he had not threatened the men and that he only was trying to collect what was legitimately due him. During the seven-week trial, the prosecutor linked the defendants with the Black Guard, an activist cadre from Philadelphia. In the context of the times, Harrison believed that he was being persecuted for his political views by a racist power structure intent on shutting him up. It came as no surprise to him when, in 1969, he was convicted of armed robbery in the incident, a verdict that he appealed but lost. Rather than serve the jail sentence, Harrison fled to Tanzania in 1970. He was pardoned in 1993.[33]

Harrison—perhaps to whites the angriest African American in Lawrence—had a profound influence on young blacks in Lawrence between 1967 and 1970. His radical rhetoric would have fallen on deaf ears without the heat of racial oppression; the crucible of white racism in Lawrence made his words very relevant and tangible to young blacks, motivating some of them to act. Many of them, such as Rick Dowdell, got caught in the middle of this power struggle.

Bill Simons and his wife were foster parents to Dowdell, whose mother had died when he was a toddler. The Simons took in Dowdell in 1967 or 1968, not long after Rick (and his uncle) had been arrested, but not convicted, of theft. Dowdell felt great personal loyalty to the Simons, but he also looked up to Leonard Harrison, whom he saw as a role model.[34] As Black Power became a significant movement within Lawrence, Harrison was at its forefront, and a few young blacks in Lawrence, including Rick Dowdell, looked to Harrison for guidance.

Jesse Milan believed that Harrison was a "strong impetus" in encouraging young blacks to become more militant in their fight for equality in Lawrence. Both Milan and Harrison emphasized black cultural identity and self-identity, but Milan, like Simons, believed that Harrison preached black separatism, which Milan opposed. Milan also labeled Harrison ineffective, a view shared by John Spearman, Jr., himself a self-proclaimed Black Power advocate. He saw Harrison as mostly an agitator who could not translate his rhetoric into accomplishments. Other African Americans disagreed. Judith Thompson, who worked with Harrison at the Ballard Center, described Harrison as "a tornado that just blew through. He wanted to rile things up a bit in Lawrence. He felt it needed it. Black people simply weren't getting their due, and he wanted to help." Cynthia Turner, another Ballard worker, believed that people who did not know him were frightened of him. Martin Luther King "prayed and Leonard demanded. I think they [the white power structure] were scared of him. That's what made people hate him, and I think frame him."[35]

Only eight or nine when she first met Harrison, Stephanie Coleman, a life-long Lawrencian whose family had settled there in the late nineteenth century, admired him. She recalled Harrison as a "nice man" but noted that there was always a "sense of violence, or mystery and intrigue" about him. Coleman's mother, who was involved in civil rights activism, was a friend of Harrison, and he was a frequent dinner guest. Coleman claimed that Harrison "threatened" the Lawrence National Bank with violence if it did not hire more blacks, and that that was how her mother got a job there. She saw Harrison frequently on the playgrounds and around town, and he often checked in on black kids to see how they were doing. She remembered that Harrison "liked to be in control of things . . . and he had answers for everything." She recalled him as a "very big man, a very loud man," "who demanded and got respect" from everyone. "This was the man who confronted Mr. Whitey," Coleman asserted, "we didn't have that" before.[36]

Harrison was not above using threats and intimidation in his activism, declaring that the "new black man can no longer call for nonviolence." Not surprisingly, most Lawrencians "either loved [Harrison] . . . or hated" him, Bill Simons declared. Ocoee Miller, the founder and director of the Penn House, a self-help center in east Lawrence for low-income residents, fell into the latter category. She once believed that she and Harrison shared the same goal of wanting to help the poor. Miller believed, however, that Harrison wanted to be the only voice for the black community in Lawrence. She recalled that Harrison was able to raise "enormous" amounts of money, which he used for projects such as a breakfast program for children from low-income families and for a legal defense fund for African Americans. According to Miller, Harrison was able to persuade local churches and "white liberals" to give willingly and frequently. But Miller also believed that Harrison got much of his money through extortion and threats and that most of the money went into Harrison's pocket. Although Milan and Spearman, Jr., did not accuse Harrison of such tactics, they, like Miller and Simons, believed that Harrison was motivated by self-interest, and that he was intent on establishing a Black Power movement in Lawrence, only if he himself could be leader.[37]

Police officer Verner Newman concluded that Leonard Harrison was largely responsible for getting the swimming pool built. His agitation and anger, Newman asserted, convinced folks in west Lawrence (by which he meant white folk) that black people were fed up, and that the pool was one way to appease blacks in Lawrence. Although he recognized Harrison's impact on the pool issue, Newman did not like him, declaring that he "put a lot of stuff in those kids' heads" and encouraged them to set fires and harass the police. "I knew black people who would volunteer to run him out town themselves," Newman declared. "I had a black man . . . tell me, 'Just give me the word and I'll tar and feather him.'"[38]

Although he liked Harrison personally, Dick Raney understood how his rhetoric could be "misconstrued." Raney noted that the more articulate voices in the black community, like Harrison, Jesse Milan, and Joane Hurst of the LHRC, provided a perspective that he previously had not considered. Although Harrison helped Raney to become aware of the "underlying problems," Raney could not support Harrison's solutions: black nationalism, separatism, threats, intimidation, and violence. Raney also knew blacks in Lawrence who rejected Harrison, fearing that his fiery actions and words would engender a backlash and threaten their own status and material comfort.[39]

The fight for control of the black community extended to Lawrence's public schools, which also became sites of cultural and racial struggle in Lawrence. Although the quality of education in Lawrence was generally good, the racism of teachers and white students made the experience for blacks less than ideal. While some black students took college preparatory classes at Lawrence High, others had to plead with school advisors to take the same courses. Helen Kimball claimed that school officials "tracked," or steered, black students away from such courses and into "work training" or vocational training. Karen Byers aspired to be a social worker, but her white advisors warned her how "hard it was for blacks to" enter any profession. One teacher even told Kimball's cousin—an average student—that "she didn't have time to help" and "as far as she was concerned . . . most blacks were supposed to be in the kitchen and cleaning and stuff like that."[40]

Even accomplished black students were socially isolated from white students. Byers remembered trying to socialize with white students at school functions, but "they would wander off and mingle with their own group." When she walked over to join them, they moved away and she felt unwelcome.[41] Comprising almost 100 out of some 1,500 total students, black students at Lawrence High were a distinct minority (about 7 percent). The 1968 *Red and Black,* the Lawrence High yearbook, dramatizes how isolated black students were. That year there were no black cheerleaders (although in previous years there had been), nor were any African Americans selected as homecoming or winter royalty. The football team and track squad had only three blacks and the gymnastics team had two, but there were none on the basketball or wrestling squads (often considered "contact sports," where the athletes' skin came in contact). Nor were blacks in the school choir, orchestra, band, or the school's theater productions.[42] Moreover, African American students rarely were taught by blacks and never learned about African American history or culture.

Perhaps worst of all, black students had to endure racial epithets. Karen Byers recalled that when she, two other black girls, and a Native American girl prepared "soul food" in a home economics class, the white teacher exclaimed she "didn't know . . . what kind of foods niggers ate." Kenneth Newman, a life-long Lawrencian, remembered the white student manager of a seventh grade theater production who in the early 1960s wanted him to play a part in the play, which Newman turned down. "Well, a nigger like you should" play the part, the manager replied. Newman walked out of school, and eventually he and his mother met with the white student and the principal. The white student apologized, saying that she "didn't mean anything about it but" she could not "have white boys . . . playing a black part." When asked why she called Newman a "nigger," she replied, "that's what you are supposed to be called," and the principal agreed. An unidentified student claimed that a teacher told her, after she was unable to finish an assignment properly, "You niggers can't do anything right." Lawrence High principal William Medley did not defend the use of such language, but believed that "teachers sometimes can have a slip of the tongue that doesn't necessarily indicate prejudice."[43]

It is not surprising, given these conditions, that in May 1968 some fifty black students and their parents met with Medley and six counselors and teachers to discuss their frustrations in coping with such an odious environment. They also raised several other concerns: alleged discrimination by school faculty and staff, the racially biased selection process for athletic teams and cheerleaders, the lack of communication between black students and officials, and the absence of black history and cultural studies courses. John Spearman, Jr., explaining that African American students did not identify with the curriculum, requested that a "Negro history course" become part of the required history program. Spearman insisted that "white people as well as Negroes should know about Negro history," and Medley agreed, conceding that "[s]uch a course might even be more valuable for white students than for Negroes."[44]

The students also pointed to the shortage of black teachers and counselors at Lawrence High. "There are just some things we need to discuss with another Negro," Spearman said, explaining that only another black could understand the feeling of being oppressed. Medley scoffed at this remark, claiming that he personally had experienced oppression because he was "redheaded." Max Stalcup, the head counselor at Lawrence High, took the comment personally, and remarked that the students were saying they "would rather talk to a Negro" than to him. Another student, Beverly Southard, assured Stalcup that "we don't mean to be critical" but "a Negro would understand some of our problems better."[45] The students were respectful, almost deferential, to the administrators, and there was no hint of latent violence or charged emotion.

The meeting suggested a nascent awareness of cultural pride and identity. By asking for a course on black history, the students embraced black cultural consciousness and pride. Spearman would later admit that at the time of this meeting, he was a committed adherent of Black Power. He did not point to a specific event that resulted in his transformation, but said it was a culmination of things, including the continued episodes of racism, the failure of the traditional civil rights movement, and the desire to have control of his own life. The following fall Spearman enrolled at the University of Kansas, helped to found and became president of the Black Student Union there, and worked to unite the black community and gain political power for blacks.[46]

For his part, Medley believed the meeting had been a success, although he stressed he had made "no promises of commitments." Medley agreed to meet regularly with the black students, beginning in the fall, to discuss their concerns. As evidence of his resolve, in the fall Medley noted that over forty books on black history and culture had been added to the library (although black students claimed they were sitting in boxes collecting dust); discussions continued over increased black participation in sports, cheerleading, and other extracurricular activities; and Chester Loomey, an African American, had been hired as a part-time counselor. Additionally, it appears that in April school officials had tried to recruit black teachers to Lawrence. Robert D. Ramsey, an assistant administrator, told Dr. Carl Knox, superintendent of Lawrence schools, that it was "too late in the year" to lure new teachers to the district and, moreover, no "blacks [had] expressed an interest in a teaching position in Lawrence."[47] Citing these efforts as evidence, Medley believed that race relations at his school were improving.

Thirty-seven African American students, however, did not agree. Sensing that they would have to force meaningful change, on September 25, 1968, the students, led by John Spearman's younger brother Mike, gave school officials a resolution demanding black representation on the cheerleading squad, a black homecoming queen, more black teachers and administrators, courses about black history and culture, and a black student union, essentially the same items discussed at the May meeting. They then walked out of school in protest. School officials were taken aback by the students' actions. Why, they wondered, given the seemingly successful May meeting and the apparent willingness of school administrators to continue discussion of black student concerns, did the walkout occur?

After they left the school, senior Rick Dowdell explained the students' goals. They wanted black history and literature courses, and they suggested eliminating "half the teachers and make the new ones black." Dowdell remarked that the one black teacher at LHS was a "Negro, he's not a black and there is a difference." Mark Dowdell, Rick's brother, told reporters, "we'll not return to LHS until our demands are met . . . we're not just asking for these things, we're demanding them." Similarly, Vanessa Collins declared that "we are a peaceful group" but "if we don't get [our demands] . . .

we'll have to use other means. . . . We haven't decided what but it won't be pleasant."[48] Collins's threat alarmed white citizens who feared the outbreak of violence.

Medley was out of town on the day of the protest, but on his return, he suspended the black students and declared that they would not be reinstated until each student and his or her parents had met with him. The students, however, were determined to be treated as a group. Rick Dowdell believed if they were sent "back to school one by one, they're going to make fools of us one by one."[49] Medley was adamant that he would only consider each student individually.

Their parents and other members of the community, especially Leonard Harrison and John Spearman, Jr., provided emotional support for the students. Parental support for the students was most evident at the October 7 school board meeting, which was devoted entirely to discussion of the walkout and attended by an estimated 1,500 people. "We are not ashamed or disapproving of their actions," said June Walker, the mother of a protesting student who spoke for all the parents, "but proud that our children have the awareness, the pride and the determination to make the effort through traditional democratic processes to fight against racism and discrimination." The black students' parents were "disappointed and disgusted" by the administration's response, and they claimed that the May meeting was nothing more than "a period of procrastination and half-hearted pallatives [sic]" by administrators who hoped the matter would disappear. The black parents believed that their children had "demonstrated their willingness to work with the administration" but that it chose to "ignore" the students and failed to "implement the recommendations." Walker absolved the students of any culpability for the current crisis. "Black students, after having exhausted all orderly and conventional means of protest," had no other choice but to walk out. Leonard Clark, the only black teacher at Lawrence High, agreed, asserting that the administration ignored the black students' demands prior to the walkout.[50]

As director of the Ballard Center, Leonard Harrison had a close relationship with many of the students. Together, Harrison, the students, and their parents created alternative institutions to address their needs. The day after the walkout, around fifty black students, their parents, and other African Americans formed a "revolutionary" and "'symbolic black school,'" which was taught by several black volunteers, some parents, and a few accredited teachers. Among the classes offered at the new school was black history.[51]

Harrison also met with Lawrence school superintendent Carl Knox to mediate the situation. He told Knox "that black students need a black cheerleader and pictures of black heroes on the walls so they can have someone with whom they identify." Harrison emphasized building black identity and pride, to which Knox, like other whites, showed little sensitivity or understanding. "Leonard, this is bigger than color," Knox replied, "[t]his is Americanism." Schools were "the greatest place in the world for real democracy to grow and thrive," Knox claimed, adding that "choosing a student for a position according to race is not consistent with the principles of our American way of life. We don't discriminate neither do we go out of our way to hand pick for special consideration because of race, color or creed." Nor was Knox sympathetic to the creation of a black union of students, preferring instead a "union that includes both" races. Knox continued: "We've got a system going for us that is so good, that has so many merits and values about it that we don't want to throw it out without something to replace it." Harrison coldly responded: "If the method had worked, we wouldn't be here today."[52] Harrison and the students protested a system that did not meet their needs. Knox, however, rejected the students' actions as undemocratic and defended the system as the embodiment of Americanism and individualism. Significantly, Knox not-too-subtly defended the existing racial boundaries as "our American way of life."

The language used by Knox—however well-intentioned he may have been—was not unlike that used by the defenders of segregation and opponents of fair housing legislation in Lawrence earlier in the decade. This discourse clearly defended the existing racial boundaries, with whites as the arbiters of when and if those boundaries would be shifted. For example, Knox and Medley, like many other whites, equated the students' demands with the imposition of racial quotas. While both Knox and Medley were tactful in condemning the students' demands, other whites displayed no such restraint in opposing quotas, which they denounced as preferential treatment. In a letter to the *Journal-World,* one white resident wrote: "the demands of Negro students at Lawrence High School, as well as demands of national Negro leaders, have reached a state of unbelievable irrationality. . . . they are demanding that there be racial quotas established. They want Negroes assigned to these positions for reasons of their race."[53]

The black students were not seeking special treatment, however, but were trying to find ways to cope in a predominantly white environment in which there were few black faces in positions of authority or status. White faculty and staff members, even those with the best of intentions, did not understand the social and cultural questions raised by the students because they could not know what it meant to be black. "White teachers and adults did not try to understand black youths," one unidentified black student complained, while Danny Mumford, another protesting student, claimed, "it don't move me to see a white girl cheering for my black brothers out there."[54]

The KU-BSU offered advice, but, as John Spearman, Jr., made clear, it did not organize or encourage the action. The LHS students organized the protest, wrote their own demands (which clearly were inspired by similar movements across the country), and set their own goals and objectives. Additionally, the protesting students received vocal support from several white KU students, who offered to baby-sit children of parents teaching at the alternate school. In a display of their new militancy and growing self-confidence, the black students abruptly rebuffed the white group, saying that whites "should worry about their own problems as white members of the community."[55]

Most whites, however, were indifferent or opposed to the students' goals. Both Medley and Knox received many phone calls and lots of correspondence encouraging them to remain resolute. Knox received forty-nine petitions—signed by over 600 "tired tax payers"—approving the administration's position and condemning the walkout. A local businessman recommended that Knox hold his "ground because the large majority of the people are behind you in doing what's right." Representative Morris Kay, from Lawrence's 14th legislative district, voiced his approval, as did the Lawrence Education Association. J. R. Haney, a columnist for the *Lawrence Outlook,* called the students' demands "completely ridiculous." Ed Abels, also writing in the *Outlook,* remarked, "Of course they did wrong" by following an "example set by radical and ignorant college students." Abels also believed that the walkout "placed renewed emphasis on the need for more industrial and practical courses in the high schools for those who do not want to go to college," which presumably referred to African Americans.[56]

Petitions supporting the black students garnered a mere forty-five signatures at Lawrence High School, and, according to LHS student president Mike Roark, most whites disapproved of the black students' actions. Moreover, he believed that "now they've hurt their cause." While Roark conceded that some of the demands were "reasonable," he felt that others were "just too far out," and that if the administration granted any of the demands now, the black students would never be "satisf[ied]." "Colored girls didn't even try out for cheerleader [*sic*]," Roark noted, ignoring the biased selection process, and he claimed that the homecoming queen demand was "out of the question because there are only about 100 black students" at Lawrence High.[57]

Most of the community approved of both the suspensions and Medley's conditions for reinstatement, but there were those who supported the students. About fifteen whites urged superintendent Carl Knox to treat the blacks as a group and give them a chance to be heard, fearing that "killing their spirit . . . may incite violence." Elaine Oser Zingg, a committed antiwar activist, insisted that the black students deserved to be "taken seriously and treated with respect." The probationary conditions placed upon their return to school did "not reflect their status as young adults who should be encouraged to take responsibility for their own self-determination."[58] These opinions expressed some sensitivity to the situation and revealed efforts to understand the students. It is clear, however, that Zingg's was not the dominant view. Moreover, it is not clear if those who supported the students were motivated by altruism or simply wished to avoid what they believed was a potentially violent racial conflict.

The walkout ended abruptly on September 29, when the black students, without explanation, returned to classes according to Medley's conditions. The administration made no guarantee of black representation on the cheerleading squad, although it did agree to amend the selection process so that ability, and not solely popularity, would be a factor. School officials also agreed to increase efforts to hire more black teachers, coaches, and administrators and to consider the feasibility of a black history course. Medley regretted that the students chose to protest by walking out, and he hoped that all students would "gain confidence in using the suggested procedures for effecting necessary and desired change."[59]

Although most whites believed that the "concessions" given to the black students were more than adequate, they fell short of the students' demands. Two years later, John Spearman, Sr., said that "this is the problem. Unless you are black, what America is doing seems impressive. But while it looks fair to you if you are white, it looks to the black like they're really not giving an inch where it counts."[60] Years of peaceful struggle had failed to resolve any of the black grievances. To many, radical new approaches had to be adopted.

Jesse Milan believed that the increase in black awareness and identity fostered by Black Power was positive. He felt that many young African Americans found Black Power and militancy more relevant than the mainstream civil rights movement, and their embrace of these ideas were sincere, even if misguided. Using John Spearman, Jr., as an example, Milan thought "that little Johnny legitimately did what he thought was right to do, even though his parents were on the other side of the tracks. . . . Little Johnny was representative of a lot of kids that fell into that new nationalism and that new surge of Black Power" and "it served its purpose: to get people to react and black kids involved."[61] Moreover, the walkout illustrated an effort by African Americans to take greater command of their lives and the institutions that shaped their world. Black Power provided a language for them to claim space that they could control. While this excitement did not stimulate all black students to action—the protesting students were only about one-third of all blacks at LHS—the cultural aspects of the movement were ubiquitous and very enticing to some young blacks.

The contrast between the May meeting between the black students and school officials and the September walkout was striking. In September, the students demanded change, were less polite and respectful of the administration, referred to themselves as "black," and were contemptuous of the label "Negro." There was an implicit hint of violence in their tone. The demands they made of Lawrence school officials reflected their identification with Black Power, pride in being black, and cooperation in taking control of their own lives.

As African American students walked out of classes at Lawrence High in the fall of 1968, black students at the University of Kansas, including John Spearman, Jr., pursued similar goals by organizing the BSU. Over the next three years, the BSU exemplified Black Power and black radicalism in Lawrence. The BSU employed divergent tactics to accomplish two primary goals: unifying blacks and gaining control of their own community. Using the Black Panthers' Ten-Point Program as a model, and under the leadership of Spearman, Jr., the BSU built black self-identity and pride and enacted a measure of African American control over their community.[62]

The BSU also created new cultural spaces in Lawrence by promoting African history and culture, sponsoring black poetry readings and art displays, and bringing prominent black speakers to campus, such as H. Rap Brown in December 1969. Denied sufficient access through mainstream media, the BSU created its own publications. Within a year of its founding, the BSU began publishing *Harambee,* or *For Our People.* Alongside defiant threats and bombastic maxims, *Harambee* filled its pages with short stories and poems by black writers who emphasized black Americans' African heritage and affirmed black pride, self-assertiveness, independence, and solidarity. The paper endorsed African-style clothing, jewelry, and cuisine and carried advertisements from stores that sold these items. It celebrated the distinctiveness and beauty of African people, extolling their dark skin and suggesting ways to wear and care for Afro hairstyles. *Harambee* was a crucial component of the most important, and lasting, legacy of black power: the promotion of black culture, which in turn prepared the way for a "psychological liberation" of African Americans that transformed Lawrence's racial discourse and redrew its racial boundaries.[63]

While the BSU and *Harambee* promoted black culture, they also alienated the white establishment, which led whites to defend their whiteness and traditional racial boundaries. The BSU's verbosity maddened many in the white community and eventually even those sympathetic to the cultural goals of the movement, like University of Kansas chancellor E. Laurence Chalmers. In October 1969, the BSU demanded that it be allowed to crown a black queen during the half time of the homecoming football game, that the university recruit more black students, faculty, and administrators, and that it create a dean of black students, a dean of black student affairs, a black disciplinary board, and a department of black studies. Chalmers refused the homecoming demand outright, though he did agree that there should be "some recognition of the black community during Homecoming," and the BSU crowned their black queen during pregame ceremonies. K. S. (Boots) Adams, Chairman Emeritus of Phillips Petroleum, assailed Chalmers for allowing the "colored minority communistic group" to dictate university policy. Another alumnus urged Chalmers to mobilize the state and local police if necessary to insure that his "homecoming football weekend would be pleasant."[64]

Two weeks after homecoming, Chalmers rejected the other demands—which essentially would have created a separate black college within the university—as economically and politically unfeasible. Again in February, the BSU, calling itself the "University component of the Black Liberation Struggle," reiterated its demands, which this time also included the construction of a Malcolm X building to house the black studies department. Each time, Chalmers repeated that KU was doing, and would continue to do, all it could to meet the "legitimate needs" of black students. He emphasized the university's efforts to recruit and hire black teachers and administrators and acknowledged that black studies was a desirable aspect of the college curriculum. In early March Chalmers chastised the BSU for chasing "short-range demands" instead of addressing "long-range goals," adding that "reasoning men and women would not question goals consistent with equal opportunity." Spearman, Jr., insisted that the BSU's goal was to unify and assert black control over all aspects of black student life, rather than to inflame racial tensions, but the incendiary words and demands of the BSU eventually wore thin on potential allies, including center-liberals like Chalmers.[65]

Like the Black Power movement, the BSU was enigmatic and terrifying to whites. Sometimes it worked within the existing structure and achieved significant gains for the black community. In 1970, for example, the BSU received over $14,000 from the University Student Senate to create new black institutions, such as a black cultural center it named the Afro-House; scholarships for African American students; a breakfast program for young black children; and a Big Brothers/Big Sisters program in Lawrence. It also helped to get a black studies program started at KU.[66]

At other times, however, the BSU preached violent, armed revolution and, just as Leonard Harrison had, used intimidation and threats. In 1970, the BSU and Harrison tried unsuccessfully to take over the Pennsylvania House, or Penn House, as it was known. Ocoee and Keith Miller moved to Lawrence from Carbondale, Illinois when Keith accepted a teaching position in the psychology department at KU. The Millers, who were white, began Penn House in February 1969. In Carbondale, Ocoee Miller had been a civil rights activist and community organizer, working to improve the lives of low-income people through self-help cooperatives operated by and for poor people. When Frances Horowitz, chair of KU's department of family life and human development, learned of Ocoee Miller's experience, she offered her the use of a house the university owned in east Lawrence to start a similar program in Lawrence. The only stipulation was that Miller had to hire KU students to work in the program. Keith Miller received a $100,000 grant from the Office of Economic Opportunity (OEO), and Ocoee was named the project director. Keith Miller and KU students used Penn House as a laboratory, studying which projects helped the poor and why.[67]

Black and white women, all of whom were receiving Aid to Families with Dependent Children (AFDC), were organized into six self-help clubs. There was an all-black group (the Jets) and an all-white club (She-Lions), but the other clubs (Busy Bees and Victorious Friends) were racially mixed. The club members governed Penn House, overseeing matters such as membership and programs. Ocoee Miller helped the club members learn their rights at the county assistance office and taught them how to balance a checkbook, prepare meals economically, and acquire job skills. Her goal for Penn House was to put "democracy in action" and to help the poor help themselves through education and support. It also had an emergency food, clothing, and medicine fund.[68]

Because of its mission, Penn House worked with similar agencies in Lawrence, especially the Ballard Center and the CCBC, of which Harrison was director and a member, and the Black Presidents of Pennsylvania House, the group that oversaw Penn House activities. The Ballard Center, for example, set up a credit union for low-income families and a tutoring program, which later moved to Penn House for lack of space. Ocoee Miller was confident that Penn House was helping Lawrence's poor, and there was great demand to join the project. Moreover, she believed that Penn House and the Ballard Center had a good working relationship. They shared equipment and staff, and when Harrison told Miller he could not meet payroll, Penn House paid the salary of Cynthia Turner, a Ballard Center employee. In 1970, however, the relationship between Penn House and the Ballard Center deteriorated. Keith Miller described the relationship as "one-sided"; Penn House gave but the Ballard Center did not reciprocate. When the OEO grant ran out, Ocoee Miller told Harrison she could no longer pay Turner's salary. Allegedly, Harrison told Miller "You'd better not run out of money. You'll be sorry." Miller claimed that shortly thereafter she was shot at and Penn House was bombed, which she blamed on Harrison and his "cadre of three or four thugs who did his dirty work for him."[69]

Publicly, Harrison praised the "good spirit of cooperation and communication" between the center and Penn House, and Penn House's willingness to cooperate with the Ballard Center.[70] Privately, however, Harrison and the BSU believed that Keith and Ocoee Miller and Penn House were condescending and patronizing toward blacks, and that Keith Miller, a behavioral psychologist, was using the project to do behavioral research on black folk. A power struggle for control of the Penn House project ensued. In December 1969, with the OEO grant to run out soon, Penn House applied for funds from the CCBC, which initially rejected the proposal because it included "ambiguous language" that "stereotype[d] Black people." The CCBC, after long deliberation, agreed that Penn House served Lawrence's low-income residents well. It agreed to fund Penn House if it hired a black project administrator, a black secretary, and three black research assistants (out of six total); used African Americans in the community as consultants; and revised the offending language in the proposal. Keith Miller agreed to all of the recommendations. Duane Vann, who had been a research assistant since October, was appointed project administrator "in training," and took over for Miller's wife Ocoee in February.[71]

The struggle for control of Penn House continued. Keith Miller felt that Vann and Cynthia Turner, who had been hired as a research assistant, did almost no work at Penn House and only came by to collect their salaries. Vann was fired in March, after Ocoee Miller claimed that he had only clocked in at Penn House once between December and February, for fifteen minutes. Ocoee and Keith Miller also had to refute rumors, reportedly discussed at BSU meetings, about themselves, and what Penn House was trying to accomplish. It was alleged, for example, that the Millers were "run out" of Carbondale, Illinois and that they were "using behavior modification and other psychological tricks to brainwash and control black people."[72] The Millers denied the allegations, but the claims created concern about the Millers' credibility among Penn House's clients.

Ocoee Miller claimed that Harrison tried to persuade Penn House members not to join the group. Harrison, according to Miller, wanted "to be the only voice for blacks" and black institutions in Lawrence. Harrison saw Penn House as an institution that primarily served blacks in Lawrence, and thus should be controlled by blacks. As the struggle for control of Penn House continued, Keith Miller became the target of verbal attacks by BSU, in meetings and on the street. The BSU declared that this "peckerwood faggot and others like him have to be treated like mad dogs and removed from the black community by whatever means necessary." A few weeks before Rick Dowdell was killed, Penn House was bombed, which Ocoee Miller believed could have been the work of black militants or white vigilantes, both of whom disliked the project and its goals. Ocoee and Keith Miller saw the struggle this way: They had to either cede total control of the project to Harrison and his faction or fight; they chose to fight. The Millers and Penn House clients discussed having blacks use the house in the morning and whites in the afternoon, but they decided that they were "all mamas, we have a common bond, we got this far together; we'll fight and die together." Ultimately, control of Penn House remained with its members, and it still operates that way today.[73]

By the late 1960s, Black Power and black nationalism had become an alternate path to equality, one that emphasized creating black-controlled institutions and self-affirming black consciousness. It had found a warm reception among Lawrence's young black population, exacerbating fears and prejudices among whites. Black Power was an important element of Lawrence's sixties experience and it significantly redrew the community's racial boundaries and transformed its political culture. In 1967, for example, the anger of black teenaged Lawrencians stimulated the city to open a temporary integrated swimming pool and influenced the passage of the swimming pool bond issue in November. Students at Lawrence High School walked out of classes and demanded courses on black history and culture, which forced the administration to hear them and united much of the black community. Their assertiveness laid the foundation for future protests, and, moreover, changed the town's racial discourse from a white, liberal approach to an agenda set by blacks and focused on the needs of black people.

This was the real strength of Black Power. As an ideology, it was as much a cultural and psychological movement as it was a political one. There was a clear change in attitude among many young African Americans in Lawrence, first apparent in August 1967 and even more so thereafter. African Americans used the language of Black Power to create institutions that addressed the concerns of people of color and gave them a measure of political power. The Black Student Union at the University of Kansas, the Afro-House, and the newspaper *Harambee* are examples, as are the scholarships and breakfast program the BSU established. Additionally, African Americans sought to take control of existing institutions, such as the Ballard Center and the Penn House in east Lawrence, through a variety of legal and extralegal means, and to use them to serve the black community.

Although some whites tried to understand Black Power, it utterly confounded most, including the well-intentioned liberals. More significantly, at the same time that Black Power filled many blacks with racial pride and gave them a language with which to challenge existing power structures, it provided many whites in Lawrence with a target against which to defend their whiteness and the boundaries of their identity, creating a racial dynamic that became more confrontational, more intense, and more dangerous. The threat of violence, real or perceived, was a powerful element in transforming the community.

In Lawrence, the threat of black violence, made more real by race riots across the country, was an important factor in winning the swimming pool bond election and in gaining white support for moderate reforms. Rather than impeding the cause of civil rights these radical voices improved the bargaining position of moderates.[74] African Americans challenged the racial status quo by taking control of and creating black institutions, adopting militant tactics, and shifting the racial discourse to their own terms. As they did this, long-standing goals, like a municipal swimming pool open to all citizens, were realized. While it is likely that Lawrence would eventually have built a city pool, it would not have happened in 1967 without the threat of black violence.

Both Black Power in Lawrence and its most vocal champion, Leonard Harrison, were enigmatic. Harrison shook up the town's entrenched power structure, startled whites out of their lethargy, and raised money for helpful programs for the black community. He also used threats, intimidation, and violence to achieve those goals; some critics suggest that he extorted money for personal gain. Understanding Harrison as a revolutionary who used "any means necessary" to gain political and social power for African Americans provides a rationalization for his actions. Years of liberal programs and legislation had made little difference in the lives of men such as Harrison. He saw that the best way to get his share of the system was to take that system on and use the same tactics on whites that they had used on blacks for centuries. At the same time, Harrison's rhetoric and actions were sure to alienate much of the community.

Similarly, Black Power further polarized a community already divided over race. The evolution of black radicalism and the embrace of Black Power by African Americans in Lawrence during the 1960s were significant developments. Threatening the white power structure and the town's racial boundaries was empowering for African Americans, but it also transformed the entire community.

1. In 1967, Don and Jacqueline Speakman and their two sons hold a vigil to protest communism in America. A local network of fraternal and civic organizations, church and work associations, and personal relationships, which were loosely affiliated with national organizations, helped a grassroots anticommunist movement flourish in Lawrence throughout the 1960s and into the 1970s. Anticommunism was a significant countermovement to the struggles for meaningful social change in the community throughout the decade. (Courtesy University of Kansas Archives)

above 2. The civil rights movement was national in scope but was given expression in hundreds of local venues such as Lawrence. Although blacks in Lawrence could vote and Jim Crow laws were largely absent, African Americans still confronted racial discrimination in housing, jobs, and education, as well as exclusion from many places of public accommodation. Here African Americans march down Massachusetts Street in downtown Lawrence not only in support of activists in the South but also to protest racial inequality in their own community. (Courtesy University of Kansas Archives)

right 3. Lawrence did not have a public swimming pool open to all residents until 1968. Private swim clubs filled the void for whites but excluded African Americans from swimming. In July 1960, the Jayhawk Plunge was picketed by black residents, including many students. Rather than open her doors to blacks, the pool's owner sold it to a group of investors, who reopened the pool under a different name a week later. (Courtesy *Lawrence Journal-World* Collection, Kansas Collection, Spencer Research Library, University of Kansas)

4. Members of the Civil Rights Council picket outside of Strong Hall in March 1965. Over one hundred students conducted a sit-in inside Chancellor W. Clarke Wescoe's office to protest racial exclusion in fraternities and sororities, as well as racially discriminatory advertisements in the student newspaper. The protesters achieved most of their demands but the demonstration did little to change racist attitudes or assumptions on campus. (Courtesy University of Kansas Archives)

5. The peace movement provided the initial opposition to the United States' involvement in the Vietnam War, and remained the core constituency of the antiwar movement. This October 15, 1965 Student Peace Union protest against the Vietnam War underscores the pacifist roots of the antiwar movement in Lawrence. (Courtesy University of Kansas Archives)

above   6. A picket against the Vietnam War, part of a national "Mail-In" referendum on the war, took place on Easter Sunday, 1967. As these photographs suggest, a cross-section of the Lawrence community—not merely college students—was opposed to the war by then. (Courtesy *Lawrence Journal-World* Collection, Kansas Collection, Spencer Research Library, University of Kansas)

right   7. Not all college students in the sixties were radicals or protested against the Vietnam War; many supported the U.S. military effort in southeast Asia. Conservatism was strong on the KU campus, although it was not as visible as other forms of activism. (Courtesy *Lawrence Journal-World* Collection, Kansas Collection, Spencer Research Library, University of Kansas)

above 8. Symbols of American patriotism were in full force during the annual Veteran's Day parade down Massachusetts Street on November 12, 1968. The veneration of the nation's symbols by these "Young Patriots," as the *Journal-World* called them, were held up by many locals as emblematic of the "American Way of Life." (Courtesy *Lawrence Journal-World* Collection, Kansas Collection, Spencer Research Library, University of Kansas)

right 9. This march by young Lawrencians stands in sharp contrast to the "Young Patriots." Antiwar activists marched down Massachusetts Street to protest the war a few hours after the 1968 Veteran's Day parade; the *Journal-World* called their action a "March Against the Military." (Courtesy *Lawrence Journal-World* Collection, Kansas Collection, Spencer Research Library, University of Kansas)

above 10. Student activists called for a campus-wide general strike in April 1970 to support two professors denied tenure because of their leftist politics. The strike was to coincide with the appearance of the colorful leader of the Youth International Party (Yippies), Abbie Hoffman, at Allen Fieldhouse. Not all students supported the call to strike, however, as this photograph suggests. (Courtesy *Lawrence Journal-World* Collection, Kansas Collection, Spencer Research Library, University of Kansas)

right 11. Leonard Harrison was a significant player in Lawrence politics between 1967 and 1970. Harrison personified the enigmatic qualities of Black Power. He was at once articulate, proud, and charismatic, but often used threats, intimidation, and violence to achieve his goals. (Courtesy *Lawrence Journal-World* Collection, Kansas Collection, Spencer Research Library, University of Kansas)

above   12. Racial tensions were acute after a walkout by black students at Lawrence High School in April 1970. Further contributing to the tense situation were strained relations between African Americans and the Lawrence Police Department. With good reason, blacks in Lawrence had long complained about police surveillance and brutality. (Courtesy University of Kansas Archives)

right   13. On April 20, 1970, arson engulfed the University of Kansas Memorial Union, doing an estimated $3,000,000 damage. For three nights after the fire, Lawrence was under a dusk-to-dawn curfew, and the Kansas National Guard patrolled city streets. Critics of student activism blamed the fire on student revolutionaries who thrived under lax campus administration; KU administrators blamed the fire on "outsiders." The arson was never solved. (Courtesy *Lawrence Journal-World* Collection, Kansas Collection, Spencer Research Library, University of Kansas)

14. Arrests were commonplace during the April curfew in Lawrence, particularly in the Oread neighborhood near the university. Here a group of young people is detained by Lawrence police officers while National Guardsmen stand to the side. (Courtesy *Lawrence Journal-World* Collection, Kansas Collection, Spencer Research Library, University of Kansas)

15. Two ponies pull a make-shift hearse, on which rests the casket bearing the body of Rick Dowdell. Dowdell had been shot by a Lawrence police officer a few days earlier, and his comrades in the Black Power movement—some pictured here dressed in black d e n i m — s w o r e vengeance. The mourners marched from the church through the streets of Lawrence to a local cemetery, while curious, mostly white pedestrians passively watched. (Courtesy *Lawrence Journal-World* Collection, Kansas Collection, Spencer Research Library, University of Kansas)

left 16. Dowdell became for many young blacks a martyred symbol of the struggle for racial justice and equality, as shown at this December 1970 demonstration. (Courtesy *Lawrence Journal-World* Collection, Kansas Collection, Spencer Research Library, University of Kansas)
above 17. While other students mill around, a woman pensively sits near the spot where Nick Rice was shot and killed by high-powered rifle, just three days after Rick Dowdell was killed. An investigation into Rice's death was inconclusive; witnesses claimed the police were the only ones with carbines. (Courtesy *Lawrence Journal-World* Collection, Kansas Collection, Spencer Research Library, University of Kansas)

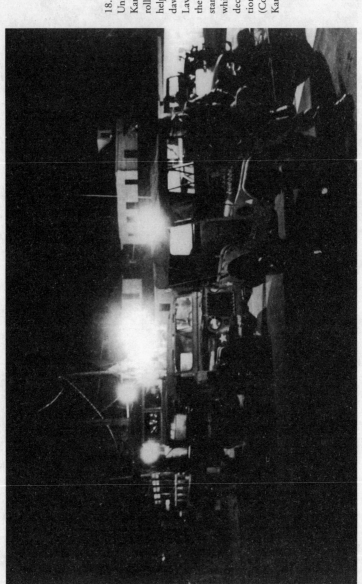

18. After the Kansas Union fire in April, the Kansas National Guard rolled into Lawrence to help enforce a dusk-to-dawn curfew. Some Lawrencians cheered the move as a strong stand for law and order, while the street people decried the "occupation" of their turf. (Courtesy University of Kansas Archives)

19. The street people, as members of Lawrence's counterculture called themselves, claimed Oread Avenue and such hangouts as the Gaslight Tavern and the Rock Chalk Café as their own, which lead to frequent clashes with local police. Here George Kimball, who ran for Douglas County sheriff on the Democratic ticket, talks with a Lawrence police officer at the height of the July crisis. (Courtesy *Lawrence Journal-World* Collection, Kansas Collection, Spencer Research Library, University of Kansas)

20. In February 1972 a group of women calling themselves the February Sisters occupied a university building, making several demands of the university, including a daycare facility on campus for faculty, staff, and students. Here a young Sister looks on as her mother addresses other women who participated in the demonstration. (Courtesy University of Kansas Archives)

CHAPTER 6

"THE AMERICAN WAY"

In January 1962, native Lawrencian and U.S. Representative Robert F. Ellsworth conducted a survey to check the political pulse of his constituents. Among the many questions on the survey was the following: "Should the United States send their [*sic*] own troops to South Viet Nam if this be necessary to prevent that country's seizure by communists?" Although the United States had not yet made a significant troop commitment to South Vietnam, communist advances in Vietnam, coupled with the escalated Cold War tensions in Cuba and Berlin, had increased the likelihood of a larger American presence in Southeast Asia. Of those surveyed who answered "yes" or "no," in Kansas's second congressional district—which included Lawrence—three out of four respondents replied "yes," the United States should commit troops to South Vietnam to prevent a communist takeover.[1]

Although the question was written to induce a "yes" response and Ellsworth's tabulations suggest there was a consensus on committing troops to turn back communism, most of those surveyed actually wrote "I don't know" or did not respond, suggesting an ambivalence or ignorance about the war and Vietnam. Of those who did reply, a range of opinions was evident. R. T. Schwanzle, a manager at Spencer Chemical Company, declared that the United States should send enough troops to Vietnam to halt the communists, while John Garcia, an art teacher in the Lawrence public schools, opposed greater troop commitments, even to prevent a communist seizure of power. KU's Dean of Foreign Students Clark Coan proved to be the most prescient. He feared that a greater military commitment would get the United States "bogged down in a jungle war in Vietnam. With the Chinese so close to the Commies it could be an almost unending conflict."[2]

Few events in American history have so divided the United States as the Vietnam War. As early as 1962, well before the war dominated daily news reports, Vietnam was a topic of public debate in Lawrence. As troop levels and American spending on the war increased, an antiwar movement began to grow in Lawrence between 1962 and 1969. The movement, which included but went beyond draft card burning, marches, teach-ins, and other symbolic episodes of public protest, blurred the boundaries between the town and the campus.[3] The stereotypical images of 1960s antiwar protestors are of longhaired young people carrying peace signs or angry college students defiantly burning their draft cards. These popular images obscure our understanding of the antiwar movement in particular and the sixties in general. Angry radicals did protest the war, but the core of Lawrence's antiwar movement were pacifists who opposed war and militarism out of their religious convictions and personal beliefs. The antiwar movement also included church groups and more genteel dissenters, who protested not by marching but by writing letters to the president, members of Congress, and senators, or by using their connections and friendships with politicians to influence the debate.

Opposition to the Vietnam War was an eclectic, and largely grassroots, activity, and grew out of the peace and the civil rights movements that provided the organizational and rhetorical roots for an ad hoc antiwar movement. Moreover, the new radicalism and youth activism in the United States infused the antiwar movement with a "distinctive ethos."[4] After the ratification of the 1963 Nuclear Test Ban Treaty, peace advocates turned their attention to the escalating American presence in Vietnam. The loose coalition of peace advocates and antinuclear protestors coalesced into an inchoate antiwar movement by 1965. The burgeoning movement began to set the terms of the nation's involvement in Vietnam and helped to bring the issue into focus for many previously ambivalent Americans. By 1965, the fledgling movement challenged President Lyndon B. Johnson for control of America's political center.[5]

Pacifist and religious organizations, both in the community and on campus, were the first to critique the war and American intervention and were among the first to frame the war as a moral issue. Using church buildings as meeting places and their religious beliefs as a moral foundation, these protestors took antiwar dissent into Lawrence's public sphere by picketing the draft board and the Sunflower munitions plant east of Lawrence. Others claimed public space to publicize the war by organizing and sustaining for several years the Silent Vigil for Peace in South Park, near downtown. As we have already seen, between 1963 and 1966 college students and faculty at the University of Kansas began to question America's involvement in Vietnam, using the campus as a forum on the war. By the end of the decade, antiwar protest had become an almost daily event and was given public expression through direct action, including civil disobedience, vandalism, and guerilla street theater.

Not all dissent, however, was public. In Lawrence much of the early opposition to the war was expressed privately, through traditional democratic practices, such as letter-writing and petitions to Congress, meetings with elected officials, or political contributions. These private expressions of dissent often were accompanied by public expressions, too; some of the most prolific letter writers were very vocal and active antiwar leaders and organizers, but their numbers also included older, established citizens, business owners, and white-collar professionals, dissenters who were not stereotypical antiwar protestors. Opponents of the war did not always frame the war in moral terms (as did many who protested from religious convictions), but often viewed the conflict and the United States' role in it within the context of economic growth and development, fiscal and budgetary responsibility, and other material concerns. Although they expressed their dissent in private correspondence to elected officials, this correspondence reflects another side to the war and to protest and provides a window to examine how Lawrencians viewed their world. Both "hawkish" and "dovish" citizens expressed their ideas and concerns about the war to their elected representatives, illustrating "citizenship in practice."[6]

There were two crucial moments that changed the public mood about Vietnam in Lawrence. In early June 1963, the *Lawrence Daily Journal-World,* along with countless other newspapers across the country, carried a photograph of Thich Quang Duc, a Vietnamese Buddhist monk who immolated himself in the streets of Hue to protest repression by the United States-backed Diem regime. It was a brief story and there was no published commentary in any Lawrence paper about the episode. The graphic image seems to have jarred the consciences of many Lawrencians, prompting them to think about the war and the United States' role in it. Thereafter, stories about Vietnam began to occur more frequently in the local papers.[7]

The second occurrence was, for millions of Americans, more significant: the commitment of U.S. troops to defend Vietnam. President John F. Kennedy in 1961 had pledged that the United States would give its "best efforts" to help the "people in the huts and villages of half the globe" fight communism. To that end, Kennedy increased the American commitment to South Vietnam; by October 1963 the number of American troops in Vietnam exceeded 16,000. That milestone marked the beginning of a constant increase in American troops in Vietnam that would not abate until it reached over 500,000 in 1968.[8]

As early as 1964, Lawrencians were becoming more aware of Vietnam, although it was not the dominant issue it would be later in the decade. A. B. Weaver, a downtown merchant, believed that the "government or State Department or someone has diverted our attention to Viet Nam which in importance is infintesimal [*sic*] as compared to Cuba." Already some Lawrencians saw the war as a moral tragedy, one from which the United States should extract itself as quickly as it could. Rebecca Coan believed that the United States' presence in Vietnam was a "tragic wrong" and a "sin on our conscience to back these ignorant peasants in years of futile war." KU students Thomas and Shirley Schmidt urged Congress to "do something about South Vietnam" because they "abhor[red]" the loss of lives there. Elizabeth Henderson, a widow, believed Vietnam was a problem for the United Nations and implored Representative Ellsworth "to keep us out of *War*."[9]

Public awareness of Vietnam grew in 1964; it exploded in 1965. A 1965 Ellsworth survey suggested that 49 percent of Lawrencians favored a negotiated settlement in Vietnam, with 39 percent opposed to negotiations and 12 percent undecided.[10]

Containing communism was, of course, a standing justification for United States involvement in Vietnam. Mrs. H. M. Brownlee avowed that America was "in the right against Godless communism" in Vietnam, "therefore we will win the war, if those brave men in our cause are sent the sinews of war and given the support of citizens here at home. Defeatist talk is shameful." Mr. and Mrs. Albin Longren (he was a carpenter at the university) did not want a "negotiated peace. If anything, we want increased United States military action." "The free world has lost so much ground in the last ten years," they declared. "Our soft pedaling must stop." Most Lawrencians supported the idea of supporting the war to contain communism. Clayton Crosier, a professor of engineering, wanted to see the war end, but thought that "ONLY by *negotiations*—from strength, of course, and patiently and smartly—have we any chance of winning anything in South Vietnam." The Dorsey-Liberty American Legion Post #14 passed a resolution condemning antiwar protests. The post believed antiwar sentiment was a minority opinion and did "irreparable harm to our country and the morale of our service personnel." The resolution encouraged all veterans "who have experienced the honor of war" to write to American soldiers and express their support and "appreciation for the[ir] devotion to the United States." In November, the legion and the local post of the Veterans of Foreign Wars began a three-day petition drive downtown. Alan Fisher spearheaded the drive as a forum for Lawrencians to support the troops in Vietnam, which he believed the majority of people would do. As Fisher made clear, the Legionnaires did not want Americans troops in combat, but "as long as it was necessary " would "support and encourage them." On Veterans Day, they gathered almost 400 signatures, decrying the "the recent demonstrations by a small but highly vocal minority" and pledging their "heartfelt appreciation" to General William Westmoreland and his troops.[11]

While the American Legion unconditionally supported U.S. policy, other Lawrencians suggested that the United States either "put up or get out." Dr.

Glenn A. Lessenden, a physician, was "amazed" that the United States could not defeat a small country like Vietnam. "What sort of political nonsense is allowing the war to drag on," he asked, "and wasting American lives (one of which is worth more than all of Viet Nam) when we have weapons which, if used, would defeat the Viet Cong?" Lessenden also remarked that if Vietnam was vital to American interests, then "[l]et's win the war and get out."[12]

By 1966, however, many Lawrencians viewed Vietnam less as a fulcrum of grand global strategy and more as a misguided, immoral, and untenable war. Social activist and Quaker Anne Moore "urge[d] Congress to seek non-military solutions to the conflict." Thomas Kruse thought the United States' participation in the war simply was "morally wrong." Helen Hartzell, a widow and an accountant at KU, believed that "[s]urely the richest and most powerful nation on earth is also big enough to admit that we have made a mistake in Vietnam without losing face."[13]

From the beginning, antiwar protest in Lawrence had a strong religious connection, and it was on that basis that many Lawrencians opposed the war. The bombing of Hanoi and Haiphong, declared Mrs. David Leonard, was "incompatible with America's love of peace, respect for sovereign nations, and honor of freedom" and "mocked the Christian principles of our founding fathers." Robert T. Howard, a metallurgist and KU professor, wrote that the issue of Vietnam is of "deep concern for Christians" who were "distressed at the brutal and inhumane manner of prosecution." Howard, who claimed he spoke for other members of the First Christian Church in Lawrence, wanted to stop "communist oppression" but warned if "our methods become as un-Christian as those of the communists, we lose the war, regardless of its military outcome."[14]

By 1967 it was clear that opposition to the war came from a cross-section of Lawrence, and not just from the university community. Some Lawrencians may have muffled their opposition to the war because they did not want to be associated with antiwar protestors. "I am not a sandal-wearing, folksinging beatnik," declared Ruth A. Eigner, "but a midwestern housewife and mother" who "do[es] not approve of our policy in Vietnam." Similarly, KU professor Theodore H. Eaton was "one more voice of protest against this barbarism, and there is a growing number of informed people in the United States who feel this way." He added, "We do not have long hair, go barefoot, or play guitars." "I have felt for two years," wrote Lawrence physician Monti L. Belot, Jr., "that I should express my concern over the war in Vietnam, but have withheld doing so because I did not want to associate myself with some of the unpatriotic groups which are making these objections." Although Belot gave President Johnson and the government his "full support," he felt "compelled to express [his] . . . concern over a war that is so costly to our lives and our economy. Could not some form of containment be undertaken?" he asked.[15]

Based on the correspondence that Senator Pearson and Representative Ellsworth received, it would appear that by 1967 a majority of Lawrencians wanted the United States to withdraw from Vietnam.[16] Moreover, after 1966, as the ranks of dissenters broadened to include a greater cross-section of the community, individual opposition melded into community-based, ad hoc organizations committed to ending the war in Vietnam.

Principal among these groups was the Kansas Peace Forum (KPF) and the Lawrence Peace Center (LPC). In December 1966, about thirty people from Emporia, Manhattan, Topeka, and Lawrence, most of whom were in academia, established the KPF. The bulk of the members were from Lawrence, including Tom and Anne Moore, and KU anthropology professor Rob Hinshaw, all of the Oread Friends Meeting. The KPF also established a committee based in Lawrence to organize a statewide workshop on community peace action, which was held in March and was co-sponsored by the Kansas University Vietnam Committee, the University Christian Movement, and the American Friends Service Committee (AFSC), which also provided financial support.[17]

The KPF was a clearinghouse for local peace activities and facilitated communication about peace activities with other groups, communities, and individuals throughout Kansas. For example, it coordinated a "mail-in" on Easter Sunday, 1967, as part of a nationwide campaign. Participants sent letters or cards to elected officials encouraging them to work for a peace settlement in Vietnam and to support United Nation's Secretary-General U Thant's proposal for negotiations, and walked as a group to the post office to mail their protests. Jean Shellhammer cast her vote against the war "on the grounds that it is immoral and a self-defeating form of American 'foreign aid.' This war has been more wasteful, and consequently, more harmful to the United States," she wrote, "than any Communist plot could ever hope to [be]. . . . Bring this insane slaughter to an end." William and Nan Scott—he was an English professor at KU—also participated, calling the war "bloody and senseless," an "unjust and stupid war" that "benefits neither the American nor the Vietnamese, who are being tyrannized over by a military regime in the south." Following the example of peace activists in Hutchinson, Kansas, the KPF encouraged the placing of a full-page signature advertisement in local papers as "a valuable first step toward peace action."[18] Full-page signature ads appeared frequently in the *Journal-World* as the movement grew.

In May 1967, the KPF, the KU Vietnam Committee, the Student Peace Union, and the Women's International League for Peace and Freedom (WILPF) held a rally on the KU campus. The slogan of the rally was "*MR. PRESIDENT, PLEASE STOP THE BOMBING NOW, AND SEEK IMMEDIATE NEGOTIATIONS.*" The KPF sent a telegram with this message to the president, signed by all in attendance, to "create more enthusiasm and support for peace in Vietnam." "The only way the war will be stopped," the organizers declared "is for the American people to voice their disapproval directly to those officials capable of bringing peace by their actions. Since the vast majority of our political representatives refuse to consider the Vietnam war in any political discussion, it is our obligation to bring the argument to them through any peaceful channel we find useful." Proceeding the rally was a march past the Union to Strong Hall; following the rally was a march to Memorial Stadium, where the protestors held a "picket-vigil" of the chancellor's review of ROTC. According to the rally's organizers, the purpose of the vigil was "to protest the draft, university complicity with the war effort, the war itself, and American foreign policy in general."[19]

The KPF and the LPC initiated a "Vietnam Summer" project in 1967, part of a nationwide initiative to attract more Americans into the peace movement. Carol Coleman, of rural Douglas County, said the Lawrence effort wanted to engage area residents in a public discussion about American goals and involvement in Vietnam. Volunteer canvassers knocked on doors and discussed the war with residents. According to Coleman, "many people appeared to not want to know any more about the war, and others refused to give any answers to the canvassers." One Lawrencian objected that the project presented only one side of the argument by calling for an immediate American withdrawal. But Sally Heeren, a participant in the project, defended the endeavor as unbiased, claiming critics of the project were only too willing to "follow along with what those in authority say is right."[20]

Protesting against the Vietnam War in Kansas was not an easy task. As the journalist Calvin Trillin observed in 1967, Kansans voiced "'virtually unanimous contempt' for draft-card burners; but they benignly accepted draft avoidance, and they were tolerant of antiwar critics. Local activists leavened their determination with caution." Most Kansans, Trillin surmised, were apathetic about both the war and protest.[21]

Trillin apparently did not visit Lawrence. The apathy he observed elsewhere in Kansas did not discourage Lawrence activists who protested out of deeply-held personal and religious convictions. This was true of the members of the KPF and LPC. Founded in October 1967 by the Oread Meeting of the Society of Friends, the Wesley Foundation at the University of Kansas, and the WILPF, the LPC had once been the Lawrence committee of the Kansas Peace Forum. Rob Hinshaw and Tom and Anne Moore, all Quakers and members of both LPC and KPF, helped the LPC affiliate with the American Friends Service Committee and immediately set up a draft counseling program and began training draft counselors. Additionally, the LPC ran classified advertisements announcing the draft counseling program, distributed literature on conscientious objection each week in KU's Memorial

Union, distributed draft literature at the Ballard Center in north Lawrence, and ran an ad in the Lawrence High School newspaper, *The Budget,* publicizing the program. It also created a speaker's bureau and, in April 1968, sponsored an appearance by Dr. Benjamin Spock, the noted pediatrician and an outspoken critic of the war.[22]

Across the nation, women were central actors in the antiwar and peace movements, bringing great energy and commitment to the effort by drawing on several resources, in particular religion and motherhood. As the testimony of Women Strike for Peace (WSP) before the House Un-American Activities Committee in 1963 made clear, women challenged both the meaning and rhetoric of the Cold War. "It has not dawned" on men, wrote WSP member Barbara Deming, "that the rapidly altering nature of the world about us has drained certain words of all former meaning." Men, especially national political leaders, "were hypnotized by these words . . . whereas the women see the cold fact that we are now willing to lay down our *children's* lives, and are already doing so." Although WSP in 1963 was concerned with nuclear proliferation, its emphasis on peace applied to antiwar activism as well. Not unlike the social activism of Jane Addams and other reformers a half-century earlier, the members of the WSP and the WILPF, and other women used their traditional role as mothers acting in the name of their children, and the idea of "household values," to struggle against war and for peace. In so doing, women offered an alternative civil voice, a "maternal pacifism," to the masculinized rhetoric and ethos of rugged individualism.[23]

The feminization of peace activism was evident in many ways. One was a vigil against the draft, which drew participants from a number of Lawrence peace organizations, including the WILPF. There are no extant records for the Lawrence chapter of the WILPF, but several of its members were the spouses of KU professors. The members of the WILPF recognized that they, as women, were not subject to the draft, but because they were wives, mothers, sisters, and friends of draft-age men, they had a "special responsibility" to give support to those who had been denied conscientious objector status or who were in jail for refusing to submit to the draft. Several Lawrence WILPF members visited prisoners of conscience in the federal penitentiary in Leavenworth, an hour's drive northeast of Lawrence.[24]

The WILPF used traditional holidays and women's roles as mothers to underscore the death and destruction of war, especially in the wake of increased American bombing of North Viet Nam. Mother's Day, for example, seemed an appropriate time for hundreds of Kansans from across the state to express their opposition to the war. A variety of cards were sent to political leaders, all of which emphasized the bond between mothers and children and how the war was tearing at that bond. The cover of one card used the familiar slogan, "War is not healthy for children and other living things." The message inside read: "In this gentle season / When men remember they are brothers / And know that all children are our children / We urge an end to killing—Now / Let it be written / Our nation found a way to peace."[25]

In May 1967, as part of a nationwide project, the KPF encouraged people to send a Mother's Day card to Kansas's senators and representatives, asking that they "work for peace" in Vietnam. Peace activists hoped a million or more cards would be sent to dovish senators such as William Fulbright, Wayne Morse, and George McGovern, who said they would carefully count the cards and publicize the numbers. The response was impressive, including a number of cards from Lawrence's women-led peace groups, such as the WILPF and an ad hoc group, Another Mother for Peace. Jane Fowler Morse sent Pearson a card in May, printed and issued by the WILPF, addressed "To the Mothers and Wives of the United States from Japanese Women." The Japanese mothers compared the United States' position of "fight[ing] communism and defend[ing] our land, to liberate Asia" Vietnam with their own suffering during World War II. Was the death of millions, the loss of sons, fathers, and husbands, "really worth the sacrifice?" the card asked. "As the mother of a young son and a daughter," Morse wrote in her own hand, "I pass this message on to you." Ada Jacobowitz, whose husband Ron was an instructor at KU, supported Another Mother for Peace in calling for a halt to the bombing in Vietnam and in "ask[ing] for Peace in Viet Nam for Mother's Day." She added that "[p]arents whose children are injured by our bombs are hardly won over by our brand of democracy."[26]

The LPC, the WILPF, the Oread Meeting, and other committed pacifists and activists worked together for a common goal: Ending the war in Vietnam. An example of their commitment was the Silent Vigil for Peace, first held in Lawrence in front of the First United Methodist Church in March 1967, and soon thereafter moved to more public and visible locations. For at least four years, it met Thursdays from noon to 1:00 P.M. in front of Watson Library on the KU campus and Sundays from 11:30 A.M. to 12:30 P.M. in South Park. The Silent Vigil For Peace had originated at the University of California at Santa Barbara in February 1966 and had quickly spread through other Friends' Meetings to some fifty communities nationwide by November. According to the Silent Vigil for Peace's newsletter, at one time as many as 300 people participated in a single vigil, the goal of which was "confrontation with [the protestors'] fellow citizens." The vigils took place outdoors, in full view of others. Participants declared they would continue with the vigil "until the killing stops." The silent, daily witness of the participants, many of whom wore black armbands or ribbons each day as symbols of mourning, and their commitment to peace were inspired by the Gandhian principle of *satyagraha* (holding firm to the truth).[27]

Although it had no formal organizational affiliations, in Lawrence the Silent Vigil for Peace grew out of the AFSC Peace Action Workshop and was supported by the WILPF, the Oread Meeting of Friends, the LPC, and the LCPV. One flyer publicizing the vigil illustrates the commitment to silent witness and the moral basis of the protest: Five bold peace signs with the caption in bold, black letters, "PUT YOUR BODY ON THE LINE." The flyer also asked Lawrencians to join the "vigil line to remind Lawrence and KU that the war is still going on still killing people week after week after week." As Anne Moore and Elaine Zingg, the wife of campus minister Otto Zingg, made clear, the vigil was silent "to make clear that it is actions rather than men that are being criticized."[28]

Many of the participants in the Silent Vigil for Peace had long used their religious and moral personal convictions to resist all war and militarism. As draft calls steadily increased after 1965, Lawrencians unleashed a torrent of protests, including some from previously silent segments of the community. For many, the draft brought the war home, personally touching their lives.[29] Perhaps three-fifths of Americans in the early years of the war supported the draft, which had been in existence since World War II, in part because call-ups were few given the low troop commitments. By 1967, that had changed. World War II veteran Perry E. Puderbaugh, a woodworker at Reuter Organ Company, expressed the thoughts of many older Lawrencians, especially those men who had seen military service. Drafting nineteen-year-old boys, he claimed, was the "worst [crime] of all." "[S]peaking from experience," Puderbaugh lamented that a draftee would see "a war before even becoming legal age, too young to vote, too immature for marriage and [without] even the opportunity to finish his education." His wife Lola's letter was even more heartfelt. Recounting her husband's service, which began at age nineteen, Lola Puderbaugh wanted Senator Pearson to know "the torment this man has suffered. I've awakened many nights by his nightmares of reliving the war. He has swing [sic] his arms and hit the bed until his hands were actually bleeding. Can you imagine what it is like to try and live a normal life, and raise a family . . . with a man whose nerves have been shattered by . . . fighting in a war before he is old enough to vote, mature enough to marry, or even given an opportunity to complete his education[?]" Although Lola Puderbaugh opposed the lottery, she added her belief that the United States should either "fight this war to win or else get out. It is certainly a gross sin to keep sending our boys over to be killed so our leaders can gain more prestige and money."[30] The contradiction in Lola Puderbaugh's thought—that she was aware of the tragedy of war to young men but supported fighting to win—illustrates the complexity of the war and why it ripped at the fabric of American society.

For a time, Lawrencians gave little thought to Vietnam, which was half a world away and affected their lives little, if at all. But the Vietnam War hit many Lawrencians close to home in 1967. "The first body of a local boy was being shipped home," wrote Betty Lessenden, the wife of a Lawrence physician, to Senator Pearson in May. Deeply saddened by the loss, Lessenden also reflected the ambivalence many Americans felt about the war, uncertain whether to withdraw and own up to a tragic mistake or to continue fighting to the end. "Can it be," she asked rhetorically, "that the United States finds it impossible to admit to a mistake and remove itself from a 'goof', or . . . admit its commitment to a military involvement and proceed to a military victory?" Vietnam, Lessenden avowed, was "not worth one more American life," but, like millions of other Americans, she was unsure which path the United States should take.[31]

The young man to whom Lessenden referred was probably Marine Pfc. James R. Cooper, the nineteen-year-old son of Ray, a sales agent for Phillips Petroleum, and Pat Cooper. Jim Cooper had died on May 10; he had been in Vietnam only sixteen days.[32] Corporal John V. Hughes, a Lawrence High classmate and part of the same marine division as Cooper, believed that his friend's death was not in vain: "God bless all young men like Jim, and help us keep our country free." Glenn Close, another marine comrade, had carried Cooper to the helicopter that evacuated him from the battlefield. He wrote to the grieving parents that they should take comfort in "knowing that Jim has laid down his life . . . for the life we are able to lead in America."[33]

Jim Cooper's death provided an opportunity for many Lawrencians to express their thoughts on the war, the draft, antiwar protests, and Americanism, and several citizens publicly poured out their heart. Prompted by the death of her friend, eighteen-year-old Sharon Ireland could "not possibly keep quiet any longer" about "this business of draft dodging." Ireland declared that she was "strongly opposed to all those foolish, unpatriotic kids who think they are being cute by burning their draft cards, protesting by rioting, and dodging the draft." Convinced that protestors were only seeking "attention," Ireland and other Lawrencians argued "that if it weren't for those who were willing to give their lives for our country," like Jim Cooper, "there would not be any 'individual rights' as we know them." Moreover, she declared that it was not "important whether we are doing the right thing by being in Vietnam, at least not as important as accepting the fact that we are there and we must fight to win." Cooper's death, obviously, touched her deeply. As she directed her anger at antiwar protests she also revealed the values on which she constructed her own identity as an American. Cooper's sacrifice was not in vain, she believed, because he and thousands of other Americans were preserving "our way of life. We can not throw away their sacrifice, making their deaths without cause," she averred, "we have to continue fighting, if we must, to spread freedom throughout the world."[34]

Although many Lawrencians accepted Cooper's death as part of the price of fighting communism and preserving American values, others disagreed. Hamilton Salsich, a teaching assistant in English at KU, a conscientious objector to the war, and a self-proclaimed "draft-dodger," responded to Sharon Ireland. He wrote that there "can be no greater anguish" than losing a loved one, but it was "a similar anguish—and utter horror—over the loss of 10,000 American lives that has prompted the protests of many of our 'draft-dodgers.'" Like other dissenters, Salsich saw the war as a "senseless slaughter . . . contrary to the moral and political traditions of our country." Salsich also noted the loss of his own friends, who were languishing in prison because they opposed the war. Salsich believed that both he and Ireland "champion[ed], in our own confused ways, the same basic freedoms—the freedoms for which" Jim Cooper "gave his life and the freedoms for which" war protestors "went to prison."[35]

Lawrencians searched to understand why the war was being fought and why so many people close to them were dying or suffering because of the conflict. With each American death, the war, and the politics of waging it, became more personal, and Americans responded in more passionate ways. Additionally, Vietnam provided an opportunity for the meaning of patriotism, honor, duty, and freedom to be contested and debated in a public forum.

This was never clearer than in April 1967, when the *Journal-World* published a photograph of an unidentified young woman, probably a KU student taking part in a "be-in" on campus, with an American flag wrapped around her.[36] The woman may have been warding off the fifty-degree chill, or perhaps, as many believed, she was making a statement about the United States and its participation in the Vietnam war; apparently no one from the *Journal-World* or any other media asked her about her actions, nor did she come forward later with an explanation. Whatever her intentions, the incident touched off a firestorm of protest and discussion in the community that illustrated how the war became a referendum on what it meant to be an American.

The Lawrence be-in itself was a peaceful happening, probably modeled on the well-publicized first "Human Be-In" or "A Gathering of Tribes" held in San Francisco on January 14, 1967. Although more a cultural celebration than a radical political statement, the event had political consequences, as hippies and radical politicos carved out new spaces for themselves in the city and used alternate life choices to challenge traditional norms, behavior, and social identities.[37] By 1967, in Lawrence and elsewhere, Americans were considering personal lifestyles and behavior to be political acts.[38] The nascent Lawrence counterculture, now appropriating its own space in Lawrence, was melding with the widening antiwar and student movements to create a powerful political and social force that was reshaping the community. Whether she meant to or not, the "flag girl" made an overt political statement by wrapping herself in the United States flag, a statement that initiated an extended public debate in Lawrence.

The *Journal-World* launched the first salvo in the "flag incident," as it became known. In an editorial entitled "Pitiful Taste," the *Journal-World* lambasted the young woman in particular and the emerging "hippie culture" in general. The low point of the be-in, the paper noted, was the "flag incident." The young woman was trying to draw attention to herself, "or to show just how liberal and open-minded she is." The *Journal-World* then cut to what it considered the real issue: It wondered if the young woman had "any idea just what that flag means, or stands for, or if she really cares." The incident was symptomatic of "extremist activity in our country in recent years," a trend that has made "many citizens reluctant to speak out on matters of patriotism—for fear of being branded as being red-hot. This is too bad. There still is plenty of room in our society for sincere expressions of patriotism, and it is understandable that a lot of citizens—vocal or silent—are quite disturbed by" the incident.[39]

Not all Lawrencians were appalled by the incident, and many used the opportunity to express an alternative patriotism. Kenton Craven, a KU student and a be-in participant, wondered why a flag could be draped on a casket, or worn by Uncle Sam or Miss Liberty, but could not "be draped around the sacred body of a live human being[.]" He also asked why the *Journal-World* was intent on splitting Lawrence "into two factions, the good Americans who love sports, and the bad Americans (or is it the non-Americans?) who love poetry, songs, and celebration of the human soul." To KU student James McCrary the flag "symbolize[d] . . . a foul, meaningless war in Vietnam," "the worst kind of poverty," "a country torn by racial unrest [and] disabled by strikes and labor disputes," and "a President blaming the anti-war protestors for prolonging the escalating war."[40]

Despite these rejoinders, most Lawrencians who publicly voiced an opinion agreed with the *Journal-World*. In early May, Alan Fisher, the new commander of Lawrence's Dorsey-Liberty American Legion post, agreed that the woman had "every right" to protest, "but no citizen has a right under any circumstances to tear asunder our great symbols." Not surprisingly, to the legion the flag represented a good deal more than just a symbol of the state: It embodied the values and ideals of the nation. As Fisher declared, "This flag is only pieces of cloth that has [been] sewn together by loving hands until someone cherishes the land for which it stands, until you and I stand together to defend it, until our blood stains its stripes red, until our love chastens and purifies its [stripes] white, and until we hold it so high that the blue sky and the stars mold into its union. When these things happen this flag becomes your country, your home, your family, and even yourself, and woe be to them who try to destroy it for they are trying to destroy you."[41]

Fisher clearly linked the flag to his and the Legionnaires' personal identities as Americans, homeowners, fathers, and husbands. He linked the flag incident to Vietnam, antiwar protests, the death of Jim Cooper, and what he saw as a declining sense of duty and responsibility in the nation, all of which were serious threats. "Yesterday, I had the sad duty of extending my sympathy and paying my respects of this post" to Jim Cooper's parents, Fisher recalled. And, although he wanted to honor Cooper, rather than deal with the slain man as a person the speech raised symbolic issues about patriotism and Americanism: "[T]his young man, and thousands like him today are deserving of our endearing gratitude for his unselfishness and willingness to serve when there are so many others who cow before this privilege of serving with the flimsiest of excuses." That same night, the legion passed a resolution condemning the "gross disrespect to the flag" and asked that the woman be prosecuted under a Kansas law that prohibited flag desecration.[42]

Nonveteran groups were also outraged by the woman's actions. As "law-abiding and loyal citizens," the Lawrence High-Twelve Club, affiliated with the Masonic Lodge, demanded that the young woman's "defiance" be punished. The Lawrence Federation of Women's Clubs (LFWC) expressed its "hostility for the desecration of our revered flag." The LFWC held to the adage "Our Country and our Flag—right or wrong—where right to be kept right—where wrong to be made right." The stars and stripes, according to the federation's president, Ruth Findley, had been "the banner of Hope and Freedom for generation after generation of Americans. So long as men hold respect for their country, for the privledges [sic] bought with blood of our forefathers—so long as these principles of truth, justice and charity remain deeply rooted in human hearts—shall Americans, worthy of the name, revere and cherish these symbols displayed in Old Glory. Woe be to those who desecrate it!" Marine Major Thomas J. Glidden, a professor of naval science at KU, called the woman's display "boorish and rude and in execrable taste" and likened the wearing of "The Flag" to "paint[ing] swastikas on synagogues and burn[ing] crosses."[43]

The flag incident widened the debate on Vietnam to include the counterculture, student activism, and feminism, but at the heart of the discussion was a discourse on America's symbols and the meaning of patriotism. Eric Rundquist, a sophomore at Lawrence High School, was confused about the motives and intentions of "dissenters and their ilk." Rundquist admitted that the United States had "made a mistake" in Vietnam but wondered: Could antiwar protestors not "keep their big mouths shut and let us find our own solutions?" "What good is their protesting going to do," he inquired, "if they have no solutions to begin with?" A high school classmate, Kathy Schott, agreed. Schott sincerely believed that war protestors were trying to create "in-security in American society" and "ruining the image that other countries have" of the United States. Like many of their elders, Rundquist and Schott believed that there was in the United States a "trend toward 'unpatriotism' and [that] American ideals [were] slowly disintegrating." They thought that "many of these protestors are off-beats who only desire attention, who would protest anything at the drop of a hat." Schott also believed that many anti-war demonstrators were "influenced by Communists who are using them for their own purposes." She allowed that "[p]erhaps we shouldn't be there in the first place, but let's face it. We're there, and we should support our men, not turn our backs. Once we had run, where would we hide?"[44]

Veneration of the nation's ideals and symbols, such as the flag, became more pronounced during the Vietnam War. Any fears that ordinary folks may have had about current problems—Vietnam, crime, violence, and stu-dent unrest, for example—were mediated by the nation's dominant narrative of steady progress and "orderly transitions." People looked to the past to in-vest the present with meaning and to give expression to their own sense of self. Supporting the American nation in Vietnam became a way to express not only that identity, but also what they believed to be "the American way of life."[45]

There was support for the United States' involvement in Vietnam, though in Lawrence such support expressed a particular brand of patriotism, an Americaness drawn from the past. The American flag and unwavering support for the nation's male warriors, who were defending the nation's core values of freedom, democracy, and liberty, formed the rhetorical and sym-bolic core of this identity. Conversely, dovish Lawrencians believed that they were as patriotic as any hawk in the community but that they defined their patriotism in distinctly different ways. Ironically, they both drew upon sim-ilar symbols, icons, and rhetoric to proclaim their Americaness. The debate over Vietnam, like the discourse on race, feminism, and a host of other is-sues became a debate about what it meant to be an American. Vietnam thus gave opponents of the war opportunities to convey their own sense of self and define an alternative patriotism.

With each passing month, and with each additional American death in Vietnam, Lawrencians became more aware of the war, yet were not always sure what should be done. KU student Robert E. Ireland, from Valley Cen-ter, Kansas, was concerned about the Vietnamese refugees; his humanitari-anism, however, did not mean that he was opposed to the war. "Intelligent men are saying much on both sides of the question," he lamented, "and I frankly cannot decide with side is closer to being right." Even the *Journal-World* by 1967 was beginning to question the Johnson administration's han-dling of the war, a position that perhaps reflected the paper's distrust of

Johnson's Great Society programs rather than opposition to the war. "How can the Johnson Administration expect Americans to be enthusiastic about 'preserving the freedom' of the South Vietnamese," read an April editorial, "when these people are not particularly interested in defending themselves?" The *Journal-World* did not call for immediate withdrawal of American forces but did demand a clear statement from Johnson on American objectives and goals for victory in Vietnam.[46]

On the other hand, the *Journal-World* did not endorse antiwar demonstrations any more than it had civil rights protests. The paper criticized Martin Luther King, Jr., for declaring that civil disobedience might "be necessary as a form of protest" against the war. The editorial claimed that the "big problem" in Vietnam is "that the people and the nations involved cannot settle on rules or 'laws' to follow. What good could be served by people in our country engaging in the same type of faulty thinking and disobeying existing laws in protest? Let's hope Dr. King and his followers think things over carefully before they get carried away with some foolish program of 'civil disobedience' that will do far more harm than good." In a May editorial, the *Journal-World* linked the two most pressing issues of 1967, race and Vietnam. Taking umbrage at boxer Cassius Clay's (Muhammad Ali) refusal to report for induction, the *Journal-World* dismissed as irrelevant criticism from African Americans that blacks were shouldering a disproportionate burden of the war. "Whether one is for or against the Vietnam War or U.S. involvement in helping other nations," the paper opined, "it is not difficult to see irony in the fact that at a time when Negroes are doing such an outstanding job in serving their country their efforts are being detracted from by members of their race who are too irrational and emotional in their crusading."[47]

More Lawrencians were questioning America's involvement in Vietnam, and many hesitations were driven by economic concerns. Arly Allen, a vice-president of the Allen Press, asserted that the war threatened the United States economy. The deficit could be reduced, he argued, "by eliminating the $25 billion dollars spent, or rather wasted, in Vietnam." Ada Jacobowitz, the wife of a KU mathematics professor, agreed. If those billions of dollars were spent on domestic concerns, she wrote, they "could help with Head Start, water and air pollution control, help to small farmers, hospitals, etc., as well as cutting inflation." Additionally, Lawrencians were growing increasingly frustrated with politicians. Josephine Hutton, the KU financial aid office manager, wrote Pearson that when "you say you back Johnson's policies in Viet Nam you do not speak for me nor for my friends nor for the many Kansans I have talked to." Hutton, like her neighbors, wondered why the United States was fighting in Vietnam, and she, too, expressed concern about the cost of the war. Tax increases may not hurt you, she told Pearson, "but it will certainly hurt everyone I know out here." Like other Lawrencians, Hutton connected Vietnam with the social problems facing the United States. "And what is it for—Viet Nam? Space program? War on Poverty (!)? Great Society? What's great about it—riots? hippies? draft dodgers? Mississippi? Medicare? . . . I think it's time for you people who represent Kansas to have the guts to stand up and speak right for us and get counted."[48]

By 1967 opposition, in a variety of forms, to the Vietnam War included a large cross section of the Lawrence community, a trend that did not escape the attention of some residents. Rebecca Coan, the wife of KU's dean of foreign students, urged Congress and the president to "consider" that a "great, great many" opponents of the war are "educated, middle aged, thinking people." Others noted that opposition to the war was no longer limited to a radical few. Emily and Angus Wright, both KU students and "long time Kansans," listed the diversity of dissenters in Lawrence: "a contractor's son, [a] farmer's wife, a minister . . . a priest . . . a clothing store owner . . . and many others." These people, Angus Wright declared, were not "confused and resentful" but were "simply too frightened or bewildered to express misgivings about governmental policy." Wright hoped that Pearson was beginning to appreciate "this same swell of opposition." Penelope Hanna, whose husband was a mathematics professor at KU, previously had seen the United States' involvement in Vietnam as part of the "domino theory." She now was convinced that "we have gone too far in expenditures of both men and of money" and demanded negotiations and withdrawal. Hanna also noted that there was a "growing dissatisfaction with America's stance" in Southeast Asia, which she believed came from "not just some east coast minority. It is, surprisingly, the Kansas milkmen and the Kansas grocery clerks who are speaking out now."[49]

In 1968, public opinion about the war remained somewhat mixed, although more Lawrencians were turning against the war. Some opposed the war because it was costing too much money, that they believed could be better spent fighting poverty, hunger, and crime. For others, the war, especially the failure to win, was a blow to American prestige and self-esteem. A growing majority, however, viewed the war in moral terms: It was illegal, immoral, and barbaric. KU student Sandy Bair appealed to Pearson to do all he could to end the war, "for the lives of my brothers, the lives of the men over in Viet Nam, and for the freedom we are suppose[d] to be fighting for in Viet Nam."[50]

The 1968 Tet Offensive was one factor motivating many Lawrencians to express their opposition to the war. In March, at the end of the offensive, according to a WDAF (Kansas City) television poll, nearly three-fourths of area residents agreed that the United States "should not be fighting" in Vietnam. Denis B. Lardiner, Sr., a supervisor at the Hercules (formerly Sunflower) ammunition plant, agreed and encouraged Congress to end "the killing and bring our boys home." Elizabeth Henderson, who was retired, asked Pearson to "[p]lease do something to stop the killing in Viet Nam. It is terrible. How can it pay?" KU student Judy Wonn, from Independence, Kansas, wondered "[h]ow can we possibly believe we are 'winning' when [Vietnamese] cities from north to south are vulnerable to attack [by communists]?" Wonn was highly skeptical of official reports on the conduct of the war, hinting at the growing credibility gap between the president and the public. She also saw in Vietnam lost opportunities to address serious social problems in the United States. "If Vietnam continues to get top priority to the neglect of our internal needs," she warned, "we may find that we have little country left to fight for." Wonn claimed she "would rather see the tax payer's [sic] money spent in programs for prevention rather than [in] rebuilding burned cities or for wounded and homeless citizens."[51]

Despite the growing opposition, many Lawrencians continued to support the war. Richard Nixon, who had been elected President in 1968 in part on his promise to end the war, in 1969 actually widened the war. Nonetheless, many Lawrencians approved of the president's handling of the war. Mr. and Mrs. Alfred J. Graves, both retired, gave Nixon their "wholehearted support" for a "satisfactory end" to the war. Similarly, Ray and Marsha Goff of rural Lawrence were "convinced" that Nixon could achieve "an honorable peace *if* he is given the support he needs in Congress." Like other supporters of the war, the Goffs believed they spoke for the "majority of Kansans" in their support of the president. Mrs. Grace Reisner, a widow, asserted that Nixon needed "our support" and believed those "who call themselves doves seem to have done more harm than good in bringing peace." William C. Elbrader, a research worker, was dismayed with Congress's lack of support for the president. Praising Kansas Senator Robert Dole's support for Nixon, Elbrader claimed that "the minority has been conducting a massive campaign to stop the war," and "their motives are suspect, to say the least; their judgement, patriotism, and loyalties are highly questionable and borders [sic] on treason." Vernon Harrel, a detective with the Lawrence Police Department, and his wife Patricia told Pearson that "*we strongly support our President Nixon* on his Vietnamese policies. We feel he has made the right choice." The Harrels declared that they were "just two of a large majority of loyal American supporters of President Nixon and our great American government."[52]

As the war dragged on, Lawrence, and the nation, remained divided over Vietnam, and the discourse on the war became more intense. Vietnam increasingly became part of daily life in Lawrence, and its residents continued to debate the meaning of citizenship. In the fall of 1969, a new wave of antiwar activism resulted in the October 15 Moratorium and the New Mobilization (New Mobe) in November, which together were the greatest antiwar protests in American history. Both the Moratorium and the New Mobe generated a great deal of popular momentum for the United States to withdraw from Vietnam.[53] The success of these demonstrations resulted directly from the local people who organized hundreds of local groups as part of a nationwide protest. In Lawrence, the Moratorium had widespread support, due largely to the efforts of the Lawrence October 15th Committee and the KU October 15th Committee. The Lawrence Committee was created in early October, at a meeting held at the First United Methodist Church. Chaired by Arthur Katz, dean of the School of Social Work at KU, it planned the day's activities in the community, coordinating its efforts with the student October 15th Committee, which focused on the campus.[54]

In calling for all Americans to take a one-day break in "business-as-usual" to contemplate and protest the war, the Moratorium hoped to create public support for an immediate American withdrawal from Vietnam, or perhaps a fixed date for withdrawal. In Lawrence the rhetoric of democracy, freedom, peace, and justice ruled the day as thousands of Lawrencians paused to reflect on the war. KU students milled about the campus, some selling and wearing back armbands in memory of the dead in Vietnam, others distributing and reading antiwar literature, and many signing petitions to end the war. A workshop on nonviolence was held, faculty used class time to discuss the war, and local musicians added an air of festivity to the activities. Officials estimated that up to five thousand students participated in the demonstration, marching peacefully down Jayhawk Boulevard past Strong Hall to the Kansas Union. The *Kansan* hailed the Moratorium as an overwhelming success, and the *Lawrence Outlook* described it as "peaceful."[55]

Off campus, the day began with a "Breakfast of Reconciliation" at the First Christian Church. Several films about the war were shown in local theaters, and a luncheon was held at the Eldridge Hotel. Students at Lawrence High School held workshops and discussions about the war, while downtown, Danna Santee distributed antiwar literature from a recessed store entrance. That evening, former mayor and school board member James V. Owens moderated a town meeting titled "Vietnam Withdrawal," which included three KU professors who spoke on the moral and social impact of the war on the American people and society.[56]

About 130 people attended the town meeting, which turned from a discussion about the war to a debate over the "town and gown" split. The *Journal-World* portrayed the event as "not much of a 'town gathering'" and noted that many people "complained bitterly about the lack of non-university people who showed interest" in the war. Rosella Pratt, a self-described "newcomer" with no ties to the university, told the crowd that "she did not feel the need for faculty to interpret" the meaning of the war for her. There were, Pratt estimated, more than 25,000 Lawrencians not connected with the university, whom she described as "the people who go about their daily business and can't be bothered with moralistic principles. 'Self interest, not high moral principles, governs people,'" she declared. Although deeply concerned about Vietnam, Pratt apparently resented the manner in which the university community was discussing the matter. "Self interest for the average woman between 30 and 60," she explained, "is expressed through children not intellectual[s]." Although Pratt, a socialist, was perhaps not a representative community spokesperson, others shared her views. Pratt concluded that a "lot of people are for peace, not for high minded ideas, but for material reasons in terms of their own jobs," which received "applause and responses from some who objected to the division of the 'university' and 'town' people." Another woman agreed, requesting that the discussion be "concerned with less academic considerations."[57] The "town-gown" division was artificial; KU faculty lived in Lawrence, paid taxes to local government, shopped in local stores, bought houses, sent their children to local schools, and attended local churches, and many lived until their deaths in Lawrence. It was a real division in the minds of many Lawrencians, however, which contributed to their resentment of "outsiders" telling them what they should do or what was wrong with their country.

Other Lawrencians were simply fed up with protests and demonstrations. R. Wayne Nelson, the coordinator for cultural and fine arts in the Lawrence school system, and his wife Trena claimed to speak for the "'silent public'" who were upset with antiwar protests. On October 15, the Nelsons "flew the flag, did no marching, signed no petitions, gave no money." Richard Nixon "clearly" was elected as president, the Nelsons argued, and as commander-in-chief was "doing his best with an inherited war." Similarly, the *Journal-World* reported that "the people," by which it meant most Lawrencians, did not participate in the Moratorium. Harold V. Siegerst, a vice principal in the Lawrence public schools, claimed that "the people" spoke loudly by ignoring the protest. "They spent the day or night working and home-making as usual," he declared, "making appropriate responses as they thought to the 'call' to dissent (or hold a 'moratorium' meeting—a more suave phrase—which didn't trick the majority of clear-thinking citizens)." Siegerst thought that the actions of those who did not join in the Moratorium spoke as loudly as the actions of those who did. Ed Abels agreed, claiming that on November 11, Armistice Day, "there were more flags and more expressed concern about patriotic loyalty to the nation." Abels gave much of the credit for this to the "activity of the dissenters," who were "stirring deep and sincere resentment among those who believe in the American way." Believing that most protestors were merely "misinformed rather than disloyal," Abels declared that "the loyal citizens . . . must take a stand against the troublemakers."[58] As Abels and others' comments suggest, the demonstrations challenged conventional notions of patriotism and what it meant to be an

American. The CIA reported to President Richard M. Nixon, who was un-settled by antiwar protest, that "the real problem" with the Moratorium was not the "usual troublemakers" but that "prominent people regarded as loyal Americans have instilled the day with respectability and even patriotism."[59]

"This Day is Different" was the headline of a full-page advertisement paid for and signed by 152 peace activists. Several times in October antiwar activists placed full-page signature ads in the *Journal-World,* including one signed by 318 people. A quick analysis of those people who in this ad pub-licly declared their opposition suggests that while KU students and faculty remained the core of antiwar dissent in Lawrence, voices of protest came from throughout the community. They included an insurance agent, a sheet metal worker's wife, a sales representative, several widows, a pathologist, a city librarian, a lawyer, a florist, a downtown health food store owner, pub-lic school teachers, a writer for Centron Corporation, and a local film maker. Signers of a second ad included a maid, a nurse, an electrician, a waiter, a leather worker, the owner of a leather goods store, the manager of a hard-ware store, the manager of a grain elevator, and an automobile mechanic. A third ad was signed by the wife of a printer, a public school teacher, an em-ployee in the KU printing service and his wife, the owner of a sports car business, and the wife of a lumber yard worker. In addition, many of these signers were business owners and provided frequent financial support for several local antiwar organizations.[60]

The Moratorium also signaled the beginning of a sustained, organized peace effort in Lawrence. Although there had been organizations committed to peace before 1969—the SPU, the Kansas Peace Forum, the Lawrence Peace Committee, the Oread Meeting of Friends, for example—the Mora-torium brought their activities together into a unified effort, one which drew in Lawrencians from a wide range of backgrounds. The October 15th Com-mittee soon evolved into the Lawrence Committee for Peace in Vietnam (LCPV, later renamed the Lawrence Committee for Peace in Indochina, or LCPI), which was chaired by Bob Charlton, an insurance agent; Danna San-tee, a mother of three and the wife of a former marine lieutenant and famous American mile runner; and I. J. Stoneback, the chair of the Lawrence Na-tional Farmers Organization. None of them had any direct affiliation with the university. Also fighting against the war was the Lawrence Peace Action Coalition (LPAC), a branch of the National Peace Action Coalition. LPAC members included the WILPF, the Student Mobilization Committee, the LCPI, the LPC, and area businesspeople, farmers, and high school and col-lege students. The Lawrence Peace Action Coalition (LPAC) and the Lawrence Committee for Peace in Indochina (LCPI) supported Nixon's peace initiative, which called for a cease-fire, complete withdrawal of U.S. troops, the release of all American POWs, and meaningful negotiations to settle the political situation. In support of the proposal the LPAC and LCPI planned a "Walk for Peace" from Central Park to South Park, a "Rally for Peace" in South Park, and a twenty-four-hour "Silent Vigil for Peace" along Massachusetts Street near South Park.[61]

At the same meeting in Washington that a national Vietnam Moratorium Committee (VMC) was created, the New Mobilization Committee to End the War in Vietnam (New Mobe) was formed. Intent on creating a "more disciplined, responsible coalition" than previous left, antiwar organizations, the New Mobe was more radical than the VMC. It declared that Vietnam was the "pivotal issue" that obstructed social reform in other areas of American life. To that end, the New Mobe planned a national demonstration in Washington in November.[62]

The KU Student Mobilization Committee to End the War in Vietnam (KU New Mobe) coordinated local activities for the November demonstration. While some of its members planned to march in Washington and a few others in Topeka, most focused their energies on Lawrence. The KU New Mobe held its meetings at the United Campus Christian Fellowship (UCCF), whose advisor was peace activist and campus minister Otto Zingg.[63] While the October 15 Moratorium in Lawrence had been peaceful and without incident, the November protest, organized almost exclusively by KU students, was a different matter. In October, the Moratorium maintained an air of patriotism, albeit a non-jingoistic version, and many of the day's events were largely out of the public's eye. Student involvement remained confined to the campus, and other activities were held in churches, hotels, and school buildings. Since October, however, students had taken antiwar activity into the streets of Lawrence, thus constituting a direct threat to the town's traditional boundaries and a threat to the personal identity of many Lawrencians.

This was vividly illustrated on November 11, Veterans' Day, when a group of about seventy-five veterans held a "patriotic ceremony" in South Park (where the Silent Vigil for Peace was also held on Sundays). In a speech, the Reverend Harold G. Barr, dean emeritus of the KU School of Religion, decried the upcoming moratorium because it was "attacking servicemen and ridiculing what has been accomplished by the servicemen here today and the servicemen across the country." Most telling, Barr told the veterans the demonstrations were "attack[s] on us, what we stand for, what we have always stood for and America itself." Although Barr allowed room in the United States for dissent, he believed "there should be a line drawn between dissent and treason," and that Lawrence's dissenters were stepping over that line. During Barr's speech, John Hensley, a KU junior from Wichita, flashed the peace sign to the group. After a twenty-one-gun salute and the playing of "Taps," Hensley began talking to a smaller group of the veterans. Hensley told them that "Communism is not the same everywhere and we don't have to fight a war to the end everywhere in the world." Ed Young, the commander of the rifle firing squad, began chasing Hensley around the park and eventually punched him in the jaw, leaving Hensley bleeding. Young refused to talk to the *Journal-World* and several veterans warned the paper not to report the incident. Hensley declined to press charges.[64]

A few days later, as part of the November Moratorium, a "March Against Death" took place in Washington with about 300 Kansans participating, each wearing the name of a dead soldier from the state. In Lawrence, as part of the same protest, about 150 people marched in frigid, "bone-chilling" weather from South Park, down Massachusetts Street, and on to Central Park, west of the downtown. Several people proclaimed their Americanism by carrying a banner that read "Patriots For Peace Now." Before the march, several speakers braved the weather to advocate American withdrawal from Vietnam. On campus, an estimated 300 students participated in a teach-in and discussed the war in Hoch Auditorium, where KU chancellor Laurence Chalmers refuted claims that dissenters were committing treason. "It is not treason we commit today. Far from it," Chalmers avowed. "It is a constitutional privilege predicated upon a respect for the rights and freedom of every individual in our society," a declaration which the students roundly cheered. According to the *Journal-World,* there "appeared" to be fewer activities and participants than in the October 15 Moratorium. The weather was partially to blame, as was a lack of publicity surrounding the event. Additionally, many of KU's antiwar activists had traveled to Washington to march there.[65]

The *Journal-World* commended the marchers, who "expressed themselves in a rational and dignified manner without allowing violence to erupt," although a few "carr[ied] . . . things too far" by carrying North Vietnam or Viet Cong flags. The paper allowed that "[b]y now it is established that an individual can be opposed to the war in Vietnam and can disagree with national policy and still be patriotic." It simply did not "make sense," the paper opined, to label such people as traitors or "treasonous." But the *Journal-World* also believed that such protests had outlived their usefulness. "It is doubtful that any great good will be accomplished by" marches or moratoriums. Moreover, these type of activities gave "aid and comfort to the enemy" (which is one definition of treason), and they were unlikely to affect national policy. The "longer moratorium advocates drag out their project, the less support they will have." To the *Journal-World,* then, the protestors had made their point—they were not traitors but in fact patriotic Americans—and it was time to end these kinds of protests before "they do harm to the national climate."[66]

As a show of opposition to the November demonstrations, "real patriotic Americans" were encouraged to display their loyalty and patriotism by flying the flag. Fred E. Johnson, who was retired, declared "that in these violent upset days every loyal United States citizen should fly the American flag from his home on every legal holiday. If I am wrong so be it. I intend to do so myself from now on." Jo Barnes, a public school teacher, encouraged all Lawrencians to "get behind President Nixon—and be real Americans!" She claimed that antiwar protestors had lost their "common sense" and were "dupes of the communists." Barnes urged other Lawrencians to join her in refusing to support antiwar protests and in "discouraging them in any way we can. I'd like to see the Stars and Stripes flying all over the town all week" as they had been on Veteran's Day. "I thought how grand it would be if our city could leave them up the whole week, supporting our country as strongly as we do the football team!"[67]

The debate had come full circle from the 1967 "flag incident." Supporters of the war claimed the flag as a marker of their own patriotism and identity as Americans. As several dissenters noted, however, this action politicized a national symbol: One was a true American only if one flew the flag. Judith Daily objected to the symbolism because, "as a patriotic American, who now finds it hard to fly the stars and stripes because it puts me in a 'Pro-Nixon-and-None-Other' position, I still treasure that flag and the democracy that it stands for." KU student Stephen J. Schroff of Shawnee Mission, Kansas, suggested that using a national symbol to make a political statement "prostituted its meaning" and was as "disrespect[ful]" as flag burning. Moreover, for some Americans prowar symbolism had caused the flag to cease to be a "symbol of which they can . . . be proud." Similarly, Roberta R. Nixon continued to fly her flag but also wore a peace button. She was distressed by the dichotomy on which many red-hot patriots insisted. "For too long most of us have been apathetic," Nixon wrote, "settling for symbols to speak for us. Now we are called upon to consider deeply what the American flag and the Peace Symbol and support and dissent really mean to us—and act according[ly]."[68]

As Americans debated the wisdom of fighting in Vietnam, it became increasingly difficult to separate the war from other domestic concerns: racial unrest, urban riots, and poverty, to name a few. KU professor of zoology John Cairns, Jr., for example, was in Detroit during its 1967 riots. "Surely the $28 billion a year being spent in Vietnam could be better applied to provide better housing, education, and vocational training for slum people. It might not stop the riots entirely but then $28 billion doesn't seem to have brought victory in Vietnam either." Cairns saw the war as a waste of lives and money. The $500,000 "now spent to kill each Viet Cong," he claimed, "might save the life of a citizen here." Similarly, but from an opposite ideological perspective, Jacqueline Speakman wanted to "bring back a little sanity to our nation, our boys back from Vietnam, and our tax dollars from out of the hands of foreign aid programs." Speakman sensed a malaise in the nation, one brought on not only by Vietnam, but also by the riots, urban unrest, and dissension in the country. Moreover, she believed it emanated from the top of the government down through the citizenry. "We are being let down by our commander-in-chief," she said, "who will not speak out to let his countrymen know he is not in accord with this criminal element now running free in our cities' streets." The nation's police "cannot touch them for fear of civil rights violations or some such piece of trash, while innocent people, both black and white are forced to stand by and watch helplessly while their life's work is destroyed in a matter of minutes." Speakman believed that "[a]s long as Stokely Carmichael and his ilk are free to preach and practice this filth and incite these murderous riots, every boy who died in Vietnam died in vain, shame and degradation. Don't remind me of free speech, I'll be remembering that in November" during the national elections.[69]

Although by January 1970 there was more opposition to than support for the war, Vietnam had clearly polarized the community. At one extreme were radicals on the Left, who not only wanted to end the war but saw the conflict as symptomatic of the greater evils in American society: American imperialism, impersonal capitalism, and dehumanizing racism. These self-proclaimed revolutionaries believed that the only solution was the destruction of American institutions and capitalism. At the other extreme were prowar advocates unwilling to criticize American policy. In the middle were thousands of Lawrencians who, for moral, political, religious, or economic reasons, either supported or opposed the war.

Between 1965 and 1969, antiwar sentiment in Lawrence grew far beyond the boundaries of the academy to encompass a broader cross section of the community, and even some previously hawkish Lawrencians called for a negotiated settlement to the conflict. Although there had been opposition to the war before 1967, the bulk of it had come from people affiliated with the university and religious groups. A substantial portion of the community, led by veterans organizations, civic and service groups, and hard-line cold warriors, believed that the country was not doing enough to win the war and contain communist aggression. They generally supported the administration.

After 1967, however, retired pensioners, businesspeople, and some working-class people joined the chorus of voices to speak out against the war. The draft lottery, the increased number of American troops in Vietnam, and the mounting death toll partially explain this change, especially as millions of teenaged men faced the prospect of military conscription. There were other explanations, too. The gradual cracking of the Cold War consensus left America's mission in Vietnam less clear, and the seeming lack of progress in winning the war wounded American pride. Additionally, televised coverage of the war brought body counts and gruesome battle scenes into Americans' living rooms. At the same time, domestic unrest (particularly the urban riots in Watts, Detroit, and Newark), crime and poverty, antiwar protests, and youth cultural rebellions, among other things, signaled to some Americans that the United States needed to put its own house in order; to others it signaled a loss of traditional American values.

Indeed, it is clear that during this period there was a great and growing rift among the people of Lawrence, a rift that often centered on American symbols and what constituted and defined "traditional American values." While some Lawrencians defined their patriotism and loyalty through their peace efforts, which they believed best embodied the true values of the United States, others defined the same ideas through the nation's strength and a willingness to defend freedom and liberty. Lawrence's debate over the Vietnam War provides an opportunity to examine the limits of dissent and how Lawrencians defined their patriotism.

As the war dragged on, antiwar protestors claimed and transformed public spaces in Lawrence. Patriotic symbols of Americaness were challenged and defended, claimed and co-opted, reified and redefined. By the end of 1969, civil rights, cultural change, the youth and student rebellions, urban unrest, economic change, and shifting gender roles combined with the tragedy of Vietnam to create a volatile social context in which Lawrencians struggled to define themselves and their community. Social and political conflict in Lawrence was not simply the product of America's participation in the war in Southeast Asia; much of it resulted from problems, such as racial tensions, that were indigenous to the community. But for Lawrencians to admit the local origin of their problems would mean acknowledging their own culpability in creating those problems. Thus, by 1967 and thereafter, Lawrencians tended to blame an easier and more distant target, the war in Vietnam.

Because the war had become so personal to so many Americans, at the core of the disagreement among Lawrencians over Vietnam was a greater public debate over the meaning of Americanism. Lawrencians constructed competing narratives of what it meant to be an American, what the core values of American society were, and how those values should be expressed. Thus, whether one supported or opposed the war, and, moreover, the manner in which one chose to do either, became markers of identity in the community and either challenged or defended social boundaries, which contributed to a great social division in the town. Furthermore, as antiwar demonstrations became more frequent and came to encompass a larger portion of the community than just the university, opponents and advocates of the Vietnam War made public spaces within the community sites for contestation. Antiwar activists sought out public spaces in which to express their views on American society and its values, while others struggled to hold on to that space to preserve and defend their own identity as "Americans." This process was transforming the community and the politics of dissent.

The public discourse about the Vietnam War transformed Lawrence, in large part because the politics of the war became personal and touched their lives. A close examination of this debate, which engulfed the entire community, reveals important insights into American society, and it helps us to examine the conventional wisdom and myths that we as a nation share about the war. Vietnam seemed to cut each Lawrencian to the bone, for it called into public scrutiny fundamental assumptions about the United States, its values, and what it meant to be an American. Thus, the Vietnam War became as much a battle for the hearts and souls of Americans as it did for those of Vietnamese peasants. To some Lawrencians, the war was unwinable and immoral; to others, defeat was anathema. This polarization suggests the parameters of the debate on what it meant to be an American.

Religious beliefs, and particularly pacifism, were crucial sources that provided a language and a space through which opponents of the war could speak out and act. For Quakers, Mennonites, and other pacifists in Lawrence the war was an abomination to their deeply-held religious values. For hundreds of older Lawrencians, Vietnam meant a replay of the horrors of war that they had experienced some two decades earlier. Others, however, were more pragmatic, viewing the war not in moral terms but as an economic question, one that exacerbated their fears of a bloated federal bureaucracy, a massive budget deficit, and a growing national debt. It is not surprising that many of these opponents also opposed Lyndon Johnson's Great Society. Still others saw Vietnam as part of their patriotic duty—and their sense of self—to support without question the policies of the United States government. In Lawrence and across the United States, Vietnam revealed deep fissures in American society.

CHAPTER 7

"THIS IS AMERICA? THIS IS KANSAS? THIS IS LAWRENCE?"

Between 1960 and 1969, Lawrence had changed a great deal. Citizens previously shut out or marginalized by the political system made their voices heard, while the established political order struggled to hold onto power. The community had weathered this transformation well and without any significant violence, although the threat always had been present. In 1970, however, the strain from years of cultural, social, and political conflict and shifting demographics stretched to the breaking point. That year the city exploded into a civil conflict, culminating in two deaths, numerous injuries, and millions of dollars of property loss. The turmoil of that year forced many residents to ask, "is this really America?"

In January 1969, the *Lawrence Daily Journal-World* reported the top local news stories of 1968 were the town's record economic growth, increased crime, and a greater participation of citizens in community affairs. Along with economic fortunes and a growing population, however, came problems, including more crime, housing shortages, and increased demands on city services. Those problems were exacerbated in 1969. Although Lawrence's population had grown slowly during the 1960s, from about 33,000 to 45,000, a significant portion of the growth was attributed to "hippies" who made up the so-called street community. Thousands of young people, a diverse and eclectic congregation of so-called freaks, street people, radicals, revolutionaries, and hippies commonly known as the counterculture, had come to Lawrence.[1] The counterculture, from gentle hippies and dropouts to violent Leftist revolutionaries, carved out new spaces to live in and created new institutions to serve its needs. The large number of new faces, especially those with beards, long hair, and different clothing from the mainstream, concerned many Lawrencians. The hippies, they believed, were outsiders responsible for the community's increased crime rate, were unfairly making demands on the community's social services, and were simply giving Lawrence a bad name.

A young hippie from Ohio said she came to Lawrence because "there are good vibes here," adding that "she had 'retired a couple of years ago' and was in town 'between festivals.'" Eighteen-year-old Saith Lappan lived with thirty-five other people at 1406 Tennessee in an "activist commune" called the Campus Improvement Association (CIA), a project initiated by Penn House's Keith Miller. The CIA was also home to the Lawrence Liberation Front (LLF) and was where the radical newspaper *Oread Daily* was published. "I'm here in Lawrence to rest," Lappan said, "There is always food somewhere and there aren't as many hassles here as in most towns."[2]

Like Lappan, hundreds of students, hangers-on, radicals and nonradicals, dope-smoking hippies, and revolutionary foot soldiers lived close to the university in the Oread neighborhood, mostly in subdivided houses and communes on Ohio, Tennessee, Kentucky, and Louisiana Streets that once were among the town's most fashionable homes. Most of the communes appeared between 1968 and 1970, coinciding with Lawrence's population increase. A few students lived there, but most of the residents—the majority of whom were white—were not affiliated with the university. But street people found places to crash all over town. Eight freaks, for example, lived in an eight-by-forty-foot trailer called the "Blue Max." Others chose to live in rural Douglas County in old farmhouses, where some grew low-grade marijuana and held frequent gatherings, like the annual "drug 'n' drink 'n' fuck picnic" called the "Big Eat." Some of Lawrence's freaks were known as the "Rock Chalk Society," while another group went by the "Kaw Valley Hemp Pickers." Oread, commented one freak, was a "good street scene where people can smoke their dope and play their guitars."[3] Although the locals derisively called the area "hippie haven," Oread was evidence that the counterculture had claimed part of the city for itself.

The university environment and youth culture were lures for former students or dropouts, and once the counterculture community was established it grew steadily. "As the word about Lawrence spread," recalled one former hippie, "the town became known as a friendly place for wayward freaks. . . . Lawrence was like the Oregon trail for hippies." Drugs flowed freely in Oread and for the most part the police did not crack down on drug use until about 1970. Located in the middle of the country, near a major interstate highway, Lawrence also was a stopping off point for drug traffic, or as one hippie stated, it "was on the Silk Route for drugs. . . . We thought of Lawrence as Baghdad on the Kaw." One fringe of the Lawrence counterculture embraced the use of hallucinogenic drugs, free love, communal living, and fun-seeking "reckless experimentation." By their own account, "[n]othing was forbidden. This was the social contract of the Kaw Valley hippies."[4]

The spread of the drug culture concerned many Lawrencians. Former Lawrence mayor Dick Raney, who owned a chain of pharmacies and was on the board of Headquarters, a drug information and counseling center, noted an increase of narcotics usage in the community around 1967 and witnessed several bad trips. Dr. Raymond Schwegler, the director of health services at KU, admitted in 1969 that his staff had been treating LSD users for many years. He claimed that only a few KU students used "hard narcotics," but that a "high-percentage" used speed, LSD, and marijuana. Moreover, he noted in 1970 that narcotics use by KU students had declined but more high school and junior high students were taking drugs.[5]

The counterculture was an important and enigmatic part of the sixties experience in Lawrence. The counterculture reshaped Lawrence by claiming part of it as their own, undermined traditional institutions by creating alternate ones, and challenged traditional forms of authority by not fulfilling the roles American society expected of its youth.[6] The broad rubric "counterculture," however, does not satisfactorily explain the range of experiences and diversity of alternative youth cultures in Lawrence. Some freaks arrived as runaways, disgruntled with parents, society, school, and other forms of authority. Others adopted the countercultural lifestyle for purely idealistic and sincere reasons, such as the desire to live a simpler, more egalitarian and communal lifestyle, perhaps, or to reform American society through how they lived their lives. Many came for the fun and the thrills that this lifestyle offered but found it also included vandalism, violence, and destruction. Some of the men enjoyed fighting with the locals, while others abused their girlfriends or wives, or sold illegal firearms and ammunition. Several became hippie capitalists, selling material goods in alternative stores or bales of low-grade "K-pot" on the east and west coasts. As one freak recalled, the "love-and-flowers angle of the Haight-Ashbury didn't ever happen here." Many arrived from small Kansas towns, where "[t]hey might have been the nastiest guy" in town. "They were not lightweights. Creeps, but not lightweights."[7]

There is little question that the community had changed since the early 1960s, and even some of those in the counterculture noticed the difference. Gary Brown, a 29-year-old sales clerk at Strawberry Fields, where cigarette papers, hashish pipes, and incense were sold, noted that in 1965 Lawrence had "a very small colony of gentle hippies smoking grass." By 1970, Brown claimed, "the whole thing ha[d] . . . mushroomed—it's full of mad dogs and crazies. It's really kind of frightening, even for me." Brown was concerned about the frequent bombings, arson, and vandalism that took place in 1969 and 1970, which the locals blamed on the left-radicals, black militants, hippies, and the "gypsies," vagabond revolutionaries who migrated to Lawrence to be part of what they believed was the coming revolution against "pig Amerika."[8]

With the arrival of thousands of new people and increased social and political activism during the decade, "law and order" became watchwords in 1969 and 1970. In August 1969, the Lawrence Police Department announced that crime was up 25 percent in the city for the first half of the year, although it did not say who or what was to blame. There were other signs, too, that Lawrence was becoming more dangerous. Between March 1968 and September 1969 there had been at least forty fires directed at symbols of authority and resulting in property damages of over $200,000. In February 1969, a Molotov cocktail was hurled into the office of Marine Colonel John P. Lanigan, head of Naval ROTC at KU, damaging the walls and carpeting. An arson attempt at the Lawrence public library in April resulted in only a few burnt papers, but later that month a piece of concrete and a bottle of acid were thrown through a window of Douglas County District Court Judge Frank Gray's house.[9]

Additionally, personal conflicts, especially racial fights, became more frequent. In September 1969, separate gunfights between motorists occurred in east and north Lawrence, both following traffic accidents. Bouts of violence between black and white students were common at Lawrence High School, recreational centers, and other public spaces. The town celebrated the opening of its new swimming pool in June 1969. More than 3,000 people used it in the first five days, but later in the summer it was the scene of several fights between blacks and whites. The Black Power movement led to greater police surveillance of blacks, while narcotics busts escalated tensions between the police and the street community. Increasingly, the police became targets of aggression. In early September, Harry Rayton, Jr., was arrested and charged with the felonious assault of Lawrence police officer William Garrett, the fifth assault against a police officer in Lawrence in a month.[10]

The war in Vietnam continued, killing more young men and further dividing the community. In January, Army Lt. Lynn Highley, 22, became the area's first Vietnam casualty of 1969, and in August Pfc. Timothy Mohler became the thirteenth Lawrencian to die in Southeast Asia since the war began. Protests against the war increased. Pacifists and peace activists, on campus and in the community, continued their diligent and peaceful efforts to end the war, evidenced by the weekly Silent Vigil For Peace, then in its third year. Some activists, however, turned to more confrontational, and even violent, means.

The violence of 1969 paled beside what happened in 1970. Arson and bombings were almost daily occurrences, almost all went unsolved, and only occasionally did anyone, like the Students for a Democratic Society (SDS) splinter group Weatherman, claim responsibility. Most Lawrencians, however, heaped blanket responsibility on New Left radicals, antiwar activists, black militants, and dropped-out hippies, making no distinction among these groups or their goals. Moreover, most Lawrencians refused to acknowledge the indigenous sources of tension and violence in the community: racism, vigilantism, and the preservation of the status quo. It was more palatable for Lawrencians to blame the community's problems and bursts of violence on Vietnam, communists, outsiders, hippies, and black militants. State and local law enforcement reinforced these perceptions, claiming (with some justification) that agent provocateurs from the Black Panthers and Weatherman had come to Lawrence in 1970 to instigate an armed revolution against the community and the United States.[11] The underground press also fed these perceptions. The *Vortex* claimed the arson and bombings were revolutionary "class warfare" against "pig Amerika." The alternative press, especially the *Vortex,* the *Oread Daily, Disorientation,* and *Harambee,* further inflamed these fears by defending the revolution, rationalizing the attacks, and providing periodic information on guerilla warfare, explosives-making, self-defense, first aid, and how to survive a tear gas attack, among others.[12] A significant minority in Lawrence believed that an armed revolution against mainstream American society was possible and perhaps imminent; indeed, it appears that in 1970 some had already initiated this war. Whether or not the editors and writers of *Vortex* or *Harambee* knew who was responsible for the bombings (and they probably did), most Lawrencians accepted the talk of revolution as true.

Racial identity, both black and white, and the defense of and challenge to racial boundaries, were at the heart of the struggle. For years, the community's racial lines had been in flux. The civil rights movement and, later, the Black Power movement and black culturalism became powerful social and political forces in Lawrence, directly challenging white privilege, white identity, and the boundaries prescribed by whites and whiteness. Whites resisted these challenges, however, polarizing the community along black and white racial lines.

The extent to which the town was divided over racial issues was evident early in 1970. The University of Kansas had few African Americans on the faculty, and the limited number of available black teachers and a lack of interest by black candidates in coming to Lawrence hindered its efforts to recruit more. When the political science department hired Leonard Harrison, the director of the Ballard Center in east Lawrence, as a lecturer and consultant for a course on "Political Revolutionary Theory," a barrage of outrage ensued from across the state. The cries grew louder when Harrison's 1961 conviction for burglary in Oklahoma and a recent armed robbery conviction in Wichita (which was under appeal) were revealed.[13] Even without a criminal record, Harrison's hiring would have been controversial. The episode was the first salvo in a year of increasingly contentious race relations in Lawrence, revealing both the enigmatic nature of the Black Power movement and the differences between black and white perceptions of racial problems.

Harrison lectured on "Black Revolutionary Thought," a topic for which the university acknowledged he was qualified. Whatever expertise and experiences he brought with him to the classroom, and certainly, his was a perspective few white, middle-class students would have known or experienced, an outcry from whites against his employment, and the course content, was likely. The course focused on the various strains of black nationalism, the concept of Black Power, and the prospect of a black revolution, all of which most white Lawrencians viewed as inflammatory. Additionally, students participated in group projects that considered, for example, the attitude of local clergy on the payment of reparations to African Americans for their bondage in slavery, the university's recruitment of black students and faculty, and the problems of coalition building between blacks and whites.[14] Herman Lujan, the chair of the political science department, had hired Harrison, but Vice-Chancellor for Academic Affairs Francis Heller had to justify the decision. He tactfully, but with little conviction, noted that the "class deals with black politics and Harrison has a distinct contribution to make to the class both as a black person and experienced politician." Privately, however, Heller claimed that the Black Student Union, to which Harrison had close ties, was looking for a confrontation with the university's administration and "incite violence" on campus. The controversy over Harrison's hiring provided just such an opportunity.[15]

Few critics of the decision considered Harrison's qualifications to lecture on black revolutionary thought. Predictably, the controversy centered on his criminal record and the concern that taxpayers' money was being spent to hire a convicted felon. There was nothing illegal about Harrison's hiring, Kansas Governor and Lawrence resident Robert B. Docking explained to a livid James Huff of Lawrence, and student fees, not state funds, were used to pay him. Although Docking acknowledged that Harrison had "paid his debt to society" on the Oklahoma conviction and that his legal troubles in Wichita were under appeal, he was not enthusiastic about the appointment. He understood Huff's "concern" and would share his "feelings except that the decision has been made by those who are charged with such decisions." Refusing to interfere with the autonomy of the university on this matter, Docking deferred to the administration's contention that Harrison "represent[ed] a type of thinking of which students in this particular class should be aware." "At this time," he concluded, "we must assume that this is a right decision."[16]

It was not the right decision, according to Senator Reynolds O. Shultz, a Republican and a zealous cold warrior from Lawrence. Shultz, who was a longtime critic of campus demonstrations and was considering a run for governor, was contemptuous of Chancellor Laurence Chalmers and his handling of campus problems. It was simply wrong to hire Harrison, Shultz argued, because he was "a militant and his political ideas and opinions could sway uncertain students in that direction." Shultz implied that KU's appropriations might be threatened by this decision.[17]

While Shultz fumed over Harrison's hiring, the BSU offered another target for his anger. The university's printers refused to print the February issue of *Harambee*, the BSU newspaper, because they believed it contained obscene material. Although Chalmers declared that the university would not censor campus publications, the printers stood fast. Undoubtedly, most whites found *Harambee* offensive. Each issue of the paper promoted Black Power, condemned the oppressiveness of white society, and called for armed revolution and self-defense. Each issue quoted Black Panther minister of defense Huey P. Newton's declaration that "[a]n unarmed people are slaves, or subject to slavery at any given time." *Harambee* published information on weapons, ammunition, and guerilla tactics. Unquestionably, *Harambee* and the BSU were radical, inflammatory, and unconcerned with white perceptions of them or their programs.[18]

White Lawrencians saw the BSU and *Harambee* as threats to the existing order and their own sense of self. Ollie Farmer, a cook at the Dairyland Drive-In, derided the "communist backed" paper as "obscene" and called for Chalmers's dismissal. Louise Farmer, who also worked at Dairyland, believed it was "alright for the colored to have a paper but not have this kind of stuff in it." While the Kansas Bureau of Investigation noted that *Harambee* "appeared to be racist in nature," the obscenity claim, as an attorney general's opinion concluded, was unfounded. *Harambee* may have been "offensive to contemporary community standards," but it did not "appeal to the 'prurient interest in sex'" and "was not legally obscene." The opinion declared, however, that the printers risked prosecution because the paper advocated violence.[19] The state could not legally halt publication of *Harambee* on obscenity charges, but it could use the threat of personal liability to encourage the printers not to print the paper. The BSU denounced the charges, declaring that the "racist printers and the racist Attorney General ha[ve] tried to deny Black people proper news coverage." In retaliation, several blacks, led or encouraged by Leonard Harrison, gathered some 6,000 issues of the *Kansan,* threw them into Potter's Lake on campus, and drove away in a van registered to the Ballard Center.[20]

For years, the university had been both a site and an object of struggle over the values and meaning of American society, and Harrison's hiring and the *Harambee* controversy were flash points. There were others. On February 17, KU professor of communications John Wright and law professor Lawrence Velvel spoke to a crowd of students on campus about the sentences handed down in the Chicago Seven trial. Shortly after the rally, KU students, faculty, and nonstudents marched from the campus to the Douglas County courthouse. Several protesters spraypainted red and blue fists on a courthouse wall and broke one window. Believing that Wright and Velvel had incited the vandalism, Shultz called for their dismissal from the university. The Kansas Board of Regents directed Chalmers to find out if Velvel's speech was inflammatory, although nothing came of the inquiry.[21]

The following month the Kansas Board of Regents denied the promotions of Velvel and professor of drama Fredric Litto. Velvel and Litto, both political leftists, were controversial. Velvel was an outspoken opponent of the war who, on behalf of five Congressmen, had brought a suit before the Supreme Court over the constitutionality of the war in Vietnam. Litto had incurred the wrath of Lawrencians in 1969 with his production of *Kaleidoscope of the American Dream,* which a KU drama group presented overseas. Critics called the play pornographic, vulgar, and blatantly un-American, claims that Litto denied. One person even suggested that the play was "contradictory to the wholesomeness that seems to be coming from" the new Nixon administration.[22]

The Regents' decision, led by Henry Bubb, a supporter of Ronald Reagan's 1968 presidential bid and the chair of Capitol Federal Savings, seemed to be politically inspired, particularly in light of Velvel's actions the previous month. For both supporters and opponents, the matter centered on free speech and academic freedom, issues that the board and many Lawrencians felt had been taken too far and were being used by radicals as dangerous subterfuges for inciting violence. Correspondence to Governor Docking overwhelmingly denounced the two men and their political activities. Velvel and Litto's supporters, most of whom were KU faculty and students, claimed they were being denied the promotion because of their politics, an act that they decried as an infringement of academic freedom. By the end of the month, the KU Council of Deans, faculty, students, and others, including an ad hoc group called "Concerned Members of the University Community," protested in support of the two men. KU students organized an April 8 strike to support Velvel and Litto. Over Bubb's protests, the board promoted Velvel and Litto in April.[23]

Against this backdrop came one of the darkest periods in the city's history. A flurry of bombings and arson occurred. Around midnight on the first of April, a homemade bomb exploded near the front door of Judge Charles C. Rankin. No one was injured. On April 5, an unexploded firebomb was found on campus near the east door of Strong Hall. Three days later another homemade bomb exploded at Anchor Savings, just north of the university. Four windows were broken, but no one was hurt. In all, some fifty bombs and acts of arson took place in April, May, and June.[24]

Lawrencians instinctively blamed students for the bombings. The violence and strike activity focused attention on the university and, in particular, its first-year chancellor, Larry Chalmers. Reynolds Shultz, with an eye to the fall gubernatorial race, sensed that student unrest provided a ready-made campaign issue and kept up his attack on the chancellor. Shultz believed that Chalmers had not "taken a firm stand" against student protests and was "'batting pretty near zero'" in how he governed the campus. Shultz's opinion of Chalmers surely did not improve when, on April 8, KU students peacefully picketed in support of Velvel and Litto and against the war at almost every building on campus. The marchers did not worry administrators as much as the several telephoned bomb threats and arson attempts on campus. The students' activity, however, greatly alarmed the general population in Lawrence.[25]

Those fears increased later that night when the radical activist Abbie Hoffman, the leader of the Youth International Party (Yippies), spoke to a crowd of some 7,000 curious onlookers in Allen Fieldhouse. Hoffman's appearance inflamed Lawrencians who feared his radical politics and rhetoric would incite students to riot.[26] That Hoffman's trip to Lawrence coincided with the general strike seemed like more than a coincidence to many Lawrencians. His arrival in Lawrence angered Kansans, who believed that their tax dollars supported his appearance, although the Minority Opinions Forum of the Student Union Activities (SUA), paid for his speech and was financed by student fees.[27] The moment gave exasperated Lawrencians, several who identified themselves as part of the Nixon administration's so-called "Silent Majority," an opportunity to bemoan their sense of alienation from American society and culture and what they believed was the failure of American politics.

A typical view came from Robert W. Doores, the owner of a printing business in Lawrence. "CBS aired hours of venomous drivel by Jerry Rubin and Abbie Hoffman all in the same week," Doores wrote to Senator James B. Pearson. "I call this irresponsible, un-American and not even sound judgement. I think the so-called 'silent Majority,' . . . who elected Richard Nixon, is about fed up with our elected representatives stand-in [sic] around while those advocates of violence, hard drugs, etc. have free access to the air ways."[28] A female critic saw Hoffman's appearance as symptomatic of a decline in American society during the 1960s, brought on by liberal social policies, civil rights legislation, and student and youth unrest. She noted that "[e]ach time one of these 'radicals' appear you can be sure violence of one form or another will follow. . . . The 'Silent Majority' has sat by while our elected leaders and law makers have taken prayers out of the public schools, bussed students all over town, let . . . some lay . . . around and draw welfare checks [rather] than work, . . . Schools are no longer safe . . . we are no longer free to travel the streets at night. Habitual criminals are repeatedly set free to go out and commit yet another crime."[29]

Hoffman's profane rhetoric, theatrics, and colorful stunts, such as blowing his nose in a handkerchief that resembled the American flag, angered both students and townsfolk. His performance also left the crowd of students, including many left-radicals, unimpressed. One KU student, calling his appearance "theatrical," expressed "disappointment" with his speech. Chalmers agreed, saying that Hoffman had "nothing to offer" Lawrence or the university. Left-wing radicals criticized him because he was not a "serious revolutionary" and had "no plan [for] after the revolution." When he finished, Hoffman received no applause from the audience and headed out of town, calling KU "a drag."[30]

By mid-April, however, Lawrence appeared headed for the revolution that Hoffman had advocated, and an armed confrontation seemed inevitable. Guns, explosives, and other weapons flowed freely, though surreptitiously, into the community. The street people and black radicals were stockpiling weapons. One local freak claimed that George Kimball, a radical and prominent member of the street community, was running guns into east Lawrence and selling them to African Americans. On April 12, John Spearman, Jr., the BSU's president, urged African Americans to arm themselves and declared that his group was "taking responsibility for insuring the safety of all blacks on the KU campus" because "numerous threats" had been made against him and members of the organization. Moreover, the BSU declared that it had "little confidence" in the Lawrence police force. *Harambee* said that Lawrence "pigs" were embarking on a witch-hunt, "using every tactic from A to Z to commit legal genocide on BSU members." The BSU, however, was not merely encouraging blacks to arm. In March, according to Kansas Bureau of Investigation (KBI) surveillance, Monty Beckwith, the editor of *Harambee*, purchased a .30 caliber pistol and placed a .30 caliber rifle on layaway, while Melvin Jackson, rumored to be a Chicago Black Panther, ordered two 30 caliber rifles.[31]

Although the thought of armed white radicals and hippies unsettled many in the community, nothing frightened white Lawrencians more than the specter of black men with guns. It is probable that threats made against the BSU and other campus groups came from local members of the Minutemen (founded by the virulent anticommunist Robert DePugh), the Ku Klux Klan, or armed militia from Lawrence's extreme Right. The radical Right was less public than the radical Left, and identifying members and activities is difficult. There is little doubt that vigilantes existed in Lawrence, both as groups and as individuals. Richard Beaty, a worker at Acme Dry Cleaning, once was a member of the Minutemen and friend to the Ku Klux Klan, although he later claimed to have renounced his racist views. In 1970, however, Beaty was carrying a gun, as were his friends and acquaintances.[32] Mostly, however, Beaty and the Minutemen "sat around and talked about what we would do 'if' [blacks or hippies got out of line] and stockpiled weapons." According to Beaty, the Minutemen numbered around 100 and bought their own weapons, but they also pooled their money to buy illegal automatic rifles, grenades, and explosives. Unlike the purchases made by the BSU and blacks, the Minutemen's weapons buildup was not accompanied by a public denouncement, nor does it appear that the police monitored their activities closely; some evidence suggests that several police officers were involved with the Minutemen. The Minutemen stored their weapons in a barn in an area south of Lawrence, where, Beaty claimed, they also took target practice. The Minutemen had no organizational structure. When "something would happen," he recalled, several "self-appointed" leaders called for a meeting, word of which was relayed to others and which twenty-five to fifty people attended. Meetings became more frequent during April and July 1970, when the town experienced acute racial problems. Beaty and his colleagues were aware that blacks and white radicals were also armed.[33]

With Lawrencians armed and tensions high, it seemed likely that violence would follow. The threat was never more likely than during a racial confrontation at Lawrence High School. On April 13, several black students at Lawrence High forced their way into Principal William Medley's office, demanding to speak with him. They gave him a list of demands, similar to those which black students had made during the 1968 walkout and almost verbatim to demands made by the KU-BSU to Chalmers in October and February. They included the addition of black history and literature courses, a black homecoming queen and black cheerleaders, and the hiring of ten new black teachers, not, as one student remarked, "those colored teachers we have now."[34]

Mike Spearman, one of the protesting students and the brother of the KU-BSU president, allegedly shoved Medley and told him they were taking over his office, while another student kicked in the outer door to the office. Medley claimed the demands were made in a "loud and boisterous manner" and that many "rude and sarcastic remarks" were made about him and his staff. He rejected the demands outright and ordered the students back to class. They ignored him. Some milled around his office while others pounded on classroom doors with bricks, rocks, and clubs. Teachers locked their doors to keep the black students out; several claimed that the black students threatened white students. The black students told Medley that he had better come up with "some answers" to their demands before John Spearman, Jr., Leonard Harrison, and others arrived. John Spearman, Jr., did arrive, as did his father, school board member John Spearman, Sr. Someone called the police, who arrested, among others, John Spearman, Jr., Rick

Dowdell, and Danny Mumford, all KU-BSU members. John Spearman, Sr., convinced the students to meet in the cafeteria, where he talked with them until 3:00 P.M. Medley immediately suspended the black students.[35]

Two days later, the racial situation at Lawrence High remained tense, and Medley feared further confrontations. Police patrols allowed only students not under suspension into the school building. On April 15, black students gathered across the street from the school in Veteran's Park while, at the same time, white students amassed in the cafeteria parking lot. Small groups of blacks broke out classroom windows and fights erupted between blacks and whites that resulted in several minor injuries and one serious injury. Medley blamed the disturbance on "outsiders," by which he meant the KU-BSU and Harrison.[36]

During the week-long high school crisis, Richard Beaty recalled that the Minutemen, including several police officers, learned through the "underground" that blacks were planning to "take" the high school. In response, Beaty, allegedly armed with a submachine gun, and some fifty other "well-armed" colleagues presented a public "show of force" at the school, although it is not clear when this might have happened. Beaty and his comrades felt that "there comes a time when the only way to stop violence is with violence."[37] Whether Beaty's claims were true is not clear, but they seem probable.

The high school was closed the following day, and, on April 20, an estimated 1,500 people attended a special school board meeting to consider the students' demands and the school's race relations. Black students and their parents, many who were members of the Lawrence Concerned Black Parents, walked out of the meeting when the board did not reinstate the students or take any action on their demands. After the meeting, the administration building adjacent to the high school was firebombed. Lawrence police warned Medley and Superintendent Carl Knox that their homes also were likely targets of firebombs. Medley asked the board of education to provide protection for his family and property at night, and both Knox and Medley took their families to motels.[38]

Although many Lawrencians, including twenty-three Lawrence clergy, urged amnesty for the suspended black students, the school board rejected the plea. Its position had broad support throughout the community. A Lawrence teacher claimed he had never seen "such near-complete support" for the administration as he saw among the local business owners. One resident called the pleas for amnesty "pure nonsense" and called the board's decision "the only one which makes sense in a society which says it wants law and order." She added, "[m]ind you, this isn't a black vs. white issue with me." Robert D. Ramsey, a former administrator in the Lawrence schools, was "concern[ed]" about the racial violence and asked Knox if "our old nemesis, Leonard Harrison, [was] behind the current unrest[.]" A survey of white high school students suggested that they did not think the school system was racist, and if it was, one student commented, "the niggers made it that way."[39]

To make matters worse, late on April 20 a multimillion dollar arson gutted the Student Memorial Union at the University of Kansas. The FBI and the KBI believed the arsonists were a group of young black men, seen leaving the Union shortly before the fire was discovered, but they were never identified. Minuteman Richard Beaty did not rule out the possibility that a right-wing white radical, intent on stirring up more trouble, had started the fire. Some Lawrencians believed that white radicals or some hippies set the fire, a direct consequence of Abbie Hoffman's appearance earlier in the month. The arson, however, was never solved. On April 21, Governor Robert B. Docking, at the request of city officials, placed the city under a dusk-to-dawn curfew that was extended for two additional nights. No one was allowed on the streets without a pass between 7:00 P.M. to 6:00 A.M., alcohol sales were limited, and the sale and transportation of flammable liquids, firearms, and explosives were prohibited. Arson, firebombings, and sniper fire continued during the curfew period, however, including another fire at Lawrence High School.[40]

On the morning of April 21, racial violence again erupted at Lawrence High. About 150 black high school and junior high students, parents, and other supporters, many carrying clubs and baseball bats, again assembled in Veteran's Park. They crossed the street, passed by police officers, and broke school windows. Helmeted Lawrence police formed a line in front of the administration building (adjacent to the high school), used teargas to disperse the demonstrators, and made several arrests. Black students who did not participate in the walkout were caught in the middle of the fray, threatened by both white students and the protesting black students. *Harambee* proclaimed the high school disturbance as "THE WEEK THAT WAS."[41]

A resolution of sorts was reached in late April when black and white student representatives, after earlier rejecting a plan that would allow the high school's BSU to choose two of the five varsity cheerleaders, accepted an alternative plan that increased the number of cheerleaders to eight instead of the traditional five, with two members selected from minority groups. But a week later, a cross section of black leaders, including Leonard Harrison, John Spearman, Sr., and Vernell Sturns, all agreed that little progress had been made on the students' demands, despite Knox's and other administrators belief that things were getting better. Harrison commented, "I'd say at this point that the issues are not resolved. I don't know, in fact, what the consequences might be." He added a prescient warning: "[W]hen you create a situation like this and don't resolve it immediately, you may not get more disruptions today or tomorrow or next week. But the next time there is a confrontation, it'll probably be worse."[42]

Although the crisis at the high school had not been resolved to blacks' satisfaction, in the aftermath of the Union fire the community's focus shifted to the KU campus, only a few blocks away. The arson and the curfew were psychologically devastating.. Chalmers, who had been in Washington, D.C. when the fire broke out, quickly returned to Lawrence to assuage fears that a student revolution was imminent. Chalmers did not believe the arson was the work of students, and he pointed out that many students had helped the fire department by providing them with water and sandwiches and removing furniture and artwork from the Union. Chalmers claimed the media, including the national networks, *Time,* and *Newsweek,* misrepresented the arson, portraying it as the work of student revolutionaries and depicting KU students as radicals trying to shut down the university. The greater problem confronting the community, Chalmers believed, was the influx a few days later of radicals, or "gypsies," as he called them, from both coasts, enticed to Lawrence by the promise of an impending revolution and media coverage of the fire. His assertions were shared by much of the community and supported by intelligence gathered by law enforcement agencies. The KBI, the Lawrence Police Department, and the Douglas County sheriff all believed that the firebombings and arson were the work of nonstudents. The KBI claimed that during the crisis "Militant Weatherman and Black Panthers" were in Lawrence "to join in the disturbances," and that three-fourths of those arrested during the curfew were "testing" the police and National Guard.[43]

To Lawrencians, the high school disturbance, bomb threats, the Union fire, and the curfew, were all logical consequences of what they perceived as Chalmers's, and the entire nation's, liberal toleration of student radicalism and left-wing extremism. Permissive liberal social policies, they argued, designed to help only racial minorities at the expense of the white Silent Majority, and an unwillingness to preserve law and order, had created chaos in Lawrence and threatened to undermine legitimate authority. "This is America? This is Kansas? This is Lawrence?" Lee Scott plaintively asked. The owner of Carol Lee Products in Lawrence, Scott had spent the first night of the curfew guarding his business with a fire extinguisher and shotgun. Like other Lawrence residents, Scott was "getting tired, Damned Tired!" of "lawlessness and the destruction of . . . property," which was not "an answer to our Civil Rights problem. *Law and Order must be respected and returned. . . . I am tired.*" Bernard K. Freeman, the owner of Rogers Electric Co., who also spent the night in his business, claimed that he fired his shotgun and .38-caliber pistol at vandals who tried to set his business on fire. He pointed to multiple bullet holes in the wall behind his counter as evidence.[44]

The police held "outsiders" responsible for the violence. Lawrence police supervisor Charles Greer, who described Lawrence as "a safe haven" between the "real radicals" on the east and west coasts, believed that "hippies" and radicals stopped in Lawrence and stayed in "crash houses" in the community. But as Lee Scott noted above, in linking "lawlessness" with the nation's civil rights "problem," race was at the heart of Lawrence's problems, and race was an indigenous problem. Although locals perpetuated much of the actual violence, police lieutenant Verner Newman believed they were inspired and led by "outsiders." Newman, who was African American, felt that local blacks were only doing what some white student agitators goaded them to do.[45] Most Lawrencians, even Verner Newman, who had firsthand experience of racism in his hometown, refused to acknowledge the local roots of racial conflict in their community, instead preferring to put the blame on outsiders, left-radicals, and agents provocateurs.

Moreover, it seems clear that the student radicals and street people had a distinct Kansas flavor. While there were non-Kansans among the street people, native Kansans and Lawrencians were significantly represented. It was easier for Lawrencians to believe that other communities' children, and not their own, rejected middle-class, white America and sought to change or destroy it. This was evident during the April curfew, as the street people staked a claim to Oread and resisted encroachments and intrusions from police and the university into what they believed was their turf. For years, the university, through its Endowment Association, had been buying up the property surrounding the campus, especially along Oread Avenue, where many radicals and hippies lived. During the curfew the street people in Oread offered serious resistance to city and university officials, and turned the entire neighborhood into a site of political and cultural struggle. Defying the police and other symbols of authority, living communally and behaving unconventionally became political acts. The experience radicalized many young people and seemed to unify the area's residents. The *Vortex* called the White House, a commune on Oread between the Gaslight Tavern and the Rock Chalk Café, a "symbol of a unified and growing political consciousness" among the street people. "What started as a group of freaks living together and sharing together," the paper reported during the April curfew, "turned into the first site of battle and open rebellion in Lawrence by the white people."[46]

Gerry Riley, a KU student who lived in Oread, was in the middle of the confusion there in April. He helped to remove art and furniture from the Union during the fire. A few days later, during the curfew, the Department of Public Safety (DPS) arrested him and two black men, allegedly for carrying a Molotov cocktail. The three men soon became the prime suspects in the Union arson. Riley asserted he was set up, and after a lengthy and expensive legal battle he was exonerated.[47] Riley believed that the police assumed that he must have been the ringleader because he was white. Riley claimed that police and the DPS "excessively manhandled" him, including hitting him with a rifle butt. At the jail, Riley recalled that it was "[s]ort of a party atmosphere . . . because it was all full of people."[48]

At his arraignment, Riley remembered that there was a "whole gallery of people—a lot of them I knew, a lot of them I didn't know—street folks—doing all this incredible, 'Right on,' and 'Hang in there, man,' and 'Power to the people' stuff. And I thought, 'Oh lordy, you know, just what I need.' Kind of a scene at the courtroom." Riley got "an extraordinarily high bond" from Judge Charles C. Rankin, whose home had been damaged by an explosion a few weeks earlier. Even some of his friends in the Oread area believed that Riley had set the fire, and he became something of a folk hero, which he found "real disgusting. I mean, I got . . . lots of attention, lots of free goodies, psychoactive substances, lots of kind adulation, lots of sexual attention . . . all for something that . . . I hadn't done." Riley and his wife received threatening telephone calls from "some right-wing groups" who apparently believed that he was the Union arsonist.[49]

Riley accused the police, the DPS, and the Kansas National Guard of knocking down doors and getting "rough with a some people" during the curfew. Additionally, he claimed that the police stole personal property, which further angered Oread residents. Riley thought that officials simply "panicked" when they declared a state of emergency after the arson. The prevailing assumption in the community was that it was SDS, the antiwar movement, or some radical student group that set the blaze, which Riley thought was ridiculous. Most students, he believed, saw the campus as their home. Moreover, Riley felt that before and during the curfew Lawrence police focused too much of their attention on the Oread area, which then became a "war zone." With plenty of drugs being used, something "between hysteria and euphoria" engulfed the area. Many students, Riley said, simply wanted to get out and enjoy the spring weather, while others saw the engagement with the police and the National Guard as a kind of game.[50]

To a few leftists in Lawrence, however, it was more than a game; it was a guerilla struggle between them and the police over control of their own space. A mimeographed flier distributed by an unidentified left-radical group claimed that "[l]ast week in Lawrence our streets were . . . occupied and our brothers are jailed." The *Vortex* asked its readers in late April or early May, "Are we demonstrators or revolutionaries? . . . We should take a lesson from the first American Revolution: when [the] people met the troops head on they got vamped on, but when they took to the woods and sniped at 'em they wiped those cocksuckers out!" The paper added, "a Molotov Cocktail under a pig car will usually do the trick, and if they're on foot an M-80 dipped in hot wax and rolled in B. B.'s can really do some paralyzing. And if you've got some guns, they should be employed." How large a group in Lawrence adhered to armed revolution is uncertain, and it is not clear how much credibility can be put in the bombastic rhetoric of the *Vortex*. Regardless, many people in Lawrence—on both the Left and the Right—sincerely believed that an armed revolution was underway across the country, and that Lawrence was one of the front lines. "The pigs intend to wipe us off the planet," the *Vortex* concluded, "[w]e're battling for survival, and the only way to off armed pigs is through armed struggle."[51]

Riley felt that some of the "real serious" revolutionaries, whom he called "the real Chairman Mao Red Book types," were "kind of a joke." He recalled that one of the leaders of this group was living on six or seven hundred dollars a month from his parents. There also was a less serious group, who were the "street guerilla theater fun folks"; he included himself among this group and noted that friction developed between the two.[52]

The Lawrence police were on the front lines of the struggle and were seen as the enemy by black militants and leftist radicals. Their jobs were difficult, to say the least, during the April crisis. "Have you ever had a sack of shit thrown in your face?" asked Charles Greer, a LPD supervisor. " Did you ever have a baseball bat with 16 penny nails [sticking through it] . . . flying at your head[?]"[53]In April, the street people in Oread threw frisbees at and taunted police officers (whose nerves already were on a hair-trigger) and National Guardsmen patrolling the area. Former mayor Dick Raney and Verner Newman claimed that some radicals set booby-traps by stringing piano wire at leg and neck height in darkened alleys, and then setting small fires to attract police and fire fighters.[54]

From April 8 to 23, Greer had only one day off out of sixteen, logging eighty-three hours of overtime. On April 18, he worked seventeen hours; April 19, twenty; April 20, fifteen; on April 21 and 22, the first two nights of the curfew, he worked back-to-back twenty-four-hour shifts, which he remembered as typical of other members of the force. To Greer, the town seemed in a constant state of tension. He said that he and the other police walked the streets "hoping nobody's going to shoot you," and on several occasions police cars had their windows shot out. "To be quite honest," Greer declared, "people are lucky in this town that the police didn't shoot a whole bunch of people."[55]

Verner Newman, who as the identification officer was responsible for the fingerprinting and processing of those arrested, also worked twenty-hour shifts during the curfews. He recalled that on the way to his home (not far from Oread) he would drive down Tennessee Street, where people shot at him from the darkened windows. Newman sent his family away during the crisis, put mattresses around the bedroom windows, and kept his pistol, rifle, and shotgun at hand.[56]

Dozens of arrests were made during the crisis, mostly for curfew violations, but some, like Gerry Riley, were arrested for possession of incendiary devices. Leftists and civil libertarians established a Legal Self-Defense Fund to help protect the civil liberties of those arrested. KU students Joan Irvine and Candy Reeves confirmed Riley's allegations of police assault. They claimed that several people were dragged out of their houses and arrested because of their political beliefs or because they were in the wrong place and the wrong time.[57]

The curfew pleased few in the community, and most people, especially business owners, were eager for a return to normalcy. The third night of the emergency, April 23, the curfew was delayed until 9:00 P.M. City officials reported that the curfew was being "phased out," but most likely it was pushed back so that the downtown merchants could stay open on their traditional Thursday late-sales night.[58] The curfew was lifted after the third night, and it seemed as if the crisis had passed.

Amid the violence and racial strife of April, protests by pacifists and students against the Vietnam War continued. There had been a town meeting on April 13 moderated by the Lawrence Committee for Peace.[59] On April 15, the National Anti-War Day was marked in Lawrence by a peaceful march across campus. Student radicals continued to protest the war and began planning for a general strike early in May. On April 30, President Richard M. Nixon praised American military men and denounced "these bums blowing up the campuses," which many in Lawrence took personally. That same day, U.S. military forces invaded Cambodia in an effort to attack the Viet Cong's supply lines, which touched off a heated round of antiwar protests on the nation's college campuses, including Kent State University in Ohio. Around noon on May 4, while forty students from the KU Committee for Alternatives (KUCA) were organizing a "Day of Alternatives" to discuss the war, National Guardsmen in Kent shot and killed four KSU students. Ten days later, police in Jackson, Mississippi killed two black students at Jackson State University, which garnered fewer headlines and less attention than the Kent State shootings. The tragedies set off even more protests across the nation, including several in Lawrence.[60]

While racial and cultural issues precipitated the April crisis, the May crisis was primarily about Vietnam. The murder of four students, not by revolutionaries or left-radicals but by the state, gave the struggle to end the war a greater sense of urgency for peace activists; for Left revolutionaries it further justified the righteousness of their cause against Amerika. The solid core of Lawrence's antiwar and peace movements rallied to mobilize additional support for ending the war. Peace activist Anne Moore, for example, went to Washington, where she got a view on the war from each member of Kansas's congressional delegation. Chalmers reiterated his opposition to the war but called for peaceful protest. KU history professor David Katzman's call for a general strike and his condemnation of violence as a means of protest received cheers from more than 1,500 students gathered in Hoch Auditorium. Additionally, Katzman, along with colleagues Walter H. Crockett, Bruce Molholt, and Norman R. Yetman, organized a Peace Commencement Fund to divert antiwar sentiment into political action. A civil disobedience workshop was held at KU that focused on tax resistance by encouraging people to withhold their federal excise tax from their telephone bill. An organizational meeting to collect blood for Vietnamese civilians was called for May 14, 1970. *The Coalition,* an alternative student paper which had backed the April strike supporting Velvel and Litto, also encouraged people to bottle up the operations of local draft boards by mailing worthless material to tie up office staff and space. It also suggested that women write a letter refusing to register and sign it with only an initial and a last name. "The boards will go crazy trying to catch the 'draft resisters.'"[61]

The timing of the Cambodian invasion, coming on the heels of the Union fire and the high school disturbance, was, as Chalmers put it, especially "lousy" for Lawrence. Like other communities across the nation, Lawrence and KU bore its share of the fallout from the Kent State and Jackson State tragedies. Chalmers was besieged by horrified and angry students and a disgruntled citizenry. The pressing issue on campus was whether the university would remain open for the last three weeks of the semester. Onetime Chalmers supporter Governor Robert B. Docking averred that he would "not tolerate the closing of any campus institution." The Board of Regents issued a statement declaring that the "University would remain open," and that there were "no options for faculty." Chalmers believed that Docking's statement only served to inflame moderate students, resentful of anyone interfering with the university or attempting to tell them what to do.[62]

The more radical factions, such as the KU-SDS and the BSU, supported an unequivocal shutdown of the school. The KUCA preferred instead that classes be dismissed "to allow teach-ins and discussion of events in Southeast Asia." Initially, Chalmers told students that the university would make no "plans for formal dismissal" of classes, but students and faculty could attend teach-ins or other discussions about the war, if their work was made up.[63] Neither moderates nor radicals accepted this proposal.

The situation on campus deteriorated in the days after the Cambodian invasion. On May 7, at least two hundred youths attacked the military science building with rocks, breaking out windows. The Kansas Highway Patrol sent additional troopers to relieve weary Lawrence police. The Kansas National Guard stationed watchmen in most of its armories, including the one in Lawrence, only a few blocks from the southwest edge of campus, for fear of attacks. One hundred students sat down and blocked Highway 59, a major north-south artery through Lawrence that runs along the west edge of campus, before police in riot gear dispersed them. Approximately

500 demonstrators gathered in front of Strong Hall to protest the Cambodia invasion and the Kent State tragedy, and demanded that the campus be shut down. Demonstrators again pelted the military science building with rocks.[64]

In many respects, the crisis of April and May was as much a fight over ownership of the university, and thus a fight over American values, as over the war or racial issues. The university meant different things to different people. To Kansas taxpayers, who believed their money made the university possible, the problems on campus were symptomatic of the permissiveness and decline of authority in the United States, which they thought were responsible for creating the crisis. They argued that the free exchange of ideas, the essence of the liberal university, meant little if law and order were not preserved. In contrast, *The Coalition* claimed that the "University belongs to the People, not to Phillips Oil or Capital Federal Savings and Loan [of which Regent Henry Bubb was Chair], or to the Kansas Legislature. YOU are the people. KANSAS UNIVERSITY BELONGS TO YOU."[65]

University officials huddled to conceive of a plan that would keep the university open and appease outside critics but that would allow for discussion of the war and other social problems, and to which campus radicals would agree. They canceled the Tri-Service Review of ROTC (formerly the Chancellor's Review) scheduled for later in the week. Given the political climate on campus and the military connection with the Kent State student's deaths, and despite the fact that the cadets' right of free expression was circumvented, it was an appropriate decision. Chalmers's willingness to sacrifice the cadets' ceremony to prevent an almost certain confrontation suggests that he was willing to exchange the free exchange of ideas, which he had long championed, for security. The decision was criticized unreservedly. Faculty and students lamented the cancellation, and some 322 of them signed a petition to give the cadets "whatever protection necessary" to hold the review. A few weeks later, KU faculty proposed a policy to prevent any future ROTC review cancellations. (Adding insult to injury, the names of the ROTC commandants were left off of the university-wide commencement program.) Docking promised not to interfere in university operations but was publicly displeased with the decision.[66]

The question of closing the university, however, remained unresolved. The Senate Executive Committee (SenEx), empowered to act for faculty and students in emergencies, suggested students have a number of options: finishing their classes as usual; take credit/no credit for work already done; take an Incomplete; or skip classes to participate in alternative work—teach-ins or discussions about the war, for example—and take the grade they had earned thus far in the course. Although the SenEx proposal needed no further input than Chalmers's approval, he called a convocation for May 8 in

Memorial Stadium to, in his words, "put . . . the University back together." An estimated fourteen to fifteen thousand filled the stadium amid tight security and fears of further confrontation. Chalmers presented the already-approved proposal, asked those assembled to vote, and declared the proposal passed by acclamation. The BSU, SDS, and left-radicals demanded to speak, but Chalmers, who clearly controlled the event, refused. There was no discussion of the proposal and he gave a signal to shut off the microphone if any group or people tried to take the stage.[67]

According to a student news release, by May 16 less than 20 percent of the students had left campus. During finals week, there were over 100 workshops on topics, including antiwar protests, the do's and don'ts of civil disobedience, what to do if you are arrested, women's liberation, off-campus housing problems, and white racism. A schedule of "Free School Activities" or "Free University Workshops" listed topics similar to those above but also men's liberation, "Malcolm X and the *Harambee*" (with Monty Beckwith of the BSU), "Urban Guerilla Warfare," a "Crash Course on Draft Counseling," and an "Open Forum" with Dolph Simons, Jr., of the *Journal-World*.[68]

Not all students and faculty supported the day of alternatives. The KU Coordinating Committee argued that the "alternatives" did not give faculty the option of going on strike and using their class time to discuss peace activities and the war. Chalmers declared the convocation a "success" and basked in what he called the "overwhelming response of students and faculty" to keep the university open. Vice-chancellor Francis Heller remarked wryly,"[a]ny observer of the campus scene would be justified in concluding that, while K.U. had not closed, it certainly had not continued normal operations." Like Heller, state politicians and local media also questioned Chalmers's definition of "open." Governor Docking noted that there was "'great, great agitation'" to fire Chalmers and offered the chancellor only grudging support, remarking "[w]ell, I haven't started a movement against him."[69] Chalmers and his supporters affirmed that the alternatives given to students met a "variety of needs," the greatest of which was avoiding further violence. If that was his goal, then Chalmers's plan was successful. The campus escaped serious violence; there were no deaths, only minor injuries, and, apart from the Union arson, minimal property damage.

Whether this was due to Chalmers's actions is unclear, but his supporters gave him the credit. Petitions signed by approximately 8,000 KU students claimed that the chancellor had prevented the "University of Kansas from becoming another Berkeley." One hundred seventy faculty members praised him for his "positive, open-minded and conciliatory response to student-faculty demands." Chalmers also drew accolades from several newspaper editors around the state, with most of the comments applauding him for preventing violence. The remarks of Raymond A. Schwegler, director of the

Watkins Health Clinic at KU, were typical. He lauded Chalmers for demonstrating "courage few possess" by standing in front of such a large crowd, which contained what Schwegler described as perhaps "three or four hundred mentally disturbed persons."[70]

In contrast to his support from the university community, Chalmers received unbridled criticism from townspeople, alumni, and politicians for his handling of the situation in May, and, more generally, for his handling of student unrest since he had arrived in Lawrence the previous year; several critics even blamed Chalmers directly for the Union arson. N. Tom Veatch, a KU alumnus and partner in the engineering firm of Black and Veatch in Kansas City, asked rhetorically, "What can [Chalmers] expect after allowing a man like Hoffman to come to the campus? . . . [Hoffman] advocated violence and burning the campus and both have resulted." Other critics condemned student organizations like SDS—which they believed was a "communist front"—and censured Chalmers for allowing it to remain on campus. Another typical response came from a "disgusted taxpayer," Robert L. Elder, the owner of Western Home Builders, Inc., who was fed up with student demonstrations and Chalmers's handling of them. "If the students are going to run the schools why pay the salary to staff members?" Elder was upset that the ROTC review was canceled for "a small minority." Chalmers was not "qualified for the job," Elder declared, and he wondered "[w]hy are the dirty hippies allowed on campus as agitators when they are not registered students. I couldn't get away with tearing down or burning public property."[71]

Regent Henry Bubb also denounced Chalmers. Like California governor Ronald Reagan, whom he supported in the 1968 presidential campaign, Bubb took a hard line on campus disturbances. Bubb declared that there could not be academic freedom "without academic safety." He, like Reynolds Schultz, believed student demonstrations at KU were "a tool of communist organization[s]" and that Chalmers did not have the ability to "control events in Lawrence." Bubb had been opposed to Chalmers from the very start, primarily due to their divergent political views. Largely at Bubb's insistence, in the summer of 1970 the board unanimously passed a resolution directing state university administrators to "suspend all employees, faculty, or students engaged in disruptive activity."[72]

The Day of Alternatives did not, of course, resolve the divide in the community over the proper role of the university or the Vietnam War. The United States' invasion of Cambodia coalesced several streams of thought and activism on campus. It appears that students, if not a majority then at least a significant minority, used the occasion to express their discontent with the Vietnam War, racism, poverty, American imperialism, and other problems facing the country. Their responses were not all radical, although certainly some were. Many used education and discussion, in the Free University Workshops, for example, as a potential springboard into further social activism on campus and in the community. A special *Vortex* street edition called for radical students to support and reach out to other students, especially the "moderates" who were born into "whitemiddleclass" society and were unaware of their own oppression.[73]

Although Vietnam and the Kent State and Jackson State shootings were the focus of activity on campus during the first part of May, race remained the salient issue throughout the community. A few days after the Kent State shootings and the memorials and vigils to honor the dead students, nine black children in Augusta, Georgia, were killed in an explosion set by a white racist. The BSU organized a vigil in honor of the children, but very few people showed for the memorial, and almost no whites. Although the BSU had joined with whites for the Kent State memorial, more white students chose to attend a rock concert on campus instead of the vigil. Blacks charged whites with "apathy" and called them "unconcerned" about the plight of black people.[74]

On May 10, a dozen African American men disrupted Sunday services at the First United Methodist Church and demanded $75,000 for Lawrence's black residents. Bryce Rivers, the chair of the Coordinating Committee of the Black Community (CCBC), presented the demand, citing the "role of the church" in "the exploitation of Black People." The CCBC declared, "a little over $25 per nigger is not too much to attempt to amend the wrongs you committed against us for so long." A few days later, First United rejected the demand but appointed a six-person committee to explore ways to resolve some of the problems facing minorities in Lawrence. After the church turned down the reparation demand, the CCBC declared that the "members of First United Methodist Church 'do not want to pay their debt to the Black People.'"[75]

While the negotiations were going on for the Day of Alternatives, outgoing BSU president John Spearman, Jr., talked to around 500 students at a rally on campus that was called because the university would not provide funds and space for the BSU to publish *Harambee*. Spearman told BSU members, amid police surveillance, to develop new strategies and tactics to transform the university, which he called part of the "white racist structure." He also addressed the white students, expounding on the goals of BSU. Black Power, he told them, was the way to "meet the needs of blacks" and for blacks to have "power over the education, the politics, and economics of black people." Spearman allegedly claimed that "[w]e can no longer negotiate for our freedom and liberty; we can take it."[76]

As Spearman and the BSU tried to unite and take control of the black community from whites, white Lawrencians retrenched to defend themselves against what they believed was a threat to their own identity and the town's traditional racial boundaries. As Richard Beaty, the erstwhile Minuteman and KKK ally, recounted, "our [white] rights were being taken from us. We couldn't go to our place[s] of business" and "the streets weren't free anymore . . . it wasn't the same free streets as it'd always been." Beaty explained the "rights" philosophy that guided him and his colleagues. "[Y]ou have a right to do anything you want to do as long as it don't interfere with my rights . . . to do what I want to do," he declared. And "I should not do anything that interferes with your rights."[77] Beaty and his comrades blamed their perceived loss of "rights" and space on blacks and students.

Beaty compared Lawrence's troubles to other urban areas. During the 1964 Watts riot, Beaty was living in Los Angeles and he felt that African Americans there and in Lawrence "really had it pretty well made." He blamed the imposition of curfews in Watts and Lawrence on blacks, who were "stepping on his rights." A self-described "warmongler [sic]," Beaty claimed that when blacks and white radicals in Lawrence "were bombing Anchor Savings, when they was [sic] burning the Union, when they were burning businesses[,] . . . I see that as costing me, as threatening my way of life." Civil rights and Black Power activism was especially galling to Beaty. Moreover, as he professed his whiteness and defined the boundaries of that identity, Beaty also claimed the identity of "American" for himself and other whites. Rejecting black culturalism and race and ethnicity as the primary marker of identity, Beaty declared that blacks were "no longer servants, [or] slaves," just as he was "not a German or an Irish. I'm just an American."[78]

Blacks were Americans, in Beaty's mind, as long as they accepted the status quo in Lawrence and did not demand more from the system. What most angered Beaty, however, was the race traitor, the "white activist" who was "pushing to get things going under the guise of helping the blacks." Beaty did not care what blacks did as long as they did not infringe on his "rights," or threaten his family or property. The curfew threatened his "right" to go wherever he wanted, which infuriated him. Had the curfew lasted longer or had things not quieted down, Beaty believed the Minutemen would have taken some action. As it was, they only talked about "what [they] were . . . going to do about it and who [they] were . . . going to string up." He thought the biggest reason that the Minutemen did not take any action was because several members were afraid of "being exposed."[79]

Beaty's narrative is a racist and extreme view, but more moderate Lawrencians expressed similar thoughts over their perceived loss of rights and public space. Ronald Peters, a worker at Hallmark Cards, had declared in June 1969 that it "has become apparent that the colleges and universities of this country are gradually losing control over students that . . . is rightfully theirs." Peters had "felt secure that it would never happen in Kansas," but since it had, the chancellor and regents had to act at once to stop the "further growth" of "this subversive action." Like others in Lawrence, Peters believed the "time has come that the majority be heard . . . instead of such a small minority."[80]

In May 1970, Nancy Sampson, a secretary at Hercules, Inc., declared that the "time has come for the silent majority to speak up." "I have to work eight hours a day," she wrote, "and do not have time to demonstrate, picket and cause utter chaos to voice my views." Lawrence's recent problems had been frequent topics in her home, and her family believed that "the time is past due for action on the part of law enforcement, National Guard and school officials." Sampson's family felt that students who did not wish "to live with the regulations" of the university should be expelled. She wondered if the regents would "wait until the whole University is burned and destroyed before action is taken[.]"[81] Similarly, Pauline V. Hunn, who also worked at Hercules, identified herself as one of the "Silent Majority, silent because I had faith in people, silent because we had laws and administrators who with their education combined with our American Heritage could make but one decision, silent because never did I believe violence would be condoned as 'kids doing their thing.'" Hunn had discussed these issues with at least 200 people, and she had "yet to find one citizen who approves of the administration or the Chancellor at KU."[82]

The "Silent Majority" did not emerge solely in response to urban unrest, increased crime rates, campus disturbances, or antiwar demonstrations. Moreover, it was not silent. Since at least the beginning of the decade the people who claimed to be part of it had been complaining to politicians and newspaper editors about the growth of the welfare state, high taxes, declining national morals, and "special rights" given to racial or ethnic minorities. Antiwar protests and campus disturbances merely gave them a pubic target at which to direct their anger.

Despite some grumbling that radicals were using the commencement exercises to protest the war, the traditional walk down Mount Oread during the graduation ceremony seemed to mark an easing of tensions in the community. Chalmers admitted that "mistakes" had been made in the use of university "systems and property" during the alternative finals period. Despite threats from politicians, parents, and alumni that enrollments and university funding were in peril, a record number of students signed up for summer classes at KU, and, in the fall, enrollments reached record levels again. Part of this could be attributed to Chalmers's efforts to bind up the university's wounds. At the urging of John Conard, who had recently been named director of university relations, and Dick Wintermote, director of the KU Alumni Association, Chalmers spent the summer touring the state trying to restore the university's image, reassuring alumni of the university's commitment to academic freedom and order on campus, and keeping financial contributions flowing into the endowment. He assured KU alumni that students would not get time off for political causes in the fall.[83]

The university was not only a site of struggle, it became the object of a struggle to define the values and meanings of citizenship and what it meant to be an American. Moreover, that struggle spilled into the streets of Lawrence as the community tried to come to terms with a community in flux. After graduation, Lawrencians optimistically hoped that the worst was behind them and that the town could begin to heal its wounds. The relative quiet in June fed those expectations; it all came unraveled in mid-July.

CHAPTER 8

"THIS TOWN WILL BLOW AWAY"

The crisis in Lawrence in April and May of 1970 had been brought on by a combination of events: the Union fire, racial conflict, the radicalization of both the Left and Right, and stronger antiwar sentiment, as well as the growing dissatisfaction of the so-called "Silent Majority." City and campus officials were optimistic that the end of the semester would result in a cooling-off period and ease strained relations throughout the town. Those expectations evaporated during a two-week spree of violence in July that brought Lawrence to the brink of full-blown riot. More than a decade of racial conflict, cultural ferment, and wrenching demographic changes culminated in the shooting deaths of two teens by police, leaving in its wake a bewildered and confused community.

Although Lawrence seemed less volatile in June and the first half of July than in April and May, tensions continued to simmer and threatened to boil over at any time. White residents reported several assaults by African American juveniles to police, while a member of the Coordinating Committee of the Black Community (CCBC) told police he had been assaulted by four white men, although he refused to sign a complaint. Rumors continued to circulate, adding to the fears of many. One Lawrencian reportedly overheard a "group of 'hippies'" discussing how they could attack and burn the city with toy airplanes. There were real threats, too. On July 14, the driver of a propane delivery truck discovered twenty-three sticks of dynamite attached to the rear of his loaded vehicle, an ominous sign.[1]

The relative calm came unraveled on the night of July 16.[2] Late in the evening, an unidentified black man sitting on the porch of Afro-House, a black cultural center established earlier in the summer by the Black Student Union (BSU), was wounded by buckshot, while a few houses away a white woman was shot in the leg. When Lawrence police officers Lloyd Jones and Kennard Avey responded to the shootings around 10:15 P.M., snipers fired at them, shattering their car windows. Officer William Garrett and his partner Gale Pinegar responded to Jones's call for backup. Believing Afro-House to be the probable source of the gunfire, they turned their attention there. Garrett and Avey reportedly saw a Volkswagen, driven by Franki Cole, a KU student, park in front and two or three people go into the two-story house. BSU member Gary Jackson, Cole's boyfriend and a recently hired assistant to the Dean of Men at KU, told her "it wasn't a good time to visit" because he believed vigilantes were attacking Afro-House. As she was leaving, Rick Dowdell asked Cole for a ride to the KU campus to see a friend. He never reached Mount Oread.[3]

Rick "Tiger" Dowdell was a tall, lanky nineteen-year-old and a native of Lawrence. A good basketball player with artistic promise, Dowdell had participated in the 1968 walkout by black students at LHS. After graduation, he joined the BSU at KU and later became close to Leonard Harrison. Like many other African Americans in Lawrence, Dowdell had had many altercations with the local police. In August 1967, before the Lawrence Human Relations Commission, he complained of police harassment. Dick Raney remarked that after Dowdell worked for him and went to college, "something happened to him." He and his brothers were suspected of committing several crimes, and the police kept a close watch on him. Dowdell had been arrested or stopped by police at least ten times since February 1969, when he was a senior at Lawrence High. The previous night, Officer Garrett had stopped him for a broken taillight. Rick's brother claimed that Garrett had threatened the family, vowing that he would "get one of you Dowdells yet." The officer denied the allegation.[4]

When Cole and Dowdell left Afro-House for Mount Oread, Garrett, joined by Avey, followed. Cole recalled that the police car did not have its headlights, siren, or flashing lights turned on. According to the police report, they were turned on when Cole violated several traffic laws and drove recklessly. Given the level of mistrust between Lawrence police and local blacks, and considering in particular Rick Dowdell's experiences, the threats made by white vigilantes, and that night's gunfire in east Lawrence, it is not surprising that Cole did not heed the officer's signals to stop.

After a short chase, Cole headed east on Ninth Street, trying to get back to the safety of Afro-House on Rhode Island Street. As she turned sharply down the alley between Rhode Island and New Hampshire, the car struck a curb and stopped. Dowdell jumped out and headed down the darkened corridor toward Afro-House, with Garrett in pursuit. The officer claimed Dowdell had a long-barrel revolver in his left hand as he ran (Dowdell's relatives swore he was right-handed). Garrett ordered him to stop and fired a warning shot. By the officer's account, Dowdell disappeared into the shadows, then reappeared along an old garage, about twenty-five feet from the officer. Garrett claimed that when he again ordered Dowdell to drop his weapon, the youth shot at him. Garrett fired back, hitting the garage. All the while, Dowdell and Garrett were alone in the alley. Avey had cuffed Cole and left her in the custody of other officers who had come to the scene. Avey said he could hear Garrett's voice, see the muzzle blasts, and hear the shots. Garrett saw Dowdell jump out from the shadows, heading down the alley toward Afro-House. The police officer squeezed off three more rounds from his .357 magnum, one of which hit the young man in the back of the head. As Garrett continued down the alley, he stumbled over Dowdell's body. He and Avey both checked for a pulse but could find none. The Douglas County coroner pronounced Dowdell dead at the scene.

Rick Dowdell's death at the hands of a Lawrence police officer, no matter the circumstances of the shooting, destroyed any remaining shreds of racial cooperation in the town. It was the kind of precipitating incident that had led to race riots in Watts, Newark, and Detroit a few years earlier; many residents feared it could be the beginning of something similar in Lawrence. Dick Raney knew that Lawrence had vigilantes, or "rednecks" as he called them, as well as "some wild black kids." He feared that the two would cross paths in the streets, armed and willing to shoot. "A confrontation isn't going to help a thing," he noted.[5]

As Dolph Simons, Sr., the publisher of the *Lawrence Daily Journal-World,* prepared to tell Lawrencians about Rick Dowdell's death, he reminded his staff that the paper had "no business inflaming the situation." The *Journal-World* called for "sober thought and understanding," and noted that Lawrence's "racial situation . . . is better today than it was ten years ago, five years ago or a year ago." Despite the paper's call for calm, in the days following the shooting, rumors added to residents' fears: "Carloads of blacks are comin' over from Kansas City." "They're gonna burn down the university." "Someone said a Lawrence nigger was in Kansas City this afternoon and bought $200 worth of ammunition and paid for it with a university check." Allegedly, even the Hell's Angels were on their way to Lawrence to participate in further disturbances.[6]

In the early morning of July 17—a few hours after Dowdell had died—explosions and shooting racked east Lawrence and recurred later that night. The Kansas Highway Patrol (KHP) claimed the bombings were the work of "hippies" in retaliation for Dowdell's death. City officials, apparently fearing a repeat of the April curfew, did not make any emergency plans for the seventeenth. Around noon on July 18, fifty people, mostly African Americans, marched on the police station and demanded Garrett's suspension; he was temporarily relieved of his duties two days later.[7]

On the night of the eighteenth, snipers shot out police car windows and streetlights and fired at police cars and fire engines responding to calls. They also took potshots at Dolph Simons, Jr. (the *Journal-World*'s editor), Arden Booth, the owner of KLWN radio, and several other people in South Park. Lt. Eugene Williams of the Lawrence Police Department was seriously wounded in a gun battle near Afro-House, reportedly with around fifty blacks "employing guerilla tactics." The next day twelve business owners, led by Bernard Freeman, whose glass company had been victimized by bombs and gunfire during the April crisis, asked the city for police protection. Freeman and two other men had exchanged gunfire with several blacks the night before. His store had forty or fifty slugs in its walls as evidence. At the time of the shootings, Lawrence police were occupied elsewhere and did not respond to Freeman's calls for help, nor could they promise any protection. Ignoring the racial undertones of Dowdell's death, Freeman believed "[t]hose idiots in the university" had caused Lawrence's most recent crisis.[8]

The nineteenth remained relatively quiet, with only minor incidents, mostly in Oread. The KHP attributed the calm to Dowdell's father, who, after his arrival from Spokane, Washington, encouraged angry young blacks to "cool it as they had got his boy killed and there would be others."[9]

Not enough people heeded the elder Dowdell's advice, which proved to be prophetic. Since Rick Dowdell's death, tension between the police and the street people in Oread had been building. According to George Kimball, the Defense Chairman of the Lawrence Liberation Front, the freaks turned on fire hydrants, set small fires, and shot off fireworks as "diversionary tactics" to draw the police into Oread and take the heat of off Afro-House and blacks in east Lawrence, a practice that continued into the night of July 20. Early that evening the police had fired tear gas at a crowd gathered at the Rock Chalk Café. As the throng—perhaps sixty or more people participating in the "confrontation" and another 100 spectators— dispersed, the police retreated to a position a block or so away from the tavern. Part of the group, which included many high school aged people, then set trees and shrubs on fire and opened fire hydrants. The crowd's mood was, according to one eyewitness, "light-hearted but with an ugly and tense edge." Several spectators believed that part of the crowd "was definitely" provoking the police, who were on a "hair trigger." When several people tipped over a red Volkswagen and tried to set it on fire, three or four officers armed with shotguns and M-1 rifles marched up Oread toward 13th Street. Suddenly, bystanders recalled, the police yelled "Shoot them, shoot the motherfuckers!" Witnesses saw several "bright flashes," heard "sharp, crackling" sounds and a woman's plaintive wail, and then saw a limp body sprawled on the pavement. Most observers claimed the police lowered their weapons and fired wildly into the crowd, a charge the officers vehemently denied. Amid the confusion, Nick Rice, a nineteen-year-old white male who had just finished his first year at KU, lay bleeding in the street, dying of a bullet wound to the head. Also injured, by buckshot, was Merton Olds, a black, twenty-three-year-old graduate student. Several people tried to carry Rice into the Gaslight Tavern, but police tear gas forced them out. The police ordered onlookers, who were shouting obscenities at them, to get back to their houses "or else." By all accounts both Rice and Olds were innocent victims; neither was radical, neither had had previous encounters with the police, nor had either been involved in the altercations that brought the police to the area.[10]

A KBI investigation into the shooting was inconclusive as to whether the police had fired the shot that killed Rice. Several eyewitnesses testified that the police were the only ones with guns, while others claimed that snipers had fired at police and fire fighters. Lieutenant Charles Greer noted that after the shooting the police found several spent casings from weapons other than those used by the police. In August, an investigative team from the President's Commission on Campus Unrest (PCCU, or Scranton Commission), which had been created to investigate the causes of violence at Kent State University in Ohio and Jackson State University in Mississippi, concluded that the police had indeed fired their M-1 rifles and shotguns at "a dangerous level." One officer interviewed by the PCCU admitted he shot at someone running away, who he and the other officers believed had tried to torch the overturned Volkswagen. The commission discovered that Lawrence police officers had "no specific guidelines" for handling such situations; a Lawrence police officer believed his job, the commission concluded, "was to protect lives and property, period."[11]

An already tense situation had worsened and threatened to spiral out of control as Rice's death resulted in more bursts of violence, particularly in Oread and near the downtown. Calling the deaths "appalling," Governor Robert B. Docking warned he would "take whatever steps are necessary to protect the citizens" of Lawrence. "We cannot—and will not," Docking affirmed, "tolerate flagrant disregard for the laws of our state and nation." On July 21, he issued an emergency proclamation in Lawrence that would be enforced the following night through July 28. The proclamation prohibited the purchase, sale, or use of weapons and ammunition except by police or on one's own property, and the storage, use, or transportation of flammable materials except in automobiles. Docking also sent Kansas Highway Patrol troopers to Lawrence to relieve Lawrence police of normal routine traffic duties, a move that upset LPD officers, who thought they were being made scapegoats for the crisis.[12]

During the night of July 22 the town was relatively peaceful for a second straight night. Much of the credit for maintaining order and avoiding further violence was given to the Kansas Highway Patrol. Amid handmade signs that promised revenge ("Ten Pigs for Our Brother"), Colonel William

L. Albott of the KHP mingled with the "weirdos and hippie-type individuals" in Oread, reasoned with them, and defused volatile tempers. "In our first rounds of discussion," Albott recalled, the street people "called me 'pig.' But that stopped quickly and they started calling me 'colonel.'" They "seemed 'hungry' to find a 'decent' cop to whom they could talk as a fellow human being," he reported. One Oread resident was amazed that Albott had "walked right into the Rock Chalk this afternoon. I've never seen a Lawrence pig do that—never. . . . That guy's far out. I really dig him." Albott believed if the Lawrence police, who he felt were "looking for trouble," were kept out of the area, tensions would ease. Lawrence police, one source noted, frequently "opened their communication with tear gas canisters." The LPD wanted a curfew imposed. It was frustrated that it was being kept out of Oread and that the KHP had taken its place and was getting the credit for the relative calm.[13]

But the calm was illusory, as the crisis had not yet passed. Lawrence had divided into a number of armed camps. Over the next several days, the extent to which the community had become divided—racially, politically, and culturally—was easily apparent. At one extreme were left-radicals and black militants, who believed the only way to change the system was to challenge and destroy it completely. At the other extreme were vigilantes and those who wanted to preserve law at all costs, which included suspending civil liberties and shooting radicals, hippies, and other "troublemakers." In between were thousands of bewildered Lawrencians, paralyzed with fear, uncertain of what had happened, and unsure of what to do next.

William Garrett had been suspended on July 20, pending the verdict of a coroner's inquest. Two days later, an all-white panel at the inquest exonerated him of any wrongdoing in the fatal shooting. The Kansas Bureau of Investigation, the Kansas Attorney General's Office, and the Kansas State Fire Marshall corroborated the events as reported by the Lawrence Police Department. The black community refused to accept the inquest's verdict or law enforcement reports, and the militant faction threatened retaliation.[14] *Harambee,* the voice of the KU-BSU, vowed that "the Black World is aware of what Garrett has done and he shall reap what he has sown," noting that Lawrence police had been harassing Afro-House people for some time. After the verdict was read, Leonard Harrison called the inquest a "Klanwash." A letter, purportedly written by Harrison and addressed to city officials, declared that the black community would "no longer allow Black people to be brutalized" and that it would "avenge the death of our beautiful brother by any means necessary. . . . we will kill . . . any other muthafucka that gets in the way of the total liberation of our people. . . . Lawrence will become a police state if justice is denied us." The letter also demanded that the white "power structure," as a "show of good faith to the black community," contribute $50,000 to the Tiger Dowdell Liberation Center, $30,000 to the Dowdell family, and $10,000 to pay for scholarships for young blacks. Whites rejected the demands, although in October, the First United Methodist Church, which had been the target of a reparation demand by the CCBC in May, donated $10,000 to help minorities in Lawrence. Within weeks, the Liberation School was started in east Lawrence, although not all black residents supported the school. In August, the Concerned Black Parents, which had been established during the April crisis, created a scholarship fund in Dowdell's memory, but in September it denied any association with the Dowdell Liberation School or its administrators.[15]

On July 23, Rick Dowdell was buried. Most of the marchers in the funeral procession were black; many dressed in denim jeans and black shirts and wore arm bands or buttons that matched the red, white, and green flag on his coffin. An hour earlier a memorial march of about 300 people, comprised mostly of students at the University of Kansas and the street people, took place without incident.[16]

Lifelong Lawrence resident Dorothy Harvey, a member of St. Luke African Methodist Episcopal Church where the service was held, recalled that the more militant segment of the black community wanted to have a funeral that included many African-influenced rituals, and although church members were not pleased with the arrangements, they agreed because the Dowdells were members of the church. Harvey added that the Dowdell family was not "particularly happy," because their son's funeral became a "demonstration." The "militants" had dyed "the flowers, the casket, everything" black. At the church, mourners received memorial programs, with a red clenched fist on a black background with green lettering. John Spearman, Jr., understood that Dowdell's death and funeral were "political act[s]" that showed the depth of racial polarization in Lawrence. Spearman recalled that almost every black person in Lawrence attended the funeral, even those who had disagreed with Dowdell's political activities. Helen Kimball recalled that Dowdell's funeral "was the saddest" that she had ever attended" because he was so young and was from the community."[17]

As odd as it sounds, Richard Beaty, a member of the ultraright Minutemen, claimed that shortly before Dowdell died the two of them went to a nearby bar to have a beer. Beaty was a lifelong resident of east Lawrence, and the gunfire and other activity there made him concerned for his mother's safety, who lived only a few blocks from Afro-House. Beaty thought Dowdell was a "victim of circumstance." He was sure Dowdell had had a gun on him the night he was shot—"just to be a big shot"—and when the police tried to pull him over, Beaty surmised, he had panicked and "got cornered." Although he did not attend Dowdell's funeral, Beaty watched the procession from a few blocks away, albeit while armed. He also was not sympathetic to

Dowdell's political beliefs, especially the Black Power movement, which he believed was stepping on his "rights." Beaty was angry because blacks used the funeral "to again shove it down our [whites] . . . throats—the black thing. . . . A white probably wouldn't have been allowed to have the same kind of funeral."[18] Like many other white Lawrencians, Beaty believed that blacks had crossed a racial boundary and threatened white society. Lawrencians such as Beaty feared that more violence would result if those lines were not defended; moreover, they were willing to use violence to prevent such a transgression from happening.

Those fears were inflamed further when news broke that Gary Jackson, a BSU member and newly-hired assistant to the Dean of Men at KU, had purchased ammunition at a Topeka sporting goods store on July 17, the day after Rick Dowdell died and four days before the emergency proclamation was issued. That same day, LaVerta Murray, the BSU president, purchased ammunition at a Kansas City, Missouri, gun shop, using a BSU check. The twenty-seven boxes of ammunition that the two men bought reportedly were stored at Afro-House. In addition to whites' fears of blacks buying ammunition, the purchase was controversial because university funds or state money may have been used, and because Jackson was an employee of the university.[19]

Jackson and Murray claimed they had done nothing illegal; there was no emergency proclamation in force at the time, and, as Murray later noted, "blacks have a right to arm for self-defense." Their actions make sense if one accepts their contention that they had been under siege from police and white vigilantes since at least the April crisis. Whites, however, ignored their claims of self-defense, seeing the matter instead as a potential attack against whites and the community. Additionally, whites decried the timing, and the potential use of university funds for the purchases called into question the judgment of the BSU and black leaders. Why Jackson personally made the purchase is unclear, for he had to be aware that young black radicals and BSU members were under close police scrutiny. Although the BSU was unconcerned with white perceptions, public knowledge of the purchase was certain to create outrage within the white community, increasing the pressure on the group. From their perspective, Jackson, Murray, the BSU, and other blacks felt they needed to be armed to protect themselves, especially since they believed that Dowdell's death was, in effect, a state-sanctioned murder. Jackson's position at the university gave the regents leverage to move against him; they ordered KU chancellor Laurence Chalmers to fire him. Jackson, declaring that he had done nothing to justify the firing, retained a lawyer. The case dragged on until December.[20]

Black militants in Lawrence believed they were denigrated by the white community and harassed by the police; leftist white radicals made similar claims and were equally adamant in condemning Dowdell's death. The Lawrence Liberation Front (LLF), or the White Panthers, declared that "many people have had their eyes opened to the nature of this town and its racism." Echoing similar claims as the BSU, the LLF stated that "Dowdell fell as one more link in the seemingly endless chain of victims killed by a racist society where . . . minorities are 'kept in their place' by officially sanctioned police and vigilante violence." George Kimball, the minister of defense for the LLF, declared to the street people that "This is the last Goddamn non-violent march I'm going to ever take again. The response to murder will no longer be non-violent marches in the streets." He warned "[i]f the pigs come into our community, they are going to find a lot more than open fire hydrants."[21]

Like black radicals, white radicals too were stockpiling weapons. The LLF declared that the "Amerikan Revolution has come to Lawrence." Believing they were "no longer safe in Lawrence," the freaks and street people were "arming themselves to preserve their life-style and ready to eliminate any force bent upon destroying them." Moreover, the LLF wrote, "[I]n light of the police incursions and the brutal slayings, we pledge ourselves to honor their memory by effectively defending ourselves and our community." The freaks warned the "enemies of the people of this community . . . that any further attacks will be met with an appropriate response. LONG LIVE THE PEOPLE'S WAR."[22]

Their experience during the April curfew and the recent episode of violence had unified the street people. KU student body president and Oread resident David Awbrey, who spent several weeks in jail for a curfew violation during the April crisis, noted that the curfew had helped create a sense of solidarity among the residents of Oread because they felt as if they were defending "our community, our geographic homeland." Awbrey pointed out that merchants could move freely or get passes during the curfew, while "long hairs" could not. He also admitted that, after the recent killings, many people in Oread were armed. "If we didn't have the power of our guns, the rednecks would be storming up and beating up the freaks." Fellow Oread resident David Bailey concurred. He professed that while the street people simply wanted "an environment to feel human in," for their own protection they stockpiled ammunition and guns and kept guard through the night in both April and July. The street people's power was merely an illusion, Awbrey conceded, "because if it came down to it, they [the police and white vigilantes] could still win. Through guns is the only way that we relate to the outside community."[23]

The LLF also accused city officials of trying "to cover up the guilt of the murderers," the police officers who had shot Rick Dowdell and Nick Rice. This was perhaps the greatest concern of both African Americans—militants and non-militants—and the street people.[24] In the aftermath of the shootings, city officials expressed great willingness to talk to the street people, which many residents of Oread believed was disingenuous. Oread resident Wayne Probst colorfully summed up their feelings: "Dowdell gets it. The shit hits the fan. . . . Then Nick Rice gets shot, they [the city commission] shit—here they come to the Rock Chalk saying how bad they feel and wanting to open lines of communication after the thugs they hired to protect the 'citizens' of Lawrence have done two cats in. Well, shit, how are people on the hill supposed to feel? Then to make things worse, nothing is done about a murder with at least 30 eyewitnesses. The cops don't even try to talk to anyone until two days after Rice has been shot."[25]

Probst suggested that had the street people killed a police officer, an immediate and protracted investigation would have begun. For justice to be done, Probst and the other street people demanded an investigation into the shooting of Dowdell and Rice, even though "there would be a shit storm" from those residents who believed the police were justified in using force to restore law and order. Probst believed that the officers on the scene during the Rice shooting "have all got to be busted or the freaks in this town will know more than they ever have before that [the] middle class values they were taught are not for shit. And since no one seems to pay any attention to those values, well then fuck it."[26]

Rice's death generated much more sympathy and outrage from the entire Lawrence community than did Dowdell's. For example, both blacks and whites denounced the police for firing tear gas into the cafe where Rice was carried after he was shot. By contrast, public outrage came almost exclusively from the black community or the radical fringe when Dowdell was killed, and several whites even justified the shooting. Ruby Gimblett, an Oread business owner, circulated a petition that praised the "courageous action of the police officer who fired the shot that killed Dowdell." Insurance salesman Goldie Ferguson, a third-generation Lawrencian, believed both Dowdell and Rice were "bad apples." A stenographer believed "[h]ad Rick Dowdell been in jail where he belonged," none of the trouble would have started.[27]

Indeed, many Lawrencians believed the town's troubles had resulted from a lack of respect for the police department and the rule of law. Since at least the April crisis, many local residents had tried to increase public support for the LPD, and the most visible effort was that of the Lawrence Support Your Local Police Committee (LSYLPC). Composed mostly of businessmen and white conservatives and dedicated to restoring law and order in Lawrence by strengthening the police department, the LSYLPC launched a successful campaign to support law enforcement in Lawrence. Even residents not officially a member of the group thought it had good intentions and would be a positive force in the community. One resident called it the "the best thing that has happened to the Lawrence community" since William Quantrill, a Confederate terrorist who raided the city during the Civil War, "left town."

Linda S. Tuttle, a housewife who was very suspicious of the LSYLPC, nonetheless believed it was "very respected in the community . . . the *in* group—the doctors, private club members, builders, and public school superintendents belong."[28]

In addition to publicly backing the police, the LSYLPC also offered its own explanation for the violence in Lawrence and across the nation. Probably affiliated with the John Birch Society, which launched a similar program in the 1960s, the LSYLPC complained loudly about the growing permissiveness in American culture, which it blamed on liberal Supreme Court rulings and a lack of governmental "backbone" in supporting the police. The LSYLPC, and many other Lawrencians not affiliated with the group, saw the Supreme Court's decisions regarding the rights of the accused as a primary cause of unrest in America. One long-time Lawrencian, when asked who or what was to blame for Lawrence's troubles, emphatically indicted the "*SUPREME COURT.* Chief Justice Warren and his liberals [are the] #1 offender[s] which caused a break down of authority and respect for law and order." Other Lawrencians agreed, including housewife Katherine Tarr, who urged the PCCU to "investigate the Supreme Court. The Laws that we now have should be enforced to the limit." Myron D. Feuerborn argued that the "courts will have to change their logic and back the policeman or the taxpayer is just wasting his money for a police force."[29]

The day after Rice's death, the LSYLPC presented the LPD with a petition in support of Garrett, signed by 1,073 people; the following day, it delivered a similar petition with 600 signatures to city officials. The petition proclaimed that the police "should be allowed to use whatever force necessary to protect themselves and the public, and to enforce the law." Wayne Meisenheimer, a barber at the Hillcrest Barber Shop, declared "[i]f the hippies don't like the way things are done in our city, or don't like our police department, they should get out." Another barber, Dick Hamilton, encouraged the citizens of Lawrence to "use any kind of force necessary to protect their businesses and homes." Frank Alexander, an insurance agent; C. D. Turner, the vice-president of Lawrence Furniture Co.; Robert E. Walters, a DuPont Chemicals plant worker; and their wives and children concluded that if more Lawrencians "would give the police a little more respect and backing they would give some in return. If you feel you are wrongly accused of a violation . . . take it to court. After all, that is what they [the police] are for, to protect the citizen."[30]

Not all Lawrencians saw the police in that light. Shortly after Rick Dowdell died, *Vortex,* a radical underground newspaper, published Garrett's photograph with the caption, "Wanted for Murder." Not surprisingly, many Lawrencians were outraged. Assistant Douglas County Attorney Mike Elwell warned that anyone circulating the *Vortex* could be charged with defamation.

On July 22, a fight broke out at the courthouse between a man who was with a "police support group" and a youth distributing *Vortex*. "That's out and out treason," cried the man from the support group, "That's why we've got to do something ourselves."[31]

Indeed, it seemed likely that many residents were preparing to do just that. In response to the LLF's call for a "People's War," the right-wing V-Committee was "NOW prepared to take effective action" against "FREAK HILL." If the violence continued, it promised, "the power of the V will be unleashed. Believe when we say that freaks cannot imagine what forces can and will be brought forth." The V-Committee warned the street people to "ELIMINATE THE VIOLENCE AND DESTRUCTION OF PROPERTY IN THIS CITY OR THE V-COMMITTEE WILL ELIMINATE YOU!!!"[32]

While many city leaders were quick to dismiss the existence of vigilantes, there is little doubt that many white Lawrencians had become radicalized and threatened to use violence to end the unrest. In December 1970, the KHP reported on the existence of "3 known vigilantes" in Lawrence. Lawrence resident Raymond Vandeventer, who in 1971 ran for city commissioner, headed a secret organization that he claimed included "300 members in Lawrence and 1600 back-up people," and he always had at least fifteen people on patrol. Vandeventer, the manager of a rural water district, promised to use "guerilla warfare" to halt the "hippies and nigger militants," and calmly explained that he could trigger explosives to "eliminate the troublemakers without leaving evidence." He believed that the "elimination of 14 people would do much to quiet the city." Norman Ransford, a white electrical contractor, made explicitly clear the racial lines of the city. He promised if there was any more shooting in Lawrence, he would "get a group together and we'll shoot . . . If we don't stop them [blacks] in East Lawrence they'll be in [predominantly white] West Lawrence."[33]

It seemed the entire town was armed and amassing more weapons. A factory worker reported that a local sporting goods store was "selling guns quite carelessly to whites," and also that a pawnbroker was a member of the Minutemen. A frequently heard rumor was that the downtown merchants had an "arsenal of weapons and ammo on the second floor of JC Penney's." Lynn Handel, a housewife, overheard at a faculty-townspeople party that one local vigilante group was "armed and preparing for future unrest" from the "hippy-black" radicals and that another group was "in training." Handel strongly believed that one of the biggest problems facing the community was "Too many guns."[34]

Amid the turmoil, the residents of Lawrence looked for help. Some Lawrencians believed that the PCCU could help Lawrence's situation by exploring the causes of unrest there. On July 25, James Rhodes, Jr., of the PCCU visited Lawrence; that same day an unexploded Molotov cocktail was found in bushes near Oread Hall at Eleventh and Maine Streets. At his first meeting with Lawrence's "polarized groups," Rhodes heard folks calling each other "rednecks, niggers, peckerwoods, whites, hippies, freaks, blacks, pigs, motherfuckers, boys, insurrectionists, vigilantes, yippies, black militants, radicals, street people, university people, white power structure, and colored folk." The investigative team noted in its report that conditions in Lawrence combined "the racial tensions of Jackson and the university-community tension of Kent."[35]

On Rhodes's recommendation, on August 3, the PCCU sent a five-man team to Lawrence for a ten-day investigation into the roots of the town's spate of violence. The PCCU's sojourn to Lawrence was met with about equal measures of open arms and skepticism. W. G. McElvoy, a founder of the LSYLPC, feared if the commission didn't step in "this town will blow away." But Thomas H. Hart, the chair of the LSYLPC, believed that the investigation would not be "constructive" and could be "inflammatory." When the investigative team arrived, the CCBC and the Brothers and Sisters in Blackness pledged not to cooperate with it because the commission had "defamed the integrity and dignity of black people" by meeting first with university officials, and not them. A commission spokesperson verified that it had not talked to either of the black groups. In response, the investigative team stated it was in Lawrence at the request of Commissioner Rhodes and local officials to "review all of the facts concerning the violence and underlying tensions" of the recent events. The team intended to meet with "all groups" and had "no criminal or judicial charge" other than to "present a comprehensive picture" of Lawrence's travails.[36]

The PCCU made a concerted effort to listen and learn from a vast range of ideological perspectives by polling "the various segments of the community." To that end, the commission circulated questionnaires throughout the community. About 500 residents responded. Their responses are a remarkable outpouring of honest emotions, fears, and frustrations, expressing a variety of explanations for the causes of violence in their community.[37]

The PCCU talked to several individuals who had what it called the "white reactionary viewpoint," including Mr. Freed, a pawnshop owner who sold guns. Freed believed Lawrence's problems were simple: KU students were promoting socialism; Leonard Harrison was teaching blacks to hate whites; the courts had been too lenient; and KU faculty had encouraged students to stand against American values and principles. Like many other white Lawrencians, Freed was concerned that an African American reportedly had been able to buy high-powered, seven-millimeter rifle simply because he was a "registered voter." Freed noted that blacks had purchased other weapons, too, which greatly alarmed him and his friends, as did the rumors of TNT and arms stored at the Ballard Center. Freed acknowledged that he and many other citizens were "on the verge of taking the law into their own hands." Another man interviewed by the investigative team declared the problem was not race related but rested with the "family unit" and the breakdown of morality, principles, and values. "The worst thing you can do," he professed, "is give them [children] no God." Expressing a view shared by many others, he also declared that if blacks and students have "the right to break the law and burn property, then I want that right also."[38]

Other Lawrencians also offered rather narrow explanations for the unrest. A thirty-one-year-old student, declaring that "We Silent People are sick of pussy footing destructiveness," identified "THE LEFT WING ULTRA LIBERAL HIPPIE-YIPPIE STREET PEOPLE RADICAIL [sic] MILITANT POLITICAL SOCIAL ACTIVIST FACTIONS WHO ARE HELL BENT ON DESCTRUCTION & TERROR" as the source of the town's troubles. P. H. Riedel, a professor at KU, believed that "Revolutionary KU faculty, white revolutionary students, white revolutionary 'street people' . . . and black militants" were the main problems. Others agreed, adding that "outsiders" were to blame for instigating the violence. One resident declared that "99% of our trouble has been caused by the outside agitators and the local communist sympathizers or dupes who don't know they are being lead along by the communist agitators." L. V. Feurerborn, a KU Student, used similar figures, asserting that the problem was "About 1% a racial problem and 99% caused by communist agitators aided by the news media."[39]

In seeing the causes of unrest and dissension in their community as originating from the outside, few Lawrencians were willing to admit the indigenous, especially racial, roots of the turmoil. Race was at the heart of the Dowdell shooting and had been a principal cause of tension in the community since at least 1960, but most white Lawrencians refused to believe that their community had such a problem. After all, they reasoned, this was Lawrence, the free-state fortress. Moreover, as they reflected on the racial situation in the community, white Lawrencians exhibited the same paternalistic attitudes toward racial minorities that had dominated the town for over a century. A forty-nine-year-old mechanic and World War II veteran avowed that "Lawrence was born a free town. It was one of the first to have integrated schools." He continued: "If a black is decent most of the people will respect him. If he isn't, they judge him likewise. The same goes for whites. People choose their friends." A homemaker, also a lifelong resident, declared that the "colored race . . . do not realize their members are not as well qualified as those that are hired—get them to see that they need to work and help themselves—not have things handed to them." Similarly, a bank clerk felt that that African Americans in Lawrence were "[m]ostly fine people who have been discriminated against for many many years," but who now were being "terrorized by members of their own race—the Black Militants, who preach justice and equality but do not even pretend to practice these qualities when dealing with other blacks." Phillip H. Riddle, a maintenance foreman, believed that the troubles had been brought on by the "unreasoning attitude of the black people toward solving local problems." Blacks, he argued, have a "closed mind attitude and will not discuss their 'problems.' . . . The black people seem to want to demand their way to respect."[40]

Additionally, many white Lawrencians believed that civil rights legislation, court rulings, busing, and black activism had turned the racial tables. "I say the white people are the one's [*sic*] who are oppressed," declared Daniel J. Blewitt, a twenty-one-year-old stenographer. "The white people cannot walk the streets, day or night, without fear of being attacked." A Lawrence-born KU student agreed, avowing that "the white, hard working businessmen and students are being neglected" and "the most preposterous demands of the blacks are being met." John W. A. Murphy, a maintenance mechanic and forty-two-year resident of Lawrence, believed that "negroes can break any law with impunity." One native Lawrencian believed the key to understanding the unrest was the "hostility that has been instilled in the colored to *all* white people." Melvin E. Copp, a painter and Lawrence native, put it succinctly: He felt there were "a lot of good colored people in Lawrence and theres [*sic*] a lot of bad niggers!"[41]

Copp no doubt would have put Leonard Harrison into the latter category. Harrison's impact on the community was great, and he certainly contributed to the tense atmosphere. Harrison was seen as an "outsider" (he had lived in Lawrence for only three years), which, combined with his militancy and harsh rhetoric, made him an easy target for blame. Many Lawrencians believed there had not been any problems in Lawrence until Harrison arrived. A bank clerk spoke for many when she declared that Harrison's "presence and leadership" had disrupted the "tranquility of this community," and she suggested that his "removal . . . would save property and lives." As well, many people—black and white—believed Harrison was using the situation for his own personal gain, politically and financially.[42]

It is perhaps not surprising that a substantial number of those questioned believed that a communist conspiracy was responsible for the town's problems. Ed Alexander, a member of the LSYLPC and an ardent cold warrior, also believed that Lawrence was "sick to death of appeasement," especially the university and city commission's coddling of "a small minority of militant blacks and the street people." Like a good many Lawrencians, Alexander believed the community had too long "appeased" the unreasonable demands of black and white radicals; high insurance rates for property owners was but one consequence of appeasement. A thirty-six-year resident believed that Lawrence "never had any serious trouble" until "infiltration into the community by outsiders (including SDS, Anarchists, Traitors, Communists, et al) made up of students, faculty, blacks, ministers & some local do-gooders." Many residents believed that the University of Kansas had become "an indoctrination center for leftests [*sic*]."[43]

White Lawrencians, seeing the increasing tension as an issue of law and order rather than race, called for the law to crack down. From this perspective, Lawrence's problems were easy to identify and simple to fix. A group calling itself the Responsible Citizens of Lawrence called for "group action to watch for destruction of property and suspicious activity." Kenneth Tarr, the president of the LSYLPC, declared that the Lawrence "situation" was simply a "matter of law and order versus crime and lawlessness." He argued that the people of Lawrence get along well with the police, while "criminal[s] and militant[s] never do. Only to the criminal and militant [extremists] do the police become an object of violence and fear." Tarr also asserted that "there was no 'atrocity' committed in Lawrence, unless one can so call the atrocities and insults suffered by the police. We [the LSYLPC] are in direct opposition to the demands of the so-called 'black community.' And since when are a few radicals (less than 100) to be considered as representative of the real black community."[44]

Tarr was right in that Harrison did not speak for the entire black community, nor did Black Power represent the political views of most African Americans in Lawrence. Rejecting black nationalism, many African Americans disliked Harrison personally and opposed his goals. The black community, however, knew from experience that police harassment of people of color existed. Moreover, Lawrence's African Americans seemed to be unified in their sadness and anger over Dowdell's death, which they believed was unnecessary and clear evidence of how little the community valued black lives or the concerns of African Americans. Helen Kimball, a 1966 graduate of Lawrence High, believed Dowdell died not as a revolutionary or a martyr to the cause of black liberation, but rather "in self-defense." At "that particular instant" and "with the particular officer that was involved," Kimball claimed, "it could have been any" black in Lawrence. Lab technician Harold Stagg, forty-five years old and a graduate of Grambling College, and his wife Willie, who worked in a local department store, admitted that Dowdell was not an angel and may have been doing something wrong. They believed Dowdell was not, however, a "vicious" or violent person. And, like most blacks in Lawrence, Stagg did not understand why Dowdell had been killed. Harold Stagg did not believe that there were "a lot of militant kids in this town, white or black, but when they are pressured into being hostile, they'll fight back."[45]

While Lawrence's problems were mostly racial in origin, the challenges to traditional social boundaries also came from white radicals, the street people, and oppositional cultures. Lawrence city manager Buford Watson, who had assumed his duties in January, in one breath claimed he was not sure why

Lawrence was the site of so much violence but in the next placed the blame squarely on the street people, who took "advantage of last week's racial unrest in the city. We had a problem in the community and the street people have taken the opportunity to cause trouble." While Watson alluded to the community's race problems, he suggested they were not the main source of the crisis. The "Vietnam War generally is the only complaint I've heard," he professed. The radicals "want to end the war, and this is a form of protest. It's a method of creating unrest." George Kimball allowed that "Vietnam is part of it, but it is not all of it. I think everybody here recognizes that Vietnam is just part of a system. This would continue if the War ended." An Associate Press report concluded that the "consensus" among city leaders was that marijuana was the primary cause of "the radical problem" and that Harrison's "galvanizing effect on young blacks" was at the heart of "black unrest."[46]

These perceptions suggest the limited perspective of Lawrence's governing officials, which necessarily constrained their response in preventing violence in the first place and in handling the situation once the crisis was in full swing. Lawrence had long been governed by a mayor-commission form of government, but in the late 1960s switched to a manager-commission structure. Most of the commissioners had been local professionals, merchants, and business owners, although occasionally a KU faculty member served. Given this orientation, the commission primarily had been concerned with economic growth and development; social problems often were addressed in terms of how they would affect the town's image and ability to attract industry and businesses. Generally, however, the commission reacted rather than led. It had established the Lawrence Human Relations Commission in 1961 and had been among the first cities in Kansas to pass a fair housing ordinance, but both actions were in response to civil rights activism.

The 1970 city commission believed that the first sign of trouble appeared only with the black student walkout at Lawrence High in 1968, ignoring the protests and grievances of African Americans since the end of World War II. In July, Buford Watson admitted "We haven't done a damn thing to change anything, true." But, he added vaguely, "[w]e are willing to do something differently." Not surprisingly, the PCCU concluded that "the city commission had not responded "decisively and creatively" to deal with the city's problems.[47]

Many Lawrence residents agreed. The street people were suspicious of the commission's willingness to open lines of communication after Nick Rice's death. Harsher criticism came from Lawrencians on the right, who typically described city officials as "weak" and having "no back bone," especially in not allowing the police department do its job. Indeed, many Lawrencians believed that the police department was the last pillar of justice and virtue in Lawrence and had done an excellent job, even thought the commission had kept its "hands tied." Others, however, believed that the department bore much of the responsibility for the crisis. Lynn Handel offered another view: She thought the police "represent[ed] unthinking brutality and stupidity." Within the Lawrence Police Department itself, most officers, including Chief Richard Stanwyx, believed that local tensions corresponded to the civil rights movement, and that "young blacks and George Kimball" had caused most of the trouble. As did the city commission, the police department believed that Larry Chalmers also contributed to the problem, as most of the townsfolk "dislike him." The PCCU noted that Lawrence had about half the number of recommended officers for a town of its size and concluded that the LPD lacked the "necessary support and manpower to cope with new and changing needs within the community," and was thus unable to address tensions within the community.[48]

The residual emotion from the bloody summer remained as autumn neared. Fights with "racial overtones" occurred at Lawrence High throughout the fall. Reynolds Shultz, the Republican candidate for lieutenant governor, remarked during a stump speech that Lawrence "hadn't lost a thing" when Dowdell died. In response, the BSU declared it would "apply our knowledge to try and eliminate him and his kind." Shultz's remark inflamed the entire black community but won him sympathy from whites fed up with the disruptions. Shultz won the Republican nomination for lieutenant governor in the August primary, and won the general election in November, albeit by a small margin in both races. That he won at all, however, is evidence that Kansans were growing weary of racial, campus, and civil disorders and looked to leaders who promised to do something about the problem. Not surprisingly, Governor Docking had hardened his stance on campus disorders, too, and was re-elected in November.[49]

BSU members, despite constant surveillance, continued to arm themselves with rifles, pistols, machine guns, and even dynamite. Fights, explosions, and fires were frequent occurrences during October and November. Black and white militants continued to wage their revolution against power and authority in Lawrence. The FBI reported that KU's ROTC building and the Hercules Plant east of Lawrence were threatened with being blown up the week of October 12. The Kansas Highway Patrol reported that H. Rap Brown was in Lawrence, that Abbie Hoffman had made reservations at the Ramada Inn, and that members of the Weather Underground (formerly Weatherman) were hiding in Lawrence, although there is no evidence to confirm any of this. On October 22, the Weather Underground declared "We will blast and shoot our way to freedom!" Its Demolition Squad claimed to be in Lawrence as part of its "Fall Offensive" and threatened to "blow up the [football] stadium sometime" during the homecoming game, although the game went on without incident. On October 30, a bomb detonated at the LHS administration building, shattering several windows.[50]

In November, the BSU warned the Board of Regents and KU administrators that if they did not reinstate Gary Jackson, who had been fired from his administrative position at KU during the July crisis for buying ammunition, it would "take necessary actions to see that the remainder of the staff and faculty share his condition of unemployment." In December, however, regent president James Basham announced that the board would not reinstate Jackson. The BSU called for a university-wide strike in support of Jackson, which divided the campus along racial lines. Black students were more defiant; white students were weary of the confrontations. Many alumni, politicians, and townspeople believed that Chalmers and the university were kowtowing to the BSU and forsaking the white majority for an agitating black minority.[51]

The breaking point came on December 7, as the BSU prepared for its general strike. The word "STRIKE" had been spraypainted on Fraser and Strong Halls, on bus stops, and on sidewalks and cars across the campus. Around 8:30 A.M., Harry Snyder, a white senior from Topeka, approached two black men who were painting "STRIKE" on the steps and stone wall in front of Watkins Library. When Snyder tried to stop them, Keith Gardenhire pulled a pistol and shot Snyder in the throat; Snyder later recovered from his wound. After the shooting, the BSU continued to march, picket, and make speeches. Later, two male and two female African Americans allegedly beat a white secretary from KU Continuing Education. BSU president Ron Washington was "surprise[d]" when told of the gunfire but vowed that the strike would continue "until June if necessary."[52]

The next day, December 8, around 100 African Americans marched from the Union to Strong Hall. Later that day, KU police reported a fire in a Strong Hall restroom and suspected arson as the cause of a fire at the old Pi Beta Phi house, which the university was then using for offices. KU police also evacuated Templin Hall because of a bomb threat. As a show of support for the BSU, the following day around 150 students vandalized the chancellor's suite in Strong Hall, doing about $150 in damage. According to the Kansas Highway Patrol, the BSU parked stalled cars on campus (snarling traffic), occupied lecture halls, and threw stink bombs in classrooms during exams.[53]

Although the BSU suspended the strike, the violence did not end. University officials, anticipating "guerilla attacks" after the BSU strike, requested that undercover agents from the KBI and the LPD be assigned to the campus. On December 11, a small fire was discovered in Ellsworth residence hall, and the following day at 11:00 P.M., a bomb ripped through Summerfield Hall, the university's computer center, injuring three people—although none seriously—and doing almost $30,000 in damage. Governor Docking denounced the Summerfield Hall bombing as a "senseless act which can't be tolerated." A $2,000 reward was offered for information about the bombing. Chalmers, who had been "grilled" by the regents the day before about events on campus, described KU after the bombing as "calm." He said that he did not fear an impending crisis like the previous spring but was uneasy that people outside the university who perceived a problem would call for a crackdown on student autonomy.[54]

The Snyder shooting, the Summerfield bombing, and the repeated bomb threats were evidence to many whites that African Americans and white radicals had pushed the community's racial and cultural boundaries too far. Most whites believed that militant blacks and left-revolutionaries did not respect property rights, had vandalized state property with impunity, had provoked racial confrontations, and had shot and beaten innocent white citizens, all in support of their radical goals. Many Lawrencians were angry and frustrated with years of violence, and they held black and white radicals, communist subversives, outside agitators, permissive administrators, weak government officials, and years of liberal legislation and court decisions responsible for the situation. What few whites understood or tried to comprehend, however, were the underlying economic, social, and political realities that led many Lawrencians, in particular young blacks, to challenge the existing power structure.

Almost as soon as the violence of July had ended, the citizens of Lawrence began searching for ways to avoid future conflicts. The Lawrence Human Relations Commission (LHRC) undertook a study of the Lawrence High conflict and identified a lack of communication and racial inequities as the primary causes of the disturbance. Eerily similar to a 1963 LHRC report, the commission also pointed to structural deficiencies—such as limited access to public transportation and marginal economic opportunities for blacks—that had compounded the situation. Other community efforts sought to open dialogue among the people of Lawrence. After the PCCU left in early August, representatives from the National Center of Dispute Settlement of the American Arbitration Association met with various people and organizations in Lawrence. In early September, the Concerned Black Parents brought in a professional mediator to meet with students.[55]

The most significant effort at opening lines of communication within the city was a study directed by the Menninger Foundation of Topeka. In August 1970, the Lawrence Chamber of Commerce called for the creation of a task force to discuss "police-community relations" and coordinate efforts among the city, the school district, and the university in "building stronger social institutions." Heeding the call, the Lawrence city commission asked the Menninger Foundation to study the causes of violence in Lawrence and to recommend action to prevent future disturbances. The program consisted of several workshops among the various factions within the community, including the street people, the black community, and the police. In January, 1971, a steering committee met over several weekend-long workshops in a Topeka motel and helped to prepare a report. The steering committee included Chancellor E. Laurence Chalmers, City Manager Buford Watson, John Spearman, Sr., and representatives from the police and sheriff departments, city administrators, the black community, the street people, the business community, "Grass-root' citizens groups" (vigilantes), and KU students. A lack of communication, the steering committee concluded, had been a principal source of Lawrence's troubles.[56]

The workshops were not greeted with enthusiasm. All Lawrence police officers were ordered to participate in at least one, but few went willingly. The LSYLPC called it "a type of sensitivity training or brainwashing" founded on the assumption that "the policeman's difficulties stem from his own inadequacies." Charles Greer and Verner Newman, both Lawrence police lieutenants, agreed that the workshops allowed for the participants to understand one another a little better. For example, they were able to talk to a "hippie girl" who was "scared to death" of police officers. Newman surprised other police officers when he told the group that the LPD had discriminated against him. John Naramore, who reluctantly represented the street people, believed that because of the program people in Lawrence began to value others as people and not "objects." Greer thought they were successful was because the people of Lawrence "were ready for solutions."[57]

While the program opened a dialogue that began to ease tensions in the community, its conclusions merely echoed what national commissions had already concluded, what blacks already knew, and what most whites refused to admit: Racial tensions and strained police-community relations were the primary causes of the unrest and violence. In 1971, the PCCU released it findings on the causes of violence in the nation's colleges and universities. The commission noted that "many Americans consider campus unrest to be an aberration from the moral order of society. They treat it as a problem that derives from some moral failing on the part of some individual or group. The explanations of campus unrest that they adopt therefore tend to be single-cause explanations that clearly allocate blame and that specify remedies which are within the capacity of individuals, public opinion, or government to provide."[58]

Many white Lawrencians did try to comprehend the concerns of African Americans, but most simply could not understand why some blacks were dissatisfied with the civil rights "progress" that the community had made. Most whites refused to acknowledge that a problem had ever existed, or if they did, they charged blacks for creating it. Others blamed outsider agitators, such as Leonard Harrison, for inciting violence; in fact, most of the principal actors were local blacks responding to local conditions.

Blacks and whites shared responsibility for Lawrence's troubles. The Black Student Union, Leonard Harrison, and other blacks had chosen confrontation and violence as a means of resistance and a way to challenge the restrictive racial boundaries of the community. White leftist-radicals, who claimed to be an oppressed people like African Americans, also shared responsibility for the unrest and violence, as did white vigilantes. Together they, along with apathetic citizens and misguided liberals, helped to create the conditions in which Rick Dowdell and Nick Rice were killed.

CHAPTER 9

"FINALLY WE WERE DOING SOMETHING"

Around 6:00 P.M. on Friday, February 4, 1972, about twenty women and four children entered and took control of the East Asian studies building on the campus of the University of Kansas. "This action has been taken because the needs of women in this community have long been neglected," read the manifesto of the February Sisters, as the group called itself. They made six demands of the university: create an affirmative action program; establish a daycare center; provide comprehensive women's health care at Watkins Hospital, the student health center; create an autonomous women's studies department; end wage inequities and unfair employment practices; and hire more women in faculty and administration positions. Negotiations between the Sisters and members of the Senate Executive Committee (SenEx) took place twice during the night, and early the next day an agreement was reached. A SenEx resolution supported a student senate-funded daycare center and a commitment to establish a women's health care clinic, an offer that the Sisters accepted. Cheered by about sixty other women gathered around the building, they relinquished control of the building before 9:00 A.M. and proclaimed victory.[1]

While the university responded quickly to the February Sisters' action, the rest of the Lawrence community barely took notice of the occupation. Perhaps Lawrencians were jaded from a decade of protests and social activism; perhaps they recognized and accepted the legitimacy of the women's demands; perhaps they felt this was only a university problem, one that did not affect the rest of the community. Regardless, Lawrencians appeared largely ambivalent about the takeover. The *Journal-World* gave little coverage to the protest, nor were there any editorials or letters to the editor in the wake of the action.[2] In contrast to the civil rights and antiwar demonstrations of a few years earlier, the February Sisters generated little public response; support for and opposition to their action, what little there was, were about equal.

The February Sisters' occupation of the East Asian building, however, was an important moment for women at KU and left an enduring legacy for women on campus. The Hilltop Child Development Center, the women's studies program at KU, and the women's health clinic on campus all trace their origins to the Sisters. Perhaps the real significance of the event was in the impact it had on the women themselves. Years later, February Sister Mary Coral recalled "such a feeling of power" when she walked into the East Asian building. For Coral, the experience "was wonderful. It changed women's minds about what they could and couldn't do. Finally we were doing something." The women's action symbolized how intensely personal politics had become, and how grassroots organizing and action had transformed the community's political culture.[3]

In Lawrence, as elsewhere in the United States, the emergence of a women's liberation movement came from the experience of women as both part of the university and the greater community. Women affiliated with the University of Kansas, either as students, faculty, spouses of faculty, or administrators, were key players in the development and spread of feminist consciousness in Lawrence.

Like the black freedom struggle, women's liberation—the women's rights movement or the feminist movement—is difficult to define, in large measure because it encompassed a broad spectrum of activism and beliefs. Not all women supported equal rights and opportunities for women, nor did all agree on how those goals could be reached. From the beginning, women who publicly identified with the women's liberation movement in Lawrence were divided between "liberal" and "radical" feminists. These two groups worked together cautiously to achieve common goals but always seemed to eye one another warily. Further making gender such a contested notion were those women who viewed the world in such a way that put gender equality at a much lower priority than, say, defending America's borders against communism or restoring the rule of law and order, both actions that tended to buttress the traditional order in Lawrence.

Just as the black freedom struggle had confronted white authority and the dominant racial hierarchy in American society, women in Lawrence confronted male authority, prescribed gender hierarchy, and institutionalized discrimination. Between 1960 and the early 1970s, American women constructed a movement that politicized privacy and one's personal life.[4] Gender politics and the rise of a feminist consciousness posed a powerful challenge to most men, and many women, in Lawrence. As the women's movement became more politicized, the response to the movement tended to reinforce traditional gender roles, making the challenge for feminists even greater.

Redefining the relationship between men and women, and transforming accepted gender roles in Lawrence, would not be easy. The cultural assumptions that neatly divided men's lives from those of women were deeply entrenched in the community. The *Journal-World*, as it acknowledged "Business Women's Week" in 1960, noted that the typical male executive would be lost trying to conduct business "without the help and loyal assistance of his womenfolk." Not only did women do their tasks "expertly" but also "dress[ed] up the office" and provided a "particular glow never found at a stag party." The newspaper also recounted the "ideal" working woman's day, which, in addition to her duties on the job, included full responsibility for the household chores and errands, all of which was done without "a word of complaint." Equally telling, the editorial compared the "ideal" woman to the one "next door," who at noon was still not dressed and whose house reeked of "a pool hall." The other woman was "grouchy" because her maid was absent and because she did not have "a thing to wear to bridge club, which incidentally means getting out for dinner because of no time to get any groceries."[5]

On the one hand, the *Journal-World* explicitly acknowledged women's participation in the work force and the business world, although that role was narrowly (and possessively) prescribed as a man's "womenfolk." On the other hand, and most significant, the paper assumes that although women worked outside the house, they still held responsibility for their traditional obligations of managing the household economy, which the "ideal" woman was expected to do without complaint. This was even more apparent when the "ideal" woman was compared to the "other," undesirable woman, who was depicted as slothful, ungrateful, lazy, and unable to conform to the traditional expectations of maintaining a house.

Lawrencians in the early 1960s agreed that a woman's primary job should be that of a homemaker. W. H. Trippensee, the manager of a local dime store in Lawrence, opposed a proposed federal minimum wage bill because his store had nine female employees, only one of whom "actually need[ed] . . . the money" because her husband was unemployed. The other workers used their wages, according to Trippensee, as "spending money or to supplement their husband's income." While he was concerned primarily with the economic consequences the bill would have on his store, Trippensee asserted that women were not really workers, but only augmented the real breadwinner, the man of the house. A few years later, Mr. and Mrs. Bert Day asked their congressperson to enact legislation to prevent a husband and wife from both holding jobs. A "woman's place is in the home, where the Good Lord intended her to train and care for her family," the Days declared. There would be less teenage delinquency, they argued, if women did not work outside of the home. Moreover, the Days also held that any woman working outside of the home whose husband was able to work was "depriving some able bodied man of a job to provide for his family and it isn't fair."[6] Trippensee and the Days both believed that there were specific social roles for men and women: women should stay at home, tend to the house, raise the children, and provide a suitable environment for the real breadwinners, men. Women worked outside of the home, conventional wisdom held, only because of dire economic need (an out-of-work or incapacitated husband) or to earn extra cash for some frivolous purchase.

Many Lawrencians predicted dire consequences if women did choose to work outside of the home. The *Journal-World* quoted a Kansas City Catholic archbishop who declared that "women must not desire to be more like men, but more truly women." The archbishop hoped, as did the *Journal-World,* that women would carry their "good influence into public life— but woman too often has left her home unattended and evil has moved into the home."[7] The consequences of women entering the paid labor force were great; they were the principal challenge to the accepted gender roles in the community.

Although the traditional perspective on women and work was dominant in the early 1960s, it belied the reality of life for women in Lawrence, most of whom worked outside the home. Excluding the 3,351 women enrolled in school and the small number of female inmates, in 1960 more women in Lawrence worked for wages outside of the home than not. Moreover, in 1960 married women made up about 54 percent of the female civilian labor force, a proportion that remained in 1970.[8]

As might be expected, women were paid much less than men. In 1960, the median yearly income for women in Lawrence was $969, about 39 percent of men's median income of $2,493. The difference was even greater for nonwhite women, who earned only an average of $623 annually. While the median income for women in Lawrence increased by 176 percent between 1960 and 1970, men's wages increased by 132 percent, meaning that the wage gap closed only slightly. By 1970, women's median income was still only 46 percent of men's median income.[9]

This is attributable, in part, to the kinds of jobs women held, which reflected dominant assumptions about both the temporary nature and life trajectory of women's work. Women in Lawrence who worked outside of the home in 1960 were scattered in a number of occupations, the largest of which were clerical and secretarial, which had long been culturally sanctioned as work appropriate to women. Some women held positions in the professions (i.e., finance, medicine, law), manufacturing, elementary and secondary education, management and administration, and sales. A sizable number were engaged in service industries such as domestic work, cleaning, food service, and health care.

The pattern of women's employment followed a different trajectory than men's, too, which again reflects deeply held assumptions about women and the family. The greatest share of the female work force in 1960 was comprised of women eighteen to twenty-four years of age (about 32 percent of the total) and those forty-five to sixty-four years of age (25.7 percent). Women between twenty-five and forty-four made up less than one-third of the female labor force. These data suggest that women in Lawrence decreased their participation in the labor force between the ages of twenty-four and forty-five, presumably because of marriage and child rearing. Women returned to the labor force when their children were older and out of school.

This pattern highlights the paradox of women's place in society, what Betty Freidan, in her seminal 1963 book, called the "feminine mystique." There occurred after World War II a blurring of the lines between the public and the private, accelerated by the massive social upheavals during the war. Between 1945 and 1962 many American women struggled to define their own identity in a culture that provided few options for them. The key to fostering a feminist consciousness, which developed slowly over the course of the 1960s and 1970s, was the great increase in women's participation in the paid labor force. As many historians have noted, while women's roles changed after World War II, the promise of equality for women in the workplace remained elusive.

This fact forcefully challenged traditional assumptions that prescribed women's place as in the home. These assumptions, while still quite powerful, rarely aligned with the realities of most women's lives. This contradiction, combined with increasing political activism throughout the country, created an atmosphere ripe for a movement for gender equality and heightened feminist consciousness. In Lawrence, as elsewhere in the country, the Civil Rights Act of 1964, the civil rights movement, and the antiwar movement all helped to spark feminist awareness and activism among students, faculty, and women in the community.

For feminist consciousness to take root in Lawrence, a great deal of inertia had to be overcome. Despite the increased number of women in the work force and in college after World War II and a decade of social and political upheaval, especially the dynamic struggle for racial equality and the student movement, by 1970 the pull of traditional gender roles was still very strong in Lawrence. The *Journal-World* ran a society page targeted at women, filled with wedding and engagement announcements, fashion and household advice, and advertisements directed at women as household consumers. The paper objectified women, too. For example, it ran a monthly "calendar girl," featuring photographs of women students. July's issue had a KU student in a bikini, while September's had one sitting on a stack of books in her mini-skirt.

There was nothing inherently wrong with providing information about social events or offering household tips; taking care of a house and family was, and is, important and meaningful work. The underlying assumption, however, was that these were the only issues in which women were interested. This assumption becomes more apparent when one searches for other material in the local newspaper directed to or about women. For example, women's sports coverage was nonexistent, although this was mostly because there were few women sports, at the professional, amateur, or collegiate level.

Moreover, even in the most banal of news stories, women were clearly objectified. In a front-page story about the Miss Kansas pageant in July 1970, the *Journal-World* noted that KU students "must be the most shapely girls in the state." Not only did the paper report that KU student Brenda Bartel had won the swimsuit competition at the pageant, it also noted she was five feet, five inches tall, measured "37–24–36," and had brown hair and green eyes. The pageant was not totally devoid of current politics. When asked about the women's liberation movement, the new Miss Kansas, Linda Susan Edds, replied that she favored it but did not "approve of picketing" because she did not "agree with people trying to force their ideas on others." She believed that women were discriminated against, and they "should get the same pay for the same work if they are as capable as a man doing the work, and they should be treated as equals."[10]

Nationally, the women's liberation movement took form in the mid-1960s. The National Organization for Women (NOW), a liberal group of mostly middle-class professional women, sought greater gender equality in the workplace and in public life through research, education, advocacy, legislation, and favorable court decisions. By 1970, nationwide polls indicated that while most women supported the goals of the movement, such as greater access to daycare, the repeal of abortion laws, and gender equity in the workplace, those same women refused to identify themselves as feminists and were antagonistic to the movement itself. Despite the lack of widespread support among women, the movement had made significant progress in changing ideas about women and their place in society.[11]

This was most evident among college-age women. Polls suggested that by the early 1970s, women college students held "wide and deep" acceptance of the movement's values and goals.[12] It is ironic that while many women, and some men, internalized the goals and values of the movement, most refused to identify themselves as feminists or actively participate in the movement.

Most Lawrencians seemed, at best, ambivalent about the emerging women's liberation movement across the nation. The *Journal-World*'s coverage of the Women's Strike for Equality, a nationwide general strike called by NOW in August of 1970, provides an indication of this attitude. "Liberation Day Has Blahs" read the *Journal-World*'s front-page headline. While thousands of women participated across the nation in what was the largest mass demonstration by women ever, in Lawrence the response was less than overwhelming. "As you may have noticed," the story began, "the women of Lawrence didn't stay home in droves today, the date of a national women's strike for equal rights. . . . Most of them didn't even stop buying groceries. And even the women's liberation advocates at Kansas University did little to make the day different from any other." The paper recounted that several demonstrations had been cancelled, including one at the student health clinic because organizers thought there would be too few passersby "to make the action worthwhile." According to the *Journal-World,* most women students at KU were wary of the strike's purpose and goals. One student opposed it because she did not want to be drafted, while another simply remarked "I don't know what they've got to gain." Another student (who, the *Journal-World* noted, sported the "new braless look") agreed, and another claimed the strike would "hurt them more than help them." These young women sharply distinguished themselves from "them," the women participating in the general strike.[13]

The following day, the *Journal-World* ran an editorial cartoon about the strike, dripping with sarcasm, which typified the paper's view of the women's movement. It depicted a group of women office workers reading the paper, drinking coffee, and chatting, while the male boss says "Strike? What strike? They're like this every day." The implication, of course, was that women do not really work, even when they hold jobs outside of the home.[14]

By 1970, the women's movement in Lawrence (if it could accurately be called a movement) found much of its strength on the campus of the University of Kansas. Between 1960 and 1972, women at the university were successful in changing rules and policies that affected personal behavior, such as the closing hours of women's campus housing units. But they also raised a number of other extremely personal issues—birth control, women's health, day care, and equal pay—that remained to be addressed. On campus, Watkins Hospital did not have a women's health clinic nor were contraceptives dispensed freely to female students who wanted them. Although female students could go to the Douglas County health department, it only dispensed birth control pills and did not provide full examinations.[15] Additionally, by the beginning of 1972, the university still had not implemented an affirmative action program to meet the requirements of Title IX of the 1964 Civil Rights Act, contrary to a federal mandate (nor, of course, had most other institutions). Female students, faculty, and staff continued to lobby the university for a campus daycare center.

Although many feminists in Lawrence had been New Left activists, there is no clear evidence that their dissatisfaction with the goals of or their place in the New Left moved some or most of them into the women's liberation movement. While some women were involved in New Left organizations like the KU chapter of Students for a Democratic Society, their numbers were small (although the records left by the group makes an accurate count impossible). Only occasionally does the name of a woman appear as a spokesperson for the group in local newspapers. Women across racial and class lines had been active in the Lawrence civil rights movement; indeed, the strength of the traditional civil rights movement had always been women and the church. Women had been officers in groups such as the Lawrence chapter of the Congress of Racial Equality and the student-based Civil Rights Council. Even within the highly masculinized rhetoric of the Black Power movement, embodied in Lawrence in the KU Black Student Union, women sometimes held positions of authority and spoke on behalf of the group.

In the fall of 1968, several KU students formed the Women's Liberation Front, but there is little extant information about the group, its members, or activities. As well, by the spring of 1970, a number of women's consciousness-raising groups had been formed in Lawrence, although one women's advocate called the movement in Lawrence "unorganized." The women who published a special issue of *Vortex* (a radical, left-wing, underground paper) on feminism asserted that women's liberation, "as a specific group doesn't exist in Lawrence, at least at this time. Most women who are interested in this type of thing have divided their energies among a variety of different liberal and radical organizations."[16]

On KU's campus, however, young women were beginning to organize in the struggle for gender equality, with the Women's Coalition (WC) and the Commission on the Status of Women (CSW) at the forefront. (CSW, formerly the Associate Women Students [AWS], had represented all women's living groups on campus.) The WC was generally conceded to be the "more radical" group, while CSW took a more "academic approach" to addressing issues of gender inequality. In general, the CSW focused on what it called the "practical" aspects of women's rights, while "women's liberation groups," such as the Women's Coalition, addressed "human responses and the effects of socialization." The CSW evolved out of the organizational structure of the AWS, which it replaced in 1970, and the NOW-style liberal feminism of Dean of Women Emily Taylor. The CSW sought to treat female students as individuals, rather than as members of a living group. An organization designed only to deal with regulations pertaining only to women, such as curfew hours, seemed anachronistic to many women on campus, thus the name change to the Commission on the Status of Women, the first such campus organization in the nation.[17]

The CSW was the larger of the two organizations. Its mailing list numbered around 500, and about a third of the recipients were men. Cindy

Hird, the CSW president, attributed the growth to a change in attitudes rather than to specific CSW programs. Compared to other schools across the country, the University of Kansas appeared to be ahead in addressing the concerns of gender equality on campus. Many schools, Hird noted, were still addressing the question of closing hours for women. Perhaps one reason for the wider support of the CSW was the group's fairly traditional image and approach to gender inequality. "A handful of women, most of them chicly-dressed sorority members, are changing the image of women's liberation at the University of Kansas," began a 1971 feature article on several CSW officers. The bulk of the CSW's programs focused on education, particularly on economic and employment discrimination. Since the mid-1960s, for example, the AWS had examined the extent that female graduates were using their degrees professionally, as well as gender differences in various campus departments. The CSW found, in a 1969–1970 study, that women and men had equal access to all of the educational, social, and cultural activities the university provided. While the university shielded women from the inequities of the outside world by providing equal leadership, scholarship, and educational opportunities, it also replicated that world: Women held a very small percentage of full-time teaching positions at KU, and only two women chaired their academic departments. The CSW also sponsored a series of seminars on human sexuality, which drew 750 to 1,000 people to each workshop. Topics included "Male and Female Sexual Response," "Birth Control Methods," and "Abortion." A CSW board member avowed that "men need to be educated, too" and that the world needed to be "feminized, that is, to emphasize the softer traits associated with womanliness."[18]

While the other notable feminist group on campus, the Women's Coalition, emphasized the same goals and programs as the CSW, it offered an alternative, more radical, route to women's equality. This was due, in part, to its origins, which were rooted in the experience of women in the counterculture and communes of Lawrence.[19]

The day before Rick Dowdell died, several women from the WC requested funds from the KU Student Senate to establish a women's center. As she announced the request, Patti Spencer, a recent KU graduate in English, one of the WC's founders, and a contributor to *Vortex,* demanded "an end" to the university's discrimination and "oppression" of women. The proposed center would provide child care facilities, childbirth counseling, and a self defense program, as well as information on birth control, abortion, and, and, women's studies. Rather than being run on the masculine model of a "strict" organizational hierarchy, Spencer insisted that the women's center would be operated by "a coordinating committee," by women for women. Two days later, the CSW asked the Student Senate for funds to pay the salary of a counselor-coordinator for the Human Sexuality Educational Center, where women could receive advice on abortion, birth control, and venereal disease and get referrals for treatment. The CSW acknowledged that its request was similar to the WC, but noted that its center would be "an alternative source of information and aid" to women who did not want to go to the center run by the WC.[20]

Regardless if one or both groups received funding, the prospect of a women's health and counseling center on campus was ludicrous to the *Lawrence Daily Journal-World*. In an editorial, the paper warned of "Two More Extremes." Such projects as the Gay Liberation Front (which earlier had asked to be officially recognized by the university so that it could receive funding from the Student Senate) and the women's center, the paper opined, "are just the kinds of things that parents want to hear about when they help their youngsters select a school. Because of the unrest and violence of recent months, parents and students are apprehensive about enrolling at KU, or coming back. Now we have two more excellent examples of why there is understandable concern. . . . [KU] is going to need all the greatness it can muster to weather the current storm without irreparable damage."[21]

In hindsight, the newspaper's fears appear unwarranted and perhaps a bit silly. The university did not disintegrate, despite the fact that both the women's health center and the gay liberation movement have a strong and vibrant presence on campus today. At the time, however, many Lawrencians believed that both threatened the mores and traditional gender boundaries of Lawrence society. Providing female students access to contraceptives challenged deeply held constructions of female sexuality by a male-dominated society. Likewise, gay liberation challenged the entire notion of heterosexuality and patriarchy, posing an alternative and oppositional model to a male world. Thus, the editorial, in large measure, reflects the pessimism of the town's elite as it struggled to hold on to its power and position in the community.

Spencer declared that her participation in the women's movement grew from her "caring for people" and directly from her "experiences as a woman. I'm fairly confused now about a lot of things. I think a lot of people are." The response to the women's center among Lawrence residents was minimal. Only two letters appeared in the *Journal-World* in favor of the center; none opposing it were published.[22]

The WC was instrumental, in 1971, in establishing Women's Self-Help, a women's health group that encouraged women to give themselves pelvic examinations. The WC also helped in launching a women's studies program at KU in 1972. By the fall of 1971, it also provided speakers to community groups, and had begun a speaker's bureau, a gay caucus, and a women's media committee. The latter put out a newsletter and published editorials in the *Journal-World*. The WC's "most effective" program was a self-defense course, which enrolled thirty-five women and was funded by Student Senate. The WC also sponsored a rape victim counseling program, which was less effective, possibly due to funding cuts by the university.[23]

While both the CSW and the WC pursued equal rights for women, they often took different paths toward that goal. Dean of Women Emily Taylor argued that there were really "two movements" for gender equality: one, represented by the CSW, that emphasized equal rights and opportunities, the other, represented by the WC, that was a "more extreme liberation movement." Proponents of the latter, she explained, were not struggling for gender equality, which they equated with "entering the same rat race" as men. In Taylor's mind, women's liberation was too radical because it focused on "upsetting the economic system and rearranging social patterns such as the family," neither of which, she believed, would appeal to most women. For Taylor, individual choice was "woman's most important right and obligation," and meant that "neither traditional roles nor their rejections are right for all women." As she had been doing since her arrival in Lawrence in the 1950s, Taylor encouraged young women to "discover the wide range of choices open to them and, through awareness and enlightened self-concern, to make the individual choices right for" themselves.[24]

Other women activists had more practical concerns about the women's liberation movement, such as it was in Lawrence. Sharyn Katzman, a faculty spouse with young children, was an early WC member who believed that the talk of revolution permeating the community was a "great influence" in moving women to organize. Katzman, who described herself as "a fairly rigid, traditional woman" who "wanted to get things done," left the WC, citing a lack of women her age, her responsibilities as a mother and wife, and "problems" with the WC, although she did not elaborate. Barb Krasne left the WC because she felt the group had not made any progress for women. She grew frustrated because the WC increasingly did not want to work with the CSW, in part because WC members rejected the formal structure of CSW and did not want to "spin their wheels" in such a setting. Suzanne Bocell, the president of the CSW, explained that she "sympathized with women's liberation groups" but that she had grown weary of their "radical techniques" and lack of effectiveness. Bocell noted the contrast between the CSW's and the WC's reactions to sexist ads in the *University Daily Kansan* the previous year. While the WC "burned" the papers in protest, the CSW appealed directly to the *Kansan* board, which Bocell believed was a better, more constructive approach.[25]

Publicly, however, Bocell's comments were as far as anyone from either group would go in condemning or attacking the other. The WC commended the organization and energy of the CSW and admitted that a radical position would be "impossible" for a university-recognized group. Moreover, the WC was partially dependent upon the CSW, as funding for the women's center flowed from the Student Senate through CSW and then to the WC.[26] One consequence of this symbiotic relationship, however, was a blurring of lines between the two groups, often to the chagrin of more conservative CSW members.

The fact that the campus was the locus of women's activism resulted in no small measure from the presence of Emily Taylor. Taylor formed the Commission on the Status of Women as a committee of the AWS shortly after she arrived in Lawrence in 1956, five years before President John F. Kennedy created a national body of the same name. Taylor was a member of, and a frequent speaker and organizer for, the National Women's Political Caucus, the Women's Equity Action League, the National Organization of Women, the Intercollegiate Association of Women Students, the American Association of University Women, and the National Association of University Women Deans and Counselors. She also moderated a half-hour radio program on the campus station called "Feminist Perspective."[27] By the early 1970s, Taylor was also working to expand the offerings in women's studies.

Taylor identified herself as a "conventional feminist" concerned mostly with equal opportunity for women in work and educational markets. She rejected the term "women's liberation," which she believed carried an unfavorable "emotional connotation" to the New Left of the 1960s. Taylor believed that the phrase made many women uncomfortable, in particular those content with fulfilling traditional gender roles, who feared that "someone is going to force everybody to get out and work, to force them to give up the choice they have made." Taylor preferred the terms "women's movement" or "women's rights movement" because they more accurately described the focus of her activism.[28]

Increasingly, university women committed to the cause of gender equality felt it necessary to distance themselves from the radical wing of the feminist movement. "Because of the recent misrepresentation created by the news media, the K.U. Commission on the Status of Women feels it necessary to explain the difference between the K.U. Commission and the Women's Liberation Movement," began a 1970 letter to the Kansas Board of Regents. The letter pointed out that the CSW no longer represented the interests of all women at KU but was now "an active body" of like-minded women. Similarly, in the first issue of *Comment,* the CSW newsletter, the editors pointed out that while the CSW was "fighting for women's equality," it did not "follow 'bra burning' tactics. . . . We want women to have the choice" A column later in the same issue also addressed the matter. It stated that women's rights activists were "not merely trying to arouse male hostilities" but were attempting to "broaden" the "very narrow horizons" available to women. These feminists wanted "the freedom to choose any career, to marry or stay single, to raise a family or not raise a family, and to live a life style that suits their individual needs." The author continued: "The struggle to rebuild the attitudes of society cannot be easily won by alienating the current ruling class—the males."[29]

Even the traditional, mainstream feminism of the CSW, however, threatened many Lawrence women, especially older women. Boydston admitted that when the CSW met with women's organizations in the community, the older women often felt "threatened" by the "questioning of their daily roles." The CSW found its greatest reception with professional women, who had experienced first-hand wage and employment discrimination. Fears about sexuality—both heterosexuality and homosexuality—also confronted the CSW. Casey Eike, an assistant to Taylor in the Dean of Women's office, said her office often was criticized for dispensing information about birth control. "There are still people out there who are very much against us thinking that people have sexual lives at all."[30]

Despite the ambivalence many Lawrencians felt about women's liberation, a growing feminist consciousness was evident in some parts of Lawrence. Among the most common women's organizations in Lawrence in the 1960s were book and social clubs, such as the Zodiac Club, which had been organized in 1878. The Zodiac Club was not a bastion of radical feminism, but the group's programs in the late 1960s and early 1970s reflect a growing engagement with social and political issues. In 1967–68 the club focused its discussions on such topics as the "History of Vietnam" and "The Role of the United States in Southeast Asia." In 1972, the "year of the woman" was the club's annual theme. It hoped to better understand the place of women in contemporary society and to explore the prospects for changing attitudes and expectations regarding women's place in society. Perhaps a more telling indication of feminism's growing influence was the way in which members were identified. Women's names in the club's programs were traditionally all listed as "Mrs. (husband's first and last name)." In the 1972–73 program, however, for the first time each woman's first name was used.[31]

On September 26, 1970, the Zodiac Club welcomed Professor Wil Linkeugel of the KU speech department, who spoke about the "Rhetoric of the Women's Movement." Linkeugel told the Zodiac Club that he had identified three branches of the women's movement. In addition to the moderate NOW, which wanted "total equality by legislation," Linkeugel noted two other women's liberation groups, one from Chicago that grew out of SDS and one from New York. The Chicago group, according to Linkeugel, believed capitalism reinforced gender inequality and that "we must have communism." The New York group saw the problem as "strictly a battle between the sexes and that women must pull away entirely, find themselves, and then come back together in unisex." To underscore his point, Linkeugel declared that one had only to look at women wearing jeans and men with long hair to "see that the unisex idea has gone a long way." Linkeugel concluded his presentation by claiming that radical feminists would not give women the choice to work or stay at home; "they would have us all leave home."[32]

Linkeugel's understanding of radical feminism suggests the difficulty in the women's movement obtaining widespread popular support. Out of necessity, a more radical feminist critique emerged in the early 1970s that challenged the foundations of patriarchy and male privilege in the United States. Whether it was class-based, with capitalism as the principal agent of women's oppression, or sex-based, with patriarchy as the main culprit, it was undoubtedly radical. It questioned the traditional ordering of American society, including marriage and the family.

The first phase of 1960s women's activism was modeled on the civil rights movement, in part because many women had gained experience in that struggle, including many in Lawrence.[33] By the end of the decade, however, a new phase, radical feminism, had appeared in Lawrence, drawn largely from the city's counterculture. Radical feminists, like their sisters elsewhere, had come to draw comparisons between their own oppression and that of African Americans and other minorities. By 1970, several women had organized feminist consciousness-raising groups, a women's issue had appeared in the underground paper *Vortex*, and the *Lavender Luminary*, a lesbian paper, began publication. Radical feminists cast relationships between men and women in political terms, arguing that sex, not race or class, was the key to understanding, and ending, women's oppression. Moreover, radical feminists offered a "provocative" analysis of the family, love and marriage, heterosexuality, and rape that challenged conventional gender roles. While they used different means, radical and liberal feminists frequently worked toward the same ends. Both sought greater access for women to contraceptives and abortion rights, demanded child-care centers, and called for an end to the objectification of women in the media and throughout the larger culture. To achieve their goals, radical feminists often employed a technique they called "consciousness raising," which was quite effective in attracting women into the movement and building solidarity among women. Increased numbers and greater unity within the movement were evident in Lawrence by 1970.[34]

This transformation continued into the 1970s and beyond. If anything, political and social issues became more intense and more personal after 1970. This was due, in no small measure, to the spread of feminist consciousness and to the fact that, subsequently, women's bodies became sites of cultural struggle. As a result, women in Lawrence had developed more radical critiques of American society and had organized to liberate themselves from male dominance. Radical feminism, like other radical movements such as

Black Power, pushed the discussion beyond the accepted bounds of mainstream political discourse. Radical feminists challenged fundamental American values and institutions, whether in their critique of the economic system or the family structure. They claimed, with much justification, that marriage and the prescribed social roles expected of women severely constrained the options available to women. Heterosexuality similarly was limited, and homosexuality offered an alternative way to order and live one's life.

Their critique was valid: Male privilege was very real, and societal expectations did limit women to very narrow social and economic roles. Radical feminism, however, became an unacceptable path for many women, including many women sympathetic to the principle of gender equality. The rhetoric of radical feminism was well outside the bounds of acceptable political discourse for many women, because its critique directly challenged the roles that many women embraced and the social structure that gave them comfort.

In February 1972, the radical feminist and noted author Robin Morgan spoke on campus to a crowd of some 350 people, including 100 men. Morgan declared that the "'serious' part of the women's movement" was "radical feminism," which did not allow men to participate. The ideology of radical feminism was "very clear," Morgan said, "the priority is women. It's not warmed over Marxism." Morgan sneered at the mainstream women's organizations, such as the liberal National Organization for Women, derisively calling it the NAACP of women's movements in seeking legislation and political compromises in the quest for gender equality. She urged women to get "in touch" with their "own pain" and struggle on their "own terms in terms of . . . [their] own oppression." Morgan also demanded that Lawrence women stop—"by any means necessary"—a women's history course being taught by Linkeugel, "make" Watson Library purchase a $900 collection of historical documents about women, and "organize anti-rape squads" to provide collective protection for women. After her speech, Morgan asked the men in attendance to leave, and she and several women gathered and held a closed meeting.[35]

From that meeting the February Sisters, a group of students, faculty, and women affiliated with the university, were born. Morgan's appearance had a galvanizing effect on women in Lawrence. February Sister Mary Coral recalled that during the women-only meeting after Morgan's speech, she found that two or three other groups in the community were trying to address the same issues that interested her, especially access to birth control and day care. One of the Sisters remarked years after, "Morgan didn't organize the February Sisters, but her presence brought together women from all over the campus who discovered in Morgan's rap session that others were organizing over the same injustices, including pay disparity between male and female faculty, a lack of child care on campus, and the inability of female students to receive a full range of gynecological services at the student health center. Their collective anger, their shared frustrations birthed the February Sisters."[36]

The details of that closed meeting were never revealed, but the following day the February Sisters met to plan the occupation of a university building. Fearing that the FBI or KBI had planted a spy in the group, only three of the women knew that the East Asian building was the target. Their preparation was meticulous and precise; the East Asian building was selected because it was the easiest to secure with chains and locks, and the windows could be easily covered with boards. The Sisters brought bedding and blankets with them, arranged for food to be delivered to them by comrades on the outside, prepared press releases giving their demands and reasons for the demonstration, and planned an escape route once the occupation ended.[37]

For several of the February Sisters, their action flowed from their previous involvement in the antiwar and civil rights movements. Mary Coral was a faculty wife and chair of the Women's International League for Peace and Freedom. For Christine Leonard, the sit-in was the "culmination" of nearly a decade of political activism spent protesting against the Vietnam War and for civil rights in Lawrence. Leonard arrived in Lawrence in 1964, working in the library as a clerk-typist. By 1972, she was separated from her husband while struggling to support her two children. Childcare, she noted, was both scarce and expensive, so both her children accompanied her during the sit-in. The other Sisters chose Leonard to negotiate with the university administration. She recalled being both scared and exhilarated during the meetings. The thing she remembered most, however, was the look on the faces of the male administrators when she declared the Sisters were "'not just students. We're employees, and we're faculty wives.' This ripple of energy went out. You could see every man there deciding whether he knew where his wife was."[38]

The February Sisters were an ad-hoc group, created solely for the one-night occupation of the East Asian building. After that action, and a few news conferences over the next several weeks, they never met again as a group, although many of the participants remained active in other feminist organizations. Their need for anonymity was typical of many radical feminists around the country, who preferred not to acknowledge a leader or spokesperson. Women activists, in general, preferred anonymity and avoided the charismatic leadership role that men sought, working instead to build relationships and a sense of community within the movement.[39] Their experience in the New Left and civil rights movements had left many of them resentful over the clash of personalities and the leadership battles that ultimately obscured the goals and tactics of those movements. National feminist leaders believed what women "were doing was making a women's movement," and were "not out to make individuals involved in that movement famous."[40]

Of their six demands, they believed they had obtained one: A woman they endorsed would chair the affirmative action program. The SenEx's support of the day care and health care demand was also seen as a positive, although SenEx also "decried" the Sisters' tactics. The Sisters were largely "satisfied" with ongoing negotiations on the daycare center and the creation of a women's health clinic, but warned that they expected "additional action" from the administration by the end of March or "the February Sisters will rally and move again."[41]

For its part, the university claimed that it had been working on most of the Sisters's demands and had made progress in implementing them. John Conard, director of university relations and development, admitted that the university "may have been at fault for not publicizing its efforts more, as the women were unaware of many steps the university had taken." Not surprisingly, given his experience during his first year in office, Chalmers was eager to avoid publicity and moved quickly to protect the school's image. On February 4, Chalmers announced a series of affirmative action plans, including a new staff position to address the needs of women on campus. The other demands were not to be quickly met. On February 16, the student senate rejected SenEx's recommendation and turned down a request for a daycare center, claiming it would rather seek a long-term solution to the matter rather than a quick fix. The senate also questioned the "advisability" of funding "a group which had demonstrated its irresponsibility by occupying a university building." Despite the senate's action, a plan and funds were found, and in the fall, Hilltop Child Development Center opened on campus.[42]

Those few individuals who voiced an opinion about the February Sisters displayed little sympathy for the women's goals, tactics, and critique of their place in society. In fact, several writers blatantly illustrated the sexism and attitudes that the Sisters were trying to overcome. An example came from John Overbrook, a student from Oskaloosa, Kansas, whose tirade accused the Sisters of being "the most untogether group I have ever seen." Overbrook pointed out that the university had been working on the problems the Sisters addressed and criticized their action as unnecessary and grandstanding. He continued:

That poor oppressed group of about 30 human beings have taken it upon themselves to educate their half of the human race to the fact that they are oppressed and it's all the other half's fault and that the University of Kansas had better do something about it. . . . To the dismay of these idealistic broads, their demands were already being worked on. But I have no fear that given time, a whole new list of demands can be compiled. Long live the oppressed. Don't worry though, girls, because I am fully prepared and qualified as a male chauvinist pig sexist to admit that my half of the human race is at fault. It just gets a little hard, though, when one of yours in a tight sweater and tight jeans walks by. She must be one of the uneducated sisters who is still working under the antiquated system, headed by marriage. Have no fear, because that sister will change as soon as she gulps down 30 minutes of hard sell from Robin Morgan. Look what that cataclysmic catalyst did for the February Sisters, who were ready to castrate everybody starting with Chalmers. I'll never open another door for anybody but myself.[43]

Not only were Overbrook's remarks sexist, hostile, and insensitive to women's needs, but they evoked many of the criticisms angry and threatened whites had directed at the civil rights movement. As well, he felt personally threatened by the Sisters's actions.

Other comments were just as sarcastic and echoed a similar defense of traditional gender boundaries. "I just wanted to publicly commend the February Sisters for repressing the cause of liberation for women and men on this campus," read a letter from one male student, with tongue firmly in cheek:

Of course, there is a great deal of logic in seizing a campus building of such great stature and then putting forth a list of six demands, all of which were being dealt with in a concrete way before the "dramatic effect" of the seizure hit the news. Done that way, you can be sure that you will be able to say that you succeeded. . . . I am tired of hearing the blame for the problems of women being placed on the "male chauvinist pigs." A great deal of the blame may be given to the millions of "female chauvinist pigs," call them Hefner's silent majority if you will, who are more than content in their subservient role handed down by countless generations. Equal rights for women would indeed be a good thing. It would eliminate the loathsome task of living up to the masculine or feminine stereotype. . . . However, since men are in charge right now, they will hang on very tightly to their financially and authoritatively superior positions until all women, including Hefner's silent majority, are ready and willing to take on equal responsibilities along with their equal rights.[44]

On February 21, Peter George, a KU graduate student, filed a complaint against the Sisters with the university ombudsman. While George claimed he did not question the "validity" of the Sisters' grievances, he took exception to their "extra-legal action," which he believed set a "dangerous precedent." George said he supported all of the Sisters' goals except one; the appointment of a woman vice-chancellor. "[T]hat's reverse sexism," he declared.[45]

A *Kansan* editorial claimed that the Sisters only wanted publicity. He also criticized their anonymity, which he declared was "a right to which no newsmaker is entitled: that of dictating what the public could know about them. They sought to influence public opinion and openly demanded University funds, yet they refused to even identify themselves. They sought to manage the news and this is inexcusable." He also accused them of using "thug tactics." Although he argued it was not the university's place to provide daycare and health services (the city should), he acknowledged that "[t]hey have focused attention upon a situation that too long has been ignored and which now can be acted upon. . . . Brash and theatrical as their methods sometimes were, they succeeded in informing us about the plight of many women in this community."[46]

According to Christine Leonard, the protest was largely symbolic. The police could easily have removed the women. The support among women on campus for the Sisters's action appeared to be nearly unanimous. Women on the staff and faculty praised the Sisters, especially their goals. Although the Sisters were a minority of women on campus, Leonard believed they represented the views of most women on campus. "We knew how deep the sentiment was and the support was pretty incredible," she recalled.[47]

It did appear that the Sisters had near-unanimous support among women faculty and staff, who rejected the administration's claims that the needs of women on campus were being addressed. Joan Handley, chair of KU's Committee on the Status of Women and the KU Association of American University Professors, asserted that she had been trying to get an affirmative action office going by "patiently" working "within the system" for some time. She noted that "[w]e have had promises and no results. I applaud the courage of the women who, by their action last weekend, achieved something that others were not able to achieve" through traditional means. Handley noted with irony that it often took dramatic action to compel action. What the Sisters accomplished was to open "lines of communication which are serving to unite women in many areas of the University community. It is no longer (if it ever was) a matter which concerns a 'poor oppressed group of about 30.'"[48]

The Sisters's demand for a comprehensive women's health clinic on campus was perhaps the most controversial, because it was fundamentally about women controlling their own sexual and reproductive rights. The advent of the birth control pill in the early sixties had promised a "sexual revolution," but prescribing the pill for unmarried women, especially college students, raised moral issues that were applied exclusively to women. Thus, prescribing or not prescribing birth control pills, along with women's health in general, involved a struggle to define and maintain traditional roles for women.[49] Dr. Raymond Schwegler, the director of student health services at Watkins Health Clinic, had refused to dispense contraceptives to students through the clinic, remarking that "this is old fashioned, mid-Victorian . . . [b]ut Watkins will not contribute to the recreational activities of the campus." Women who requested gynecological examinations or birth control at Watkins often received a "morality lecture" instead. Moreover, pelvic examinations and pap smears were not covered by student health insurance, which was a refusal on the university's part to "acknowledge [that] women's sexual and reproductive organs were legitimate parts of their bodies." The Sisters's actions, therefore, made women's bodies a point of struggle. Schwegler resisted the implementation of a women's health clinic, citing a "lack of funds, space and qualified personnel."[50]

The February Sisters shifted a masculinized discourse focused on morality and the proper roles for women to one centered "on and of women." A women's health clinic eventually was added to Watkins, but as Schwegler remarked twenty years later, all he did was add the title of "clinic" to the women's health program. "We didn't even change offices," Schwegler recalled, adding that the women "were very outspoken, but they could have gotten what they wanted without asking for it. It was going to happen anyway."[51] While Schwegler downplays both the women's health clinic and the Sisters's role in its creation, real change did occur. Watkins began dispensing birth control pills soon after the Sisters's action, and soon developed a more comprehensive women's health program.

Along with the Hilltop Child Development Center (which began taking children in the fall of 1972) and the increased women's health services, perhaps the most lasting legacy of the February Sisters was the creation of the women's studies program at KU. Although the Sisters demanded a Department of Women's Studies, the university created only a program, which still exists. The affirmative action program, already in the works but tangled in university bureaucracy, would have been in place in a matter of time. While it is clear that the takeover of the East Asian building in 1972 was not the only reason that programs like affirmative action were implemented at the university, it seems apparent that that very public action, at the very least, sped up the process.

Within a year of the occupation of the East Asian building, women in Lawrence formally organized to address gender inequality. On campus, the Office of Affirmative Action for Women had been staffed. Activists also formed two community-based organizations, a Lawrence chapter of the National Organization of Women and the grassroots Lawrence Women's Political Caucus (LWPC). The fledgling NOW chapter counted thirty members in 1973 but hoped to double or triple that figure within a year. Bonnie Patton, NOW president, promised the group would research Kansas statutes that had been superceded by national legislation. She also believed attitudes had changed in the recent past, particularly over the issue of abortion, which Patton thought was at the core of the women's movement. The LWPC vowed to watch the Kansas Legislature's action on abortion laws, child daycare, and civil service requirements. The caucus also wanted to see more women appointed to state boards and commissions.[52]

The February Sisters's campaign split the WC, and many of the older members dropped out. The leaders of the February Sisters assumed leadership of the WC. Another February Sister, Barb Krasne, an Overland Park junior, felt a "letdown" after the takeover of the campus building. With students gone over the summer, a lot of the energy dissipated, and members went on to work on their own "personal projects." As a result of the February Sisters, Spencer noted, the WC became much more political. As well, the WC also focused much of its activity around issues of concern for gay women, which some WC members viewed ambivalently. Spencer saw the gay presence as a source of strength for the coalition, while Ann Francke, a one-time coordinator for the WC, feared that homophobia would weaken the movement. "I think Women's Coalition is imploding," Francke declared. Women are refusing to "confront their bigotries, their fear of gay women that are working in Women's Coaltion."[53]

Gay liberation and sexual freedom were but two strands of the women's liberation movement, but, as they offered the most radical challenge to the status quo, were the most feared and resisted. For some women, lesbianism was a liberating experience that moved them away from the dominance of men. The women's liberation movement gave sustenance to a gay liberation movement that challenged "the tyranny of heterosexuality," one of the most entrenched aspects of male supremacy. Lesbianism held tremendous "political power" for many women because it allowed them to reject the established order of heterosexuality.[54]

While some women in Lawrence saw homosexuality as the path to equality, many others shared the views of KU Dean of Women Emily Taylor, who believed that the most important tool for achieving equality was the Equal Rights Amendment (ERA). Taylor thought the ERA was a "significant and necessary step" in assuring equality for women in America."[55] By the time the amendment passed through Congress in 1970, more women—and in particular women with college degrees and those in the professions—were aware of the inequality they faced in the workplace and in American society. Like Taylor, many saw the ERA as a way to address that inequality. The public debate over the ERA, however, revealed deep divisions with in American society over the proper role of women, in which opponents of the ERA painted the modest goals of liberal feminists with the rhetoric of radical feminism.

Clearly, women were discriminated against because of their gender. Despite the provisions of the Equal Pay Act of 1963, women in Lawrence still earned less than half of men's wages. There were other, more subtle forms of inequality, too. One woman, for example, claimed the Veterans Administration would not consider her income when she and her husband applied for a home loan because she was "of child bearing age" and was assumed to leave her "career one day to raise a family." She wanted Kansas senator James Pearson to support the ERA. "As a professional person with a master's degree, I find this insulting to my intelligence and to my sense of responsibility, particularly in view of the number of methods of birth control available and the more intelligent laws concerning abortion recently enacted in Kansas and other states."[56]

Overwhelming support for the ERA came from professional women in Lawrence. Vivian Rogers McCoy, the director of student services at KU and the wife of a KU history professor, supported the ERA because she had "encounter[ed] many Kansas women now experiencing serious job discrimination, educational bias, and psychic and financial insecurity because of their sex." Many women from the Lawrence Business and Professional Women's Club, including administrative assistants and several realtors, supported the ERA "without any weakening amendments."[57] The Kansas Legislature responded to ERA supporters and became the sixth state in the nation to ratify the amendment by an overwhelming margin.[58] There was little debate on the Kansas House floor, although several legislators feared that the amendment had not been given sufficient attention. Additionally, there had been little public discussion of the ERA in Kansas, and newspapers gave limited press coverage to either the debate or the vote. By the end of 1972, twenty-two of the thirty-five states required for ratification had approved the amendment.

Surprisingly, there was virtually no public opposition to the ERA in Lawrence in 1970. Perhaps the town's attention was diverted elsewhere. Opponents to the ERA did emerge, however, after the Kansas Legislature passed it in 1972. A grassroots movement led by energetic ERA opponents made sure their voices were heard, and in 1973, a resolution was introduced in the Kansas House to rescind the ERA. By 1974, a grassroots movement to overturn Kansas's ratification was in full bloom. Although the effort was unsuccessful, it does illustrate the ways in which Lawrencians were engaged in a continuing political discourse on acceptable social boundaries for American women.

In general, opponents of the ERA in Lawrence espoused the same arguments used by national ERA opponents such as Phyllis Schlafly. Mr. and Mrs. Robert R. Burk's opposition was typical. They opposed it because they believed it would "equally subject women to the draft and military service and it would allow homosexuals to marry, adopt children, and teach in public schools." They encouraged Pearson to "[p]lease vote to get this recinded [sic] in Kansas." Larry Shambaugh, a lineman for Kansas Power and Light, and his wife Mary, predicted the ERA ultimately would "destroy our American way of life. There will not be any free choice for women, it will be a mandatory way of living." The Shambaughs also believed the ERA would "subject women to the draft," and for them the "thought of what could happen to a women P.O.W. is almost unbearable to consider." Mrs. Elmer Rollins opposed the "many repugnant things" the ERA would do, particularly reducing American women "to the status of Russian women." As did many of the ERA's opponents in Lawrence, she included one of Phyllis Schlafly's "Pink Sheets" with her letter. In addition to her concerns about women being subject to the draft and homosexuals marrying, Mrs. A. W. Luallin, whose husband was retired, opposed the ERA because it would "finalize abortion on demand." She also believed if a wife did not provide half of a couple's living expenses, "her husband can use it as grounds for divorce." She thought there would be other consequences, too. Churches would be "required to hire women preachers. Please work to get this recinded [*sic*] in Kansas," she begged Pearson. Alice M. Smith, a widow and cook at Delta Gamma sorority, opposed the ERA because women would be "subject to draft and combat" and homosexuals would be able to marry.[59]

Mildred Catlett, whose husband worked for the city of Lawrence, wanted Congress to "refuse tax funds to the Committee on International Woman's Year, which will be used for the ratification of the E.R.A." Catlett supported the principle of equal pay for all working women, but believed "that isn't what the Equal Rights Amendment is about at all." Nanette Alexander, whose husband was an engineer at Sunflower Ordnance Plant, also was concerned that federal funds were being used by "proponents of ERA" such as the National Organization for Women. "As a taxpayer and opponent of ERA I object to these funds being used by pro ERA forces and wives of gov[ernment] and state officials influencing legislatures." She wanted to know "how equal money can be made available for those who wish to lobby against ERA." On another occasion, Alexander noted that there had been a "hasty vote on the ERA" in Kansas. She opposed federal funds going to the International Women's Conference and enclosed several of Schlafly's Pink Sheets.[60] Using language similar to that used by opponents of the New Deal, civil rights legislation, black nationalism, youth activism, antiwar protests, and a host of other challenges to traditional authority, the ERA's opponents wrote that it threatened the identities that Lawrencians had constructed for themselves, especially what they defined as the "American way of life."

Additionally, opponents of the ERA, many of whom were women, rejected the new roles that the feminist movement had helped to create for women. One woman declared that she wanted "the protection, privileges and courtesies that I enjoy as a woman. I would have to get down off my pedestal to be equal with men. The ERA will not bring an equality of rights but a loss of rights" for women. Additionally, ERA opponents brought religion into the debate, which made the issue much more personal for them and let them argue that Christianity provided separate roles for men and women. Debbie Barnes Miles, a former Miss America who lived in Eudora, Kansas, in Douglas County, averred that as "a Christian and a believer in the Bible, I can't say I want to be equal to a man." Miles, on another occasion, insisted that the Bible demands that the man be the head of the family, and that "the wife . . . obey him. It may sound old-fashioned and fuddy-duddy, but it works."[61]

Most threatening to the identity and traditional boundaries that ERA opponents constructed for themselves was their belief that the ERA would "legalize" homosexual relationships and that lesbians were the measure's biggest advocates. What this meant for society, should the ERA become law, was too abhorrent for some Lawrencians to consider, for it attacked the basis on which they constructed their own sense of self. Alice LaFrenz, whose husband was a technician at Hallmark, was "horrified at what we're being threatened with" if the ERA was ratified. LaFrenz, a mother of two, felt that this "garbage, this 'invasion' of privacy will lead to such a demoralized society, it will not be a fit place to raise a family." Connie Kamp, whose husband Roy was a laborer at FMC, remarked that she had "become aware of what the ERA really means" and was "appalled." According to Kamp, the ERA "would do away with the sacredness of womanhood, motherhood, and the home; God has never let a nation with such a demoralized society go unpunished."[62]

Much of the opposition to the amendment came from women, mainstream conservatives, and religious moderates, most of whom were working class. Many opponents were motivated by their religious beliefs, but not everyone in the anti-ERA movement was a fundamentalist. As the anti-ERA movement in Kansas "evolved into an attack on the feminists who supported it, and as their critique of the amendment evolved into a defense of the traditional family, these women helped to create the pro-family movement which became a critical component of American conservatism."[63] In calling for a return to traditional gender roles and for a defense of traditional values, opponents of the ERA offered an alternate narrative of the American experience, one that rejected feminism and gender equality.

It is not surprising that the feminist movement was widely opposed and aroused great hostility in some Lawrencians. As it was highly decentralized and diverse, great conflicts among activists resulted, with sexuality, ideology, and tactics and strategy providing the clearest dividing lines. Nonactivists were ambivalent about the movement; not until the passage of the Equal Rights Movement did many Lawrencians begin to express their anger and outrage with feminism. Many men felt assailed by feminism and its critique of male-female relationships, which, they believed, threatened their very sense of self. As well, many women rejected the goals and values of the women's movement, in particular those who had devoted their lives to caring for their home and raising their children.

Despite this resistance, however, in fact women in Lawrence had been pushing the boundaries of the traditional "women's spheres" throughout the 1960s, often quietly and without fanfare. Women at KU and in Lawrence were on the front lines of the fight to end double standards of behavior for men and women, to eliminate racial exclusion, and to end the war in Vietnam. In addition to these activists, women with different worldviews and goals also became politicized during the 1960s. Some of the women who protested the Vietnam War as mothers concerned for the nation's sons were, indeed, at the fore of the antiwar movement. Lawrencians who lobbied the Kansas Legislature to rescind the ERA became part of a state-wide grassroots political movement that later became a part of the New Right in the 1970s and 1980s. Their motives may have been presented as traditionally female, but their activism proved that they were engaged in and passionate about a wider world than that of their own homes.

The February Sisters's takeover of the East Asian building was a dramatic moment in the university's history and a turning point for its women. It was, however, just one more example of how women in Lawrence were, throughout the 1960s, making their voices heard by fighting for their individual values. Certainly not all women who became politically active during this period considered themselves feminists, nor did they all identify with the feminist movement. Many, in fact, were categorically opposed to the nascent feminist movement of the late 1960s and early 1970s, and were willing to become politically active only to oppose many of the changes that feminists pursued. Women's roles did not change dramatically in Lawrence in the 1960s, but by the end of the decade women on both ends of the ideological spectrum were becoming politicized by both challenging and defending society's traditional gender boundaries. In so doing, they began a debate about women's roles in our culture that continues to be argued today.

EPILOGUE

As the February Sisters's takeover of the East Asia building suggests, neither the problems that prompted social activism nor activism itself ended as the calendar flipped over to the 1970s. The antiwar movement in Lawrence continued until the last American troops were pulled out of Vietnam in March 1973, and even then the war still had its supporters in town. Lawrencians in 1974 pondered the issue of amnesty for draft resisters (or "draft dodgers" and "deserters," depending on one's politics). While many supported amnesty, others strongly disagreed, claiming it would be a slap in the face of all veterans and demean their sacrifice.

The culture wars continued, too. Shortly after taking office in 1971, Kansas's new attorney general, Vern Miller, made good on his law-and-order, anti-hippie and anti-drug campaign promise by personally leading the state's biggest ever drug bust in Lawrence. Miller's election was a political statement by the many Lawrencians who supported him in a continuing struggle to define American values and the proper ordering of society. The drug busts continued throughout Miller's tenure as attorney general, gaining him a reputation among his supporters as "Super Cop."[1] Miller's strong stance to maintain law and order symbolized the extent to which politics, social issues, and cultural dissent had become matters of personal identity, not only for activists but also for the "Silent Majority," an amorphous group of mostly white citizens of all economic classes. Seeking to restore their sense of self, those who saw themselves as part of the Silent Majority sought to reclaim the public square and return to "traditional values." Their impact would not be felt fully until the 1980s, when the nation's political agenda swung to the Right and the Silent Majority provided a ready-made political constituency for Ronald Reagan, Newt Gingrich, and other conservatives.

Lawrence has changed a great deal since the 1970s, yet in some ways it is still the same. Its population grew to nearly 53,000 by 1980, and to over 65,000 by 1990. Between 1990 and 2000, Lawrence's population swelled to 80,098, a remarkable increase of 22.1 percent. It has become a suburb of the southern Kansas City metropolitan area, with much of the rapid growth occurring to the south and west. While the population has grown substantially, the racial characteristics of the community have changed little. Whites still are the overwhelming majority, comprising nearly 84 percent of the population. Blacks number 4,078 in Lawrence, greater in numbers than they were in the sixties but still comprising about 5 percent of the population. Native Americans are still a distinct minority, comprising only 2.9 percent of Lawrence's total population.[2]

As well, the issues that Lawrencians debated and the problems they confronted in the 1960s have not gone away. The names and faces have changed, but the essence of the discourse remains the same. Since the 1960s, Lawrence has not experienced upheaval on the magnitude of the summer of 1970, but social and political activism, in a variety of forms, has continued. Perhaps more significantly, Lawrencians today continue to disagree in the public arena over the meaning of basic American values: What is the meaning of freedom, equality, and citizenship? What are the terms of civil, social, and political participation? What is the role of the government in legitimizing these claims? Two brief examples illustrate this ongoing discourse.

In 1985, the Lawrence city commission refused to read a proclamation for Gay and Lesbian Awareness Week. A recommendation by the Department of Human Relations to add "sexual orientation" to an equal rights ordinance was at first ignored by the commission. Citizens for Human Rights in Lawrence (CHRL) supported the measure while the Alliance of Citizens for Traditional Values (ACTIVE) opposed it. ACTIVE contended that businesses would be forced to hire a quota of homosexuals and that the DHR had not proven that discrimination against gays existed. The commission subsequently voted 3–2 against the measure, citing a lack of evidence of discrimination and not wanting to endorse a particular "lifestyle."[3]

The issue was revived in 1991, when a new grassroots organization, the Freedom Coalition, took the lead. The Lawrence chapter of the National Organization of Women and the Freedom Coalition, with the support of the ACLU, the League of Women Voters, the KU Ecumenical Christian Ministries, and the KU LesBiGay Services, joined forces to push for a new gay rights initiative in Lawrence, called "Simply Equal." Many businesses and churches supported the initiative, but some church leaders opposed the amendment, fearing it would lead to costly law suits and the "eroding [of] family values." The Freedom Coalition continued several years of concerted efforts, including an all-out campaign during the 1995 city elections, to see the measure passed. Its work paid off in April 1995, when Lawrence city commissioners passed the "Simply Equal Amendment." Lawrence became the first city in Kansas to prohibit discrimination in housing, employment, and public accommodations on the basis of sexual orientation. Two months later, opponents circulated a petition to repeal the amendment but failed to garner the 25 percent of registered voters required to force its reconsideration. In many ways, the impact of the amendment has been negligible, as only one complaint has been brought under the ordinance, and it was later dismissed. Its symbolic importance is significant, however, as the city commission extended its civil rights protection to more citizens, making them feel safer and more part of the community.

The other example is less uplifting, as it illustrates the darker side of life in Lawrence. Early in the morning on April 21, 1991, Gregg Sevier, the twenty-two-year old son of Orene and Willie Sevier, had been drinking heavily and was in his bedroom holding a butcher knife. Gregg Sevier was an Indian of Creek and Choctaw descent. His parents had met and married in Lawrence while they were students at Haskell Institute. That night at their house there was no fighting or shouting, only the loud music blaring from Gregg's stereo. Orene was concerned about her son's mental state and worried that he might try hurt himself. Unsure where to turn, at 2:28 A.M. she called the 911 dispatcher for help. The dispatcher asked if there was a disturbance, and Orene calmly said "no," she "just wanted someone to talk him down." About five minutes later, a Lawrence police officer arrived at the Sevier's house, followed soon thereafter by another officer. Within minutes, Gregg Sevier was dead, shot six times by Lawrence police.[4]

Gregg Sevier had been the fourth Indian to die in Lawrence since late 1988. In April 1989, the body of John Sandoval, a nineteen-year-old Navaho, was found in the Kansas River five months after he disappeared. In October of that year, Cecil Dawes, Jr., twenty-one, a former West Point cadet whose father taught at Haskell, apparently drowned in the Kaw. On March 2, 1990, nineteen-year-old Christopher Bread died as the apparent victim of a hit-and-run automobile accident.

As happened in 1970 after the Dowdell shooting, a coroner's inquest exonerated the officer who fired the shots that killed Sevier. The district attorney noted that Sevier was quite intoxicated; his blood-alcohol level was .278, more than twice the allowable limit for driving a car. The officer declared that Sevier had ignored his orders to drop the knife and then "lunged" at him. No one knows for certain Sevier's state of mind that night. In 1989, Sevier had attempted suicide, and some Lawrencians suggested this encounter was "suicide by police."

The truth may never be known, but for Native Americans and other racial and ethnic minorities, the incident further confirmed their fears that they were not safe in Lawrence. The Lawrence Police Department believed Sevier's death, as well as the deaths of Bread, Sandoval, and Dawes, resulted principally from alcohol consumption. In the aftermath, the Indian community in Lawrence interpreted this as stereotyping Indians as drunkards and thought it illustrated the low value most Lawrencians held for people of color.

Amid the turmoil and violence of 1970 in their small town, Lawrencians from all political persuasions asked, "This is America?" Indeed, this *was* America, in microcosm. Lawrence's struggle in the 1960s was but one moment in an ongoing fight to come to terms with competing visions of what America is and should be. Lawrence's experience was unique to itself, with indigenous roots expressed by local actors and local conditions. But Lawrence is also of America, and its past and present disagreements reflect a nation struggling with its past, its competing visions of the good life, and its tenuous balance between individualism and communitarianism, public and private interests, materialism and idealism.

Notes

A Note on Sources

For most of the manuscript collections I have used, I have cited the box and folder number rather than use the unwieldy folder titles found in many manuscript collections. Thus, JBP 45.1 refers to box 45, folder 1 of the James B. Pearson Papers. When the folders in a collection were not numbered, I identified the folder by its title. Many pieces of correspondence used here were not dated; I indicate this in the notes with the notation, "n.d." I have put the approximate date that I believe the letter or message was sent, based on the content in the source, in square brackets.

Introduction

1. Leonard Harrison, typed statement, attached to governor's office memo to Robert B. Docking, 22 July 1970, Robert B. Docking Papers, Kansas Collection, University of Kansas, Lawrence, Kansas (hereafter, RBD), 41.10.
2. "Street People Remain Defiant," *Kansas City Times,* 22 July 1970; *Vortex,* n.d. [July 1970]; "supporters" in "Courthouse Scene of Trouble," *Lawrence Daily Journal-World* (hereafter, *LDJW*), 22 July 1970.
3. Dorsey-Liberty American Legion Post #14 (hereafter, DLAL) minutes, 21 July 1970; petition in "Massive Ideological Chasm Apparent in Lawrence," *Topeka Daily Capital,* 22 July 1970; merchant quoted in "AP Reporter Views Lawrence Turmoil," *LDJW,* 31 July 1970.
4. Edward Morgan, *The 60s Experience: Hard Lessons about Modern America* (Philadelphia: Temple University Press, 1991), xi.
5. Richard J. Ellis, *American Political Cultures* (New York: Oxford University Press, 1993), 151.
6. I have in mind here something similar to what the historian Thomas Bender calls the creation of "public culture." Bender and others argue that public culture is created through any number of expressions of power: not only the state's institutional power but also the ability of groups, organizations, and "ordinary" people to ascribe meaning to the rhetoric, signs, and symbols of political and everyday life. This includes, he argues, "the power to establish categories of social analysis and understanding." See Bender, "Wholes and Parts: The Need for Synthesis in American History," *Journal of American History* 73:1 (June 1986), especially pages 126–136.
7. David Thelen, in *Becoming Citizens in the Age of Television* (Chicago: University of Chicago Press, 1996), makes similar use of this type of evidence;

the quote is on page 8. I have used city directories, telephone books, student directories, credit bureau reports, and other means to identity each speaker and his or her occupation. Unfortunately, I have been unable to do this for every person (especially many women who were not listed separately from their husbands) whose voice appears in this narrative.

8. "Lawrence Looks for New Frontiers to Conquer in Sixties," *LDJW,* 2 January 1960; "Lawrence's Challenge" (editorial) *LDJW,* 27 April 1960; "Bankers Expect Continued Growth for Lawrence in 60s," *LDJW,* 13 February 1960; "Industry North, Houses South and Boom in the Middle," *LDJW,* 20 February 1960; "City Hall Must Be Ready to Handle Big Future Growth," *LDJW,* 27 February 1960.

Chapter 1

1. Bert Carlyle, "Kansas Colleges Offer All of the 'Isms,'" *Lawrence Outlook* (hereafter, *LO*), 1 April 1965.

2. David Dary, *Lawrence, Douglas County, Kansas: An Informal History* (Lawrence, KS: Allen Books, 1982), 18–19.

3. In March 1855 the company became the New England Emigrant Aid Company. Dary, *Lawrence, Douglas County, Kansas,* 22, 24, 25, 27, 30. See also Samuel A. Johnson, *The Battle Cry of Freedom: The New England Emigrant Aid Company in the Kansas Crusade* (Lawrence, KS: University Press of Kansas, 1954).

4. Dary, *Lawrence, Douglas County, Kansas,* 1. Books on Quantrill's raid, particularly from the nineteenth century, abound. For a recent study see Thomas Goodrich, *Bloody Dawn: The Story of the Lawrence Massacre* (Kent, OH: Kent State University Press, 1991).

5. "Colman Heads New England Society; Means Reminisces," loose clipping, *Lawrence Daily Journal-World* (hereafter, *LDJW*), 22 December 1952, in Sons and Daughters of New England Papers (hereafter, SDNE), 1.5, Kansas Collection, University of Kansas, Lawrence, Kansas (hereafter, KC); John G. Whittier, "Emigrant[']s Hymn," in SDNE "Seventy-Second Annual Reunion" program, 9 December 1968, SDNE, 1.9. The complete poem can be found in Daniel W. Wilder, *The Annals of Kansas* (Topeka: Geo. W. Martin Kansas Publishing House, 1875), 39.

6. The "doctrine of first effective settlement" suggests that a community's character is shaped by the emigrant/cultural group, no matter how small, able to establish the first viable settlement. In Lawrence's case, it was the Yankees from New England. See Wilbur Zelinsky, *The Cultural Geography of the United States* (Englewood Cliffs, NJ: Prentice-Hall, 1973), 13–14.

7. Although there are numerous examples, the best New England history of Lawrence is Richard Cordley, *A History of Lawrence, Kansas, from the First Settlement to the Close of the Rebellion* (Lawrence, KS: E. F. Caldwell, Lawrence Journal Press, 1895).

8. James R. Shortridge, "People of the New Frontier: Kansas Population Origins, 1865," *Kansas History* 14:3 (Autumn 1991): 185; Dale Nimz, "Build-

ing the Historic City: Significant Houses in East Lawrence" (master's thesis, George Washington University, 1984), 72, (photocopy), KC; Clifford S. Griffin, *The University of Kansas: A History* (Lawrence: The University Press of Kansas, 1974), 11–13.

9. Wallace E. Galluggi to President's Commission on Campus Unrest, 11 August 1970, and attachment [*Disorientation*], in President's Commission on Campus Unrest, Records of the University of Kansas (Lawrence) Investigative Team (hereafter, PCCU), box 8, "Miscellaneous Reference Material" folder; Beth Bailey, *Sex in the Heartland*, (Cambridge, MA: Harvard University Press, 2000), 149.

10. "Haskell Students Face Discrimination," *University Daily Kansan* (hereafter, *UDK*), 13 December 1968.

11. Galluggi to President's Commission, and attachment; Bailey, *Sex in the Heartland*, 149.

12. "Contemporary Indian Affairs Class Polls Indian Affairs and Feelings," *Indian Leader*, 11 May 1972, cited in Bailey, *Sex in the Heartland*, 149.

13. Martin E. Marty, *Modern American Religion: Volume 3: Under God, Indivisible, 1941–1960* (Chicago: University of Chicago Press, 1986), 43; "town's social life" quoted in Nimz, "Building the Historic City," 72.

14. Robert Wuthnow, *The Restructuring of American Religion: Society and Faith Since World War II* (Princeton, NJ: Princeton University Press, 1988), 9–10; Robert S. Ellwood, *The Sixties Spiritual Awakening: American Religion Moving from Modern to Postmodern* (New Brunswick, NJ: Rutgers University Press, 1994), 37. Martin E. Marty agrees with Ellwood, suggesting that Congregationalists, Presbyterians, and Episcopalians, the "colonial big three," were of the elite, old-stock folk, while Methodists, the Disciples of Christ, and certain Baptists, the "frontier big three," were more of the "common folk." These class distinctions appear true in Lawrence. Church membership figures, however, are thin and inconsistent. My figures for Plymouth Congregational, Trinity Episcopal, and First Presbyterian come from Plymouth Congregational Church Papers, One Hundred Sixth Annual Report, 18 January 1961, KC; Trinity Episcopal Church, "Parish Directory of Trinity Episcopal Church, Lawrence, Kansas, 1970–1971, Douglas County Historical Society (hereafter, DCHS); First Presbyterian Church, "United Presbyterian Women, First Presbyterian Church, Lawrence, Kansas, 1971," and "Church Directory" n.d., DCHS.

15. See Aldon Morris, *The Origins of the Civil Rights Movement: Black Communities Organizing for Change* (New York: The Free Press, 1984), Doug McAdam, *Political Process and the Development of Black Insurgency* (Chicago: University of Chicago Press, 1982); and Taylor Branch, *Parting the Waters: America in the King Years, 1954–1963* (New York: Touchstone, 1988).

16. James J. Farrell, *The Spirit of the Sixties: The Making of Postwar Radicalism* (New York: Routledge, 1997); Douglas C. Rossinow, *The Politics of Authenticity: Liberalism, Christianity, and the New Left in America* (New York: Columbia University Press, 1998); on white resistance and Christianity, see Neil R. McMillen, *The Citizens' Council: Organized Resistance to the Second*

Reconstruction, 1954–1964 (Urbana: University of Illinois Press, 1971), 159–188, and Numan V. Bartley, *The Rise of Massive Resistance* (Baton Rouge: Louisiana State University Press, 1974), 295–305.

17. Zelinsky, *Cultural Geography of the United States,* 97, 118–119, and Raymond D. Gastil, *Cultural Regions of the United States* (Seattle: University of Washington Press, 1975), 29, both cited in Shortridge, "People of the New Frontier," 162, 166–167.

18. Elmer L. Craik, "Southern Interest in Territorial Kansas, 1854–1858," *Kansas Historical Collections, 1919–1922* 15 (1923): 437–48, cited in Shortridge, "People of the New Frontier," 170.

19. As quoted in Dale Nimz, *Living With History: A Historic Preservation Plan for Lawrence, Kansas* (Lawrence, KS: Urban Study Project, 1983), 63, KC.

20. On black migration to Kansas see especially Nell Irvin Painter, *Exodusters: Black Migration to Kansas after Reconstruction* (Lawrence, KS: University Press of Kansas, 1986), with a new introduction by the authors, Robert G. Athearn, *In Search of Canaan: Black Migration to Kansas, 1879–80* (Lawrence, KS: Regents Press of Kansas, 1978), and Jacob U. Gordon, *Narratives of African Americans in Kansas, 1870–1992: Beyond the Exodust Movement* (Lewiston, NY: E. Mellen Press, 1993).

21. F. W. Blackmar and E. W. Burgess, *Lawrence Social Survey: A Report to the Lawrence Social Survey Committee, Lawrence, Kansas* (Topeka: Kansas State Printing Plant, 1917), 10–11; Shortridge, "People of the New Frontier," 177; Tom Schmiedeler, "Perceptual Regions of Lawrence, Kansas" (master's thesis, University Of Kansas, 1985), 39–44; North Lawrence Civic Association, *Early History of North Lawrenee* (Lawrence, KS: North Lawrence Civic Association, 1930), in North Lawrence vertical file, DCHS.

22. Lawrence Douglas County-National Association for the Advancement of Colored People (LDC-NAACP), "Survey of the Lawrence Negro Community," September 1963-March 1964 (hereafter, NAACP "Survey," 1963), in Lawrence League for the Practice of Democracy Papers, (hereafter, LLPD), 2.14, KC.

23. Bill Moyers, *Listening to America: A Traveler Rediscovers His Country* (New York: Harper's Magazine Press, 1971), 103; *Lawrence Social Survey,* 11.

24. Katja Rampelmann, "Small Town Germans: The Germans of Lawrence, Kansas, from 1854 to 1918," (master's thesis, University of Kansas, 1993).

25. United States Bureau of the Census, *U.S. Census of Population: 1960. Volume I, Characteristics of the Population. Part 18, Kansas* (U.S. Government Printing Office, 1960), 59, table 21.

26. Institute for Social and Environmental Studies, *Kansas Statistical Abstract* (Lawrence, KS: Institute for Social and Environmental Studies, 1971), 11; *U.S. Census of Population: 1960,* 53, table 20; enrollment figures are taken from the University of Kansas, Office of the Registrar, "Annual Report of the Director of Admissions and Registrar" for the years 1958–59 through 1972–73, all of which can be found in Office of Admissions and Records, Annual Report, box 1, 1958/59-, in University Archives, University of Kansas, Lawrence, KS.

27. See, for example, Nina Postlethwaite to the editor, *LDJW,* 14 April 1960; Paul O. Johnson to the editor, *LDJW,* 22 July 1960; "Comments on Local Affairs," *LO* 8 March 1962; and "Whole City Must Benefit in Any Urban Renewal Project," *LO* 29 March 1962.

28. Dary, *Lawrence, Douglas County, Kansas,* 350–351; NAACP, "Survey," 1963.

29. NAACP, "Survey," 1963; Jesse Milan, interview by author, Kansas City, Kansas, 27 May 1994.

30. *U.S. Census of Population: 1960,* 35, table 13; 59, table 21; 180, table 53; 189, table 69; 208, table 73; 220, table 77; 222, table 78; NAACP, "Survey," 1963, (emphasis in original).

31. Milan, interview. For more on the socioeconomic status of the black community, see Rusty L. Monhollon, "'Away from the Dream': The Roots of Black Power in Lawrence, Kansas, 1960–1975" (master's thesis, University of Kansas, 1994), chapter 2.

32. *U.S. Census of Population: 1960,* 35, table 13; 59, table 21; 180, table 53; 189, table 69; 208, table 73; 220, table 77; 222, table 78.

33. Lawrence Human Relations Commission (LHRC), "A Report to the Lawrence City Commission," October 1961-September 1963" in LLPD 3.9.

34. *U.S. Census of Population: 1960,* 208, table 73; 220, table 77.

35. *LDJW,* 4 August 1942, as quoted in Dary, *Lawrence, Douglas County, Kansas,* 336, 348; Cathy Ambler, "Identity Formation in the East Lawrence Neighborhood," (unpublished paper for American Studies 770, 16 December 1991) 28, KC.

36. On the consumption habits of American youth in the post–World War II era, see Douglas T. Miller and Marion Nowak, *The Fifties: The Way We Really Were* (New York: Doubleday, 1977), 269–290. Enrollments figures are gleaned from the annual reports of the University of Kansas, Office of the Registrar.

37. *Kansas Statistical Abstract,* 24, 42–45.

Chapter 2

1. Ed Abels, "A Disgraceful Demonstration," *Lawrence Outlook* (hereafter, *LO),* 7 July 1960; Abels, "Comments on Local Affairs," *LO,* 14 July 1960; Bert Carlyle, "Kansas Colleges Offer All of the 'Isms'," *LO,* 1 April 1965; "Schultz Firm on Vow," *University Daily Kansan* (hereafter, *UDK*), 9 October 1969, 1; K. S. Adams to E. Laurence Chalmers, 24 November 1969, Chancellor's Office, Correspondence, Departmental, 1969–1970, box 1, "Black Student Union" folder, (hereafter, ELC Departmental) University Archives, University of Kansas, Lawrence, Kansas (hereafter, UA).

2. The cartoon appeared in the *Lawrence Daily Journal-World* (hereafter, *LDJW*) on 20 June 1960. Most editorial cartoons published in the *Journal-World* were drawn by Scott Lang of the *Minneapolis Tribune* and Roy Justus of the *Minneapolis Star.* See Charles Press, *The Political Cartoon,* (East Rutherford, NJ: Fairleigh Dickinson University Press, 1981), 322. The *Journal-World*'s use of syndicated cartoonists and columnists who opposed

communism suggests that grassroots anticommunism was part of a larger national culture opposed to communism.

3. Mrs. Dick Mulally to James B. Pearson, n.d. [1971], James B. Pearson Papers (hereafter, JBP), 100.10.

4. On the connection between the Cold War and civil rights reform, see Mary Dudziak, *Cold War Civil Rights: Race and the Image of American Democracy* (Princeton, NJ: Princeton University Press, 2000).

5. Circulation figures are drawn from the annual publication of *N. W. Ayer and Sons Directory of Newspapers and Periodicals* (Philadelphia: N. W. Ayer); I have used the directories for the years 1950–1969.

6. Dolph C. Simons, Jr., "The Saturday Column," *LDJW,* 23 July 1960, and 10 September 1960.

7. "How We Can Do It" (editorial) *LDJW,* 5 August 1960.

8. The fallout shelter sketch appeared in *LDJW,* 4 June 1960; "Shelter Interest Increases," *LDJW,* 25 October 1961.

9. The *LDJW* pullout section was found in "Bomb Shelter" vertical file, DCHS.

10. Here I use the term "movement" loosely. It is not my intent to subject Lawrence's anticommunists to the rigorous analysis provided by movement theory, although I believe they would meet that criteria. My point is that Lawrencians, and other Americans, organized and mobilized resources to fight communism.

11. Eric Sevareid, "Is America Ready for a Showdown?" *LO,* 20 July 1961.

12. Merle L. Jackson to Robert F. Ellsworth, 5 May 1963, Robert F. Ellsworth Papers (hereafter, RFE), 88.7; Richardson T. Conner to Ellsworth, 1 May 1963, RFE, 67.9; Mr. and Mrs. O. H. Garber to Ellsworth, 19 July 1963, RFE, 86.2.

13. Advertisement, *LO,* 27 April 1961.

14. William Pencak, *For God and Country: The American Legion, 1919–1941* (Boston: Northeastern University Press, 1989), 320. Pencak argues that the legion "has been a major form through which the important strain of the national character stressing community, sacrifice, nationalism, and unity—and opposing individualism, dissent, internationalism, and pluralism—has expressed itself" since the end of World War I. Pencak's account of the legion is sympathetic but reasonably balanced and objective. A more celebratory account is Thomas A. Rumer, *The American Legion: An Official History, 1919–1989* (New York: M. Evans, 1990). For brief examples of the organization's anticommunism, see Peter H. Buckingham, *America Sees Red: Anti-communism in America, 1870s to 1980s: A Guide to Basic Issues and References* (Claremont, CA: Regina Books, 1988), 21, 24, 31, 54, 89.

15. The *Journal-World* reported 230 in attendance; the *Outlook* set the figure at 300: see loose clippings, "Anti-Communist to Speak at KU" and "Speaker Suggests Firm U.S. Policy with Red Nations," both *LDJW,* n.d. [November 1963], and loose clipping, "Over 300 Learn More about Communism," *LO,*

n.d. [November 1963], all in Dorsey-Liberty American Legion Post #14 (hereafter, DLAL) minutes, 19 November 1963. On Skousen's philosophy, see Cleon Skousen, *The Naked Communist* (Salt Lake City, UT: Ensign Publishing Co., 1960).

16. DLAL minutes, 3 February 1964.

17. G. M. Stark to Robert F. Ellsworth, 6 September 1961, RFE, 75.9. Legislation had first been introduced in 1959 to create a Freedom Academy, but, although Congress sent a number of similar bills to committee each session until the late 1960s, to my knowledge no bill ever made it out of committee.

18. "Knowledge of Reds Vital, Leavenworth Officer Says," *LDJW,* 12 May 1961; *Lawrence Kiwanian* (newsletter of Lawrence, Kansas Kiwanis Club), 16 May 1961, deposited in the Kansas Collection, University of Kansas, Lawrence, Kansas (hereafter, KC); Alan Stewart to Robert F. Ellsworth, 19 May 1961, RFE, 67.8.

19. Herbert A. Philbrick, *I Led Three Lives: Citizen, Communist, Counterspy* (New York: McGraw-Hill, 1952). For brief descriptions of Philbrick, see Buckingham, *America Sees Red,* 226, and M. J. Heale, *American Anticommunism: Combating the Enemy Within, 1830–1970* (Baltimore: Johns Hopkins University Press, 1990), 163; Marie Abels, "Information to Loyal Citizenship," *LO,* 24 March 1960.

20. KLWN was one of five Kansas stations to carry "Life Line."

21. All quotes are from Harry Hurt III, *Texas Rich: The Hunt Dynasty from the Early Oil Days through the Silver Crash* (New York: W.W. Norton, 1981), 180, 182. H. L. Hunt always wrote LIFE LINE in all capitals, although the sources I have used did not. See also John George and Laird Wilcox, *Nazis, Communists, Klansmen, and Others on the Fringe: Political Extremism in America* (Buffalo, NY: Prometheus Books, 1992), 229–230.

22. Poucher's appearance in Lawrence is gleaned from a handwritten notation on a "Life Line Radio Program" transcript no. 310–61 (Washington: Life Line Foundation), 6 November 1961. Transcripts of many of these programs are deposited in the Wilcox Collection of Contemporary Political Movements at the Kansas Collection. Poucher's appearance in Marie Abels, "Information to Loyal Citizenship," *LO,* 7 April 1960. Munn's appearance in George and Wilcox, *Nazis, Communists, Klansmen,* 229–230.

23. These comments are drawn from President's Commission on Campus Unrest Records of the University of Kansas (Lawrence) Investigative Team (hereafter, PCCU) box 8, "Questionnaires-Community" folder, "Questionnaires-Students" folder, "Questionnaires-Miscellaneous" folder, and "Questionnaires-Community (Professionals—Businessmen)" folder.

24. Undated promotional flyer, in Anne Moore (collector), Collection of Correspondence related to the Lawrence Support Your Local Police Committee, KC. John Birch Society founder Robert Welch in the late 1960s launched a "Support Your Local Police" campaign. It is quite likely that the Lawrence group was associated with Welch's campaign, although I have only anecdotal evidence to support the implication. See Buckingham, *America Sees Red,* 142.

25. James B. Pearson, "Statement, *in re* John Birch Society," 26 April 1962, JBP, 3.40.

26. Marie R. Abels, "Information for Loyal Citizenship," *LO*, 6 April 1961 and also 4 May 1961.

27. The *Outlook* had a circulation of around 3,000 in 1960, a figure that swelled to nearly 7,500 in 1965. Abels sold the paper several times between 1959 and 1970, but on each occasion he bought the paper back and resumed publishing. When the paper's circulation peaked in 1965, the publisher was Bert Carlyle, who also owned several other small papers, including the Topeka *Pictorial-Times*. Abels's weekly column and his "Comments on Local Affairs" continued even during those times when he was not the publisher. For the circulation figures, see *N. W. Ayer and Sons Directory of Newspapers and Periodicals*.

28. I can strongly infer Abels's membership in the John Birch Society, which does not make public its membership lists. There is ample evidence, however, that leads me to this conclusion. The *Outlook* frequently quoted Birch Society speakers and sold the society's *Blue Book* from its offices. In private conversations with several area residents, I was told they believed that Abels was affiliated with the Birch Society and the Klan, but again, there is no conclusive evidence. Additionally, Abels's rhetoric and understanding of the world, particularly in regard to racial issues, tends to support this contention.

29. Abels, "Comments on Local Affairs," *LO*, 8 October 1959.

30. Details about Marie Abels were taken from Edwin A. Abels, "Marie R. Abels Passed Away Sunday" and "A Tribute," *LO*, 13 July 1961.

31. John Bodnar, "The Attractions of Patriotism," in John Bodnar, ed., *Bonds of Affection: Americans Define Their Patriotism* (Princeton, NJ: Princeton University Press, 1996), 15.

32. See Elaine Tyler May, *Homeward Bound: American Families in the Cold War Era* (New York: Basic Books, 1988), especially 92–113, and also Wendy Kozol, "'Good Americans': Nationalism and Domesticity in *Life* Magazine, 1945–1960," in Bodnar, ed., *Bonds of Affection*, 234, 241, and Wendy Kozol, *Life's America: Family and Nation in Postwar Photojournalism* (Philadelphia: Temple University Press, 1994). For challenges to the Cold War in the "age of consensus," see Wini Breines, *Young, White, and Miserable: Growing Up Female in the Fifties* (Boston: Beacon Books, 1992), and James J. Farrell, *The Spirit of the Sixties: The Making of Postwar Radicalism* (New York: Routledge, 1997).

33. Membership list of the John Pound chapter of Daughters of the American Colonists, in "John Pound chapter, Daughters of the American Colonists" vertical file, Douglas County Historical Society (hereafter, DCHS); "Hear National Defense Speaker," *LO*, 26 February 1959; loose clipping, [*LDJW*, January 1964], in "Daughters of the American Revolution, Betty Washington chapter" vertical file, DCHS. According to Peter Buckingham, during the 1920s the DAR and the American Legion were two of the most active,

intolerant, and repressive organizations in the United States. Kansas journalist William Allen White remarked that the DAR "yanked the [Ku Klux] Klan out of the cow pasture and set it down in the breakfast room of respectability." As quoted in Buckingham, *America Sees Red*, 35.

34. Barbara Truesdell, "'U.S.ness': Patriotic Rituals of the Daughters of the American Revolution," in Bodnar, ed., *Bonds of Affection*, 273–274.

35. See advertisement in *LO*, 29 June 1961; for other examples, see *LO*, 16 February 1961, and *LO*, 1 January 1959.

36. "Maddening, Isn't It?" (editorial) *LDJW*, 18 August 1960; Dolph Simons, Jr., "The Saturday Column," *LDJW*, 7 March 1960; "A Dubious Commodity" (editorial) *LDJW*, 24 January 1960.

37. James R. Thomen to Robert F. Ellsworth, 18 April 1962, RFE, 61.6, and Thomen to Ellsworth, 15 February 1963, RFE, 19.10; A. B. Weaver to Frank Carlson, 21 July 1960, Frank Carlson Papers (hereafter, FC), 92:164, "Labor" folder; Anne Gill to James B. Pearson, n.d. [July 1967], JBP, 46.16.

38. Elmer Pond to Robert F. Ellsworth, 25 June 1962, RFE, 64.4; Doris E. Nadine Zeller to Ellsworth, 10 May 1961, RFE, 81.5; Weldon H. Sickles to Ellsworth, 5 August 1965, RFE, 92.3.

39. L. W. and W. H. Blevins to Ellsworth, 18 November 1964, RFE, 64.4.

40. John Bodnar, "Moral Patriotism and Collective Memory in Whiting, Indiana, 1920–1992," in Bodnar, ed., *Bonds of Affection*, 292; Jonathan Rieder, *Canarsie: Jews and Italians against Liberalism* (Cambridge: Harvard University Press, 1985), 262–63, cited in Bodnar, ed., *Bonds of Affection*, 6–7.

41. Chester G. Jones to Robert F. Ellsworth, 29 May 1961, RFE, 67.8; Jones to Frank Carlson, 29 May 1961, FC., 92:214, "Communism" folder.

42. Mrs. H. M. Brownlee to the editor, *LDJW*, 27 February 1960.

43. Mrs. Walter McClain to James B. Pearson, 29 July 1963, JBP, 11.12. I believe the proponent of the colony was Madalyn Murray, who was a plaintiff in the Supreme Court decision prohibiting daily Bible reading and recitation of the Lord's Prayer in public schools. See *Albington School District v. Schempp* and *Murray v. Curlett*, both 374 U.S. 203 (1963). I have found no other information about the "atheist colony."

44. Mrs. Lee Morgan to the editor, *LDJW*, 19 March 1960, 4. The NCC's opposition to the prayer amendment offered by New York representative Frank J. Becker is discussed briefly in Gary K. Clabaugh, *Thunder on the Right: The Protestant Fundamentalists* (Chicago: Nelson-Hall, 1974), 200.

45. Mrs. Lee Morgan to the editor, *LDJW*, 19 March 1960, 4; Morgan to the editor, *LDJW*, 15 March 1960.

46. Mrs. Fred Reynolds to James B. Pearson, 9 August 1963, JBP, 11.13; Reynolds to Robert F. Ellsworth, 10 August 1963, RFE, 64.4 (emphasis in original); "Lawrence D.A.R. Chapter Has Annual Patriotic Tea," [*LDJW*] 15 February 1964, in "Daughters of the American Revolution, Betty Washington chapter," vertical file, DCHS.

47. Elmer Pond to Robert F. Ellsworth, 25 June 1962, RFE, 64.4. Although Pond denied being a "Bircher," he used the same language to attack Warren

as the society used in its "Impeach Earl Warren Campaign." See *The White Book of the John Birch Society for 1963*, "Bulletin For September 1963" (Belmont, MA: John Birch Society), 28–29, in the Wilcox Collection, KC.

48. Tarr and resident remarks in PCCU, box 8, "Questionnaires-Miscellaneous" folder.

49. Bert C. Carlyle, "Briefs By Bert," *LO*, 1 July 1965. On the university and the Cold War, see Ellen W. Schrecker, *No Ivory Tower: McCarthyism and the Universities*, (New York: Oxford University Press, 1986), and Rebecca S. Lowen, *Creating the Cold War University: The Transformation of Stanford* (Berkeley: University of California Press, 1997).

50. Raymond G. O'Connor to Robert F. Ellsworth, 31 July 1961, RFE, 76.2; Kenneth P. Callicott to Ellsworth, 21 December 1961, RFE, 76.9.

51. F. C. Bates, "Opinions From the Hill," *LDJW*, 7 January 1963, 1.

52. Ibid.

53. Ibid. Commenting on the article in a letter to Representative Ellsworth, Bates remarked, "[i]t has really produced a buzz around Lawrence—seems that I may have said a few things the way folks in Lawrence would have like to say them. The 'pro' reactions outweigh the 'cons' about twenty to one," Bates claimed. See Bates to Ellsworth, 24 January 1963, RFE, 45.1.

54. Lockard, Sales, Shaw, and Feuerborn's comments in PCCU, box 8, "Questionnaires-Community" folder; Tarr's are in PCCU, box 8, "Questionnaires-Miscellaneous" folder.

55. Lisa McGirr, in *Suburban Warriors: The Origins of the New American Right* (Princeton, NJ: Princeton University Press, 2001), devotes a good deal of attention to anticommunism in the formation of the New Right, while Amy Elizabeth Ansell, *New Right, New Racism: Race and Reaction in the United States and Great Britain* (New York: New York University Press, 1997), makes explicit the link between race and the emergence of the new conservatism.

Chapter 3

1. Justin D. Hill to W. Clarke Wescoe, 9 March 1965, Chancellor's Office, Executive Secretary Case Files, 1959–65, (hereafter, COES) box 9, "Hate" folder.

2. W. E. B. DuBois, *Black Reconstruction*, as quoted in David Roediger, *The Wages of Whiteness: Race and the Making of the American Working Class* (London: Verso Press, 1991), 12–13.

3. On the NAACP's founding and the LLPD's early history, consult Kristine M. McCusker, "The 'Forgotten Years' of America's Civil Rights Movement: The University of Kansas, 1939–1961" (master's thesis, University of Kansas, 1993), 72–82, and the Lawrence League for the Practice of Democracy Papers (hereafter, LLPD). The LLPD's constitution and pledge is in "The Lawrence League for the Practice of Democracy Constitution and Pledge, amended 1 July 1959, LLPD 1.1. The LLPD's membership peaked in 1950 at 650, but it remained a strong and active group until 1965. This

figure comes from George Caldwell, the LLPD, president in 1965, in a history he wrote of the organization, in LLPD 1.2.

4. Clifford S. Griffin, *The University of Kansas: A History* (Lawrence: University Press of Kansas, 1974), 210.

5. Jesse Milan, interview by author, tape recording, Kansas City, Kansas, 27 May 1994. Milan was the first black teacher in the post-*Brown* Lawrence schools. His recollections here are generally substantiated by Griffin, *University of Kansas,* 626–628, and McCusker, "'Forgotten Years,'" (master's thesis).

6. For civil rights activism at the University of Kansas prior to the 1960s, see McCusker, "'Forgotten Years,'" (master's thesis); Kristine M. McCusker, "'The Forgotten Years' of America's Civil Rights Movement: Wartime Protests at the University of Kansas, 1939–1945," *Kansas History* 17:4 (spring 1994): 26–37; and Griffin, *University of Kansas,* 627–628. On Chamberlain's role in integrating Lawrence, see Wilt Chamberlain and David Shaw, *Wilt: Just Like Any Other 7-Foot Black Millionaire Who Lives Next Door* (New York: Macmillan Publishing, 1973), 51. For more on Murphy, Chamberlain, and the civil rights movement at KU during the fifties, see McCusker, "Forgotten Years,'" (master's thesis), chapter 5 and epilogue.

7. The "sit-down" took place in Brick's Cafe, a student hangout just off of the campus; see McCusker, "'Forgotten Years,'" (master's thesis), 2–3.

8. The effort to integrate the Jayhawk Plunge is drawn from my "Taking the Plunge: Race, Rights, and the Politics of Desegregation, Lawrence, Kansas, 1960," *Kansas History* 20:3 (autumn 1997): 138–159.

9. Monhollon, "Taking the Plunge," 140.

10. Ibid., 143–149. The LLPD apparently had absorbed much of the NAACP's membership sometime during the 1950s. Jesse Milan, along with several African American ministers, revived the NAACP in the spring of 1960, at the same time the LLPD was launching the campaign against the Plunge. Unfortunately, I have been unable to track down the papers of the Lawrence-Douglas County NAACP for the years 1960–1965. The Kansas State Historical Society has on microfilm local chapters' papers to the national office, but they include only two miscellaneous letters from the LDC-NAACP after 1960. The information I have about the LDC-NAACP is taken from minutes of meetings, reports, and memoranda scattered throughout the LLPD papers.

11. The property rights' defense was used elsewhere in the country to fight liberalism and civil rights activism. See, for example, Thomas J. Sugrue, *Origins of the Urban Crisis: Race and Inequality in Postwar Detroit* (Princeton, NJ: Princeton University Press, 1996), especially 209–230.

12. Norma McCanles to the editor, *LDJW,* 13 July 1960; Charles C. Spencer, Sr., to the editor, *LDJW,* 14 July 1960; Spencer to the editor, *LDJW,* 19 July 1960.

13. Monhollon, "Taking the Plunge," 154–155.

14. Ed Abels, "Comments on Local Affairs," *LO,* 14 July 1960.

15. Monhollon, "Taking the Plunge," 157–159.

16. On the creation of the Lawrence Human Relations Commission (hereafter, LHRC), see minutes of meeting, 21 February 1961, 14 March 1961, and 3 April 1961; "City Considers Rights Group," *University Daily Kansan* (hereafter, *UDK*), 13 December 1960; "Study Body Is Set Tuesday on Race Setup," *LDJW,* 15 February 1961; "Mayor Names Rights Group," *UDK,* 15 February 1961; "City Salons Hear Civil Rights Report," *UDK,* 26 April 1961; and Monhollon, "'Away from the Dream," 81–86; Kennedy quoted in "City Moves to Desegregation," *UDK,* 20 January 1961; Godwin quoted in "City Salons Hear Civil Rights Report"; Ed Abels's comment in "Swimming Pool is Closed and For Sale," 14 July 1960.

17. On the passage of the Civil Rights Act of 1964 and the Voting Rights Act of 1965, see Hugh Davis Graham, *The Civil Rights Era: Origins and Development of National Policy, 1960–1972* (New York: Oxford University Press, 1990), esp. chapters three through six.

18. Jerome L. Himmelstein, for example, argues that conservative thought was unified not only by its opposition to the New Deal, but also by the broader goals that the New Deal represented. See Himmelstein, *To the Right: The Transformation of American Conservatism* (Berkeley: University of California Press, 1990), 29, 68–69. On what Goldwater's campaign meant to young conservatives, see John A. Andrew III, *The Other Side of the Sixties: Young Americans for Freedom and the Rise of Conservative Politics* (New Brunswick, NJ: Rutgers University Press, 1997), 209–210, 217.

19. Ann Gill to James B. Pearson, 15 November 1963, James B. Pearson Papers (hereafter, JBP) JBP, 12.25; H. A. Puckett to Robert F. Ellsworth, 1 January 1964, Robert F. Ellsworth Papers (hereafter, RFE), 21.6; M. S. Winter to Frank Carlson, n.d. [May 1964], JBP, 19.13; Warren Zimmerman to Pearson, 26 July 1963, JBP, 12.25; Zimmerman to Pearson, 15 June 1964, JBP, 19.20. Many Lawrencians would parrot the Goldwater's position that civil rights was a moral issue and "you can not legislate morality." Goldwater contended "[w]e must always make a sharp distinction between civil rights guaranteed under the Constitution and those rights of association that are basically moral issues and cannot be resolved simply by passing new Federal laws." See Barry Goldwater, *Where I Stand* (New York: McGraw-Hill, 1964), 39–40. In the 1964 presidential election, Goldwater received about 44 percent of the vote in Lawrence (a higher percentage that he received nationally). Moreover, many Lawrencians were fervent supporters of the Arizona senator, especially his stand on communism, government, and civil rights. See, for example, Galen A. Gorrill to Robert F. Ellsworth, 18 July 1964, RFE, 28.7, and Mike Jones to Ellsworth, 1 March 1964, RFE, 59.7.

20. Melvin J. Thorne, *American Conservative Thought Since World War II: The Core Ideas* (Westport, CN: Greenwood Press, 1990), 8.

21. E. W. King to Robert F. Ellsworth, 6 May 1965, RFE, 59.8; "City Moves to Desegregation."

22. Robert F. Ellsworth, form letter, n.d. [June 1963], RFE, 15.11, and Ellsworth, *Newsletter,* April 1964, RFE, 59.7.

23. Fred A. Bremer to James B. Pearson, 27 April 1964, JBP, 19.15; Harry Westergren to Pearson, 13 June 1964, JBP, 19.20; Otto Lohrenz to Robert F. Ellsworth, 17 September 1964, RFE, 64.2.

24. Mrs. Richard B. Stevens to James B. Pearson, 6 September 1965, JBP, 26.12; Eugene L. Hardtarfer to James B. Pearson, 1 June 1966, JBP, 37.5; Basil Parris to Pearson, 6 June 1966, JBP, 37.4.Victor E. Melton to Pearson, n.d. [June 1966], JBP, 37.4; Melton to Pearson, n.d. [April 1965], JBP, 25.11.

25. The building owner's comment is taken from CORE flyer, n.d. [May 1965], in LLPD 6.4; Jeanne Alexander to Pearson, 26 March 1964, JBP, 19.20.

26. Ed Abels, "Comments on Local Affairs," *LO*, 20 June 1963.

27. Dr. W.R. Palmer to James B. Pearson, 7 June 1964, JBP, 19.20.

28. Clipping, *LDJW*, 11 June 1964, attached to H. U. Sanders to James B. Pearson, n.d. [June 1964], JBP, 19.20.

29. [name illegible] to Robert F. Ellsworth, 25 September 1963, RFE, 88.7.

30. Quoted in Neil R. McMillen, *The Citizens' Council: Organized Resistance to the Second Reconstruction, 1954–1964* (Urbana: University of Illinois Press, 1971), 184.

31. Dolph Simons, Jr., "The Saturday Column," *LDJW*, 6 April 1963.

32. A good example of this can be seen in the *Journal-World*'s editorial cartoons. The paper ran many cartoons about the state of race relations in the United States, including many favorable to the movement. But all of them depict race matters not as a local problem but as a southern problem. One example showed Uncle Sam washing and scrubbing his blackened hands, which have "race" and "issue" printed on them. The caption, quoting Shakespeare, read, "Out, Damned Spot!" See *LDJW*, 23 May 1963.

33. Simons, Jr., "The Saturday Column," 6 April 1963.

34. "Churches Joining in Freedom Rally," *LDJW*, 20 May 1963. For a recent account of the Birmingham struggle, see Glenn T. Eskew, *But For Birmingham: The Local and National Movements in the Civil Rights Struggle* (Chapel Hill: University of North Carolina Press, 1997).

35. Photograph caption, "'Freedom March' on Massachusetts," and "Housing, Jobs Emphasized in Rights Meeting," both in *LDJW*, 22 July 1963.

36. "The Freedom March" (editorial), *LDJW*, 22 July 1963; Ed Abels, "Comments on Local Affairs," *LO*, 20 June 1963.

37. Lawrence-Douglas County National Association for the Advancement of Colored People, "Survey of the Lawrence Negro Community," September 1963-March 1964 (hereafter, NAACP "Survey," 1963).

38. "Imagine Yourself . . ." (editorial), *LDJW*, 17 December 1964.

39. The notion that whiteness is a form of property is an old one, dating back at least to the Supreme Court's 1896 decision in *Plessy v. Ferguson*. For a more recent assessment of whiteness as form of property, see George Lipsitz, *Possessive Investment in Whiteness: How White People Profit From Identity Politics* (Philadelphia: Temple University Press, 1998), and Lipsitz, "The Possessive Investment In Whiteness: Racialized Social Democracy and the 'White Problem' in American Studies," *American Quarterly* 47:3 (September 1995): 369–387.

40. "Imagine Yourself . . ."

41. CORE Newsletter, January 1965, in LLPD 6.4; George Caldwell to Tom [no last name given], 17 April 1965, in LLPD 4.15.

42. Forming what the sociologist Aldon Morris calls "movement centers," churches, including white churches, were emotional, spiritual, and physical resources on which activists could draw in the fight for social justice. See Aldon Morris, *The Origins of the Civil Rights Movement: Black Communities Organizing for Change* (New York: Free Press, 1984).

43. LHRC, minutes of meeting, 5 September 1962; Plymouth Congregational Church Social Action Committee, "Viewpoints on Housing: Excerpts and Condensations from Current Periodicals on the Issues of Residential Integration of the Races," May 1964 (unpublished), in LLPD 3.12; Al Sellen, "Racism and Plymouth Church, 1940–1992," n.p., n.d. (copy in my possession); loose clipping, "Housing Action Topic of Survey By Church Women," *LDJW*, n.d. [1964], in LLPD, box 3, "Civil Rights, Housing," folder; "845 Place Names on Statement of Housing Equality," *LDJW*, 23 September 1964, and Christian Social Relations Committee of the United Church Women of Lawrence to the editor, *LDJW*, 19 December 1964, both in Lawrence Fair Housing Coordinating Committee (hereafter, LFHCC), 1.5, KC.

44. Mrs. Thomas Moore, typed press release, 24 May 1966, in LFHCC, 1.11.

45. Mr. and Mrs. Richard C. Sapp to James B. Pearson, 12 August 1966, JBP 26:37.1; loose clippings, Judith Hood to the editor, *LDJW*, 22 December 1964, and Mrs. Edward Shaw to the editor, *LDJW*, 22 December 1964, both in LFHCC, 1.5; the quote is Shaw's.

46. Typed notes, 21 January 1965; Tom Maupin to Senator G. Reynolds Shultz, 16 March 1965; Maupin to George Caldwell, 16 March 1965, all in LFHCC, 1.7; on civil rights legislation in Kansas, see Joseph P. Doherty, *Civil Rights in Kansas: Past, Present, and Future* (Topeka: State of Kansas Commission on Civil Rights, 1972).

47. Geneva Simmons to Robert F. Ellsworth, 13 February 1962, RFE, 76.5; loose clipping, Lawrence Real Estate Board, "Statement of Position on Housing," *LDJW*, n.d. [April 1965], in LFHCC 1.7. Compare the LREB's statement to the one placed by the Coordinating Committee for Fundamental American Freedom, Inc., *LDJW*, 10 March 1964.

48. Ordinance 3749, City of Lawrence, Kansas, in LFHCC 1.15.

49. "The Black Dilemma," *Disorientation*, n.d. [Lawrence, KS], 14; Glenn L. Kappelman to James B. Pearson, 13 August 1966, JBP 37.1.

Chapter 4

1. "Man of the Year," *Time* (6 January 1967): 18.

2. Much of this chapter has been informed by my reading of David Farber, *The Age of Great Dreams: America in the 1960s* (New York: Hill and Wang, 1994), and the essays in Farber, ed., *The Sixties: From Memory to History*

(Chapel Hill: University of North Carolina Press, 1994), all of which address these questions.

3. David Chalmers, *And the Crooked Places Made Straight: The Struggle for Social Change in the 1960s,* 2nd ed. (Baltimore: Johns Hopkins University Press, 1996), 68.

4. Wescoe quoted in "Chancellor Proclaims 'New KU Era,'" *University Daily Kansan* (hereafter, *UDK*), 19 September 1960; the enrollment figures are taken from University of Kansas, Office of the Registrar, "Annual Report of the Director of Admissions and Registrar" for the years 1958–59 through 1972–73, all of which can be found in Office of Admissions and Records, Annual Report, box 1, 1958/59-, in University Archives, University of Kansas, Lawrence, Kansas (hereafter, UA). For an analysis of the changing role of women in higher education, see Kathryn Nemeth Tuttle, "What Became of the Dean of Women?: Changing Roles for Women Administrators in American Higher Education, 1940–1980" (Ph.D. diss., University of Kansas, 1996).

5. Howard S. Becker, Blanche Geer, and Everett C. Hughes, *Making the Grade: The Academic Side of College Life* (New York: John Wiley & Sons, 1968), cited in Helen Lefkowitz Horowitz, *Campus Life: Undergraduate Cultures from the End of the Eighteenth Century to the Present* (New York: Alfred A. Knopf, 1987), 191–192, 221; Michael P. Fisher, "The Turbulent Years: The University of Kansas, 1960–1975, A History" (Ph.D. diss., University of Kansas, 1979), 132, 159.

6. Clifford S. Griffin, *The University of Kansas: A History* (Lawrence: University Press of Kansas, 1974), 209, 629.

7. The University of Kansas YMCA-YWCA, *KU-Y Jayhawker,* 7:4 (13 October 1966), in YMCA chronological records, 1895–1981 (hereafter YMCA), box 1, "1966" folder, UA.

8. For a brief introduction to the national movement, see Leonard Clough, *Introducing the University Christian Movement* (leaflet) (New York: University Christian Movement, 1967), Archives of Appalachia, East Tennessee State University.

9. University Christian Movement, "UCM at Kansas, 1968–1969," in YMCA, "1969/1970" folder.

10. Ibid.

11. The first was the Jayhawk Cooperative House; see Kristine M. McCusker, "Interracial Communities and Civil Rights Activism in Lawrence, Kansas, 1945–1948," *Historian* 61:4 (summer 1999): 783–799, and McCusker, "The 'Forgotten Years' of America's Civil Rights Movement: The University of Kansas, 1939–1961" (master's thesis, University of Kansas, 1994), 82.

12. This brief history of the KU-Y is culled from various letters, newsletters, and ephemera in the "1960" to "1975" folders, YMCA.

13. Douglas C. Rossinow, *The Politics of Authenticity: Liberalism, Christianity, and the New Left in America* (New York: Columbia University Press, 1998), 6. The role of Christianity, interracial cooperative living, and civil

rights activism is examined in chapter four of McCusker, "'Forgotten Years,'" (master's thesis).

14. Membership figures from YMCA, box 1, "1960/1961" folder; "full support" in Bob Hartley and Judy Gray to Dear Y Member, 13 May 1960, YMCA, box 1, "1959/1960" folder; "fellowship" quote in Gayle Graham and Carl C. Peck to "Dear fellow 'Y' Members," 27 November 1962, in ibid., "1962/1963" folder; KU-YMCA-YWCA, "1961–1962 Program," in ibid., "1961/1962" folder; "fellowship" quote in Gayle Graham and Carl C. Peck to "Dear fellow 'Y' Members," 27 November 1962, in ibid., "1962/1963" folder.

15. I have never found an official membership list for the Civil Rights Council and can only infer its membership through newspaper accounts (including photographs) and the small amount of material in the CRC records in the University of Kansas Archives.

16. On CRC's investigations, see Rusty Monhollon, "'Away from the Dream': The Roots of Black Power in Lawrence, Kansas, 1960–1970" (master's thesis, University of Kansas, 1995), 67–73; Barry's years in Lawrence are noted in Clayborne Carson, *In Struggle: SNCC and the Black Awakening of the 1960s,* 2nd ed. (Cambridge, MA: Harvard University Press, 1990), 23, 24; all of the quotes are in "Students Picket Lawrence Polls," *UDK,* 9 November 1960.

17. Monhollon, "'Away from the Dream,'" 87–93.

18. "The Port Huron Statement," written by Tom Hayden in 1961, excerpted in Loren Baritz, ed., *The American Left: Radical Political Thought in the Twentieth Century* (New York: Basic Books, 1971), 385–405. The best history of SDS remains Kirkpatrick Sale, *SDS* (New York: Random House, 1973), but see also James Miller, *"Democracy is in the Streets": From Port Huron to the Siege of Chicago* (New York: Simon and Schuster, 1987), and the more personal accounts by two former SDS leaders, Todd Gitlin, *The Sixties: Years of Hope, Days of Rage* (Toronto: Bantam Books, 1987) and Tom Hayden, *Reunion: A Memoir* (New York: Random House, 1988). For studies that focus more generally on the New Left, see, for example, Maurice Isserman, *If I Had a Hammer: The Death of the Old Left and the Birth of the New Left* (New York: Basic Books, 1987), and Wini Breines, *Community and Organization in the New Left, 1962–1968* (New York: Praeger, 1982).

19. On the original CORE, see McCusker, "'Forgotten Years,'" 128–136; the quote is in "CORE Newsletter," January 1965, LLPD 6.4; on CORE's investigations, see Monhollon, "'Away from the Dream,'" 101–103.

20. Information on KU-SDS is culled from the following: James Gunn, memorandum *in re* conversation with Laird Wilcox, n.d. [1965], and Gunn, memorandum to Clarke Wescoe, 12 July 1965, both in Chancellor's Correspondence, Executive Secretary, Case Files, 1959–65 (hereafter, COES), box 9,"Civil Rights Demonstration—3/8—9/65" folder; Kansas University Students for a Democratic Society, "Constitution"; John Garlinghouse, postcard to Students for a Democratic Society, n.d. [May

1965]; Jim Masters to Gentlemen, 24 May 1965; George R. Brosi to Jim Masters, n.d. [1965]; "went south" quote in Jim Masters, "Answers to questions," typewritten, unaddressed letter, n.d. [July 1965]; Laird Wilcox to Fellow SDS'rs, 29 March 1965, all in Students for a Democratic Society Papers (hereafter SDS), 10.10, Wisconsin State Historical Society, Madison, Wisconsin.

21. David Farber contends that there were "no clear delineations" between the various social movements transforming the country. See Farber, "The Counterculture and the Antiwar Movement," in Melvin Small and William D. Hoover, eds., *Give Peace a Chance: Exploring the Vietnam Antiwar Movement* (Syracuse, NY: Syracuse University Press, 1990), 7.

22. The quotes are in "SDS Calls 1st Meeting," *UDK,* 23 September 1965; Gunn memorandum, *in re* Laird Wilcox.

23. "KU-SDS Splits with National Group Strategy," *UDK,* 19 October 1965; "National Chapter Aims, Acts Not the Same" (editorial) *UDK,* 21 October 1965.

24. Carlyle quoted in "Publisher Claims Reds on Campus," *UDK,* 27 September 1965 and "Weekly Publisher Assails Campus SDS," *UDK,* 5 October 1965; Bert C. Carlyle, "Briefs by Bert," *LO,* 30 September 1965; Bert C. Carlyle, "Who's Laughing Now?" *LO,* 21 October 1965.

25. Horowitz, *Campus Life,* 144–148.

26. McCusker, "'Forgotten Years,'" 26.

27. "KU 'Cannot' Instruct Local Renters Not to Discriminate," *UDK,* 7 March 1961; "Dean Says Sororities Have No Discriminatory Clauses," *UDK,* 5 October 1960; "Collegiate Press Service Press Release," 4 November 1964 (copy), in SDS, 10.10; "Rights Policy By Chancellor," *Lawrence Daily Journal-World* (hereafter *LDJW*), 7 March 1961; Fisher, "Turbulent Years," 78; W. Clarke Wescoe, "Report to the Board of Regents," 14 March 1965, (hereafter, WCW "Report," 1965), 3, in COES, box 9, "Sit-in Facts" folder; Francis H. Heller, "Campus in Turmoil," (unpublished manuscript, n.d., copy in my possession), 692.

28. "Letters Remain Unanswered: CRC Criticizes Greek Presidents," *UDK,* 27 April 1961; "CRC Sends Letters to Greek Nationals," *UDK,* 11 May 1961; Gunn memorandum, *in re* Laird Wilcox.

29. Civil Rights Council "Report of the Research Committee on Fraternities and Sororities," 20 May 1965, (hereafter, CRC "Report"), in Civil Rights Council, records, box 1,UA; *San Francisco Chronicle,* 13 April 1965, quoted in CRC "Report," 4; CRC "Report," 19; Mrs. Robert P. Noble, Jr. (Karen Jo Emel) to W. Clarke Wescoe, 19 March 1965, in COES, box 9, "Civil Rights . . ." folder.

30. "Clause Waived For Sigma Nu: Letter Read At ASC Meeting," *UDK,* 3 March 1965; "Wescoe Lauds Waiver: CRC Mum on Sigma Nu," *UDK,* 4 March 1965.

31. The first quote is in WCW "Report," 1965, 3; "hot session" in George Caldwell to Tom [no last name given], 29 March 1965 and 17 April 1965, in

LLPD 4.15; "less emotional" quote is in "150 Sit-In-Stand-Out by Wescoe's Office," *UDK,* 8 March 1965.

32. The quotes are in Caldwell to Tom [no last name given]. Additional material for this paragraph is taken from the following: Norma Norman, interview by author, tape recording, Topeka, Kansas, 25 May 1994; Griffin, *University of Kansas,* 628–632; "150 Sit-In-Stand-Out by Wescoe's Office"; "Arrests No Curb On Demonstrations," *UDK,* 9 March 1965; "Special Meeting Called, ASC to Discuss Sit-ins," *UDK,* 9 March 1965; "Wescoe States Past," *UDK,* 9 March 1965; "Chancellor's Statement," *UDK,* 9 March 1965; "CRC Demands," *UDK,* 9 March 1965; "Wescoe Reinstates Demonstrators," *UDK,* 9 March 1965; "Council Introduces Bill For Discrimination Board," *UDK,* 9 March 1965;"List Of Those Who Were Arrested Monday," *UDK,* 10 March 1965; "CRC Leaders Disagree; 'Cause' Gains Support," *UDK,* 11 March 1965; "Timetable of a Sit-in," *KU Today,* 10 April 1965, 1, 5; "Transcription of shorthand notes taken of the conversation between Chancellor W. Clarke Wescoe and Civil Rights Demonstrators on 8 March 1965," COES, box 9, "Civil Rights . . ." folder; WCW "Report," 1965, in ibid.; Kansas Board of Regents, "Policy on Organizational Membership," 24 September 1965, attached to Laurence C. Woodruff, memorandum, 10 November 1965, in ibid.; University Human Relations Council, "Recommendations Relative to Commercial Advertising in Student Publications," 16 March 1965, Chancellor's Office, W. Clarke Wescoe Correspondence, box 1, "ASC" folder; W. Clarke Wescoe to Mike Miner, 16 March 1965, and Wescoe to Bob Stewart, 16 March 1965, both in ibid.

33. Norman, interview.

34. CRC leader quoted in "Arrests No Curb on Demonstrations"; Griffin, *University of Kansas,* 629, 632.

35. Norman, interview.

36. See "Regents' Backing Given to Wescoe," *LDJW,* 10 March 1965; for reaction to the protest, see correspondence in COES, box 9, "Civil Rights . . . ," "Critical," "Hate," "Faculty," and "Approve" folders; Bert C. Carlyle, "Why Not Clean Up Mess In Kansas Colleges?" *LO,* 25 March 1965; "KU's Problem, " *LDJW,* 9 March 1965; "Ed Abels Column," *LO,* 10 June 1965; "Students Are Still Due For Court Visit," *LDJW,* 10 March 1965.

37. Marcia Fleagle to W. Clarke Wescoe, 10 March 1965, and Mrs. Robert D. Love to W. Clarke Wescoe, 12 March 1965, both in COES, box 9, "Critical" folder.

38. "Discrimination" (editorial), *UDK,* 4 March 1965; Roger Meyers to the editor, *UDK,* 9 March 1965; "*UDK* Under Fire" (editorial), *UDK,* 15 March 1965; "ASC Meeting" (editorial), *UDK,* 17 March 1965.

39. See Civil Rights Council, "Interview notes with social chairs of campus fraternities, 1965–1966 school year," in CRC records, box 1.

40. "First Negro Would Do it Again," *UDK,* 9 October 1969.

41. All quotes are in "Ed Abels' Column," *LO,* 19 August 1965." In May 1965, the Strong Hall protestors pleaded not guilty to charges of disturbing the

peace and requested a jury trial. The three leaders of the demonstration, George Unseld, Walter Bgoya, and Nathaniel Sims, were tried together and were found not guilty. The charges against the other defendants were dropped in August. In September, Abels commented on the circus atmosphere of the trials, noting that the courtroom was "filled with students, ex-students, civil rights activists, beatniks, bearded characters, white girls of probably righteous equal rights ideas, and Negroes." See "Civil Rights Protestors Submit Plea of Not Guilty," *UDK,* 4 May 1965; "Civil Rights Case Presented to Jury," *UDK,* 18 May 1965; "Demonstrators Acquitted By District Court," *UDK,* 19 May 1965; "Sit-in Arrests Are Costly," *LO,* 8 April 1965; "Ed Abels' Column," *LO,* 19 August 1965; "Sit-In Dismissal Foregone Conclusion 3 Months Ago," *LO,* 2 September 1965.

42. Charles Chatfield and Robert Kleidman, *The American Peace Movement: Ideals and Activism* (New York: Twayne Publishers, 1992), 107; Charles DeBenedetti and Charles Chatfield, *An American Ordeal: The Antiwar Movement of the Vietnam Era* (Syracuse, NY: Syracuse University Press, 1990), 40–42, 64. As DeBenedetti notes, there is no monograph on the Student Peace Union; he suggests consulting Howard Metzenberg, "Student Peace Union, Five Years Before the New Left" (honors thesis, Oberlin College, 1978).

43. The first stirring of opposition to the Vietnam War originated, as the Student Peace Union's example suggests, in pacifist groups and the nuclear disarmament movement. See DeBenedetti, *American Ordeal,* 9–80, James J. Ferrell, *The Spirit of the Sixties: The Making of Postwar Radicalism* (New York: Routledge, 1997), 171–187, David McReynolds, "Pacifists and the Vietnam Antiwar Movement," in Small and Hoover, eds., *Give Peace a Chance,* 57; and Nancy Zaroulis and Gerald Sullivan, *Who Spoke Up? Americans Protest Against the War in Vietnam, 1963–1975* (Garden City, NY: Doubleday, 1984), 7–12, 19.

44. The quote is in "SPU Pickets Tri-Service Review," *UDK,* 18 May 1964; additional information about SPU's activities is drawn from "US Policy in Viet Nam Criticized," *UDK,* 10 October 1963; "Professor Terms Diem Critics Naive," *UDK,* 17 October 1963; "Professors Question American Influence in Viet Nam Coup," *UDK,* 4 November 1963; and "SPU Demonstrates at Area ROTC Meet," *UDK,* 21 October 1963.

45. "War is Picketed at KU Saturday," *LDJW,* 22 February 1965; "SPU Offers Debate on VN," *UDK,* 9 March 1965; "Group Takes SPU Challenge, *UDK,* 11 March 1965; Mark Pillsak to the editor, *UDK,* 23 March 1965.

46. Donald R. McCoy to James B. Pearson, 15 January 1965, James B. Pearson Papers (hereafter, JBP), 24.10; David Leonard, et al, to Pearson, 1 May 1965, JBP, 24.9; Marc Pillsak to the editor, *UDK,* 23 March 1965; "Prof. Asks Revamp Of Foreign Policy," *UDK,* 1 March 1965; "SPU Prepares Demonstrations," *UDK,* 11 May 1965; "SDS Demands US Halt Viet Bombing," *Summer Session Kansan,* 7 July 1965.

47. "VN Teach-in Possible at KU," *UDK,* 22 September 1965; "New Committee Seeks Peace in Viet Nam," *UDK,* 23 September 1965.

48. "Student Left Will Demonstrate Saturday for VN Peace," *UDK,* 12 October 1965; "SPU To Protest U.S. Draft Laws," *UDK,* 15 October 1965; "SPU Joins VN Protest," *UDK,* 18 October 1965; the quotes are in "Emotions Aroused as University Students Picket Draft Board," *LO,* 21 October 1965.

49. "SPU Proposes Blood Drive for Viet Nam," *UDK,* 1 November 1965; "YAF Sends Letters, Clothes to Viet Nam," and "Bring The Boys Home Viet Nam Panel Says," *UDK,* 10 December 1965; "Student Unrest Helps University," *UDK,* 4 November 1965; "Lecturer Sees Win for US in VN," *UDK,* 3 May 1965; "Withdrawal-Defeat" (editorial), *UDK,* 19 November 1965.

50. Weiss quoted in "Movement at Kansas U. Backs Viet War Effort," *LO,* 28 October1965; "Some College Youngsters We Really Appreciate," *LO,* 4 November 1965; "Counter Movement—Letter Planned Backing the War," *UDK,* 26 October 1965; "Letters Of Student Support Goes [*sic*] to Troops in Viet Nam," *UDK,* 16 November 1965; "To Boost Viet Moral Letter Effort Starts," *UDK,* 28 October 1968; K.U. News Bureau, "Press Release," 17 November 1966, UA; loose clipping, "Service Gift Receptables," *LDJW,* 30 November 1967, loose clipping, "Legionnaires Ask Blood Drive Help," *LDJW,* 1 December 1967; Alan Fisher to Robert F. Dunlap, n.d. [1967]; all in Alan Fisher, personal scrapbook related to his tenure as commander of the Dorsey-Liberty American Legion Post #14, Lawrence, Kansas (in Fisher's possession, hereafter, Fisher scrapbook); loose clipping, "VFW Joining Viet Boost," [no further information provided], in "Vietnam Petition Drive" folder, Dorsey-Liberty American Legion Post #14, Lawrence, Kansas, (hereafter, DLAL) vertical files; form letter, DLAL to American GIs, n.d. [1967]; and M/Sgt. Chet Putnam to Dorsey-Liberty American Legion Post, n.d. [1968], in "Vietnam Servicemen Letters" folder, both in DLAL vertical files.

51. Wescoe quoted in W. Clarke Wescoe, "Confidential Report to the Board of Regents," June, 1969, Chancellors Office, W. Clarke Wescoe Correspondence, State Board of Regents, Governor, box 1, (hereafter "Confidential Report, 1969") UA; additional information on the demonstration is compiled from Address by W. Clarke Wescoe, University of Kansas, Lawrence, Kansas, 16 October 1990, Heritage Lecture Series (hereafter, Wescoe Address), UA; Audrey Curtis, "The Disruption of the 1969 Chancellor's Annual Review of the ROTC" (unpublished paper for History 616, 1989, copy in my possession), *UDK,* 10, 23, 31 October 1969; Fisher, "Turbulent Years," 128, 130–131; "KU Petition Condemns SDS," *Topeka Daily Capital,* 12 May 1969; 1970 *Jayhawker,* 79.

52. Wescoe Address (emphasis in original); Fisher, "'Turbulent Years,'" 130–131.

53. For more on the controversy over the release of the protestor's names, see Curtis, 16–19, or the daily accounts in the *UDK* in September and October.

54. E. Laurence Chalmers, Installation Address, 15 September 1969 (emphasis in original), Chancellor's Office, Speeches, box 2, UA.

55. Address by E. Laurence Chalmers, Kansas City, Missouri, 25 September 1969, in Chancellor's Office, Speeches, box 1, UA.

56. Tom Leathers, " Lots of Chiefs-Not Enough Indians," *The Squire,* 14 April 1966 (emphasis in original), loose clipping attached to Mr. and Mrs. Melford Monsees to Mrs. John Hughes, n.d. [April 1966], in Chancellor's Office, W. Clarke Wescoe Correspondence, box 11, UA.

57. "Our Moral Slips" (editorial), *LDJW,* 23 December 1960.

Chapter 5

1. Dick Raney, interview by author, tape recording, Lawrence, Kansas, 8 October 1996.

2. Quoted in Bill Moyers, *Listening to America: A Traveler Rediscovers His Country* (New York: Harper's Magazine Press, 1971), 88.

3. The National Advisory Commission on Civil Disorders, *Report of the National Advisory Commission on Civil Disorders* (New York: Bantam Books, 1968), 2.

4. Although there were distinctions between the Black Power and civil rights movements, I use Clayborne Carson's formulation and consider them to be part of the same freedom struggle. Many blacks did not distinguish between the two, and, for most whites, there was no difference between the rhetoric and ideas of Martin Luther King, Jr., and Malcolm X, or between the goals of the civil rights movement and the black power movement. Additionally, as Timothy B. Tyson has recently suggested, many of the tenets of Black Power—"independent black political action, black cultural pride, and . . . armed self-reliance"—sprang from the same soil as more traditional struggles for African American freedom. See Tyson, "Robert F. Williams, 'Black Power,' and the Roots of the African American Freedom Struggle," *The Journal of American History* 88:2 (September 1998): 540–570; quotes from p. 541.

5. Stokely Carmichael and Charles V. Hamilton, *Black Power: The Politics of Liberation in America* (New York: Vintage Books, 1974), 44.

6. Clayborne Carson, *In Struggle: SNCC and the Black Awakening of the 1960s* (Cambridge, MA: Harvard University Press, 1981), 244.

7. Kathy King and Marilyn Beagle, "The Historical Development of Obtaining a Public Swimming Pool in Lawrence, Kansas," (paper prepared for Sociology 165, fall, 1970, University of Kansas), in "Swimming Pool File," Douglas County Historical Society, Lawrence, Kansas (hereafter, DCHS); Jesse Milan, interview by author, tape recording, Kansas City, Kansas, 27 May 1994; "Lookout," *Lawrence Outlook* (hereafter, *LO*), 1 August 1963; "Club-Hotel at 23rd and Iowa St." *LO,* 3 August 1961.

8. Lawrence Human Relations Commission (hereafter, LHRC), minutes of meeting, 6 April 1966; "Tuesday Voting Sets City Mark," and "The City Election" (editorial) both in *Lawrence Daily Journal-World* (hereafter, *LDJW*), 3 April 1963.

9. "Advisory Group Set to Move," *LDJW,* 5 January 1967; "Bond Project Given Okay," *LDJW,* 13 January 1967; "City's Move on Pool Aid Is Rejected," *LDJW,* 25 July 1967; "Bond Voting Setup Given Dual Okay," *LDJW,* 12 September 1967.

10. "Public Pool Plan Inaugurated Here," *LDJW,* 9 August 1967; the other account is King and Beagle, "Public Swimming Pool," 9; Troelstrup quoted in "Police Policies Topic of Meet of Rights Body," *LDJW,* 24 August 1967.

11. Milan, interview.

12. Milan, interview; "Public Pool Plan Inaugurated Here."

13. John Spearman, Jr., telephone interview by author, tape recording, 9 October 1994.

14. Milan, interview; Spearman, Jr., interview; "Cleanup Starts for Swim Pool," *LDJW,* 10 August 1967; "Public Pool Plan Inaugurated Here"; Dowdell's complaint in Moyers, *Listening to America,* 96.

15. "Officials Hold Meeting," *LDJW,* 8 August 1967; Milan, interview.

16. "Public Pool Plan Inaugurated Here"; "Cleanup Starts for Swim Pool"; Milan, interview.

17. "Cleanup Starts for Swim Pool"; "Cleanup Continuing At Pool Site," *LDJW,* 11 August 1967.

18. "Lessons Offered at Pool Here," *LDJW,* 12 August 1967; *LDJW* photograph in *LDJW,* 14 August 1967; corrugated pool in *LDJW* photograph, *LDJW,* 25 August 1967.

19. Mrs. V. R. Rody to the editor, *LDJW,* 17 August 1967; Roberts quoted in "Cleanup Starts for Swim Pool."

20. "Police Policies Topic of Meet of Rights Body"; Verner Newman, interview by Marian J. Weeks, Lawrence, Kansas, 9 March 1989, in Marian J. Weeks, "Lawrence, 1970: A Narrative and Oral Histories Surrounding Three Crises" (master's thesis, University of Kansas, 1990), 195–198.

21. Charles Greer, interview by Marian J. Weeks, Lawrence, Kansas, 1 September 1990, in Weeks, "Lawrence, 1970," 144.

22. Raney, interview by author; Bill Simons, interview by Marian J. Weeks, Lawrence, Kansas, 20 September 1989, in Weeks, "Lawrence, 1970," 178–179.

23. Milan, interview; King and Beagle, "Public Swimming Pool," 9, 10; Dick Raney, interview by Marian J. Weeks, Lawrence, Kansas, 1 September 1990, in Weeks, "Lawrence, 1970," 253–254; James L. Postma to the editor, *LDJW,* 24 November 1967, 4; "'Hall' Meeting a Hit," *LDJW,* 20 September 1967; "Churches Back Pool," *LDJW,* 16 November 1967; "Swimming Pool Can Give Community Total Aquatic Program," *LDJW,* 17 November 1967; "The Bond Vote," *LDJW,* 20 November 1967; see also several letters to the editor, *LDJW,* 24 November 1967.

24. "Voters Okay Fire House, Swim Setup," *LDJW,* 29 November 1967; King and Beagle, "Public Swimming Pool," 10.

25. Milan, interview. The headlines can be found in *LDJW,* 5 August 1967; 7 August 1967; 1 August 1967.

26. Roy Hicks to James B. Pearson, 6 April 1967, and Pearson to Hicks, 9 April 1967 (emphasis mine), James B. Pearson Papers (hereafter, JBP), 52.9.

27. Carson, *In Struggle*, 227, 244; Carmichael and Hamilton, *Black Power*, 41, 52–3.

28. William L. Van Deberg, *New Day in Babylon: The Black Power Movement and American Culture, 1965–1975* (Chicago: University of Chicago Press, 1992), 9, 17, 28.

29. Simons, interview by Weeks, 165–166.

30. "Coming Home: Governor's Pardon Clears Way for Return of Black Activist," *LDJW,* 22 August 1993.

31. Simons, interview, 169–170.

32. Ibid., 172–174, 177.

33. Gretchen Cassel Eick, "'Lift Every Voice': The Civil Rights Movement and America's Heartland, Wichita, Kansas, 1854–1972" (Ph.D. diss., University of Kansas, 1997), 217–218; "No Black Guard Exists, According to Attorney," *Wichita Beacon,* 31 October 1968. Harrison's criminal record is taken from a memo from Raymond Nichols to E. Laurence Chalmers, 13 January 1970, which Nichols reportedly received from Douglas County Attorney Dan Young. See Chancellor's Office, E. Laurence Chalmers, Correspondence, General, 1969–70, box 1, "Leonard Harrison" folder (hereafter, ELC General), University Archives, University of Kansas (hereafter, UA); Harrison's pardon in "Coming Home."

34. Simons, interview, 170–171, 172, 175.

35. Milan, interview; Spearman, Jr., interview; Turner quoted in "Coming Home."

36. Stephanie Coleman, interview by author, tape recording, Lawrence, Kansas, 24 September 1996.

37. Harrison quoted in "Coming Home"; Simons, interview by Weeks, 170–171, 172, 175; Ocoee Miller telephone conversation with author, 4 November 1998; "Oral History Interview with Ocoee Miller," by Louis George Griffin III (transcript) 19 September 1975, in Douglas County Community Improvement Association Papers, (hereafter, DCCIA), box 18, Kansas Collection, Lawrence, Kansas (hereafter, KC); Milan, interview; and Spearman, Jr., interview. An anecdote in David Ohle, Roger Martin, and Susan Brosseau, eds., *Cows are Freaky When They Look at You: An Oral History of the Kaw Valley Hemp Pickers* (Wichita: Watermark Press, Inc., 1991), 113–116, tends to support Miller's assertions. The speaker tells about "Major M, *the* big bad black man in town, the one who had all white liberals absolutely, completely snowed," which in all likelihood was Leonard Harrison. The story also suggest that "Major M" coerced and hoodwinked whites into giving him money to run the Ballard Center and other programs, "[a]nd a lot of that money disappeared. This town was taken for a ride."

38. Newman, interview by Weeks, 206.

39. Raney, interview by author.

40. Helen Kimball, interview by Mr. Nether, n.d., Douglas County Historical Society, Lawrence, Kansas (hereafter, DCHS); Karen Marie Byers, interview by Mr. Nether, 5 July 1977, DCHS.

41. Byers, interview transcript.

42. I am grateful to Ellen Garber, of Lawrence, for providing me copies of the Lawrence High School yearbooks.

43. Byers, interview transcript; Kenneth Newman, interview by Mr. Nether, n.d., DCHS; Medley quoted in "Negroes At LHS Air Concerns," *LDJW,* 22 May 1968.

44. "Negroes at LHS Air Grievances."

45. Ibid.; Spearman, Jr., interview.

46. Spearman, Jr., interview.

47. William Medley, "A Report to the Parents of Lawrence High School Students," n.d. [probably October 1968] (hereafter, Medley "Report," 1968), in Max Rife, personal collection of materials related to student activism at Lawrence High School, 1968–1970; LHRC, minutes of meeting, 4 September 1968; Robert D. Ramsey to Jack Zimmerman, 1 May 1968; and "Note-o-gram" to Dr. Knox, 17 April 1968, both in "Black Walkout 1968" folder, DCHS.

48. "Black Students Walk Out to Protest LHS Policies," *LDJW,* 25 September 1968.

49. "LHS Black Student Demands," *University Daily Kansan* (hereafter, *UDK*), 26 September 1968.

50. Copy of statement read by June Walker at Unified School District 497 board meeting, 7 October 1968, "Black Walkout 1968" folder, DCHS; "Black Students Return: Promised Black Union," *UDK,* 30 September 1968.

51. "Negroes Set Up School: Blacks Leave LHS," *UDK,* 26 September 1968; "Lawrence Board Attacked, Praised Over Walkout," *UDK,* 8 October 1968.

52. "Negroes Will Meet with LHS Officials," *UDK,* 27 September 1968; "Black Students Walk Out to Protest LHS Policies."

53. "Letter to the editor," *LDJW,* 28 September 1968.

54. "Black Students Walk Out to Protest LHS Policies."

55. Spearman, Jr., interview; "KU Group Meets to Discuss LHS," *UDK,* 27 September 1968.

56. Bill D. Haas to Carl Knox, n.d.; and miscellaneous phone messages and ephemeral material, both in "Black Walkout, 1968" folder, DCHS; "On the Street," *LO,* 26 September 1968; "Ed Abels' Column," *LO,* 30 September 1968.

57. "White Student Reaction: LHS Black Walkout Hurt Cause," *UDK,* 2 October 1968.

58. "White Group Voices Plea to Schoolmen," *LDJW,* 26 September 1968; Elaine Oser Zingg to James Owen, n.d., "Black Walkout, 1968" folder, DCHS.

59. Medley "Report," 1968, 5; Martin Modricin, "The Black Student Movement at LHS: A Study of the 1970 Black Student Demonstrations" (unpublished history honor thesis, University of Kansas. n.d.), KC. Assistant Superintendent Dr. Robert Ramsey, in a September 30 memo, told LHS vice principal H. C. Stuart to "inventory materials in the LHS library" for a black history course and to set up the course; see memorandum, Ram-

sey to H. C. Stuart, 30 September 1968, "Black Walkout 1968" folder, DCHS.

60. Quoted in Moyers, *Listening to America,* 104.

61. Milan, interview.

62. Spearman, Jr., interview.

63. See, for example, *Harambee* 1:2 [1970]. The University of Kansas Archives has several issues of *Harambee.* I am not sure how many issues were published. Many issues are not dated but can be identified by the topics they cover. On the BSU's campus speakers, see Black Student Union, Records (hereafter, BSU), box 1, "1968" folder, UA; the quote is from Van Deberg, *New Day in Babylon,* 26.

64. The demands are in BSU, box 1, "1969/70" folder; K. S. Adams to E. Laurence Chalmers, 11 November 1969, and Fred Benson, Jr. to E. Laurence Chalmers, 4 November 1969, both in Chancellor's Office, E. Laurence Chalmers Correspondence, Departmental, 1969/70, box 1, "Black Student Union" folder, UA (hereafter, ELC Departmental).

65. This paragraph is taken from the following: E. Laurence Chalmers, interview by author, tape recording, San Antonio, Texas, 1–2 April 1994; Chalmers to Daryl Bright, 14 November 1969, in ELC Departmental, box 1, "Black Student Union" folder; untitled, unsigned manuscript, 26 February 1970, and "Press Release" from the Chancellor's Office, undated [5 March 1970], both in BSU, box 1, "1969/70" folder; Francis Heller, "K.U. Notes 1948–1972" (unpublished manuscript, n.d. [1973]), 727–728, UA; and Spearman, Jr., interview. Spearman admitted that he and the BSU had put so much pressure on Chalmers that it probably contributed to the chancellor losing his job a few years later.

66. "Senate Funds BSU Project," *UDK,* 14 May 1970.

67. The background information on Penn House is taken from the following: Human Development and Family Life, department files, "Penn House" folder, UA; Douglas County Community Improvement Association, assorted correspondence, box 1, "1969–1971" folder; Ocoee Miller, conversation with author; "Oral History Interview with Ocoee Miller"; "Penn House Helps Women to Help Themselves," *LDJW,* 5 September 1969; "'Penn House' Plans Ahead," *LDJW,* 26 March 1970; "Young Rules Bomb Cause in $100 Fire," *LDJW,* 6 July 1970.

68. "Penn House Helps Women to Help Themselves."

69. Simons, interview, 168; Leonard Harrison and Lenore Findlay to "Gentlemen," 4 December 1969, and Keith Miller, "Relationship Between Ballard Center and Penn House," both in DCCIA, box 1, "Correspondence: C.C.B.C. (1969–1970)" folder; "Oral History Interview with Ocoee Miller."

70. Simons, interview, 168; Harrison and Findlay to "Gentlemen," 4 December 1969, and [Keith Miller], "Relationship Between Ballard Center and Penn House," both in DCCIA, box 1, "Correspondence: C.C.B.C. (1969–1970)" folder.

71. Vernell Sturns to Keith Miller, 17 December 1969, and Keith Miller, "Very Brief Summary of Relating with CCBC," both in DCCIA, box 1, "Correspondence: C.C.B.C. (1969–1970)" folder.

72. Keith Miller, "Rumors Regarding Penn House and Its Staff," in DCCIA, box 1, "Correspondence: C.C.B.C. (1969–1970)" folder.

73. "Oral History Interview with Ocoee Miller"; Leonard Harrison to Keith Miller, n.d. [January 1970], in DCCIA, box 1, "Correspondence: C.C.B.C. (1969–1970)" folder; "peckerwood" in *Harambee,* n.d. [probably May 1970]; Margaret Wedge, "Grass Roots in Action," (unpublished paper for Social Work 969, December 1978), KC; "Young Rules Bomb Cause in $100 Fire."

74. Herbert H. Haines, *Black Radicals and the Civil Rights Mainstream, 1954–1970* (Knoxville: University of Tennessee Press, 1988), quoted in Van Deberg, *New Day in Babylon,* 306.

Chapter 6

1. Robert F. Ellsworth, "Tabulated results of Questionnaire," Robert F. Ellsworth Papers, (hereafter, RFE) 59.2. Ellsworth claimed that he sent out over 118,000 questionnaires and that the response was "overwhelming," although the exact number was not revealed and only a few of the surveys are extant.

2. Tabulated results, opinion ballot, RFE, 59.2; R. T. Schwanzle to Ellsworth, n.d. [January 1962], RFE, 26.10; John Garcia to Ellsworth, 17 January 1962, RFE, 75.1; Clark Coan to Ellsworth, 11 March 1962, RFE, 59.2.

3. I take as a beginning definition of the antiwar movement one provided in Charles DeBenedetti, with Charles Chatfield, in *An American Ordeal: The Antiwar Movement of the Vietnam Era* (Syracuse, NY: Syracuse University Press, 1990). DeBenedetti draws on the work of the sociologist Charles Tilly, who defines a social movement as a "sustained *interaction* in which mobilized people, acting in the name of a defined interest, make repeated broad demands on powerful others via means which go beyond the current prescriptions of authority." I include as part of this movement all those people who opposed the war and who made a declaration of that opposition, either publicly (as in a march or vigil) or privately (by writing letters to their elected officials, for example). DeBenedetti, *American Ordeal,* 1, quoting Tilly, "Social Movements and National Politics," in Charles Bright and Susan Harding, eds., *Statemaking and Social Movements: Essays in History and Theory* (Ann Arbor: University of Michigan Press, 1984), 313 (emphasis in original).

4. DeBenedetti, *American Ordeal,* 2.

5. DeBenedetti, *American Ordeal,* 2–3.

6. Although mail to the president is often skeptically viewed as unrepresentative of public opinion, mail to congressional or senatorial offices is generally regarded as an accurate indicator of the district's opinion. See Barry B. Hughes, *The Domestic Context of American Foreign Policy* (San Francisco: W.H. Freeman, 1978), 101, cited in Melvin Small, *Johnson, Nixon, and the*

Doves (New Brunswick: Rutgers University Press, 1988) 11, 238 n. 38. The final quote is from David Thelen, *Becoming Citizens in the Age of Television* (Chicago: University of Chicago Press, 1996), 8–9, whose creative use of constituent correspondence is a model that I try to emulate here.

7. The photograph appeared in the *Lawrence Daily Journal-World* (hereafter, *LDJW*) on 11 June 1963.

8. Kennedy's quotes are from his first inaugural speech; troop figures are from DeBenedetti, *American Ordeal,* 81–86, 240; George Donelson Moss, *Vietnam: An American Ordeal,* 3rd ed. (Upper Saddle River, NJ: Prentice Hall, 1998), 446, and Stanley Karnow, *Vietnam: A History* (New York: Penguin Books, 1983), 681.

9. A. B. Weaver to Robert F. Ellsworth, 17 January 1964, RFE, 73.1; Mrs. Clark Coan to Robert F. Ellsworth, 20 March 1964, RFE, 27.1; Thomas and Shirley Schmidt to Ellsworth, 1 November 1964, RFE, 27.1; Elizabeth Henderson to Ellsworth, 7 August 1964, (emphasis in original), RFE, 27.1.

10. Robert F. Ellsworth, questionnaire, 1965, RFE, 59.8.

11. Mrs. H. M. Brownlee to the editor, *Lawrence Outlook* (hereafter, *LO*), 5 August 1965; Mr. and Mrs. Albin Longren to James B. Pearson, 17 February 1965, James B. Pearson Papers (hereafter, JBP), 24.12; Clayton M. Crosier to Pearson, 17 April 1965, JBP, 24.11. Dorsey-Liberty American Legion Post [Lawrence, Kansas], Resolution, 19 October 1965; handwritten notes, 12 November 1965; Petition, n.d. [November 1965], all in "Vietnam Petition Drive" folder, Dorsey Liberty American Legion vertical files, Lawrence, Kansas (hereafter, DLAL). The Legionnaires may have been right. Nancy Zaroulis and Gerald Sullivan cite a Harris poll taken in December 1967 that found that about 75 percent of Americans thought antiwar protests gave the communists encouragement, and that 70 percent thought they were acts of disloyalty. Fifty-eight percent favored fighting the war to the end. See Nancy Zaroulis and Gerald Sullivan, *Who Spoke Up? Americans Protest Against the War in Vietnam, 1963–1975* (Garden City, NY: Doubleday, 1984), 147.

12. Dr. Glenn A. Lessenden to James B. Pearson, 17 February 1966, JBP, 45.13.

13. Anne H. T. Moore to James B. Pearson, 22 December 1966, JBP, 45.15; Thomas Kruse to Pearson, 21 February 1966, JBP, 45.14; Mrs. Helen Hartzell to Pearson, 22 February 1966, JBP, 45.11.

14. Mrs. David Leonard to James B. Pearson, 29 June 1966, JBP, 45.15; Robert T. Howard to Pearson, 5 February 1967, JBP, 54.14.

15. Ruth A. Eigner to James B. Pearson, 14 April 1967, JBP, 54.7; Theodore H. Eaton to Pearson, 15 April 1967, JBP, 54.7; Monti L. Belot, Jr., to James B. Pearson, 6 July 1967, JBP, 54.11.

16. According to DeBenedetti, "[a]pathy mixed with ambivalence in a way that made public opinion both unstable and hard to assess." See DeBenedetti, *American Ordeal,* 179.

17. Tom Moore to Leonard Tinker, 11 December 1966, Kansas Peace Forum (hereafter, KPF), newsletter, 25 March 1967, and loose clipping, "To Discuss

Vietnam," *University Daily Kansan* (hereafter, *UDK*) 10 March 1971, all in Lawrence Center for Peace and Justice Papers, box 3, "Kansas Peace Forum" folder, Kansas Collection, University of Kansas (hereafter, LCPJ).

18. Tom Moore to Leonard Tinker, 11 December 1966, and KPF and KU Vietnam Committee to Dear Friend, 4 May 1967, both in LCPJ, box 3, "Kansas Peace Forum" folder; Jean Shellhammer to James B. Pearson, 15 April 1967, and Dr. and Mrs. W. O. Scott to James B. Pearson, 17 April 1967, both in JBP, 54.7.

19. "Dear Friend," unsigned letter, 15 May 1967, LCPJ, box 3, "Kansas Peace Forum" folder.

20. "Vietnam Summer Project Launched by Town Canvass," *LDJW,* 15 June 1967; Robert E. Maness to editor, *LDJW,* 8 August 1967; Sally Heeren to editor, *LDJW,* 12 August 1967.

21. Calvin Trillin, "The War in Kansas," *New Yorker,* 22 April 1967: 101,122, as cited in DeBenedetti, *American Ordeal,* 179.

22. Tom Moore to Leonard Tinker, 11 December 1966, LCPJ, box 3, "Kansas Peace Forum" folder; Lawrence Peace Center (LPC), minutes of board meetings, October-November 1967, December 1967, March 1968, 14 May 1968, and "April-May Report," in Lawrence Peace Center Papers (hereafter, LPC), "Current Correspondence" folder, Kansas Collection, University of Kansas, Lawrence, Kansas (hereafter, KC).

23. Barbara Deming, "Letter to WSP," *Liberation 8* (April 1963): 18–21, quoted in James J. Farrell, *The Spirit of the Sixties: The Making of Postwar Radicalism* (New York: Routledge, 1997), 135; on maternal pacifism and the WSP, see Amy Swerdlow, *Women Strike for Peace,* (Chicago: University of Chicago Press, 1993), and Farrell, *Spirit of the Sixties,* 130–135. After 1963, WSP expanded its efforts to oppose the war in Vietnam. The WILPF and WSP joined together in a "Mother's Lobby" in 1965 and soon adopted the slogan "Not Our Sons, Not Your Sons, Not Their Sons," which, Farrell points out, emphasized "the importance of soldiers as persons in families." The significance of personalizing the war's destruction was made more poignant as the United States stepped up its efforts to conscript soldiers. Farrell, *Spirit of the Sixties,* 175.

24. The information about the WILPF is taken from the Kansas Free University bulletin, spring 1968, in the Kansas Free University, Records, University of Kansas Archives, Lawrence, Kansas (hereafter, UA). On the WILPF, see Catherine Foster, *Women For All Seasons: The Story of the Women's International League for Peace and Freedom* (Athens: University of Georgia Press, 1989), and Carrie A. Foster, *The Women and the Warriors: The U.S. Section of the Women's International League for Peace and Freedom, 1915–1946* (Syracuse, NY: Syracuse University Press, 1995).

25. See, for example, Mrs. John Cairns to James B. Pearson, n.d. [May 1967], JBP, 54.5; Wayne and Lynn Sailor to Pearson, n.d. [December 1967], JBP, 54.7; Gene, Judy, and Jeffrey Bonny to Pearson, n.d. [December 1967], JBP, 54.7.

26. KPF and KU Vietnam Committee to Dear Friend, 4 May 1967, LCPJ, box 3, "Kansas Peace Forum" folder; Jane Fowler Morse to James B. Pearson, n.d. [May 1967], JBP, 54.5; Mrs. Ronald Jacobowitz to Pearson, n.d. [May 1967], JBP, 54.6.

27. Stewart Nowlin to the editor, *LDJW,* 29 May 1967; flyer, n.d., LCPJ, box 3, "Kansas Peace Forum" folder; Informational Clearing House for the Weekly Vigil For Peace, *Newsletter, no. 2,* 9 November 1966, LPC, "Vigil" folder. On the origins of the silent vigil, see Charles Hubbell, *The Weekly Vigil for Peace: Suggestions for the Conduct of Recurrent Silent Witness* (Santa Barbara, CA: Charles Hubbell, 1967), in LPC, "Vigil" folder.

28. Flyer, n.d., LCPJ, box 3, "Kansas Peace Forum" folder; Mrs. Tom Moore and Mrs. Otto Zingg to the editor, *LDJW,* 7 March 1970.

29. The best study of the Vietnam-era draft is Lawrence M. Baskir and William A. Strauss, *Chance and Circumstance: The Draft, the War, and the Vietnam Generation* (New York: Knopf, 1978), but see also Sherry Gershon Gottlieb, *Hell No, We Won't Go!: Resisting the Draft During the Vietnam War* (New York: Viking, 1991), and G. David Curry, *Sunshine Patriots: Punishment and the Vietnam Offender* (Notre Dame: University of Notre Dame Press, 1985).

30. Perry E. Puderbaugh to James B. Pearson, 27 March 1967, JBP, 52.29; Lola M. Puderbaugh to Pearson, 27 March 1967, JBP, 52.30.

31. Mrs. Glenn Lessenden to James B. Pearson, 19 May 1967, JBP, 54.4.

32. "Lawrence Marine Killed in Vietnam," *LDJW,* 15 May 1967. It appears that at least one other Lawrencian had been killed in Vietnam before Cooper. Army Captain David Gibson, 28, had been killed by artillery fire in early April. According to the *Journal-World,* Gibson had come to Lawrence as a student at KU and became a "permanent resident" when he joined the real estate firm of Haverty and Hedges and Hird in 1963. Mrs. Lessenden may have seen Cooper as a "local boy" because he and his family had lived in Lawrence since 1951 (although Cooper graduated from Raytown [Missouri]), High School). See "Dave Gibson Dies in Viet," *LDJW,* 12 April 1967.

33. Cpl. John V. Hughes, Jr. to the editor, *LDJW,* 25 May 1967; Glenn Close to Mrs. Cooper, *LDJW,* 1 June 1967.

34. Sharon Ireland to the editor, *LDJW,* 18 May 1967.

35. Hamilton J. Salsich to the editor, *LDJW,* 23 May 1967.

36. The photograph appeared first in the *LDJW* on Saturday, 22 April 1967. On April 24, the paper reprinted the photo on the editorial page, above a number of angry letters from residents.

37. Todd Gitlin, *The Sixties: Years of Hope, Days of Rage* (Toronto: Bantam Books, 1989), 206–214; the quote is on 208. See also Abe Peck, *Uncovering the Sixties: The Life and Times of the Underground Press* (New York: Pantheon Books, 1985); W. J. Rorabaugh, *Berkeley at War: The 1960s* (New York: Oxford University Press, 1989); and David Steigerwald, *The Sixties and the End of Modern America* (New York: St. Martin's Press, 1995).

38. The notion that the "personal is political" is not new. Sara Evans illustrates the point in her study of the 1960s women's liberation movement. See Sara

Evans, *Personal Politics: The Roots of Women's Liberation in the Civil Rights Movement and the New Left* (New York: Vintage Books, 1980). Recently, James J. Farrell has forced a reconsideration of the 1960s and political radicalism through the lens of "personalism" or "personalist politics" in his *Spirit of the Sixties.*

39. "Pitiful Taste" (editorial), *LDJW,* 24 April 1967.

40. Kenton Craven to the editor, *LDJW,* 25 April 1967; James McCrary to the editor, *LDJW,* 29 April 1967.

41. Alan Fisher, "Remarks as Installation as Post Commander," May 1967, in Alan Fisher, personal scrapbook related to his tenure as commander of the Dorsey-Liberty American Legion Post #14, Lawrence, Kansas (in Fisher's possession, hereafter, Fisher scrapbook).

42. "Remarks as Installation as Post Commander"; and DLAL "Resolution," May 1967, both in Fisher, scrapbook.

43. Lawrence High Twelve Club to the editor, *LDJW,* 26 April 1967; Mrs. W. R. Findley to the editor, *LDJW,* 5 May 1967; Thomas T. Glidden to the editor, *LDJW,* 26 April 1967.

44. Eric Rundquist to the editor, *LDJW,* 23 May 1967; Kathy Schott to the editor, *LDJW,* 26 May 1967.

45. John Bodnar, *Remaking America: Public Memory, Commemoration, and Patriotism in the Twentieth Century* (Princeton, NJ: Princeton University Press, 1991), 246; Michael Kammen, *Mystic Chords of Memory: The Transformation of Tradition in American Culture* (New York: Alfred A. Knopf, 1991), 5.

46. Robert E. Ireland to James B. Pearson, 31 October 1967, JBP, 54.10; "Our War" (editorial), *LDJW,* 4 April 1967.

47. "An Unsound Approach" (editorial), *LDJW,* 4 April 1967; "Who Won't Go?" (editorial), *LDJW,* 3 May 1967.

48. Arly Allen to James B. Pearson, 14 August 1967, JBP, 54.13; Ada Jacobowitz to Pearson, n.d. [April 1967], JBP, 54.6; Mrs. J. Hutton to Pearson, 22 July [1967], JBP, 54.13.

49. Mrs. Clark Coan to James B. Pearson, 24 April 1967, JBP, 54.6; Angus Wright to Pearson, 14 April 1967, JBP, 54.7; Mrs. Martin S. Hanna to Pearson, 23 March 1968, JBP, 60.18.

50. Ms. Sandy Bair to James B. Pearson, 23 December 1968, JBP, 60.17.

51. WDAF poll cited in Denis B. Lardiner, Sr. to James B. Pearson, n.d. [March 1968], JBP, 61.1; Elizabeth Henderson to Pearson, 27 February 1968, JBP, 60.17; Judy Wonn to Pearson, 9 March 1968, JBP, 61.1.

52. Mr. and Mrs. Alfred J. Graves to Richard M. Nixon, 6 November 1969, JBP, 71.15; Ray and Marsh Goff to Pearson, 3 November 1969 (emphasis in original), JBP, 71.21; Grace Reisner to Pearson, 29 September 1969, JBP, 71.22; William C. Elbrader to Robert Docking, c.c. to James B. Pearson, 1 October 1969, JBP, 71.14; Mr. and Mrs. Vernon Harrel to Pearson, 10 November 1969 (emphasis in original), JBP, 71.15.

53. DeBenedetti, *American Ordeal,* 248–250, 253.

54. "Citizens Group Making Oct. 15 Activity Plans," *LDJW,* 2 October 1969, loose clipping in LPC, "Lawrence Oct. 15th Committee" folder.

55. "Student strike, protest, activism" folder, David M. Katzman personal collection of materials related to student activism at the University of Kansas, 1969–1971 (hereafter, DMK); USD 497, Board of Education Memos, 1969–1970, box 11 (unsorted material), KC; "Peace Demonstrations are Peacefull [*sic*] in Lawrence," *LO*, n.d., loose clipping in LPC, "Lawrence Oct. 15th Committee" folder.

56. Information about the Lawrence October 15th Committee and the planning of the Moratorium are taken from loose clipping, "Citizens Group Making Oct. 15 Activity Plans," *LO*, 2 October 1969; loose clipping, "Local Group Seeks War's End," *LO*, 6 October 1969; loose clipping, "Meetings Mark Oct. 15 Protest," *LO*, 13 October 1969; loose clipping, full-page advertisement, *LDJW*, n.d. [October 1969], all in LPC, "Lawrence Oct. 15th Committee" folder.

57. Loose clipping, "Town Absent in Discussion," *LDJW*, n.d. [October 1969], LPC, "Lawrence Oct. 15th Committee" folder.

58. Mr. and Mrs. R. Wayne Nelson to James B. Pearson, 12 November 1969, JBP, 71.18; loose clipping, Harold V. Siegerst to the editor, *LDJW*, 20 October 1969, and loose clipping, "Ed Abels' Column," 1 November 1969, *LO*, both in LPC, "Lawrence Oct. 15th Committee" folder.

59. As cited in DeBenedetti, *American Ordeal*, 249–250, 253.

60. Loose clipping, "Citizens Group Making Oct. 15 Activity Plans"; "Local Group Seeks War's End"; "Meetings Mark Oct. 15 Protest"; and full-page advertisement, all in LPC, "Lawrence Oct. 15th Committee" folder.

61. "Peace Leaders Named," *LDJW*, 23 October 1969; "Peace Parade, Long Vigil Part of Weekend Activities," *LDJW*, 30 October 1969; "Lawrence Peace Action Coalition and Lawrence Committee for Peace in Indochina, "Advertisement," *LDJW*, 28 October 1969, all loose clippings in LPC, "Lawrence Oct. 15th Committee" folder.

62. DeBenedetti, *American Ordeal*, 250–251.

63. "War Protestor Speaks Tonight," *LDJW*, 30 October 1969, loose clipping in LPC, "Lawrence Oct. 15th Committee" folder.

64. "Veteran's Ceremony Marred," *LDJW*, 11 November 1969, loose clipping in LPC, "Lawrence Oct. 15th Committee" folder.

65. "Leaders Condemn Action," *UDK*, 12 November 1969; "150 in Parade for Peace," *LDJW*, 15 November 1969; and "Moratorium Called Anticlimactic," *UDK*, 18 November 1969, loose clippings in LPC, "Lawrence Oct. 15th Committee" folder.

66. "Moratoriums" (editorial), *LDJW*, 17 November 1969, loose clipping in LPC, "Lawrence Oct. 15th Committee" folder.

67. Fred E. Johnson to the editor, *LDJW*, 10 October 1969, and Mrs. Jo Barnes to the editor, *LDJW*, 12 November 1969, both loose clippings in LPC, "Lawrence Oct. 15th Committee" folder.

68. Judith A. Daily to the editor, *LDJW*, 12 November 1969; Stephen J. Schroff to the editor, *LDJW*, 14 November 1969; and Roberta R. Nixon to the editor, *LDJW*, 12 November 1969, and, all loose clippings in LPC, "Lawrence Oct. 15th Committee" folder.

69. John Cairns, Jr., to James B. Pearson, 1 October 1967, JBP, 54.10; Cairns to Pearson, 18 November 1967, JBP, 54.11; Jacqueline Speakman to Pearson, 16 August 1967, JBP, 54.13.

Chapter 7

1. On the counterculture, see Theodore Roszak, *The Making of a Countercul-ture* (Garden City, NY: Doubleday, 1969), and Timothy Miller, *The Hippies and American Values* (Knoxville: University of Tennessee Press, 1991).
2. "New Campus Problem: Young Drifters," *New York Times,* 10 November 1970; Credit Bureau of Lawrence, Kansas, Inc., *1968 Directory* (Topeka, KS: Capitol Service Bureau, Inc., 1968); Credit Bureau of Lawrence, Kansas, Inc., *1970 Directory* (Topeka, KS: Capitol Service Bureau, Inc., 1970); R.L. Polk and Co, *Polk's Lawrence (Douglas County, Kansas) City Directory, 1969* (Kansas City, MO: R.L. Polk and Co., 1969).
3. "New Campus Problem"; David Ohle, Roger Martin, and Susan Brosseau, eds., *Cows are Freaky When They Look at You: An Oral History of the Kaw Valley Hemp Pickers* (Wichita: Watermark Press, Inc., 1991), xi, 3; "street scene" quoted in Bryce Nelson, "Kansas: Police-Student Violence Imperils University," *Science* 169 (7 August 1970): 568.
4. All quotes are from Ohle, et al., *Cows are Freaky,* xii, 5.
5. Raymond Schwegler, "Some Brief Remarks on the Functioning of the Mental Health Clinic of the Student Health Service at the K.U. During the 1969–70 Academic Year," Office of Student Affairs, Health Services folder, 1/3/69–12/30/69,76/0, box 5, University of Kansas Archives, Lawrence, Kansas (hereafter, UA); Dick Raney, interview by Marian J. Weeks, Lawrence, Kansas, 1 September 1990, in Marian J. Weeks, "Lawrence, 1970: A Narrative and Oral Histories Surrounding Three Crises" (master's thesis, University of Kansas, 1990), 253–272; Ohle, et al., *Cows are Freaky,* xi, 124, 71–74; *The Coalition* (Lawrence, Kansas), 1:2, 7 April 1970, in "Student Pubs" folder, David M. Katzman personal collection of materials related to student activism at the University of Kansas, 1969–1971 (hereafter, DMK).
6. James J. Farrell, *The Spirit of the Sixties: The Making of Postwar Radicalism* (New York: Routledge, 1997), 212.
7. Ohle, et al., *Cows are Freaky,* xii, 5; see also Beth Bailey, *Sex in the Heartland* (Cambridge, MA: Harvard University Press, 2000), 143–146.
8. Brown, quoted in "New Campus Problem"; "pig Amerika" in *Vortex* 3:1 (July-August 1970).
9. Kansas State Fire Marshall, "Investigative Report, 3/13/68–9/9/69," Robert B. Docking Papers (hereafter, RBD), 41.10; "1969—It Began with Miami Heartbreak," *Lawrence Daily Journal-World* (hereafter, LDJW), 31 December 1969.
10. "1969—It Began with Miami Heartbreak."
11. Merwyn V. Purdy to Ed Collister, 2 June 1970, RBD, 41.11.

12. See, for example, *Vortex* 2:5 (29 April–12 May [1970]).

13. For more background on Harrison, see chapter five. Raymond Nichols to E. Laurence Chalmers, 13 January 1970, Chancellor's Office, E. Laurence Chalmers, Correspondence, General, 1969–70, box 1, "Leonard Harrison" folder (hereafter, ELC General), UA.

14. Leonard Harrison, syllabus for Political Science 164, "Political Revolutionary Thought: Black Revolutionary Thought," spring semester 1970, Douglas County Community Improvement Association (hereafter, DCCIA), "Penn House Correspondence, C.C.B.C., 1969–1970" folder, Kansas Collection, University of Kansas, Lawrence, Kansas (hereafter, KC).

15. Francis Heller to E. Laurence Chalmers, February 1970, attached to Black Student Union resolutions, 26 February 1970, in Black Student Union Papers (hereafter, BSU), 1.7, KC.

16. Robert B. Docking to James Huff [copy], 30 January 1970, in ELC General, "Leonard Harrison" folder.

17. "Shultz Opposes Hiring of Harrison," *University Daily Kansan* (hereafter, *UDK*), 10 February 1970.

18. Ibid.; on *Harambee*'s content, see, for example, 1:1, 1:2, and 1:3, in the Kansas Collection.

19. Ernest C. Ballweg to Kent Frizzell, 10 June 1970, RBD, 41:10, summarizes several attorney general opinions of campus publications, including one of *Harambee*'s content; Ollie Farmer to Robert B. Docking, n.d. [February 1970], RBD, 41.15; Louise Farmer to Robert B. Docking, n.d. [February 1970], RBD, 41.15; Gerald Nye, Kansas Bureau of Investigation Report, n.d., attached to attorney general report, RBD, 41.10.

20. *Harambee,* n.d. [May 1970]; Kansas Highway Patrol (KHP) Intelligence Report, 24 February 1970, RBD, 41.10; KBI Investigation Report, 10 June 1970, RBD, 41.11.

21. "Day-By-Day Chronology of Exciting Local Year," *LDJW,* 31 December 1970.

22. "Velvel, Litto 'Frozen,'" *LDJW,* 20 March 1970; Darrel D. Masen to James B. Pearson, 7 February 1969, James B. Pearson Papers (hereafter, JBP), 67.18.

23. "'Strike' Is Goal At KU," *LDJW,* 3 April 1970; "KU Officials Conferring On Strike Policy" *LDJW,* 4 April 1970; "Day-By-Day Chronology of Exciting Local Year"; Darrel D. Masen to James B. Pearson, 7 February 1969, JBP, 67.18. For other critics of Velvel and Litto, see Mrs. William H. Quakenbush to James B. Pearson, 14 February 1969, JBP, 67.16 and correspondence in RBD, 41.15; strike material taken from "Student strike, protest, activism" folder, DMK; "Velvel, Litto Promotions Okayed By State Regents," *LDJW,* 24 April 1970.

24. Kansas State Fire Marshall, "Investigative Report, 4 June 1970," RBD, 54.22; "'Strike' Is Goal At KU"; "Strike Challenged," *UDK,* 7 April 1970; "Fear of Violence Voiced at KU Strike," *LDJW,* 7 April 1970; "Uneasy Calm Noted After KU Arson Try," *LDJW,* 8 April 1970; "Chalmers Says KU Called About Attempt at Arson," *LDJW,* 8 April 1970; "Non-Violence Pleas

Unheeded," *UDK,* 8 April 1970; "Day-By-Day Chronology of an Exciting Local Year."

25. "Fear of Violence Voiced at KU Strike"; "Uneasy Calm Noted After KU Arson Try"; "Chalmers Says KU Called About Attempt at Arson"; "Sigh of Relief Follows Quiet 'Strike' at KU" *LDJW,* 9 April 1970; "Day-By-Day Chronology of an Exciting Local Year."

26. For examples of these responses, see Ronald Eugene Johnson, "Student Unrest and the Kansas Press: Editorial Reactions to Violence in Lawrence and at the University of Kansas in 1970" (masters thesis, University of Kansas, 1982), 59–63.

27. "Profanity-Packed Talk Fails to Excite Students," *LDJW,* 9 April 1970; "Nose Blowing Investigated," *LDJW,* 9 April 1970.

28. Robert W. Doores to James B. Pearson, 6 May 1970, JBP, 91.13.

29. Mrs. Marvin Meyer to James B. Pearson, 27 April 1970, JBP, 89.1.

30. "Profanity-Packed Talk Fails to Excite Students"; "Nose Blowing Investigated"; "Hoffman Says Degree Useless," *UDK,* 9 April 1970; Dennis Embry and John Miller, "Racial And Student Disturbances: Documentary, Lawrence, Kansas, 1970," (audio tapes), tape 5, side A, KC; Chalmers quoted in Bill Moyers, *Listening to America: A Traveler Rediscovers His Country* (New York: Harper's Magazine Press, 1971), 101; "drag" quote is from *Kansas Alumni,* 16 May 1970, 6.

31. Ohle, et al., *Cows Are Freaky,* 25; "Blacks Urged To Take Arms," *LDJW,* 10 April 1970; City Negroes Don't Trust Police," *LDJW,* 11 March 1970; "Threats Spark Reaction," *UDK,* 13 April 1970; *Harambee,* n.d. [May 1970]; "BSU Achieves Monumental Gains," *UDK,* 13 May 1970; *Harambee,* 1:2 (1970); *Harambee,* 1:3 (1970); "KHP Report, 28 March 1970," in RBD, 41.11. Jackson was later arrested in Chicago with BSU member Ron Washington for illegal possession of firearms, driving a van that belonged to KU law professor Charles Oldfather.

32. Richard Beaty, interview by Marian J. Weeks, Lawrence, Kansas, September 1989, in Weeks, "Lawrence, 1970," 230–231.

33. Ibid., 235, 240.

34. "LHS Disturbance Prompts Arrest," *UDK,* 15 April 1970; "LHS Disruption Results in Charges, Suspension," *LDJW,* 14 April 1970.

35. William Medley, handwritten report to Superintendent Carl Knox, 13 April 1970; handwritten statements from Lawrence High teachers, n.d. [April 1970]; and other ephemeral material, all in Max Rife personal collection of material related to student activism at Lawrence High School, 1968–1970; Lawrence Human Relations Commission, "A Study of the Lawrence High School Confrontation in April, 1970," December 1970 (hereafter, LHRC "Study," 1970), Lawrence Public Library; "Black Walkout, 1970," vertical file, Douglas County Historical Society (hereafter, DCHS); "LHS Disturbance Prompts Arrest"; "LHS Disruption Results in Charges, Suspension"; "High School Fights Erupt, Students Hurt," *LDJW,* 15 April 1970; "Medley Calls For Normal LHS Classes," *LDJW,* 15 April 1970; Martin

Modricin, "The Black Student Movement at LHS: A Study of the 1970 Black Student Demonstrations" (unpublished history honors thesis, University of Kansas, n.d.), KC.

36. "LHS Disturbance Prompts Arrest"; Modricin, "Black Student Movement"; LHRC "Study," 1970; "High School Fights Erupt, Students Hurt"; "Medley Calls For Normal LHS Classes"; "LHS Is Tense But Quiet As Two Meetings Are Set," *LDJW,* 16 April 1970.

37. Beaty, interview, 224–225, 239, 243.

38. "LHS Disturbance Prompts Arrest"; "LHS Is Tense But Quiet As Two Meetings Are Set"; "LHS Students Due Vote on Proposals," *LDJW,* 17 April 1970; "Classes On Monday, Knox Asks Normalcy," *LDJW,* 18 April 1970; "Proposal at LHS Beaten By Students," *LDJW,* 20 April 1970; "Violence At School Center," *LDJW,* 21 April 1970; "Police Disperse Blacks at LHS," *UDK,* 17 April 1970; "Bombs Explode At LHS," *UDK,* 21 April 1970; Modricin, "Black Student Movement"; LHRC Study, 1970; William Medley to Carl Knox, 23 April 1970, Max Rife personal collection.

39. Jeff Weinberg to Carl Knox, n.d.; "Statement of Lawrence Clergy," n.d.; Mrs. Kim Griffin to Board Members, 29 April 1970; petition to the board of education; Robert D. Ramsey to Carl Knox, 22 April 1970; and miscellaneous letters, all in "Black Walkout, 1970," vertical file, DCHS; LHRC Study, 1970.

40. Beaty, interview, 241; telegrams from Donald E. Metzler and Daniel A. Young to Robert B. Docking, 21, 22, 23 April 1970; gubernatorial proclamations, 21, 22, 23 April 1970; Kansas Bureau of Investigation (KBI) investigation report to Kent Frizzell, 10 June 1970; list of subjects arrested in Lawrence, 21–23 April 1970, attached to Merwyn V. Purdy to Ed Collister 2 June 1970, all in RBD, 41.11; "Guardsmen Activated To Quell Snipers, Fires," *UDK,* 22 April 1970; "Dusk to Dawn Curfew Ordered By Docking," *UDK,* 22 April 1970; "All Roads Into Lawrence Patrolled," *UDK,* 23 April 1970; "Arson Suspected in $1 Million Union Loss," *LDJW,* 21 April 1970; "Curfew Set, Rumor Unit Established," *LDJW,* 21 April 1970; "Snipers, Arson Tries Mark Overnight Action," *LDJW,* 22 April 1970; "Curfew Set Again in City For Tonight," *LDJW,* 22 April 1970; "Union Arson Theory: Inside or Outside?" *LDJW,* 22 April 1970; "No Movies, Burgers—Lawrence An Eerie Ghost Town," *LDJW,* 22 April 1970; "Rumor Center Phones Busy," *LDJW,* 22 April 1970.

41. Handwritten notes attached to Vernell Sturns to Carl Knox, 28 April 1970, and Knox to Sturns, 30 April 1970, in "Black Walkout, 1970," vertical file, DCHS; *Harambee,* n.d. [April or May 1970]; "Violence At School Center," *LDJW,* 21 April 1970.

42. "Report on Black Programs By School Supt. Carl Knox," *LDJW,* 24 April 1970; "Board States Policy Plans," *LDJW,* 24 April 1970; "LHS Student Council Plans For 'Leader,' Queen Policy," *LDJW,* 1 May 1970; "Lawrence Blacks Agree, Demands Still Not Met," *LDJW,* 7 May 1970; "Vern Sturns Critical Of Handling LHS Riot," *LDJW,* 7 May 1970.

43. See list of subjects arrested in Lawrence, 21–23 April 1970, attached to Merwyn V. Purdy to Ed Collister, 2 June 1970, RBD, 41.11; "Arrests As Tension Persists," *LDJW,* 23 April 1970; "Curfew Set For 10 P.M.," *LDJW,* 23 April 1970; "Tight Security on Campus to Remain, Chalmers Says," *LDJW,* 23 April 1970; "Curfew Lifted For Tonight," *LDJW,* 24 April 1970; "18 Arrests on Thursday for Breaking of Curfew," *LDJW,* 24 April 1970.

44. Lee Scott to James B. Pearson, 24 April 1970, JBP, 89.1; "18 Arrests on Thursday For Breaking of Curfew."

45. Charles Greer, interview by Marian J. Weeks, Lawrence, Kansas, 1 September 1990, in Weeks, "Lawrence, 1970," 163; Verner Newman, interview by Marian J. Weeks, Lawrence, Kansas, 9 March 1989, in Weeks, "Lawrence, 1970," 190, 204–205.

46. "New Campus Problem: Young Drifters"; *Vortex* 2:5 (April 29-May 12 [1970]).

47. The Lawrence City Commission created the Department of Public Safety in 1969 and appointed Gilbert Smith to oversee and coordinate both the police and fire department. The commission eliminated it soon after Smith resigned in April 1970. See "City Safety Director Quits," *LDJW,* 25 April 1970; "19 Police Threaten to Quit," *LDJW,* 25 April 1970.

48. Gerry Riley interview by Marian J. Weeks, Lawrence, Kansas, fall of 1988, in Weeks, "Lawrence, 1970," 105–106.

49. Riley, interview, 108, 111–112.

50. Ibid., 100–102, 103.

51. Unidentified flier, n.a., n.d. [May 1970], "Student Pubs" folder, DMK; *Vortex,* 2:5 (April 29-May 12 [1970]).

52. Riley, interview, 111–112.

53. Greer, interview, 144.

54. Newman, interview, 190; Ohle, et al., *Cows are Freaky,* xi.

55. Greer, interview, 140–141, 153–155.

56. Newman, interview, 187–189.

57. Joan Irvine and Candy Reeves, open letter to "KU Faculty," n.d., "Student strike, protest, activism" folder, DMK; "18 Arrests on Thursday for Breaking of Curfew."

58. "Curfew Set for 10 P.M."

59. *The Coalition* 1:2, 7 April 1970, "Student Pubs" folder, DMK.

60. "Nixon Raps 'Campus Bums,'" *LDJW,* 1 May 1970; "Citizens Respond to Nixon," *LDJW,* 1 May 1970; "Alternative Day Planned at KU," *LDJW,* 4 May 1970; "Protests Center On MS Area," *LDJW,* 5 May 1970; "KU Classes Might Close This Friday," *LDJW,* 6 May 1970; "Students Call for March on MS Building Tonight," *LDJW,* 6 May 1970; "KU Mob Breaks Windows," *LDJW,* 7 May 1970; "Student Senate for Discussion," *LDJW,* 7 May 1970; "Day-By-Day Chronology of an Exciting Local Year."

61. Anne Moore, typewritten notes, *in re* conversations with Kansas Congressional Delegation, Lawrence Peace Center Papers, box 2, "congressional Visits 5/6–7/70" folder, KC; Walter H. Crockett, David Katzman, Bruce

Molholt, and Norman R. Yetman, open letter to the faculty, n.d. [May 1970]; "News Release," release 4, part II, 12 May 1970, both in "Student strike, protest, activism" folder, DMK; "Day-By-Day Chronology of an Exciting Local Year."

62. E. Laurence Chalmers, interview by author, tape recording, San Antonio, Texas, 1–2 April 1995; "Committee Seeks Day of Alternatives," *UDK*, 4 May 1970: "Alternate Day Planned at KU"; "Protests Center On MS Area"; "KU Classes Might Close This Friday," *LDJW*, 6 May 1970; "Students Call for March on MS Building Tonight"; "KU Mob Breaks Windows"; "Student Senate for Discussion"; "Docking Says State Schools Won't Close," *LDJW*, 8 May 1970; "Docking Says Chalmers Job Under Fire,' *LDJW*, 9 May 1970.

63. "KU Classes Might Close This Friday"; "Student Senate for Discussion."

64. "Students Call For March On MS Building Tonight," *LDJW*, 6 May 1970; "KU Mob Breaks Windows," *LDJW*, 7 May 1970; "KUCA Plans Peaceful ROTC Demonstration," *UDK*, 5 May 1970; "KU Mourners March For Kent State Four," *UDK*, 6 May 1970; "Rally Results in Broken ROTC Windows," *UDK*, 7 May 1970.

65. *The Coalition*, 1:2 (7 April 1970), "Student Pubs" folder, DMK.

66. "Annual ROTC Review Canceled," *UDK*, 6 May 1970; "KU Classes Might Close This Friday," *LDJW*, 6 May 1970; "Student Senate for Discussion"; "Docking Says State Schools Won't Close"; "Day-By-Day Chronology of an Exciting Local Year."

67. "Chalmers Fields Alumni Questions," *Kansas Alumni*, June 1970, 4–5; Chalmers interview; Francis Heller, "K.U. Notes, 1948–1972" (unpublished manuscript, n.d.), 107–110, UA; "KU Crowd Near 13,000 Okays Alternates," *LDJW*, 8 May 1970; "'Larry' Emerges KU Hero," *LDJW*, 9 May 1970; "Docking Hails Action at KU," *LDJW*, 9 May 1970; "Thousands Back Chalmers," *UDK*, 11 May 1970.

68. "Opportunities for Commitment" and "Daily News Release of Concerned Sociologists," release 8, 18 May 1970, "Student strike, protest, activism" folder, DMK.

69. "Alternatives?" newsletter, n.d., n.p. [May 1970], DMK; Heller, "K.U. Notes," 110; "Docking Says Chalmers Job Under Fire," *LDJW*, 9 May 1970.

70. The student and faculty petitions, as well as various letters of support, are found in Chancellor's Office, Correspondence, box 3, UA; on reactions around the state, see Johnson, "Student Unrest and the Kansas Press," 54–70; Raymond A. Schwegler to James J. Basham, n.d. [May 1970], Health Services, box 5, UA.

71. N. Tom Veatch to E. Laurence Chalmers, 22 April 1970; Veatch to Chalmers, 22 April 1970; K. S. Adams, telegram to E. Laurence Chalmers, all in Chancellor's Office, Correspondence, box 4; Robert L. Elder to Elmer C. Jackson, 11 May 1970, Elmer C. Jackson Papers, 7.17 (hereafter, ECJ).

72. *KU Alumni Report*, 70 (10 October 1970), 1; loose clippings, n.d. [July 1970]; loose clipping, n.d. [September 1969], Henry A. Bubb Clipping File, volume 5, KC.

73. "Special *Vortex* Street Edition," n.d., "Student Pubs" folder, DMK.

74. "BSU Charges Apathy Over Deaths of Blacks," *UDK,* May 13, 1970.

75. "Blacks Interrupt Church Service to Demand $75,000," *LDJW,* 11 May 1970; "Black Effort for Aid Part of a Pattern," *LDJW,* 11 May 1970; "Day-By-Day Chronology of an Exciting Local Year."

76. News Release 4, part II, n.a., 12 May 1970, "Student strike, protest, activism" folder, DMK.

77. Beaty, interview, 230; 248.

78. Ibid., 216; 231, 234; 250.

79. Ibid., 228–229, 237–238.

80. Ronald Peters to James B. Pearson, 2 June 1969, JBP, 69.26.

81. Nancy Sampson to Max Bickford, 7 May 1970, ECJ 7.11.

82. Pauline V. Hunn to Max Bickford, 8 May 1970, ECJ 7.11.

83. "KU Events Don't Please Docking," *LDJW,* 28 May 1970; "Chalmers Says Mistakes Made," *LDJW,* 29 May 1970; "Drive Opposes 'Peace' Bands," *LDJW,* 29 May 1970; "Day-By-Day Chronology of an Exciting Local Year."

Chapter 8

1. "Day-By-Day Chronology of An Exciting Local Year," *Lawrence Daily Journal-World* (hereafter, *LDJW*) 31 December 1970.

2. The description of the events of July 16, unless otherwise noted, are taken from the following sources: Bill Moyers, *Listening to America: A Traveler Rediscovers His Country* (New York: Harper's Magazine Press, 1971), 83–120; Moyers, "Kansas: Lawrence, Unexpected Epitome of a Confused Country," *Harper's Magazine* (December 1970): 56–68; Kent Frizzell, "Lawrence Investigative Report," 21 August 1970 (hereafter, Frizzell "Report," 1970), in Robert B. Docking Papers (hereafter, RBD), 41.10; Marian J. Weeks, "Lawrence, 1970: A Narrative and Oral Histories Surrounding Three Crises" (master's thesis, University of Kansas, 1990), 33–60; "Youth Killed in Gun Battle," *LDJW,* 17 July 1970; "Woman, 61, Shot in Leg During Overnight Incident," *LDJW,* 17 July 1970; "Patrolman Shot Answering Call," *LDJW,* 18 July 1970; "Franki Cole Claims Only One Shot Fired in Killing," *LDJW,* 23 July 1970; "Full Text of KBI Report on July 16–20 in Lawrence," *LDJW,* 22 August 1970.

3. Weeks, "Lawrence, 1970," 41–42.

4. Moyers, *Listening to America,* 96; Moyers, "Kansas: Lawrence," 59; Garrett quote from Frizzell "Report," 1970.

5. Raney quoted in Moyers, *Listening To America,* 97–98.

6. "Sound Thinking Vital" (editorial) *LDJW,* 17 July 1970; Moyers, "Kansas: Lawrence," 59; William H. Albott, Kansas Highway Patrol memorandum (hereafter, Albott memo), 23 July 1970, RBD, 41.10.

7. "Garrett Relieved of Police Duties," *LDJW,* 19 July 1970

8. "guerilla tactics" taken from KHP Report, 20 July 1970, in RBD, 41.10; "Youth Is Killed in Gun Battle," *LDJW;* "Sturns Can't Foresee What Might

Happen," *LDJW,* 18 July 1970; Frizzell "Report," 1970; "Citizens Group Asks Protection," *LDJW,* 18 July 1970; Freeman quoted in "Citizens Support Police," *Kansas City Star,* 21 July 1970.

9. "KHP Report," 20 July 1970, RBD, 41.10; "Day-By-Day Chronology of An Exciting Local Year."

10. The account of Rice's death, unless otherwise noted, is taken from "Statement of James S. Dukelow, Jr.," "Statement of Allen E. Miller," "Statement of James Milligan," "Statement of Mike Frame," "Statement by Martin Joseph Mendoza," and "Statement by Wayne S. Probst, Jr.," all 21 July 1970, in President's Commission on Campus Unrest, Records of the University of Kansas (Lawrence) Investigative Team (hereafter, PCCU), box 7, "Eyewitness Statements of the Rice Killings" folder; Frizzell "Report," 1970; Charles Greer, interview by Marian J. Weeks, Lawrence, Kansas, 1 September 1990, and Gerry Riley, interview by Weeks, Lawrence, Kansas, fall of 1988, both in Weeks, "Lawrence, 1970," 100–164; "City Declares 'Emergency,'" *LDJW,* 21 July 1970; "Leawood Youth Killed in Monday Flareup," *LDJW,* 21 July 1970; "Probe Continuing in Rice Shooting," *LDJW,* 24 July 1970; George Kimball, "This Little Yippie Ran for Sheriff," *The Realist* 88 (January/February 1971): 16.

11. Jerry Fill, "Meeting with Patrolman Stroud," 10 August 1970, PCCU, box 7, "Law Enforcement Incidents" folder.

12. Daniel A. Young and James W. Black, telegram to Robert B. Docking, 21 July 1970; Gubernatorial Proclamation, 21 July 1970; both in RBD, 41.10; Docking quoted in "Quiet But Tense Climate in City," *LDJW,* 22 July 1970; Greer interview, 141.

13. "Ten Pigs," is taken from Bryce Nelson, "Kansas: Police-Student Violence Imperils University," *Science,* vol. 169, (7 August 1970): 567; Frizzell "Report," 1970; Albott, memo; Oread resident quoted in "Albott 'Raps' with Youths and Climate Is Surprising," *LDJW,* 22 July 1970.

14. "Garrett Relieved of Police Duties"; "Coroner's Jury Exonerates Garrett," *LDJW,* 23 July 1970; Frizzell "Report," 1970. Many blacks claimed that the revolver was "planted" on Dowdell's body. A paraffin test conducted by the KBI confirmed Dowdell had recently fired a weapon, although it did not confirm that he had fired at Garrett.

15. *Harambee,* 19 July 1970; "klanwash" taken from photo caption, *LDJW,* 23 July 1970; [Leonard Harrison?], typed statement, attached to a Governor's Office memorandum to Robert B. Docking, 22 July 1970, and "KHP Report," 2 October 1970, both in RBD, 41.10; "Day-By-Day Chronology of An Exciting Local Year."

16. The account of the Dowdell funeral, unless otherwise noted, is taken from the following: "Dowdell Coffin on Wagon to Lead Funeral," *LDJW,* 22 July 1970; "Dowdell Rites Concluded after 2 Orderly Marches," *LDJW,* 23 July 1970; "Respectful Silence for Slain Youth," *Kansas City Star,* 24 July 1970; and "Memorial March Peaceful," *Summer Session Kansan* [Lawrence, Kansas] 24 July 1970.

17. Dorothy Harvey, interview by Mr. Nether (transcript), 22 June 1977, Douglas County Historical Society (hereafter, DCHS); John Spearman, Jr., telephone interview by author, 9 October 1994; Helen Kimball, interview by Mr. Nether (transcript), n.d., DCHS.

18. Richard Beaty, interview by Marian J. Weeks, Lawrence, Kansas, September 1989, in Weeks, "Lawrence, 1970," 220; 222–223; 230; 245–246.

19. General sources for this paragraph and the next include "KHP Report," 17 July 1970, and Kansas City, Missouri Police Department Interdepartmental Communication, 17 July 1970, both in RBD, 41.10; anonymous, handwritten note to Elmer C. Jackson, n.d. [July 1970], Elmer C. Jackson Papers, Kansas Collection (hereafter, ECJ),15.8; "Event Topic of Chalmers, Regent Talk," *LDJW,* 25 July 1970; "KU Halls Having Trouble Increase," *LDJW,* 25 July 1970; "BSU Choice Main Factor in Key Posts," *LDJW,* 24 July 1970; Kansas Board of Regents, "Minutes of Special Meeting," 26 July 1970, and E. Laurence Chalmers, memorandum to Keith Nitcher, 27 July 1970, both in RBD, 54.22; Max Bickford to Board of Regents, 31 July 1970, RBD, 54.20; Robert H. Nates telegram to Chalmers and Regents (copy), 30 July 1970, RBD, 54.20. "Gary Jackson Ponders Statement," *LDJW,* 30 July 1970; "Jackson Denies Cause for Firing at KU," *LDJW,* 1 August 1970; Bickford to Kent Frizzell, 27 July 1970, and Frizzell to Regents, 28 August 1970, attached to Regents to Robert B. Docking, 4 September 1970, both in RBD, 54.21.

20. Murray quoted in "Gary Jackson Ponders Statement."

21. Lawrence Liberation Front, [Lawrence, Kansas], *Disorientation,* n.d. [July 1970], 13, Kansas Collection; Nelson, "Police-Student Violence," 569; "Street People Remain Defiant," *Kansas City Times,* 22 July 1970; Kimball quoted in Joseph Rhodes, Jr., to the President's Commission on Campus Unrest, RE: Lawrence/University of Kansas, n.d. [29 July 1970], PCCU, box 7, "Rhodes Report" folder.

22. Lawrence Liberation Front, "Pigs Riot," n.d. [22 July 1970], PCCU, "Drafts of Final Report, RE: Lawrence" folder.

23. John Gaventa, "Conversation with David Bailey, August 5, 1970"; Gaventa, "Conversation with David Aubrey, 6 August 1970," both in PCCU, box 7, "Student Interviews" folder.

24. "Pigs Riot."

25. Wayne S. Probst, "Observations," n.d. [August 1970], PCCU, box 7, "Eyewitness Statements of the Rice Killings" folder.

26. Ibid.

27. "Say Police Denied Aid to Dying Student," *Kansas City Times,* 22 July 1970; Gimblett petition in "Massive Ideological Chasm Apparent in Lawrence," *Topeka Daily Capital,* 22 July 1970; "Petition Backs Officer Garrett," *LDJW,* 22 July 1970; Goldie Ferguson quoted in "Questionnaire," and stenographer quoted in Anonymous, "Questionnaire," both in PCCU, box 8, "Questionnaires-Community" folder.

28. L.V. Feurerborn, "Questionnaire," PCCU, box 8, "Questionnaires-Students" folder; Linda S. Tuttle, "Questionnaire," PCCU, box 8, "Questionnaires-Miscellaneous" folder.

29. Anonymous, "Questionnaire," and Katherine Tarr, "Questionnaire," both in PCCU, box 8, "Questionnaires-Miscellaneous" folder; Floyd L. Shields, "Questionnaire," and Myron D. Feuerborn, "Questionnaire," both in PCCU, box 8, "Questionnaires-Community" folder.

30. "Petition Backs Officer Garret"; Meisenheimer and Hamilton quoted in "Citizens Support Police," *Kansas City Star,* 21 July 1970; Mr. and Mrs. Frank Alexander, et al., to the editor, *LDJW,* 23 July 1970.

31. *Vortex* [Lawrence, Kansas], n.d., n.p. [July 1970]; "Courthouse Scene of Trouble," *LDJW,* 22 July 1970; "Vortex Sale Said Illegal," *LDJW,* 22 July 1970.

32. The V-Committee, "Warning to Commies Hippies Freaks" n.d. [July 1970], PCCU, box 7, "Drafts of Final Report, RE: Lawrence" folder.

33. "'Vigilante Spirit' Here but Solid Facts Elusive," *LDJW,* 16 January 1971; "KHP Report," 31 December 1970, RBD, 41.10; Vandeventer and Ransford quoted in "Fear Forms in Kansas Community," loose clipping, *San Francisco Chronicle,* 26 December 1970, in Anne Moore (collector), Collection of Correspondence related to the Lawrence Support Your Local Police Committee, KC; "KHP Report," 31 December 1970, RBD, 41.10.

34. Anonymous [three], "Questionnaire," and Lynn Handel, "Questionnaire," both in PCCU, box 8, "Questionnaires-Miscellaneous" folder.

35. Rhodes to PCCU, RE: Lawrence/University of Kansas; Morey Myer, et al., "Report from the Lawrence Investigation Team," August 1970, both in PCCU, box 7, "University of Kansas (Lawrence) Team, Report from the Lawrence Investigation Team, August 1970" folder.

36. McElvoy quoted in Rhodes to PCCU, RE Lawrence/University of Kansas; Hart quoted in "Day-By-Day Chronology of Exciting Local Year"; "Presidential Board Might Study Lawrence Violence," *LDJW,* 27 July 1970; "Study Group Due Next Week," *LDJW,* 30 July 1970; "Commission Staff Group Begins Parleys on Campus," *LDJW,* 4 August 1970; "Blacks Here Denounce D.C. Group," *LDJW,* 5 August 1970; "No Meetings Set as Yet with City Black Groups," *LDJW,* 6 August 1970; "KHP Report," 6 August 1970; and Coordinating Committee of the Black Community and Brothers and Sisters in Blackness, "Press release," 5 August 1970, both in RBD, 41.10 President's Commission on Campus Unrest, "Press Statement," 4 August 1970, 5 August 1970, and 7 August 1970, PCCU, box 7, "Press Releases" folder.

37. PCCU, "Press Statement," 4 August 1970, August 1970, and 7 August 1970, PCCU, box 7, "Press Releases" folder. Many of the respondents did not reveal their names, although they did provide some background information, such as occupation and years residing in Lawrence. I have cited those who gave their names; those who did not I cite simply as "Anonymous."

38. "Meeting With Mr. Freed, et al," 7 August 1970, PCCU, box 7, "Community Interviews" folder.

39. P. H. Riedel, "Questionnaire," PCCU, box 10 "Exhibits of the Lawrence Investigative Team, August 1970" folder; Anonymous, "Questionnaire," PCCU, box 8, "Questionnaires-Miscellaneous" folder; L. V. Feurerborn, "Questionnaire," PCCU, box 8, "Questionnaires-Students" folder.

40. Anonymous [three], "Questionnaire," PCCU, box 8, "Questionnaires-Community" folder; Phillip Riddle, "Questionnaire," PCCU, box 10, "Exhibits of the Lawrence Investigative Team, August 1970" folder.

41. Daniel J. Blewitt, "Questionnaire," PCCU, box 8, "Questionnaires-Community" folder; Anonymous, "Questionnaire," PCCU, box 8, "Questionnaires-Students" folder; John W. A. Murphy, "Questionnaire," PCCU, box 8, "Questionnaires-Community" folder; June[?] Jackson, "Questionnaire," PCCU, box 8, "Questionnaires-Community" folder; Melvin E. Copp, "Questionnaire," PCCU, box 8, "Questionnaires-Community (Professionals—Businessmen)" folder.

42. Anonymous, "Questionnaire," PCCU, box 8, "Questionnaires-Community" folder; Lauren McClure, "Questionnaire," PCCU, box 8, "Questionnaires-Community (Professionals—Businessmen)" folder.

43. Jerry Fill, "Visit With the Chancellor," 3 August 1970, PCCU, box 7, "Interviews with KU Administration" folder; Anonymous [two], "Questionnaire," PCCU, box 8, "Questionnaires-Miscellaneous" folder.

44. "Ideological Chasm Seen for City," *LDJW,* 22 July 1970; Mr. and Mrs. Kenneth L. Tarr to the editor, *LDJW,* 22 July 1970.

45. Helen Kimball, interview transcript, DCHS; Stagg quoted in Moyers, "Kansas: Lawrence," 61.

46. "Massive Ideological Chasm Apparent in Lawrence"; "Street People Remain Defiant"; Watson and Kimball quoted in loose clipping, "Why Lawrence? Many Theories on the Violence, No Answers," *Hutchinson (Kansas) News,* 22 July 1970, in RBD, 54.21; "AP Reporter Views Lawrence Turmoil," *LDJW,* 31 July 1970.

47. John Gaventa, "Notes from Meeting with the City Commissioners on Tuesday, August 4, 1970," PCCU, box 7, "Community Interviews" folder.

48. Anonymous, "Questionnaire," and Lynn Handel, "Questionnaire," both in PCCU, box 8, "Questionnaires-Miscellaneous" folder; Jerry Fill, "Visit With the Chancellor," 3 August 1970, PCCU, box 7, "Interviews with KU Administration" folder.

49. "KHP Report," 18 September 1970, RBD, 41.10; "Schultz Statement Repudiated," *University Daily Kansan* (hereafter, *UDK*) 23 September 1970; "BSU Statement," *UDK* 9 September 1970; "Day-By-Day Chronology of An Exciting Local Year"; Elwill M. Shanahan, Secretary of State, State of Kansas Election Statistics, 1970 Primary and General Elections (Topeka: State of Kansas, 1970).

50. "Day-By-Day Chronology of An Exciting Local Year"; "KHP Report," 3 September 1970, 9 September 1970, 11 September 1970, 18 September 1970, 25 September 1970, 2 October 1970, 13 October 1970, 23 October 1970, 30 October 1970; Weather Underground, "Communication," all in RBD, 41.10.

51. The BSU's warning is from "Ultimatum of BSU Served," *LDJW,* 24 November 1970; Regent's stance in "No Regent Plan to Rehire Gary Jackson to KU Post," *LDJW,* 1 December 1970.

52. Details of the Snyder shooting can be found in "KHP Report," 11 December 1970, RBD, 41.10; "Shot Wounds KU Student Near Library," *LDJW,* 7 December 1970; "BSU Chief Vows Strike to Continue," *LDJW,* 7 December 1970; Washington quoted in "KU Regents Invite Blacks to Meet," *LDJW,* 7 December 1970. The Board of Regents later commended Snyder for "protecting state property"; see Kansas Board of Regents, "Minutes," 14 December 1970, ECJ 7.23.

53. "KHP Report," 11 December 1970, RBD, 41.10; "Events Listed Leading Up to Friday's Blast," *LDJW,* 12 December 1970.

54. Docking quoted in "Docking Calls KU Bombing Senseless Act," *LDJW,* 12 December 1970; Chalmers quoted in "Chalmers Says Campus 'Cool,'" *LDJW,* 16 December 1970; additional information about the bombing can be found in "Three Injured in Bomb Blast on KU Campus," *LDJW,* 12 December 1970; "Cause for Joy by 3 Victims," *LDJW,* 12 December 1970; "Watson Sees No Emergency," *LDJW,* 12 December 1970; "$2,000 Reward Set Over Center Blast," *LDJW,* 14 December 1970; "KHP Report," 31 December 1970, RBD, 41.10; "Regents Grill Chalmers on KU Events," *LDJW,* 15 December 1970; "Near-Normal Pace For Campus Today," and "Bulletin," both in *LDJW,* 16 December 1970.

55. Lawrence Human Relations Commission, *A Study of the Lawrence High School Confrontation in April, 1970* (December 1970), Lawrence Public Library; "Day-By-Day Chronology."

56. Lawrence Chamber of Commerce, "Chamber of Commerce in Action," August-September, 1970, KC; Lawrence Police-Community Relations Steering Committee, "Lawrence Police-Community Steering Committee Recommendations," 15 June 1971, Lawrence Public Library.

57. LSYLPC statement in "Petitions Out Backing Police," *LDJW,* 15 January 1971; Weeks, "Lawrence, 1970," 81–86; Newman interview, 192.

58. United States President's Commission on Campus Unrest, *The Report of the President's Commission on Campus Unrest* (New York: Avon Books, 1971), 51–53.

Chapter 9

1. This account is drawn from the following: "'Sisters' End Sit-in after KU Talks," *Lawrence Daily Journal-World* (hereafter, *LDJW*), 5 February 1972; Judith Galas, "Nighttime Takeover Births Women's Programs: Looking Back with a February Sister," *News & Notes* (autumn 1991): 1, 3, in scrapbook, Women's Students Program, University of Kansas, Lawrence, Kansas (hereafter, WSP); "A History of the Seizure and Occupation of the East Asian Studies Building by the February Sisters, or What It Takes to Make Men Move," ephemeral material, 7 February 1972, WSP; Beth Bailey, *Sex in the Heartland* (Cambridge, MA: Harvard University Press, 2000), 127–130.

2. The *Lawrence Journal-World* ran a front-page story on the February Sisters on 6 February 1972, and a page-three article on 7 February 1972, but I

could find no editorials or letters to the editors for the months of February and March.

3. Galas, "Nighttime Takeover," 3.

4. Sara Evans, *Personal Politics: The Roots of Women's Liberation in the Civil Rights Movement and the New Left* (New York: Vintage Books, 1980), 21.

5. "Wonderful Women," (editorial) *LDJW,* 5 October 1960.

6. W. H. Trippensee to Robert F. Ellsworth, 6 March 1961, Robert F. Ellsworth Papers (hereafter, RFE) 75.1; Mr. and Mrs. Bert Day to Robert F. Ellsworth, 30 April 1964, RFE, 87.1.

7. Quoted in "'More Truly Women,'"(editorial) *LDJW,* 13 August 1960, 4.

8. U.S. Bureau of the Census, *U.S. Census of Population: 1960. Volume I, Characteristics of the Population. Part 18, Kansas* (U.S. Government Printing Office, 1960), 208, table 73; 222, table 78.

9. Ibid., and *U.S. Bureau of the Census, U.S. Census of Population: 1970. Volume I, Characteristics of the Population. Part 18, Kansas* (U.S. Government Printing Office, 1970), 323, table 105.

10. "KU Coeds Dominate Swimsuit Competition," *LDJW,* 11 July 1970; Edds quoted in "No Diets for Miss Kansas," *LDJW,* 13 July 1970.

11. The polling information is taken from William H. Chafe, *The Unfinished Journey: America Since World War II,* 4th ed. (New York: Oxford University Press, 1999), 434.

12. Ibid.

13. "Liberation Day Has Blahs," *LDJW,* 26 August 1970.

14. Editorial cartoon, *LDJW,* 27 August 1970.

15. See Bailey, *Sex in the Heartland,* 127, and Bailey, "Prescribing the Pill: Politics, Culture, and the Sexual Revolution in America's Heartland," *Journal of Social History,* 30:4 (summer 1997): 827–856.

16. Judy Browder, "Women's Decade of History," WSP; *Vortex* (Lawrence, Kansas) 2:2, 1970.

17. Loose clipping, Peggy C. Scott, "Participants Trace Women's Groups' Past," *University Daily Kansan* (hereafter, *UDK*), 19 October 1973, in Dean of Women, Records, Subject: Female Studies-Kansas Union (hereafter, DOW), box 7, "Feminism 1972–1974" folder, University of Kansas Archives, Lawrence, Kansas (hereafter, UA); loose clipping, "Coeds Attack Stereotyped Status of Women," *Wichita Eagle and Beacon,* 31 January 1971, 1E, in Commission on the Status of Women (CSW), Chronological Records, 1969/70—, box 1, "1970/71" folder, UA.

18. Hird's comments found in "Participants Trace Women's Groups' Past"; "handful of women" and "emphasize the softer traits" found in "Coeds Attack Stereotyped Status of Women"; University Commission on the Status of Women, "Reports of the Associated Women Students Commission on the Status of Women, 1969–1970," in CSW, box 1, "1969/70" folder.

19. "Coeds Attack Stereotyped Status of Women."

20. "Women's Center Asks Student Fee Support," *LDJW,* 16 July 1970; "KU Woman's Unit Requests Funds," *LDJW,* 18 July 1970.

21. "Two More Extremes" (editorial), *LDJW,* 24 July 1970.
22. Spencer quoted in "Participants Trace Women's Groups' Past"; on response to the Women's Center, see letters to the editor, *LDJW,* 28 and 29 July 1970.
23. "Participants Trace Women's Groups' Past."
24. Taylor quoted in "Coeds Attack Stereotyped Status of Women"; the final quote is taken from Emily Taylor, "Choice and Change," Kansas University Commission on the Status of Women, *1970–71 Handbook,* in CSW, box 1, "1970/71" folder.
25. Katzman and Krasne in "Participants Trace Women's Groups' Past"; Bocell quoted in "Coeds Attack Stereotyped Status of Women."
26. "Coeds Attack Stereotyped Status of Women."
27. Loose clipping, "Emily Taylor: Committed to Equal Rights for Women," *UDK* 19 October 1973, in DOW box 7, "Feminism 1972–1974" folder.
28. Ibid.
29. Suanne Bocell and Suzanne Kelly to the University of Kansas Regents, 27 August 1970; Susie Bocell, "K.U. Commission 1970," *Comment* 1:1 (October 1970); and Karen Hink, "Comment," *Comment* 1:1 (October 1970), all in CSW, box 1, "1970/71" folder.
30. Boydston quoted in "Coeds Attack Stereotyped Status of Women"; Eike quoted in "Participants Trace Women's Groups' Past."
31. Zodiac Club [Lawrence, Kansas], "Program, 1967–1968," and "Program, 1972–1973," in Zodiac Club Records, Kansas Collection, University of Kansas, Lawrence, Kansas (hereafter, KC).
32. Zodiac Club, minutes of meeting, 26 September 1972, Zodiac Club Record Book, 206.
33. Evans, *Personal Politics.*
34. Radical feminism in Lawrence taken from Bailey, *Sex in the Heartland,* 127; "provocative" quote and "consciousness raising" taken from Alice Echols, *Daring to be Bad: Radical Feminism in America, 1967–1975* (Minneapolis: University of Minnesota Press, 1989), 3–4.
35. Morgan quotes taken from "Writer Critiques Feminism," *LDJW,* 3 February 1972. According to Linkeugel, in his presentation to the Zodiac Club, Morgan said women in Lawrence must "persuade him to stop, or bribe him, or threaten him, or if necessary, kill him." See Zodiac Club, minutes of meeting, 26 September 1972.
36. "Morgan didn't organize" taken from Galas, "Nighttime Takeover"; additional information about the Sisters's founding is found in Debra Graber, "Beyond Closed Doors: A Sit-in That Stands Out," *Report From the University of Kansas* (spring 1987), 2–3; and "February Sisters Panel Discussion," 1987, transcribed by Gina Witt and Sherry Fugitt, "February Sisters Information" (notebook), both in WSP.
37. "A History of the Seizure and Occupation of the East Asian Studies Building."
38. Graber, "Beyond Closed Doors" and "February Sisters Panel Discussion."
39. There is a growing literature on the civil rights movement that examines the different leadership roles and styles of men and women and expands our

understanding of leadership away from the "charismatic male" model, embodied in Martin Luther King, Jr., that has dominated earlier histories of civil rights. See, for example, Charles M. Payne, "Men Led, But Women Organized: Movement Participation of Women in the Mississippi Delta," and other essays in Vicki L. Crawford, Jacqueline Rouse, and Barbara woods, eds., *Women in the Civil Rights Movement: Trailblazers and Torchbearers* (Bloomington: University of Indiana Press, 1993), and Charles M. Payne, "Ella Baker and Models of Social Change," *Signs* 14 (1989): 885–899; consult also Payne's *I've Got the Light of Freedom: The Organizing Tradition and the Mississippi Freedom Struggle* (Berkeley: University of California Press, 1995). For more recent assessments, see the sociologist Belinda Robnett's *How Long? How Long? African-American Women in the Struggle for Civil Rights* (New York: Oxford University Press, 1997), and Belinda Robnett, "African-American Women in the Civil Rights Movement, 1954–1965: Gender, Leadership, and Micromobilization," *The American Journal of Sociology* 101:6 (May 1996): 1661–94.

40. For example, a Washington, D.C. feminist, Marilyn Webb, was removed from the coordinating committee of the D.C. Women's Liberation because the media was able to identify her as a leader of the organization. See Echols, *Daring to be Bad,* 205.

41. "February Sisters," *LDJW,* 1 February 1987, loose clipping in WSP; "'Sisters' End Sit-in after KU Talks," *LDJW,* 5 February 1972.

42. Conrad quoted in "'Sisters' End Sit-in after KU Talks"; Chalmers quoted in "Chancellor Lists 'Action' Plans," *LDJW,* 4 February 1972; "Senate Tells 'Sisters' No," *LDJW,* 17 February 1972.

43. John Overbrook to the editor, *UDK,* 8 February 1972.

44. Darras L. Delamaide to the editor, *UDK,* 8 February 1972.

45. Loose clipping, "KU Student to Drop Action Against Sisters," *LDJW,* 6 March 1972, in "February Sisters Information" (notebook), WSP.

46. Chip Crews, "A Few Sour Notes" (editorial), *UDK* 8 February 1972.

47. Graber, "Beyond Closed Doors" and "February Sisters Panel Discussion."

48. Joan Handley to the editor, *UDK* 12 February 1972.

49. Bailey, *Sex in the Heartland.*

50. Schwegler quoted in Clifford S. Griffin, *The University of Kansas: A History* (Lawrence: University of Kansas Press, 1975), 634; "Sisters Stress 'Necessity' of Women's Health Services," *UDK,* 15 February 1972.

51. Bailey, "Prescribing the Pill," 833–842; Schwegler quoted in "Six Demands That Never Left Campus," *UDK,* 2 March 1990.

52. Loose clipping, "February Sisters Mark Anniversary with Satisfaction," *LDJW,* January 1973, in "February Sisters Information" (notebook), WSP.

53. "Participants Trace Women's Groups' Past."

54. Linda Gordon, *Woman's Body, Woman's Right: A Social History of Birth Control in America* (New York: Grossman Publishers, 1976), 410.

55. Emily Taylor to James B. Pearson, 25 September 1970, James B. Pearson Papers (hereafter, JBP), 84.15.

56. (Mrs.) Elaine Eklund to James B. Pearson, 25 September 1970, JBP, 84.15.
57. Vivian Rogers McCoy to James B. Pearson, 25 September 1970; Mrs. Evelyn M. Kipp to James B. Pearson, n.d. [September 1970]; Ruth Mitchell, telegram to James B. Pearson, 2 September 1970; Virginia E. Detter to James B. Pearson, 2 September 1970; Erma L. Morgan to James B. Pearson, 2 September 1970; Iris W. Aller to James B. Pearson, 2 September 1970; all in JBP, 84.15.
58. The Kansas House of Representatives ratified the ERA by a comfortable margin of eighty-six for to thirty-seven against. The Kansas Senate approved the bill by an even larger margin, thirty-four for and five against.
59. Mr. and Mrs. Robert R. Burk to James B. Pearson, 19 March 1975, JBP, 163.15; Larry E. and Mary E. Shambaugh to Pearson, 17 February 1975, JBP, 163.16; Mrs. Elmer Rollins to Pearson, 27 January 1975, JBP, 163.17; Mrs. A.W. Luallin to Pearson, 21 January 1975, JBP, 163.17; Mrs. Alice M. Smith to Pearson, 16 January 1975, JBP, 163.17.
60. Mildred Catlett to Pearson, 16 July 1975, JBP, 163.15; Nanette Alexander to Pearson, 12 February 1975, JBP, 163.16; Mrs. E. A. (Nantette) Alexander to Pearson, 18 March 1975, JBP, 163.16.
61. The first quote is taken from "Groups Tries to Undo 'Hasty' ERA Action," *LDJW*, 6 February 1975; Barnes quoted in "Varied Opinions Emerge At Anti-ERA Gathering," *LDJW*, 5 March 1975, both cited in Sonja L. Erickson, "In Defense of the Family: The Fight to Rescind the ERA in Kansas, 1974–1979" (master's thesis, University of Kansas, 1995), 44, 49.
62. Alice LaFrenz to the editor, *LDJW*, 7 March 1975; Connie Kamp to the editor, *LDJW*, 18 March 1975, both cited in Erickson, "Defense of the Family," 57.
63. Erickson, "Defense of the Family," 11.

Epilogue

1. "Miller Leads Drug Raids," "Biggest Raid For Kansas," "Bond Posted By Suspects After Raids," and "Miller's Morning Raid 'Just the Beginning,'" *Lawrence Daily Journal-World* (hereafter, *LDJW*), all 26 February 1971; "Miller 'Pleased' Over Raid," and "Infiltrating Drug Culture Easy, Young Agent States," both *LDJW*, 27 February 1971.
2. Population data available online at http://www.census.gov/prod/cen2000/dp1/2kh20.pdf.
3. For this paragraph, I draw on Marcelo Vilela, "Changing the face of Lawrence: Simply Equal Five Years Later," *The Liberty Press Online*, July 2000, available online at http://www.libertypress.net/kansas/ksarchives/ks2000/ksjuly00.html.
4. This and the next paragraph are drawn from Jerry Thomas, "HITCHITA! The Documented Story of the Gregg Sevier Homicide," available online at http://cybold.com/hitchita/index.html.

SELECTED BIBLIOGRAPHY

A Note on Sources

I have not listed newspapers in this bibliography, as they are cited in full in the notes. I have arranged the material by archive or repository, rather than by type of material.

Also, I have used materials from the personal collections of many individuals. These materials are in the possession of the collectors of the material, and, as of the publication of this book, have not been deposited in any archive or library.

Kansas Collection, University of Kansas, Lawrence, KS (KC)

Manuscript collections

Bubb, Henry A. Clipping File, vol. 5.
Docking, Robert B. Papers. (RBD)
Douglas County Community Improvement Association, Lawrence, Kansas. Papers, 1969-. (DCCIA)
Jackson, Elmer C. Papers. (ECJ)
Lawrence Center for Peace and Justice. Papers. Lawrence, Kansas. (LCPJ)
Lawrence Fair Housing Coordinating Committee. Papers. (LFHC)
Lawrence League for the Practice of Democracy. Papers. (LLPD)
Lawrence Peace Center, Lawrence, Kansas. Papers, 1967–1973. (LPC)
League of Women Voters, Lawrence, Kansas. Papers, 1931-. (LWV)
Moore, Anne, collector. Collection of Correspondence Related to the Lawrence Support Your Local Police Committee.
Old West Lawrence Association. Papers. (OWLA)
Oread Meeting of the Society of Friends. Papers.
Pearson, James B. Papers. (JPB)
Plymouth Congregational Church. Papers. (PCC)
The Sons and Daughters of New England. Papers. (SDNE)
Unified School District 497, Lawrence, Kansas. Board of Education Memos, 1969–1970, box 11 (unsorted material).
Zodiac Club. Papers.

Other material

Embry, Dennis and John Miller. "Racial And Student Disturbances: Documentary, Lawrence, Kansas, 1970" (audio tapes).

Lawrence-Douglas County National Association for the Advancement of Colored People. "Survey of the Lawrence Negro Community," September 1963-March 1964.

West Hills District brochure, n.d. Lawrence History Scrapbooks, 1870–1948, vol. 4:42.

Wilcox Collection of Contemporary Political Movements,
Kansas Collection, University of Kansas, Lawrence, KS

Campus Humor Publications. *A Basic Guide to Campusology.* Lawrence, KS: Campus Humor Publications, 1963.

Citizen's Council of Louisiana. *The Councilor.* Shreveport, LA.

John Birch Society. *The White Book of the John Birch Society for 1963.* Belmont, MA: John Birch Society, 1963.

Life Line. "Life Line Radio Program," transcripts. 1961–1964.

University Archives, University of Kansas, Lawrence, KS (UA)

Black Student Union. Artificial Records. (BSU)

Chancellor's Office, E. Laurence Chalmers. Correspondence, Departmental, 1969/70. (ELC Departmental)

Chancellor's Office, E. Laurence Chalmers. Correspondence, General, 1969–70. (ELC General)

Chancellor's Office. Executive Secretary Case Files, 1959–65. (COES)

Chancellor's Office, W. Clarke Wescoe. Correspondence. (WCW)

Civil Rights Council. Records. (CRC)

Commission on the Status of Women. Chronological Records, 1969/70. (CSW)

Dean of Women. Records. (DOW)

"Fraternity." Vertical file.

Free University. Records.

Human Development and Family Life. Department Files, "Penn House" folder.

KU-Y. Artificial Records.

Office of the Registrar. Annual Report, 1958/59–1972/73 (Serial).

Office of Student Affairs. Balfour/Anderson Correspondence, box 5.

Office of Student Affairs. Health Services folder, 1/3/69–12/30/69, box 5.

Panhellenic News Releases, 1965–1966.

"Student Activities 1966/67." Vertical file.

Student Protests, 1964–65 folder. Artificial Records.

University of Kansas. *1970 Jayhawker* (University of Kansas yearbook). Lawrence, KS.

Wescoe, W. Clarke. Address, 16 October 1990. Heritage Lecture Series.

Young Americans for Freedom. Artificial Records. (YAF)

Young Men's Christian Association. Chronological Records, 1895–1981. (YMCA)

Kansas State Historical Society, Topeka, KS (KSHS)

Carlson, Frank. Papers. (FC)

Ellsworth, Robert F. Papers. (RFE)

Dorsey-Liberty American Legion Post #14, Lawrence, KS (DLAL)

Dorsey-Liberty American Legion Post #14, Lawrence, Kansas. Minutes.
Dorsey-Liberty American Legion Post #14, Lawrence, Kansas. Vertical Files.

National Archives and Records Administration, College Park, MD

President's Commission on Campus Unrest. Records of the University of Kansas (Lawrence) Investigative Team. (PCCU)

Women's Studies Program, University of Kansas, Lawrence, KS (WSP)

Browder, Judy. "Women's Decade of History."
Scrapbook.

Lawrence Public Library, Lawrence, KS

Lawrence High School. *1968 Red and Black: Lawrence High School Yearbook.*
Lawrence Human Relations Commission, *A Study of the Lawrence High School Confrontation in April, 1970* (December 1970).
Lawrence Police-Community Relations Steering Committee, "Lawrence Police-Community Steering Committee Recommendations," 15 June 1971.

Other Collections

Fisher, Alan. Personal scrapbook and other materials related to his tenure as commander of the Dorsey-Liberty American Legion Post #14, Lawrence, Kansas, its activities, and history, 1960–1975 (in Alan Fisher's possession), Lawrence, KS.
Katzman, David M. Personal collection of materials related to student activism at the University of Kansas, 1969–1971 (in David Katzman's possession), Lawrence, KS. (DMK)
Lawrence Human Relations Commission. Minutes, 1961–1975. Lawrence Human Relations Commission office, City Hall, Lawrence, KS.
Morris, David. Collection, subseries II-B, box 4, file on University Christian Movement, 1966–68. Archives of Appalachia, East Tennessee State University, Johnson City, TN.
Rife, Max L. Personal collection of materials related to student activism at Lawrence High School, 1968–1970 (in Max L. Rife's possession), Lawrence, KS.
Students for a Democratic Society. Papers. Wisconsin State Historical Society, Madison, WI. (SDS)

Douglas County Historical Society, Lawrence, KS (DCHS)

Black Community. Vertical file
Black Walkout 1968. Vertical file.

Black Walkout, 1970. Vertical file.

Bomb Shelter. Vertical file.

Daughters of the American Revolution, Betty Washington Chapter. Vertical file.

East Lawrence Improvement Association. Vertical file.

First Christian Church. "Membership Roster, Centennial Celebration, June 16–17, 1984."

First Presbyterian Church. Church Directory, n.d.

First Presbyterian Church. "United Presbyterian Women, First Presbyterian Church, Lawrence, Kansas, 1971."

John Pound Chapter, Daughters of the American Colonists. Vertical file.

Lawrence Swimming Pool. Vertical file.

North Lawrence. Vertical file.

Old West Lawrence Association. Vertical file.

Oread Neighborhood Survey. Vertical file.

Oread Neighborhood. Vertical file.

Oread. Vertical file.

Trinity Episcopal Church. "Parish Directory of Trinity Episcopal Church, Lawrence, Kansas, 1970–1971."

University Place Neighborhood History Association. Vertical file.

West Hills Residence District. Vertical file.

Interviews and Transcripts

Personal Interviews by the Author

Brown, Vince. Lawrence, KS, 4 October 1994.

Chalmers, E. Laurence. San Antonio, TX, 1–2 April 1994.

Coleman, Stephanie. Lawrence, KS, 24 September 1996.

Heller, Francis. Lawrence, KS, 17 February 1994.

Milan, Jesse. Kansas City, KS, 27 May 1994.

Miller, Ocoee. Telephone conversation, Lawrence, KS, 4 November 1998.

Norman, Norma. Topeka, KS, 25 May 1994.

Raney, Dick. Lawrence, KS, 8 October 1996.

Shaffer, Harry. Lawrence, KS, 4 May 1994.

Spearman, Jr., John. Telephone interview, Brooklyn, NY, 9 October 1994.

Interview Transcripts, Douglas County Historical Society, Lawrence, KS

Byers, Karen Marie. 5 July 1977.

Harvey, Dorothy. 22 June 1977.

Hicks, Debra Ann Harvey. 20 June 1977.

Kimball, Helen. n.d.

Moore, Ethel May Josephine Elizabeth Lenore Johnson. n.d.

Newman, Kenneth. n.d.

Selected Secondary Sources

I have included in this selected bibliography those works I found most useful in researching and writing this book. Not every book or article cited in the notes is listed here.

Anderson, Terry H. *The Movement and the Sixties: Protest in America from Greensboro to Wounded Knee.* New York: Oxford University Press, 1995.

Andrew, John A., III. *The Other Side of the Sixties: Young Americans for Freedom and the Rise of Conservative Politics.* New Brunswick, NJ: Rutgers University Press, 1997.

Baskir, Lawrence M. and William A. Strauss, *Chance and Circumstance: The Draft, the War, and the Vietnam Generation.* New York: Knopf, 1978.

Berman, Ronald. *America in the Sixties: An Intellectual History.* New York: Free Press, 1968.

Berman, William C. *America's Right Turn: From Nixon to Bush.* Baltimore: Johns Hopkins University Press, 1994.

Bloom, Alexander and Wini Breines. *"Takin' it to the streets": A Sixties Reader.* New York: Oxford University Press, 1995.

Breines, Wini. *Community and Organization in the New Left, 1962–1968.* New York: Praeger, 1982.

———. *Young, White, and Miserable: Growing Up Female in the Fifties.* Chicago: University of Chicago Press, 2001.

Brennan, Mary C. *Turning Right in the Sixties: The Conservative Capture of the GOP.* Chapel Hill: University of North Carolina Press, 1995.

Burner, David. *Making Peace with the 60s.* Princeton, NJ: Princeton University Press, 1996.

Carmichael, Stokely and Charles V. Hamilton. *Black Power: The Politics of Liberation in America.* New York: Vintage Books, 1974.

Carson, Clayborne. *In Struggle: SNCC and the Black Awakening of the 1960s.* 2nd ed. Cambridge, MA: Harvard University Press, 1990.

Chafe, William H. *The Paradox of Change: American Women in the Twentieth Century.* New York: Oxford University Press, 1991.

Chalmers, David. *And the Crooked Places Made Straight: The Struggle for Social Change in the 1960s.* 2nd ed. Baltimore, MD: Johns Hopkins University Press, 1996.

Conlin, Joseph. *The Troubles: A Jaundiced Glance Back at the Movement of the Sixties.* New York: Watts, 1982.

Curry, G. David. *Sunshine Patriots: Punishment and the Vietnam Offender.* Notre Dame: University of Notre Dame Press, 1985.

DeBenedetti, Charles, with Charles Chatfield. *An American Ordeal: The Antiwar Movement of the Vietnam Era.* Syracuse, NY: Syracuse University Press, 1990.

Ellwood, Robert S. *The Sixties Spiritual Awakening: American Religion Moving from Modern to Postmodern.* New Brunswick, NJ: Rutgers University Press, 1994.

Evans, Sara. *Personal Politics: The Roots of Women's Liberation in the Civil Rights Movement and the New Left.* New York: Vintage Books, 1980.

Farber, David. *Chicago '68.* Chicago: University of Chicago Press, 1988.

————. *The Age of Great Dreams: America in the 1960s.* New York: Hill and Wang, 1994.

————. ed. *The Sixties: From Memory to History.* Chapel Hill: University of North Carolina Press, 1994.

Farrell, James J. *The Spirit of the Sixties: The Making of Postwar Radicalism.* New York: Routledge, 1997.

Ferber, Michael and Staughton Lynd. *The Resistance.* Boston: Beacon Press, 1971.

Fraser, Steve and Gary Gerstle, eds. *The Rise and Fall of the New Deal Order, 1930–1980.* Princeton, NJ: Princeton University Press, 1989.

Gitlin, Todd. *The Sixties: Years of Hope, Days of Rage.* Toronto: Bantam Books, 1987.

Gottlieb, Sherry Gershon. *Hell No, We Won't Go!: Resisting the Draft During the Vietnam War.* New York: Viking, 1991.

Graham, Hugh Davis. *The Civil Rights Era: Origins and Development of a National Policy, 1960–1965.* New York: Oxford University Press, 1990.

Halstead, Fred. *Out Now!: A Participant's Account of the American Movement Against the Vietnam War.* New York: Monad Press, 1978.

Hartman, Susan M. *From Margin to Mainstream: American Women and Politics Since 1960.* New York: Alfred A. Knopf, 1989.

Heale, M. J. *American Anticommunism: Combating the Enemy Within, 1830–1970.* Baltimore: Johns Hopkins Press, 1990.

Heineman, Kenneth. *Campus Wars: The Peace Movement at American State Universities in the Vietnam Era.* New York: New York University Press, 1993.

Himmelstein, Jerome L. *To the Right: The Transformation of American Conservatism.* Berkeley: University of California Press, 1990.

Hodgson, Godfrey. *America in Our Time: From World War II to Nixon, What Happened and Why.* New York: Vintage Books, 1976.

Horowitz, David and Peter Collier, *Destructive Generation: Second Thoughts about the Sixties.* New York: Summit Books, 1989.

Horowitz, Helen Lefkowitz. *Campus Life: Undergraduate Cultures from the End of the Eighteenth Century to the Present.* New York: Alfred A. Knopf, 1987.

Isserman, Maurice. *If I Had a Hammer: The Death of the Old Left and the Birth of the New Left.* New York: Basic Books, 1987.

Kessler, Lauren. *After All These Years: Sixties Ideals in a Different World.* New York: Thunder's Mouth Press, 1990.

Knight, Douglas M. *Street of Dreams: The Nature and Legacy of the 1960s.* Durham: Duke University Press, 1989.

Lipsitz, George. *The Possessive Investment in Whiteness: How White People Profit from Identity Politics.* Philadelphia: Temple University Press, 1998.

Lyons, Paul. *New Left, New Right and the Legacy of the Sixties.* Philadelphia: Temple University Press, 1996.

Marable, Manning. *Race, Reform, and Rebellion: The Second Reconstruction in America, 1945–1982.* London: Macmillan, 1984.

Matusow, Allen J. *The Unraveling of America: A History of Liberalism in the 1960s.* New York: Harper and Row, 1984.

May, Elaine Tyler. *Homeward Bound: American Families in the Cold War Era.* New York: Basic Books, 1988.

McGill, William J. *The Year of the Monkey: Revolt on Campus, 1968–1969.* New York: McGraw Hill Book Company, 1982.

Miller, James. *Democracy Is in the Streets: From Port Huron to the Siege of Chicago.* New York: Simon and Schuster, 1987.

Miller, Timothy. *The Hippies and American Values.* Knoxville: University of Tennessee Press, 1991.

Morgan, Edward P. *The 60s Experience: Hard Lessons about Modern America.* Philadelphia: Temple University Press, 1991.

Morris, Aldon D. *The Origins of the Civil Rights Movement: Black Communities Organizing for Change.* New York: Free Press, 1984.

Nimz, Dale. *Living With History: A Historic Preservation Plan for Lawrence, Kansas* Lawrence, KS: Urban Study Project, 1983.

O'Neill, William. *Coming Apart: An Informal History of the 1960s.* Chicago: Quadrangle Books, 1971.

Peck, Abe. *Uncovering the Sixties: The Life and Times of the Underground Press.* New York: Pantheon Books, 1985.

Rorabaugh, W. J. *Berkeley at War: The 1960s.* New York: Oxford University Press, 1989.

Rossinow, Douglas C. *The Politics of Authenticity: Liberalism, Christianity, and the New Left in America.* New York: Columbia University Press, 1998.

Roszak, Theodore. *The Making of a Counterculture.* Garden City, NY: Doubleday, 1969.

Sale, Kirkpatrick. *SDS.* New York: Random House, 1973.

Sayres, Sohnya et al., eds. *The Sixties Without Apology.* Minneapolis: University of Minnesota Press, 1984.

Small, Melvin. *Johnson, Nixon, and the Doves.* New Brunswick: Rutgers University Press, 1988.

Steigerwald, David. *The Sixties and the End of Modern America.* New York: St. Martin's Press, 1995.

Stoper, Emily. *The Student Nonviolent Coordinating Committee: The Growth of Radicalism in a Civil Rights Organization.* Brooklyn, NY: Carlson Publishing, 1989.

Sugrue, Thomas J. *The Origins of the Urban Crisis: Race and Inequality in Postwar Detroit.* Princeton, NJ: Princeton University Press, 1996.

Thelen, David. *Becoming Citizens in the Age of Television.* Chicago: University of Chicago Press, 1996.

Thorne, Melvin J. *American Conservative Thought Since World War II: The Core Ideas.* New York: Greenwood Press, 1990.

Tischler, Barbara L., ed. *Sights on the Sixties.* New Brunswick, NJ: Rutgers University Press, 1992.

Unger, Irwin and Debi Unger. *Turning Point, 1968.* New York: Scribner, 1988. Reissued as *America in the 1960s.* St. James, NY: Brandywine Press, 1993.

Van Deberg, William L. *New Day in Babylon: The Black Power Movement and American Culture, 1965–1975.* Chicago: University of Chicago Press, 1992.

Wilcox, Clyde. *God's Warriors: The Christian Right in Twentieth-Century America.* Baltimore: Johns Hopkins University Press, 1992.

Wuthnow, Robert. *Meaning and Moral Order: Explorations in Cultural Analysis.* Berkeley: University of California Press, 1987.

———. *The Restructuring of American Religion: Society and Faith Since World War II.* Princeton, NJ: Princeton University Press, 1988.

Zaroulis, Nancy and Gerald Sullivan. *Who Spoke Up? Americans Protest against the War in Vietnam, 1963–1975.* Garden City, NY: Doubleday, 1984.

INDEX